RUDE REPUBLIC

RUDE REPUBLIC

AMERICANS AND THEIR POLITICS IN THE NINETEENTH CENTURY

Glenn C. Altschuler and Stuart M. Blumin

PRINCETON UNIVERSITY PRESS   PRINCETON AND OXFORD

Third printing, and first paperback printing, 2001
Paperback ISBN 0-691-08986-8

The Library of Congress has cataloged the cloth edition of this book as follows
Altschuler, Glenn C.
Rude republic : Americans and their politics in the nineteenth century / Glenn C.
Altschuler and Stuart M. Blumin.
p. cm.
Includes bibliographical references (p.) and index.
ISBN 0-691-00130-8 (alk. paper)
1. United States—Politics and government—19th century. 2. Elections—
United States—History—19th century. 3. Political participation—United States—History—
19th century. 4. Political culture—United States—History—19th century.
I. Title. II. Blumin, Stuart M.
E337.5 .A48 2000
320.973'09'034 21—dc21   99-044359

British Library Cataloging-in-Publication Data is available

This book has been composed in Berkeley

Printed on acid-free paper. ∞

www.pup.princeton.edu

Printed in the United States of America

3   5   7   9   10   8   6   4

Contents

List of Illustrations

Acknowledgments

THIS BOOK originated and developed over early morning coffee and muffins at the Temple of Zeus Coffee Shop, a wonderful gathering place for faculty and students at Cornell University. In the last five years our friends and fellow Temple of Zeus regulars, Tony Caputi, Ralph Janis, and occasionally Archie Ammons, have listened with patience and episodic flashes of interest to recitations of our latest research find and to endless refinements of our thesis. Friendship, we now realize, means never wanting to say you're bored.

Several colleagues and friends read portions of various drafts, and provided challenges to our conclusions as well as fresh insights and bibliographic suggestions. Ronald P. Formisano, whose work has anticipated and paved the way for much that is in our book, provided both moral support and detailed criticism that has enriched nearly every page. Joel Silbey set aside doubts about the work as a whole, entered into our argument, and became an invaluable source of suggestions. R. Laurence Moore and Isaac Kramnick read several chapters with the care and intelligence we have long expected of them both. We have benefited as well from critical readings of our work by Harry Watson, Norma Basch, Jean Baker, Michael Holt, Sean Wilentz, and several anonymous readers who served as referees for two journals and the Princeton University Press. The responses of these readers, like the assessments of politics by nineteenth-century Americans, ranged from hearty endorsement, to skepticism, to outright hostility. We would prefer to make our critics responsible for any errors that remain in the book, but suppose we must assume that responsibility ourselves.

Two consummate professionals at the Cornell University Library demonstrated again why this institution is one of the treasures of the scholarly world. Julie Copenhagen, the impresario of interlibrary loans at Cornell, obtained every microfilm of every nineteenth-century newspaper we requested, often cajoling archivists elsewhere to send films, to extend the time for loans, and to search for material that was not listed among their holdings. Without her many triumphs, this book would have been much diminished. Elaine Engst, Associate Director and University Archivist of Rare and Manuscript Collections, was our guide to Cornell's immense collections of diaries and letters. Elaine seems to know the content of every letter in the archive: we stand in awe of her expertise. The staffs of both of these departments, and, as always, of the library's remarkable reference desk, provided indispensable service to us.

A number of students and former students were also important participants in this project. They took on time-consuming and tedious tasks, tracking down sources, detailing the images in nineteenth-century magazines, and entering and linking names in large data bases. Our thanks go to Rami Badaway, Sarah Berger, Jennifer Blumin, Courtney Boland, Becky Fagin, Jessica Flintoft, Dawn Hoffman, Cheryl and Jed Horwitt, Debra Huret, Paul Kangas, Marc Levenson, Heather Pierce, Joshua Plosky, Jon Rauchway, Annie Scorza, Lynn Swarz, and Isho Tama-Sweet.

Esther Tzivanis typed, retyped, tracked down dusty volumes in the library, and reformatted disks with a skill, speed, and intellectual curiosity that make it a joy to work with her.

Funds for research were provided to Glenn Altschuler by Cornell University, and to Stuart Blumin by the Return Jonathan Meigs Research Fund at Cornell. A National Endowment for the Humanities Fellowship for University Teachers gave Stuart Blumin much needed time away from campus responsibilities. Portions of this book were published earlier: Glenn C. Altschuler and Stuart M. Blumin, "'Where Is the Real America?' Politics and Popular Consciousness in the Antebellum Era," *American Quarterly* 49, no. 2 (June 1997): 225–67 (The American Studies Association; reprinted by permission of the Johns Hopkins University Press); and "Limits of Political Engagement in Antebellum America: A New Look at the Golden Age of Participatory Democracy," *Journal of American History* 84, no. 3 (December 1997): 855–85. For permission to reprint portions of our original essays (which may be found in various parts of the introduction and in chapters 1 through 4), we thank the editors of both journals.

Deborah Blumin has lived through all the stages of this book. Wife to one of us, friend and intellectual colleague to us both, her help has included but has also gone well beyond her many useful suggestions for improving our argument and prose.

A book is never completed, but merely abandoned, Faulkner once wrote. We have had a hard time abandoning this one, largely because it has been so stimulating, and because it has been so much fun working together. We hope that some of this stimulation and fun will somehow come through to the reader, and that our book will open up new avenues of inquiry for students of American politics.

RUDE REPUBLIC

Introduction

The View from Clifford's Window

THE POLITICAL PROCESSION that one day disturbed the customary quiet of the House of the Seven Gables touched a "powerful impulse" in Nathaniel Hawthorne's mysterious recluse, Clifford Pyncheon, to look out upon the "rush and roar of the human tide." The view was, however, a disappointing one, as the partisans, with their "hundreds of flaunting banners, and drums, fifes, clarions, and cymbals, reverberating between the rows of buildings," marched down too narrow a street and too close to Clifford's window. "The spectator feels it to be fool's play," Hawthorne explains, "when he can distinguish the tedious commonplace of each man's visage, with the perspiration and weary self-importance on it, and the very cut of his pantaloons, and the stiffness or laxity of his shirt-collar, and the dust on the back of his black coat." To be majestic, the procession must be seen from a more distant vantage point, "for then, by its remoteness, it melts all the petty personalities, of which it has been made up, into one broad mass of existence,—one great life,—one collected body of mankind, with a vast, homogeneous spirit animating it." Proximity might actually add to the effect on an "impressible person," but only should he, "standing alone over the brink of one of these processions, . . . behold it, not in its atoms, but in its aggregate,—as a mighty river of life, massive in its tide, and black with mystery, and, out of its depths, calling to the kindred depth within him."[1]

As with the parade, so too, we would argue, with the more varied and complex processes of American electoral democracy—all can be seen from up close and from afar, by more and less "impressible" observers, absorbed in the animating spirit or attentive to the "tedious commonplace of each man's visage," beholding the "atoms" as well as the "aggregate." Historians of the United States, observing closely or from a distance, have been impressed for a very long time with the animating spirit of the nineteenth-century political spectacle, and have developed a nearly consensual view of post-Jacksonian American politics as a genuinely massive activity in which the vast majority of ordinary Americans—white, voting males, most evidently—participated with an effectiveness born of enthusiasm for and deep commitment to their political party, to specific programs and leaders, and to the idea and practice of democracy itself. "There is considerable evidence," observes Jean H. Baker, "that nineteenth-century Americans gave closer attention to politics than is the case today, thereby guaranteeing a broader, deeper understanding of issues. . . .

[P]arty rallies were better attended than Sunday services or even meetings of itinerant preachers," and elections "became secular holy days."[2] This is an assessment with which more than one generation of historians would agree. Most historians would agree also that politics, and partisan commitment especially, colored many other aspects of American life. "Politics seem to enter into everything," complained a nonpartisan editor during the heat of the 1860 campaign, and William E. Gienapp has made of this the defining phrase of the penetration of politics into the lives of Clifford Pyncheon's younger and more active fellow citizens: "More than in any subsequent era," he explains, "political life formed the very essence of the pre–Civil War generation's experience." Disagreeing only with the temporal specificity of this claim, Michael E. McGerr restates it with a compelling metaphor, suggestive, again, of point of view. Both before and after the Civil War, he argues, the political party was not merely an institution for formulating public policy and organizing election campaigns, but "a natural lens through which to view the world."[3]

The campaign spectacle of parades and mass rallies, and the high energy of election days in which very large proportions of eligible voters cast ballots, were only part of the process of political engagement. Prior to these events on the political calendar were the local party caucuses open to all the party's adherents, and the various nominating conventions to which these meetings of ordinary citizens sent delegates to represent them. At its grass roots, according to Robert H. Wiebe, America's parties functioned as a "lodge democracy," in which "leaders were made and unmade by their brothers, and all parties in the process assumed an underlying equality." More than that, the process was open to all who cared to participate: "All one needed to get into politics," Wiebe insists, "was to get into it."[4] Fueling both the desire to join and the ongoing political battle, moreover, were partisan newspapers, maintained in cities and small towns throughout the nation, and functioning not only as local party mobilizing agencies and bulletin boards, but also as educators of the public, discussing political issues and providing summaries or transcripts of legislative proceedings and presidential and gubernatorial messages even during periods of political quiescence. "The pages of the press," McGerr asserts, "made partisanship seem essential to men's identity."[5] Finally, the frequency of elections assured that these periods of quiescence would not last long. The election cycle varied from place to place, but everywhere in America there were annual local elections, usually in the late winter or spring, and everywhere there was some kind of partisan election—state, congressional, presidential—each year in the late summer or fall. Frequent elections meant that Americans were "perpetually acting" in a ritual of democratic reaffirmation. The political calendar, concludes Joel H. Silbey, "ensured that Americans were caught up in semipermanent and unstinting partisan warfare somewhere throughout the year every year."[6]

This is an attractive perspective on a young and vibrant democracy, evoking the image of a political "golden age" (a phrase used from time to time to describe this era[7]), and affirming the study of politics as a relatively unmediated manifestation of democratic American culture. The view from Clifford's window is a little more unsettling. The different expressions and postures it reveals call upon us to recognize a much more variable set of political attitudes and relations, including those less likely to affirm either the democratic responsiveness or the centrality to American life and culture of the partisan political system. Some historians have gained this view, and anticipate parts of this book, by recognizing the direction and manipulation of nominations and campaigns by political leaders, the persisting deference by ordinary citizens to these leaders well into the era of "lodge democracy," and the essential role played by party organizers in stimulating broad participation in campaigns and elections.[8] What is largely missing from the historical literature, however, is any sustained analysis of the nature and depth of popular political engagement, and of the possibility, even during this period of high voter turnout, spectacular campaigns, frequent elections, and a pervasive political press, of *variable* relations to political affairs on the part of those who cannot be recognized as political leaders.[9] It is our contention that the political engagement of nineteenth-century Americans did vary significantly, over time and among ordinary citizens at any given time, and that the recognition of these variations leads to fundamental questions about Americans and their politics. How shall we understand the patterns, the sources, and the depth of political engagement among Americans, the mechanisms and popular responses to partisan mobilization, and the "fit" between political culture and culture more generally understood? Can we identify Americans who were politically disengaged, and can we take stock of the sources of their disengagement? Can we speak meaningfully of differing types of political activism, and should this typology include a relatively distinct subcommunity of "politicians"? Did party activists, in their very efforts to secure partisan identity and mobilize voters, recognize the existence of apathy and skepticism among the electorate? Might partisan loyalty, for some, have served as an alternative to a thoughtful absorption in public affairs, rather than as a vehicle for their commitment? These specific questions, and others like them, inform the overarching issue: How can we understand the "space" that politics occupied in American society and culture during this "golden age" of participatory democracy?

Political engagement is in many respects a behavioral phenomenon, consisting of participation of various sorts in the more and less institutionalized aspects of the political process. Men (and during the nineteenth century, only men) could be public officeholders, editors of political newspapers, officers and members of party central committees, convention delegates, and behind-the-scenes manipulators of political affairs. Or, they could attend caucuses, join campaign clubs, work at the polls, and vote; while both women and men could appear at campaign rallies, listen to speeches, read editorials in the partisan press, sign petitions, and argue politics with their friends and family. That they could also neglect to do these things—to absent themselves from a convention or rally, to read a book rather than a political newspaper, to discuss the weather rather than politics—requires us to relate political participation to the whole range of activities that constitutes a given social world, and in some fashion to measure its significance within that world. It requires us also to understand the cultural dimension of political engagement. If on the one hand engagement is behavioral, on the other it is a constellation of perceptions of and attitudes toward politicians, public issues, and the functioning political system. And just as political participation can vary, so too can political attitude—from enthusiasm to indifference, from belief to skepticism, from appreciation to hostility. This, too, must be measured in some way, and related to political action as something to isolate within, but not from, American life.

The political action to which we refer was, from the 1830s through the end of the century and beyond, mostly partisan in nature. There were, to be sure, important elements of public life in American communities that the political parties often could not and did not reach: more and less official and regular "town meetings" of local citizens; local elections of certain kinds (and of all kinds in some places); religious, benevolent, and reform activities of high-minded women and men; and extralegal vigilante committees in areas where public institutions were not, or not yet, well established. Particularly in the years before the establishment of strong party institutions, there were lines of political influence and loyalty that were personal rather than partisan. But if Americans experienced for a time the pre-party "meeting-place democracy" that Mary P. Ryan has recently described,[10] and if established local leaders continued to exercise a considerable personal influence, the reach of the institutionalized parties was clearly expanding across all of these domains. More ritualized and celebratory public events, such as Fourth of July parades and local agricultural fairs, retained their nonpartisan character through nearly all these years (though the passions of the Civil War years challenged some of them), and, as Jean Baker has convincingly argued, continued to contribute in a quite different way to the sense and meaning of civic life.[11] But the parties, as we will discuss, quickly assumed the organization of what virtually everyone in the nineteenth century referred to when they used the term "politics." It is to this customary and popular understanding of the term that we will subscribe, relating a narrowly defined partisan politics to other forms of influence and civic life when these shared or competed for a presence on the public stage.[12]

Several reasons for positing a more complex and conflicted relation to political affairs among Americans emerge from even a preliminary consideration of politics (understood narrowly or even broadly) as one of a number of influences, interests, and venues within the larger society and culture. Perhaps the most important of these is religion, and the fact that political democratization was paralleled in nineteenth-century America, and particularly in the antebellum era, by an increasing commitment on the part of large numbers of Americans to the beliefs and behavioral dictates of evangelical Christianity. Political historians have recognized this parallel development and have probed in considerable detail not only the ethnoreligious foundations of partisan affiliation, but also the religious roots of reform movements, such as temperance and abolition, that entered the political arena. Perhaps because of these connections, however, they have not stressed sufficiently the power of religious sensibilities to subordinate politics to what many believed were more important activities and preoccupations, and have not recognized the degree to which politics and religion could be placed by some in an adversarial relation. Richard Carwardine, for example, acknowledges that evangelicals in the 1840s railed against the new public maxim that "all is fair in politics," lamented the decline of moral standards under the rule of "maddened, wine-heated politicians," and lambasted hickory-pole and cider-barrel electioneering as a "reckless waste in useless trappings." He notes that some religious men eschewed politics entirely: "I am myself a candidate, but it is for eternal life." But these sentiments quickly fade from his narrative when Carwardine turns to the realization by evangelicals that they could not pursue their crusades against alcohol, slavery, and Catholicism by "swimming against the tide of American popular culture." Thereafter, he argues, religion and politics became parts of an "organic seamless whole."[13]

We believe, however, that what Mark Y. Hanley has called "the Protestant quarrel with the American republic" was more enduring among a broad group of conservative Christians. Hanley describes the efforts of Ezra Stiles, Francis Wayland, Charles Hodge, Horace Bushnell, and a number of lesser-known clergy to assure that a transcendent and redemptive Christianity remain uncorrupted by the new American "liberal order." What troubled these divines was an illusory "new freedom beyond faith" that included an absorption of the mind and spirit in political affairs and an arrogant conflation of political with spiritual progress: "When did [Christ] condescend to tell us that ours is the true form of government?" asked Bushnell. "When lend himself to any such mischievous flattery as this?"[14] Bushnell raised these questions in the context of the fervent presidential campaign of 1840, but evangelicals and other Protestants continued to insist throughout the antebellum era, and later, that politics be kept out of the pulpit and the religious press, and that men and women go beyond and beneath matters of state to examine the state of their souls. What effects did these exhortations have on the political commitment of ordinary Christians? Did some churchgoers vote in secular elections but also contain or compartmentalize their political enthusiasm? Did others withdraw from political affairs? Might not the borrowing of religious rhetoric by nineteenth-century politicians have been a device for attracting those whose deeper instincts were to protect themselves from political dangers?

A second reason for questioning the pervasiveness of political engagement is the tension, obvious in so many ways, between political activism and the pursuit of upper- and middle-class respectability. Just as evangelical Christianity and political democracy developed simultaneously in a partly conflicted relation, so too did the emergence of new forms and a heightened pursuit of social respectability coincide with the development of political practices that were widely perceived as disreputable. European visitors commented frequently on the coarseness of the new American politics—on the need to shake "one hard greasy paw" after another, on the "uncouth mosaic of expectoration and nutshells" (Mrs. Trollope's name for the characteristic American citizen was George Washington Spitchew)—and Robert Wiebe contends that some Americans eagerly translated this problem into the solution, indeed the defining virtue, of American politics in the Age of the Common Man.[15] Without apology they created an egalitarian politics appropriate to what we call here a rude republic—a political nation just taking shape, and one that prided itself on its challenge to deference and its disdain for the formalities of polite address. This rude republic, we believe, was formed across the nineteenth century in ways that unsettled not only visiting Europeans but also many respectable Americans. Blatant office-seeking and behind-the-scenes maneuvering, the cultivation of political loyalty among newly enfranchised workers and recently arrived immigrants, the inclusion in political organizations of saloonkeepers, street toughs, and other unsavory characters, the employment of manipulative techniques of mass appeal, and the equation of these techniques with other forms of crude humbuggery, imparted an unseemliness to politics that considerably complicated the simultaneous pursuit of respectability and an active political life. William Gienapp cites one elite Philadelphian who complained of " 'the mere chicanery of politics,' which made the pursuit of office 'attended by a degradation of character & sacrifice of principle startling enough to drive every man of taste & feeling into deeper shades of private life,' "[16] and it is clear that many social elites did find it more difficult to participate in a rude republic of voting masses and saloon-based precinct captains, of torchlight parades and vulgar oratory.[17] By no means all withdrew into "deeper shades of private life," but those elites who remained active in the party period were compelled to adjust to new and uncomfortably disreputable associations and activities.

These concerns pertain as well to those more modestly positioned individuals and families who made new claims of social respectability as part of an emerging middle class. The most complex patterns of middle-class formation were to be found in the largest cities, where politics were also perceived as being especially unseemly and corrupt. In the cities, middle-class respectability was grounded in a variety of new social environments and experiences: enlarged and refined, parlor-centered homes; similarly embellished commercial, managerial, and professional workplaces; increasingly homogeneous residential neighborhoods and business districts; a variety of new commercial and voluntary institutions providing respectable entertainment and sociability. The essence of all of these was class segregation, and in particular the insulation of middle-class individuals and families from the rough world of the native and immigrant working class.[18] Political activities of various kinds could threaten that insulation and the sense of social well-being that went with it. Indeed, at a time when theaters, retail shopping districts, and even church congregations were increasingly segregated by class, political gatherings remained among the most socially promiscuous of the city's affairs. Was this in fact a source of political disengagement among the urban middle class? And what about the far larger number of middling folk who lived in smaller towns and in the countryside, where politics was less (or less famously) corrupt and social promiscuity less (or less obviously) problematic? Richard Bushman has demonstrated the appeal of city-bred social styles in rural and small-town America, but if rustic Americans pursued a "vernacular gentility" to confirm their middle-class status, does it follow that they faced the same complications of political engagement that we have posited for their urban counterparts?[19] What, indeed, were the social implications of political engagement—and the effects on political engagement of upper- and middle-class social sensibilities—in both the city and the country?

In defining vernacular gentility, Bushman describes a rural middle class, "without pretensions to public office," that failed to develop the sense of public duty and privilege that had once been an important part of the aristocratic package of values and behavior. "The realm of the middling people was the family rather than town or county."[20] This selective importation of genteel qualities is suggestive of what historians frequently have labeled "liberalism," that political theory or sensibility emphasizing individual rights over corporate responsibilities and asserting the superiority of the free market over public activity and control.[21] Historians ordinarily discuss liberalism as a well-reasoned article of conviction, and as a mode of political action that would use politics to limit the prerogatives of the state and to enlarge individual freedoms. There is not necessarily a paradox in this, and it is surely the case that many Americans have engaged fervently in politics with just such ends in mind. But we believe it is possible to identify another kind of liberalism that did little to nurture, and much to discourage, political participation. Less theoretical or even thoughtful, more humdrum even in its description—following Bushman, we call it "vernacular liberalism"—it is no more than an unreflective absorption in the daily routines of work, family, and social life, those private and communal domains that the small governments of the era hardly touched. To be sure, there is nothing in the "realm of the family" that would have prevented its male members from an active engagement or its female members from an active interest in the larger realms of politics and the state in nineteenth-century America. But we suspect that the radical disconnectedness and "privatism"[22] observed in America by Tocqueville and other European visitors in this period translated in many instances into a primacy of self and family that confined politics to a lower order of personal commitment than is generally recognized. Tocqueville himself argued that Americans were passionately interested in politics, but he would not have seen much or many of those people to whom we refer. Neither have many historians ferreted them out from their chimney corners and workbenches. Most Americans did vote, and for many historians that has been enough. We would look more closely at "liberalism," not merely as a political theory, but also, for some, as an apolitical way of life.[23]

The republicanism that historians so frequently place in opposition to liberalism as a source or summation of American values was itself capable of complicating and even limiting political engagement. Most importantly, it fueled the antipartyism that historians have found during the earliest years of the second party system, and that, we believe, continued as a significant element of American political culture long after the more reluctantly partisan Whigs adopted the structures and campaign techniques pioneered by Democrats.[24] Indeed, the feeling that parties were corrupting the political process may have strengthened as the two major parties came to resemble each other in structure and technique, and as the party system came to dominate, seemingly permanently, the republican political process. It was in this context of party hegemony and a wary public that the cult of George Washington served to express antipartyism (the Farewell Address was this movement's basic text, and was read aloud at many public gatherings), and to offer military heroism and sacrifice as a sounder basis of patriotism and republican virtue. The parties themselves understood the potentially alienating effects of this popular contrast between the politician and the military hero. They frequently offered their presidential nominations to former military commanders with otherwise minimal political credentials, and introduced military motifs into their campaigns even when no general could be found to head the ticket (rarely a problem in the post–Civil War era). Campaign biographers, as William Burlie Brown has shown, were increasingly inclined to disavow any kind of political apprenticeship for their subjects, whether or not they had been military men, and to claim that only their opponents were politicians by trade. "The conclusion is inescapable," writes Brown, "that the basic assumptions of the biographers are that their audience believes the politician is evil and party politics is evil twice compounded."[25] And yet, inevitably, it was the party that offered military heroes and other disinterested amateurs to the voting public. No significant candidacies were mounted by such paragons of republicanism outside the party's structures and campaign machinery. Those who loathed the party and its professional politicians, therefore, had to reconcile some significantly discordant elements of the candidacy of any latter-day George Washington.

The great public-school reforms of the 1840s and beyond offer insights into this tension between party politics and a republicanism grounded in military service. School reformers developed curricula and purchased textbooks that underscored the military origins of republican virtue while making no concessions to partisan institutions. Jean Baker has argued that the experience of schooling in the antebellum era "trained young white males in their public roles of delegating power, rotating leadership, limiting power, and supporting the government."[26] None of this entered the formal curriculum, however, and the "training" Baker alludes to consisted mainly of the manner in which restive school children resisted the tyrannies of their overbearing teachers. Against this problematic inference we would place Baker's own observation that the schools "did not introduce their students to public issues or political parties, as twentieth-century civics courses would."[27] Remarkably, American school children of the antebellum era were given no political history of their nation. American history texts culminated in the Revolutionary War, and the message of this climactic event was the patriotic virtue of Washington and his men-at-arms. It is curricular decisions of this sort, made by men who were as convinced as Horace Bushnell was about the significance of early childhood nurturance in the shaping of enduring values, that seem to us most important in conveying the intended and actual effects of public schooling upon republican civic consciousness. Americans were taught to honor the American republic, but not American politics. For how many did this kind of republicanism remain a cultural resource for resisting engagement in the "affairs of party"?

The question of what types of evidence ought to inform this study is itself an interesting one. Political history is ordinarily derived from documents generated from within the political system, by people—public officeholders, party officials, partisan editors—who were the most deeply involved in political affairs, and to a lesser extent by political outsiders—clergy, social reformers—who may have commented on or attempted to influence the course of political events in some way. Sources *about* politics are surely necessary, but they are also insufficient, for raising questions about political engagement—they reinforce the impression that politics "enter into everything," for they systematically shrink the boundaries of "everything" to include just those things that politics do "enter." To place politics alongside other institutions, and to consider the "space" all such institutions occupy within the decentered world of work, family life, and informal sociability, we must turn also to sources generated outside the political nation of parties and public bodies. Many of the pages that follow, therefore, are based on the examination of a wide range of documents of the sort that do not usually enter political history—diaries and letters written by ordinary Americans who did not pursue a political career, novels, popular lithographs depicting American scenes, and the images and texts in widely circulating illustrated magazines. Reading extensively in these kinds of documents provides us with new angles of vision (including the view through Clifford's window), and a great deal of new and useful information about the contexts and meanings of political action.

Important, too, are the ways in which these sources relate to each other, and to the more specifically political documents we have also consulted. The latter include some novel or underutilized source materials, such as political humor and, more importantly, the testimony of thousands of ordinary voters before state legislative committees charged with investigating disputed elections— testimony that gives us remarkable insights into the very process and moment of voting. The popular quality of these sources contrasts with many of the writings by party leaders and propagandists used by historians to define and understand the programmatic differences between Democrats and Whigs or Republicans. Party doctrine and rhetoric may have been "shaped to appeal to those who heard or read it," as Lawrence Kohl has argued, but the extent and nature of that appeal is not to be found in the speeches of great men, or in the writings of political propagandists.[28] Seeking better ways of connecting the disseminators with the receivers of political doctrine, we have ourselves read widely in sources written by political leaders, including, for example, the auto-biographies of political men (in a few cases, the wives of such men) and, in much greater numbers, partisan newspapers published in the cities and small towns of widely varying regions. The partisan papers are, to say the least, well-worked documents in the history of American campaigns and elections, but we have read them in new ways.[29] In addition to the specifically political infor-mation and commentary, we have read the nonpolitical content of these news-papers, which were, in fact, institutions of the local community as well as of the political party. We have read the issues they published in the years of presidential elections and in the years of lesser political importance, and have read through the entire calendar, not merely the political season. Finally, we have used the local newspapers to accumulate lists of men who performed visible political and other institutional roles in their communities, and, by searching for these men's names in census manuscripts and city directories, have amassed social and economic profiles of greater and lesser activists. Here the configuration of sources is obvious, but it is everywhere of significance. We certainly do not claim to have exhausted more than ourselves in our search for both broader and closer points of view, but the latter has been our goal. We want to read the "flaunting banners," and to see the "commonplace visage" of the men who carried them. More, we want to see Clifford himself, and those like him who merely watched, or who turned away, from the great procession.

We can state this goal another way, with the help of a letter written during the summer of 1844 by Ezra Cornell, then a rising young upstate–New York inventor-businessman. It was the year of the hotly contested presidential race between James K. Polk and Henry Clay, and Cornell, an active and enthusiastic Whig, described for his family a political debate that broke out on the coach that was taking him from Ludlowville to Aurora, a few miles north of their Ithaca home. It was, at first glance, just the kind of debate that historians have pointed to in underscoring the intense political engagement of this era. "[T]he subject of Politicks was fully introduced and discussed with a spirit that would do credit to the herows of former days," Cornell began. The Democratic point of view was "espoused by a couple of gents who pitched their tone on rather a high key," inducing Cornell "to give them a shot or two from a 'long 18' . . . and at it we went broad side upon broad side until by a skillful maneuver I got the enemy divided and in a position that I could take them right and left with an effect that soon silenced their batteries." Apparently frustrated by Cornell's tactical superiority, the two Democrats proposed a straw vote, and it is here that we learn that there were not three men in the coach, but eight, three of whom Cornell designates as the "Silents," as they had not said a word during the debate, and who restricted their participation to casting votes—for Clay, Cornell gloated—when they were asked to do so. Two others had also remained quiet "for the fact of there [sic] inheriting the complection of father Ham and not having collected enough of filthy lucre to purchase the right of which they are deprived by culler."[30] Five of the eight men, in other words, were bystanders to this spontaneous and lively political debate—two because they were excluded by race, and three for reasons we do not know. In the chapters that follow we wish to examine the whole coachload, and not merely its noisiest occupants. We wish to hear the lively debate, to take notice of those excluded from it, and to understand the meaning of silence.

CHAPTER 1

Political Innovation and Popular Response
in Jack Downing's America

THE REPUBLIC established in Philadelphia in the summer of 1787 was not premised upon the active engagement of great numbers of ordinary citizens in the
affairs of state. Important elements of the old aristocratic distinction between
the "few" and the "many" suffused the new national Constitution, and shaped
electoral practices through such provisions as the electoral college and the
selection of United States senators by state legislatures. In the individual states,
too, aristocratic elements of this sort crept back into some of the more democratic constitutions that had been written and adopted in the aftermath of the
Revolution.[1] There were popular political excitements in the early republican
decades, to be sure—armed uprisings, hotly contested elections, and, in the
Republican Party and the several Democratic Republican clubs, the beginnings
of what might well be called a popular political movement. But none of these
fully realized the democratic implications (what Gordon Wood has called the
"radicalism") of the Revolution.[2] Nor would it have seemed, forty years after
the Philadelphia convention, that a broadly participatory democracy was the
inevitable result of republican self-rule. Most of the excitements of the early
decades were played out after safe passage through the seeming crisis of the
Jeffersonian challenge to Federalism and the very real crisis of American
involvement in the Napoleonic wars. By the mid-1820s, according to historian
Ronald P. Formisano, "the vast majority of citizens had lost interest in politics.
They had never voted much in presidential elections anyway, and now they
involved themselves only sporadically in state and local affairs."[3]

Voting levels in national and state elections in the new republic had, in fact,
never been high, not even in the years of greatest partisan contention. Only
some sixty-two thousand voters—fewer than a third of those who were eligible—cast ballots for presidential electors in the pivotal election of 1800, and
in all the presidential elections before 1828 the turnout of eligible voters never
exceeded 42 percent. Voter turnout in elections for congressmen and for state
governors was usually higher, but not by a great deal, ordinarily ranging, according to Walter Dean Burnham's tabulations, between about one-quarter and
one-half of the electorate.[4] Did the customary nonappearance of the majority of
the electorate express a norm of political disengagement in the early republic?
Formisano's own discussion of the continuing influence of political deference

seems especially relevant to this issue. Deference functioned not merely through constitutional forms but in the day-to-day (and election-to-election) relations between the "better sort" and the more ordinary citizens of communities all across the United States, the latter generally acquiescing in the political leadership and authority of those who successfully claimed a more general social superiority.[5] It is likely that the bases of this acquiescence had changed a good deal since the eighteenth century, and that a system originally manifesting the personal relations of patronage and clientage (never so strongly in the colonies as in the mother country) was evolving toward something more remote and more professional, and perhaps to some extent even more institutional. Edmund Morgan has suggested a different term, "leadership," to describe "a new way of determining who should stand among the few to govern the many."[6] By the 1820s deference was not so much a system as a tendency, not a culture but the survival of one, that merged with and continued to influence the more democratic ideas and practices that were taking hold within a nation moving toward a more inclusive suffrage. But this is not to gainsay its power to shape, and in particular to circumscribe, popular political commitment. If most political leaders were no longer patrons and protectors in the oldest sense, they continued to dominate the public sphere in ways that conveyed to ordinary folk the feeling that the routine conduct of politics—the selection of candidates for public office, the shaping of political coalitions, the conduct of election campaigns, the definition of the public agenda—was not really the people's business. This is what was most durable about deference, and it continued to limit popular engagement in politics through the first party period, the "Era of Good Feelings," and some years beyond.

Questions about voter turnout and the relations between leaders and ordinary citizens in the early republic tend to be swallowed up by the energies of the Jacksonian era. Andrew Jackson's challenge to what he and his followers portrayed as a revival of Federalism within the administration of John Quincy Adams fired the interest of many Americans, including large numbers who were recently enfranchised by new state constitutions. When Jackson challenged Adams in the 1828 presidential election, the total vote increased from fewer than 360,000 to more than a million, and the proportion of eligible voters casting ballots more than doubled, from 27 percent to 57 percent.[7] Turnout would remain at almost precisely this level for the next two presidential elections as well. Would Americans now build upon a natural proclivity to engage in politics, and speak as well in their own voices to promote and protect their own interests? The Age of Jackson, in the customary language of American history, is also the Age of the Common Man, and it is to a particularly politicized and decidedly nondeferential common man that this phrase refers. Alexis de Tocqueville, whose visit to the United States occurred during just these years, wrote famously of a nearly universal preoccupation with politics among

Americans, and of American democracy as the expression of a social egalitarianism that retained little or nothing of traditional distinctions between the "few" and the "many." The "political activity which pervades the United States," wrote Tocqueville, is a "universal movement which originates in the lowest classes of the people and extends successively to all the ranks of society."

> The cares of political life [Tocqueville continued] engross a most prominent place in the occupation of a citizen in the United States; and almost the only pleasure of which an American has any idea, is to take part in the Government, and to discuss the part he had taken. This feeling pervades the most trifling habits of life; even the women frequently attend public meetings, and listen to political harangues as a recreation after their household labours. . . . [I]f an American were condemned to confine his activity to his own affairs, he would be robbed of one half of his existence. . . . This ceaseless agitation which democratic government has introduced into the political world, influences all social intercourse.[8]

A tumultuous and raucous democracy (these terms, too, are to be found in Tocqueville) is just what General Jackson brought to the White House in 1829. And yet, there is an incompleteness to the Jacksonian revolution that ought to give us pause. As Tocqueville remains so important a spokesman for the forcefulness of popular democracy in the Jacksonian era, let us note that the great writer returned to France without having observed a national election, and that in the notes he kept while traveling through America (and while speaking mainly to the most prominent members of American society) is Joel R. Poinsett's answer to the question, " 'Does the nomination for President excite real political passion?' 'No. It puts the interested parties into a grand commotion. It makes the newspapers make a lot of noise. But the mass of the people remain indifferent.' "[9] Indifference, too, is the theme of a letter written by Tocqueville's traveling companion, Gustave de Beaumont, during their American visit. It is a letter that almost directly contradicts his friend's appraisal of the penetration of politics into daily life. A people with so much free land, wrote Beaumont, "does not feel the slightest disposition to be discontent with the government. Each one, on the contrary, remains indifferent to the administration of the country, to occupy himself only with his own affairs."[10]

Neither a universal passion for politics nor a universal indifference accurately describes the United States during the early 1830s. Jackson's candidacy in 1828 had filled the glass of voter turnout a little over half way, but the next two presidential elections left it nearly half empty. It is important to observe that the significant expansion of voter turnout in 1828 did not initiate an upward curve of electoral participation. Why (assuming that voter turnout is roughly indicative of more general patterns of political engagement and disengagement) did not more and more Americans interest themselves in the "ceaseless agitation" of "democratic government"? This question becomes more significant when we consider suffrage and other political reforms that would appear to reflect a continuing democratic uprising against those deferential assumptions and practices that in the past had limited popular participation. Richard P. McCormick long ago identified a "hidden revolution in the electoral environment" of the first four decades of the nineteenth century. By 1832, every state but South Carolina chose presidential electors by popular vote; voice voting and hand-written ballots were giving way to printed ballots; increased numbers of polling places made voting easier for country people; suffrage restrictions on white males had been all but eliminated; and reemerging political parties were beginning to replace legislative caucuses with nominating conventions.[11] The national Republican, Democratic, and Anti-Masonic parties all used national conventions for nominating their candidates for the 1832 presidential election, and in the years that followed, this seemingly more open and democratic means of candidate selection would spread slowly through the rest of the electoral system.[12] On the other hand, these reforms do not seem to have resulted only, or even primarily, from popular pressure. On the contrary, McCormick and other historians have stressed the role of party leaders, who turned increasingly to sponsorship of more inclusive reforms of the political process as a way of recruiting new party members in the face of competition from other parties. Nominating conventions "had the appearance of being more 'open' and more 'popular' than the caucus," for example, but they were in fact initiated and in most cases controlled by party leaders. In those states that had lacked prior forms of party organization, conventions were denounced as means for dictating nominations.[13] Suffrage expansion, too, in Chilton Williamson's estimation, was more a means of party recruitment than a popular movement for greater inclusiveness. In Connecticut and Massachusetts, he observes, suffrage expansion was followed by a slight decline in voter turnout.[14]

Did parties, then, do no more than create the appearance of popular enthusiasm? We must be careful not to dismiss nominating conventions, suffrage expansion, and other reforms as mere technical details of partisan competition. The idea of a democracy of white men was becoming more persuasive among larger numbers of ordinary people. Party leaders may well have initiated reforms for their own narrow purposes, but they may also have helped to open a Pandora's box of democratic feeling and action that they were not able to control. McCormick himself observes that democratic reforms "added greatly to the difficulties of party management," and we would note as well that the parties were still very much in an experimental stage, wherein "party management" was at once a task of encouraging, capturing, accommodating to, and controlling popular participation.[15] These tasks were challenging enough during the 1830s; they would become more so in 1840, when Pandora's box opened all the way.

THE POLITICAL REVOLUTION OF 1840:
FOUR AMERICAN COMMUNITIES

Eighteen forty is the *annus mirabilis* of American partisan democracy. In the presidential election of that year, fully eight of ten eligible voters cast ballots, a reflection not of some temporary or accidental circumstance but of a new pattern of citizen participation in national elections, and a new level of partisan activity and organization. More specifically, the once reluctant Whigs adopted and improved upon campaign techniques pioneered by Democrats, and soundly beat their rivals at their own game. Both parties were now committed to a new style of electoral politics, and the effects of this commitment would endure. The parties would soon reach a high level of institutional organization, dedicated mainly to assuring the largest possible turnout of its own voters in national, state, and in some cases local elections. And for the remainder of the nineteenth century, voter participation would in fact remain high—in presidential elections it would seldom slip significantly below the levels established in the "breakthrough" election of 1840.

This story of the conjoined triumphs of participatory democracy and the political party is well known, and needs no further summary. What it does need is validation, or perhaps qualification, through analysis that admits of the possibility that the triumphs of politics and party were neither inevitable nor complete. What we must appreciate is that this seemingly climactic event in the formation of American electoral democracy was still very much an experiment in popular mobilization and management, and that the relations between the parties and their professed or potential adherents were far from settled and known in 1840. This leads to new questions, or at least to a more specific reformulation of ones we have already asked: Would there be a new and perhaps more democratic relation between party leaders and the larger body of party voters? Should the party be open to all who would join it, or should there be some kind of test of adherence to party principles? What kinds of appeals should be used to reach out to voters, and what role should public issues play in the election campaign? Should the party educate and otherwise involve its "members" in political affairs throughout the year, or should it merely mobilize them as voters and then leave them be? What kind of an institution should the party be? What should it mean to be associated with it? To be active within it? To lead it?

Let us focus first on the early years of triumph, the first full election cycle of national, state, and local elections of the years 1840–42. The local party newspaper is the best source for examining the political process "on the ground," and the local community, where citizens read party papers, attended rallies, joined campaign clubs, and voted—and where they worked, worshipped, and raised their families—is the appropriate place for examining the relation of people to that process. We have selected for a close look at the new system of partisan democracy four American communities from which the newspapers of both political parties have survived. Greenfield, in western Massachusetts, and Marietta, in southeastern Ohio, were small county seats, among the smallest capable of sustaining two party papers. According to the 1840 census, the town of Greenfield contained 1,756 residents, a small majority of whom lived on the streets and lanes of the town center. Marietta contained 3,381 inhabitants; 1,814 in the incorporated village of Marietta, 692 within the corporation of Harmar, and 875 elsewhere in the township. The Hudson Valley town of Kingston, New York, and the Georgia cotton-belt city of Augusta were somewhat larger. The town of Kingston had 5,824 inhabitants, some 2,200 of whom lived in the incorporated village of Kingston, and approximately 1,500 of whom lived in the adjoining, unincorporated village of Rondout. Augusta's 6,403 residents consisted of 3,266 whites, 148 free blacks, and 2,989 slaves. Another 5,529 people (including 2,384 whites) lived beyond the city's borders in the remainder of Richmond County.[16] Four towns, of New England, the Mid-Atlantic, the South, and the West: they are not all of America, by any means, but they are sufficiently representative of the nation's major regions, and of the array of ordinary communities within those regions, to repay an attentive visit to their campaigns and elections during these early days of the second party system.

We would emphasize first, however, that even the smaller of these towns were the economic and political centers of their immediate regions. All were river towns, all contained most of their counties' merchants, professional men, banks, and nonagricultural producers, and, as county seats, were centers of county government and justice. As communities, therefore, they were not typical of the great majority of localities that were neither economic nor political centers. This, indeed, may stand as our first observation: politics in the various regions of the United States was *centered* in such places as these, revolving around the courthouse, law offices, and newspaper offices of county seats, and radiating outward with variable but generally diminishing force from the few blocks around the courthouse to the rest of the town and to the more remote towns, hamlets, and farms of their respective counties. Our towns may be representative of the American political nation in the early 1840s, but for this very reason they are a biased sample of the American nation as a whole. To generalize from them, or from other centers of local political life, is no doubt to overstate the role of politics in the lives of most ordinary Americans.

How, then, did the people of Greenfield and Marietta, Kingston and Augusta—the political centers of Franklin, Washington, Ulster, and Richmond counties—experience the new politics of this era? The differences among the towns, and among their regions and states, were significant, and we will need to appreciate the role of local traditions in shaping the effects of broader influences. But each town did participate in events and structural innovations that bound disparate localities and separate state parties as never before to a national system of voter organization and inspiration. Each, for example, adopted some version of the nominating convention for selecting local candidates, and for sending local delegates to conventions higher in the political system. The convention had spread through many state and local party organizations during the late 1830s. By the early 1840s it was, or was proclaimed to be, the centerpiece of an inclusive, grassroots democracy, wherein ordinary citizens met openly and frequently to choose candidates and delegates who formally represented the party's broader membership. Martin Van Buren's home state was probably the leader in party organization in this era, and it is not surprising that among our towns it was Kingston that had, by 1840, the most complete array of local conventions and town party meetings (or "caucuses," especially after that term had lost the odor of elite control) to select candidates and delegates. In the spring of 1840 both Whigs and Democrats in Kingston called town meetings to name tickets for the upcoming town election, and the Democrats held another to choose delegates to a county convention that, in turn, would send delegates to the state party convention. For local Democrats, this meant that there were three party gatherings, all in Kingston, within the space of eleven days. The Whigs would call their town meetings and county convention for the selection of state-convention delegates in June and July, Democrats went through the same process a second time in August, and both parties were at it again for congressional nominations in September. It is clear that political leaders intended these meetings to stimulate interest in and bind voters to the party, and not merely to conduct the business at hand. Extremely large delegations were named by town meetings to attend county conventions (151 from Kingston's Democratic meeting in March, for example, and this to a convention whose only business was to select two delegates to the state convention), and party papers boasted about and disputed over the attendance at every meeting. Delegates were certain to see their names in the paper, along with the other faithful. The presidential race of 1840 no doubt stimulated much of this, but the new system endured in the off years, to be called to life for any election, which in New York as in most places meant at least twice in any year. Kingston's Whigs and Democrats had built a participation pyramid out of durable stone.[17]

The caucus and convention system did not assume the same shape in all of our towns during this experimental stage of party development. In Greenfield, town party meetings sent delegates directly to state conventions, bypassing county conventions that in Kingston were occasions for building, demonstrating, and channeling partisan enthusiasm. County conventions were held for the purpose of nominating candidates for the state senate, but the towns selected small numbers of delegates (four by the Whigs in 1840, for example), so these conventions did not take on the character of mass party rallies.[18] Marietta's nominating process was less settled than that of either of our eastern towns. As in Kingston, large delegations merged the functions of nominating candidates and creating and conveying popular enthusiasm, but the caucus and convention system was not yet firmly established. In July 1840, Whig meetings were called within the townships of Washington County for the appointment of "committees of nomination," whose recommendations would be "confirmed by the people" at the following month's county convention. Votes were apportioned by township in the morning session of the convention, before candidate nominations were made in the afternoon. Who were the "people" at this convention, if they were not the township delegates or "committees of nomination"? How did this convention really work? In the following spring, Morgan County Whigs invited party members of Washington and Perry counties to join with them in nominating state legislative candidates. The language and fact of this invitation suggests that the convention they called for was not expected in due course, and it is significant that the Whig editor of Marietta expressed regret at its necessity, blaming the Democrats for the need to organize for legislative elections.[19] Whether or not he was sincere in this regret, or was merely pandering to a lingering antipartyism, is not important. The point is that even after the Tippecanoe campaign and the Whig victory it brought, the legitimacy of these party institutions, no less than their form, was not assured.

Augusta moved with somewhat more difficulty from the legislative caucus to the popular nominating convention, a fact that would seem to reflect the decidedly elitist character of Georgia politics.[20] Both parties did begin the political year in 1840 by publishing long lists of names of party members (160 by the Democrats, 152 by their "State Rights" or Whig opponents) calling for local meetings for the selection of delegates to their respective state conventions. Both, however, retained elitist forms of local candidate nomination, sometimes very thinly disguised as local party democracy. Standing nominating committees, appointed by the chair of a party meeting, selected candidates for the state legislature in the fall of 1840. The Whig committee submitted its choices to a small convention of party delegates, which approved "without a dissenting voice." The Democratic committee did not bother with this rubber stamp, and neither did the Whig committee a few months later, when it met in the office of the party newspaper to name candidates for the upcoming county election. Conventions, though, became more regular thereafter, and the nomination of candidates was, by 1841, routinely submitted to ordinary party members for approval. The locus of decision making had probably changed but little (a subject to which we will return in the next two chapters), but Augusta's political leaders made at least this concession to popular democracy.[21]

Augusta may not have wholeheartedly embraced the nominating convention, but its Whigs, and the Whigs and Democrats of our other towns, made much use of other new modes of popular political engagement. In May and early June of 1840, Augusta's Whigs formed Tippecanoe clubs in each of the city's wards, and these, more than the party's formal structures, became the initial core of the popular campaign. Soon after its founding, each Tippecanoe Club published a list of members of its Vigilance Committee (in the third and fourth wards these lists ran to exactly seventy-six names, thereby associating the Harrison campaign with the popular iconography of the American Revolution), announcing in effect that popular commitment to Whiggery was too broad and too intense to remain within the bounds of regular party channels, just as the clubs' appearance so early in the campaign announced that local Whigs could not wait to get started and that their enthusiasm could be maintained for many months. The clubs met often in the spring and early summer, inviting the members of the other clubs to meet with them, and in June formed a Central Tippecanoe Club of Richmond County, which between August and October sponsored a number of campaign barbecues and other rallies. Augusta's Whigs also sent delegates to the Young Men's National Convention in Baltimore, and convened a large meeting to hear the delegates report on the convention after their return. It was at this Baltimore convention, in fact, that the idea of forming local Tippecanoe clubs was promulgated by national party leaders, and the meetings to form Augusta's clubs began within two days of the Baltimore delegates' report.

Democrats in Augusta did not utilize such extraparty vehicles as these, but relied on the new convention system to generate "large and enthusiastic" gatherings of the party. Elsewhere, Democrats countered Tippecanoe clubs with Democratic associations, and in Kingston, again the most fully organized of our towns, both Whigs and Democrats created Young Men's associations, not merely in response to the need to send delegates to national and state Young Men's conventions, but also as ongoing local campaign organizations. Kingston's Whigs joined the campaign club with the party organization by giving substance to a new Whig icon in the form of a log cabin, twenty-four by forty feet, where party conventions and other meetings would take place between early July and the November election. Here was the perfect emblem of the popularization of political decision making, and the Whig editor was careful to emphasize that "every portion of the community—the merchants, farmers, mechanics & working men" were present, and "animated by a common impulse," when the log cabin was dedicated a day before the community's official Fourth of July celebration.[22]

Rallies and icons were important parts of the 1840 campaign, even where campaign clubs did not flourish. Greenfield's Whigs did not form a Tippecanoe Club (three towns in the county formed Democratic associations), but they did build a log cabin at their Harrison "Grand Convention" in May. In Marietta, the Whigs made the log cabin an element of the elaborate and carefully orchestrated processions of their large delegations to county and district conventions. Both parties in Marietta made significant use of liberty poles (Whig poles were topped—or "tipped"—by canoes), which invited another kind of popular participation, the chopping down of opponents' poles by partisan vandals. Party leaders wished to achieve or at least convey the appearance of popularity, even of an irresistible popular movement, in the 1840 campaign, and in some respects they succeeded beyond their dreams. Citizens in unprecedented numbers joined campaign clubs, attended party rallies, erected and destroyed liberty poles, and, above all, voted on election day. In our four towns, voter turnout ranged from 77 percent in Kingston to 89 percent in Marietta. This was a triumph, not merely of the Whigs who won the election, but of electoral democracy and its essential vehicle, the political party.[23]

The consequences of this triumph, however, were not yet clear. Would it be repeated? Would the political party be the means for generating and expressing political enthusiasm in future elections? Recognizing that spontaneity (or at least the appearance of it) was useful in an age of democracy and individualism, party leaders needed simultaneously to perfect their organization and to keep it hidden. They had to stimulate the kinds of enthusiasm that they could attach to a popular hero or an ad hoc campaign club, but also make sure that the party itself was larger and more important than any candidate, club, or campaign spectacle. Kingston's Democratic editor, Rodney A. Chipp, conveyed this clearly and forcefully after the 1840 election by urging local Democrats "to keep up the spirit of active organization." Recognizing the difficulty of sustaining interest among ordinary people who were not party activists, and who had other things to do in their day-to-day lives, he drew upon the traditions of Cincinnatus and the Minutemen to dress partisan commitment in the cloak and boots of patriotic military vigilance:

> We are aware that after the intense excitement of the late grand struggle, the public mind seeks rest, and that individuals will again devote themselves to their customary avocations, from which they have been for so long a period withdrawn. This can be done without losing sight of the cardinal interests of the country. They can carry with them to their workshops, and to the field, the principles for which they have been, and are still contending, and undisturbed by the ferocity of political opposition, can in the sanctuary of their own thoughts deliberately mature their principles and settle their plans for future action. After the convulsive heavings of the body politic, a deceptive calm will follow—the precursor of a more intense and determined struggle—a struggle involving the life and death of our political institutions—and every true soldier to the faith should be prepared at a moment's warning to obey the summons to battle.[24]

Individual vigilance, however, would not suffice. Democrats needed to "PRE-SERVE THEIR ORGANIZATION," precisely because private citizens could not be counted on to remain politically engaged without it. The party newspaper was itself an important element of ongoing partisan organization, and so too were the standing town and county committees and the caucuses and conventions they continued to summon when another election loomed. But would these be sufficient? Everything that had made the 1840 campaign such a popular success was new—including, for that matter, many of the party newspapers. (The *Ulster Republican* was not new, but three of the partisan papers of our four towns had been founded within a year or so of the 1840 election; three others were initiated in 1837.) Partisans could find some basis for confidence in the numerous permanent and temporary roles that each party created beyond those of attending caucuses and voting. These roles expanded the party outward into the community, potentially involving many adult white males in partisan affairs in ways that would bind them to the party as an institution. The extent of this expansion, therefore, and the relative concentration or diffusion of partisan roles within the community, are significant issues with respect to the "space" the new party system was coming to occupy in American life. The party's prospects as an institution of greater or lesser significance and durability were bound up with the question of how many men played greater or lesser roles within it.

To examine the actual pattern of political activism within each of our four communities we have recorded every name that appears in every newspaper for the three-year period we have been discussing, and have accumulated the list of activities, political and nonpolitical, in which each named person engaged. This method for recapturing the total pattern of activism in political and communal affairs is by no means perfect. Especially in this early, experimental phase of party organization, local partisan papers differed in their campaign reportage, and in their coverage of other communal institutions and events. Some editors took greater pains than others to record the names of those who played some role in political and communal affairs, and it is certain that none of our papers is a perfectly comprehensive record of such people. With respect to political participation, however, partisan editors had good reason to record as many names and activities as possible, and the newspapers have left us what is surely a very good record of who did what in the emerging political institutions of the early 1840s.

Kingston's papers provide us with the largest number and highest proportion of men identified with some kind of political activity. In a town with somewhat fewer than 1,400 adult white males in 1840, the Whig and Democratic papers of 1840–42 include the names of more than eight hundred partisans, fully 60 percent of the 1840 electorate, split nearly evenly between the two parties. This is an extraordinarily high proportion; indeed, it is not far below the 77 percent of Kingston's men who voted in the 1840 election. How many of these men were party activists? Before answering this question, let us observe that if newspaper coverage somewhat understates the number of such activists, the population record at our disposal—the number of men present in Kingston during the several weeks of the summer of 1840 when the census was being collected—fails to capture all the men who lived in the town as available political and communal participants during all or some part of the period 1840–42. In a youthful and highly mobile society such as the United States the number of men who came of age and who moved into and out of a town such as Kingston in a three-year period was considerable. Hence, the proportion of activists to the total adult male population may well have been lower, not higher, than the written record suggests.

Even apart from this caveat, a closer look reveals that many of the men named in the party papers ought not be considered party activists, if by that term we intend some significant and recurring (at a minimum, occasional) activity on the party's behalf. Nearly half of the men appointed to those large convention delegations we have noted (50 percent of Democratic delegates, 46 percent of Whigs) do not appear in their party's newspaper in any other context, and 10 percent of each party's large delegations are named only on one other long list. This tends to confirm our suspicion that to have been named to a party delegation in Kingston in the early 1840s meant little beyond the individual's willingness to make a public declaration of his political allegiance. Within the remaining quarter of Kingston's men, moreover, were large numbers whose names appear only once or twice (apart from the long delegate lists) in political contexts. Indeed, the unquestionably active partisans—men whose names appear several times as committeemen, convention officers, candidates, and the like—amount to approximately fifty in each party (taken together, approximately 7 percent of the adult male population of 1840), and the men who appear often enough to convey the impression of party leadership constitute a much smaller group than that. We counted seventeen Democrats and twenty-seven Whigs who we would designate "very active" in Kingston's political affairs, and a total of fifteen men from both parties who appear to have been party leaders. We must allow, of course, for the probability of considerable "back room" influence that does not manifest itself in newspapers, but it is likely that much of this influence was exercised by the men who are identifiable in the papers as party leaders. In March 1841, for example, the Whig editor accused "the Chipps" of dominating the local Democratic party.[25] There are four Chipps on our list of active Democrats, two among the "very active" seventeen, and one, editor Rodney A. Chipp himself, within what would appear to be the party leadership's innermost circle.

Augusta's party newspapers generated several long lists of petitioners, delegates, and campaign club members, and, like Kingston's, a fairly comprehensive array of reported political activities. A smaller proportion (37 percent) of the adult white-male population of 1840 appears by name in the partisan press, but the pyramid of evident activity has almost exactly the same shape as in Kingston. Slightly fewer than 60 percent of identified Whigs and Democrats appear only on one or two long lists, while 27 percent of the Whigs and 30 percent of the Democrats were only moderately active in other ways. Some seventy men, less than 5 percent of the Richmond County electorate of 1840, were significantly active in the affairs of one or the other party, and the party leadership appears to have been a little smaller than it was in Kingston. Similar patterns appear in our two smaller towns. Marietta's Whig paper mentions several large delegations, but provides names for only one, the town delegation to the February 1840 state convention. Some 40 percent of the delegates do not appear again in the paper, and the clearly active portion of the party amounts to about 4 percent of the town's 1840 electorate. And in Greenfield, the vast majority of Whigs appear only on the May list of signatories calling for a Harrison convention, while all but a few of the town's Democratic voters do not appear at all in their party's paper. There are 160 Whigs in our file of Greenfield party participants, fully 40 percent of the town's adult white men in 1840, and 149 of them signed the petition. That may have been a promising start for the Whig campaign, but fully 129 of the signatories do not appear again in the party paper during the campaign or for the following two years. Greenfield's Democratic editor challenged the list itself, claiming that Whig organizers had used deceptive means to get some men, including Democrats, to sign. (A little later, he also challenged Whig estimates of the convention's size, calling upon the story of the boy who told his mother that a hundred cats had been fighting in the garden, and, when his mother objected, whittled down the number to fifty, then to twenty, and finally to "Capting Smith's old black cat and our own, a fighting and squalling like all creation.")[26] In any case, about 13 percent of Greenfield's men appear in the town's papers as delegates, committeemen, candidates, or in some other active party role. We would count 3 percent as significant party activists. These are rough proportions, as are those that pertain to our other towns, and we must assume that they do not capture the entirety of partisan activism in Greenfield. But given the likelihood that political reporting was fairly complete at the upper end of the activist spectrum, we must assume they are high in relation to the total numbers of men present in the town during some part of the 1840–42 election cycle.

Large majorities of the voting citizens of our four communities were not, by our estimation, active party men, and in each case the distribution of formal partisan roles pyramided upward to a small coterie of Whig or Democratic leaders. But this is in the nature of local voluntary societies, and we should not be surprised to see that activism within even an important institution should be confined to a relatively small proportion of the eligible population. We would, in fact, argue that fifty, seventy, or a hundred political activists constitute a large rather than a small number in communities of this size. What we have found in our four towns is that the political party was nothing like a general and undifferentiated congregation of believers—that, in any case, would have been a most remarkable discovery—but was a formal institution, directed and staffed by a relatively distinct subset of the population it episodically mobilized in pursuit of its own version of the public good. That subset, as we will see, was large enough, and within it were men who worked hard enough, to maintain the institution after the "convulsive heavings of the body politic" (to refer again to editor Chipp's metaphor for the 1840 election) had ceased. The party's voting masses did not "preserve their organization"; it was preserved, nonetheless, by the most interested among them.

The presence in each of our communities of a sufficiently large and committed body of partisan activists did not, however, immediately settle the form of the local party as an institution, or the ongoing relations between the party and that large part of the electorate that did not regularly perform formal roles within it. For a few years, at least, some of these forms and relations remained surprisingly fluid. In some instances, for example, delegate nominations were made by campaign clubs rather than by regular party meetings, and in Augusta and Marietta the relations between these clubs, the Young Men's associations, and the permanent party were not at all clear. Did the party, as a popular institution, even have an ongoing existence? Party leaders would be there, as they always had been, behind the scenes and on standing committees, but was there an analogous role in the organization for ordinary citizens? Or would they belong only to the campaign clubs that might or might not appear before important elections? Leaders had taken pains to portray the party as a popular institution, but some of their techniques had obscured the organization itself. In Marietta, the first Whig county convention in 1840 was advertised as a "Harrison & Tyler meeting," and was called by "many citizens" for "the people of Washington County who are in favor of a reform in the administration of public affairs." Similarly, the Whig county central committee in Kingston called upon the "friends of Harrison and Tyler," not "Whigs," to hold town nominating caucuses in June of 1840, and two months later referred to itself as the "Harrison Central Committee." Augusta's Democratic leaders called a "public meeting" of those "friendly to the present administration, and opposed to William H. Harrison."[27] These were typical ways of representing the organization as a seemingly ad hoc response to public feeling, utilized by the very men who were simultaneously insisting upon the party as the necessary vehicle for building and expressing political commitment. There was a contradiction here between organization and popular engagement that had not been resolved by the 1840 presidential election.

Our four towns provide us with other significant clues as to why party activists, even in the flush of this first truly massive campaign and election, could not be certain of their role in succeeding campaigns. The immediate future, for one thing, offered nothing to compare with the excitement of the presidential election, and party men faced an understandable falloff in interest in the local, state, and congressional elections of 1841 and 1842. They did organize for most of these elections (there was still resistance to the politicization of some village and town elections), and voter turnout, though invariably lower than in 1840, remained relatively high, ranging from around 50 percent in the 1841 congressional and county races in Richmond County, to perhaps 78 percent in Marietta for state legislative elections of the same year.[28] But there were fewer rallies, and far fewer attempts to form campaign clubs. In August of 1841, Richmond County's Whig leadership asked the city wards and country districts to form Tippecanoe clubs in preparation for state and county elections—this with Tippecanoe himself four months in his grave!—but only one ward actually complied.[29] Nowhere else was this sort of thing attempted. Caucuses and conventions were actually more numerous as the parties continued to develop, and party newspapers claimed large and enthusiastic gatherings at some of them. But they also found more occasions to complain of apathy, especially with respect to town caucuses, and more frequently ridiculed the attendance claims of their rival editors. When Democrats of all the New York counties between New York and Albany gathered in Kingston in October 1841 to celebrate President Tyler's veto of the Whig banking bill, the local Whig editor claimed a gathering of only 196 local Democrats, "including boys," to meet the incoming boats, and a final procession that reached "the astonishing number of 1,511—headed by a Grand Marshal on a white horse, and trailed by an urchin riding on a stick, with a turkey feather in his hat." The Democratic editor's estimate was 12,000, and his description rather more positive, but a week earlier he had admitted that the autumn convention of Ulster County Democrats was "not as large as usual," because of both bad weather and the fact that "a very limited number of delegates were appointed by the several towns." A year later he would comment on "negligence and indifference to the town meetings" that appointed delegates to the county convention, even while finding some comfort—and the opportunity to pay back the opposing editor in his own coin—in the claim that the Whig convention had attracted five delegates, "three from the village and two from the country."[30]

Editorial complaints and attacks of this sort suggest something of the difficulty of maintaining effective party organization in the off years, especially in outlying towns. So, too, do warnings of the possible effects of falling newspaper subscriptions, which appeared in the *Ulster Republican* as early as January 1841.[31] But there are indications in nearly all of our papers that some of the difficulties the parties encountered in 1841 and 1842 were also present in 1840, however camouflaged they may have been by the many opportunities to write of Tippecanoe clubs, log cabins, liberty poles, and barbecues. Whig editors made much of the Tippecanoe clubs, for example, which were founded with much pomp, and with careful reporting in the papers of the names of officers and vigilance-committee members. The clubs were intended to meet weekly throughout the campaign, and to play a significant role in organizing and carrying out rallies and other campaign events. As we have seen, some even participated in selecting convention delegates. But it appears that in the three towns that had these clubs—Greenfield, recall, did not—their role diminished rather than grew as the campaign proceeded. In Marietta, where the Tippecanoe Club had been founded in March (with sixty-two members drawn from among the 161 Marietta delegates to the state convention), weekly meetings appear to have ceased as early as May. It is hardly mentioned in the Whig paper through the remainder of the campaign, surfacing only in December to arrange a Harrison victory festival that may not have occurred. "Upwards of one hundred" Kingston Whigs formed a Tippecanoe Club in May, again to meet weekly, but after the log cabin was dedicated in early July this club too seems to have lost any role in the campaign, and disappeared from the newspaper's election coverage. In September, "friends of Harrison and Tyler," not the Tippecanoe Club, met at the log cabin to "ratify" county nominations. Augusta Whigs had founded four ward-based clubs and a countywide club in May and June. The county Tippecanoe Club sponsored barbecues until shortly before election day, but when two of the ward clubs announced meetings on September 23 it was the first such announcement in more than three months, and the last to appear during the campaign.[32] The founding of the Tippecanoe clubs, and of Young Men's and Democratic associations as well, gave each party editor the opportunity of introducing the campaign season in his paper with specific evidences of the popularity of the Whig or Democratic mission, and of the energies that would be invested in the campaign to come. The clubs were material for good editorial propaganda, at the least, but with the possible exception of the county Tippecanoe Club in Augusta they do not seem to have been much more than that.

A similar question may be raised about the lists of petitioners calling for a local party meeting or convention, or about the large delegations selected at local party meetings in Kingston and Marietta. Signing a petition was a simple declaration of partisan allegiance, requiring but a moment's investment.[33] A more serious commitment to political affairs is suggested by service as an official party delegate. The very length of some of the delegate lists, however, suggests the possible dilution of the significance of selection. Were the 350 Kingston delegates selected for the Democratic congressional convention of 1840 really intended to represent the town in a deliberative body of party activists? Or were most of them merely named and listed in hopes that they would swell the "immense gathering" that would attend the assured nomination of John Van Buren? Were these delegates chosen by a democratic gathering of the party's voters (gatherings that appear to have been smaller than the delegations they named), or by party leaders, working from their list of the town's known or presumed Democrats? Again, what did selection mean to the "delegates" themselves? How, indeed, can we assess the meaning of any of the evidences of political participation—in party meetings, on lists of petitioners, in campaign clubs, on party committees—that we find in the local partisan press?

The meanings of party activism can be illuminated by examining various ways in which it intersected with other aspects of community life. Every community contained institutions other than political parties, and the party papers, being also town papers, frequently reported on the meetings and other activities of temperance and Bible societies, militia and fire companies, fraternal lodges, lyceums, and various other organizations; and sometimes reported as well on the election of directors to the boards of local banks, insurance companies, and transportation companies. Did partisan politics carry over into these organizations, shaping in any way their memberships or the outcomes of their own elections? We might well expect party politics to have determined the composition of local bank boards, for example, for the chartering of banks by state legislatures had become a highly politicized matter during the 1830s, during and after President Jackson's fabled "war" against the Second Bank of the United States. In Kingston, even before the new alignment of Whigs and Democrats was completed, there had been a fierce contest between Clintonian and Bucktail factions within the old Republican Party over the question of who should control a second local bank, the first having fallen into the hands of the Clintonians. This local "bank war" dominated Kingston's politics during the mid-1830s, and resulted in another Clintonian victory (or betrayal, in the minds of the Bucktails, who thought they had achieved a deal that would even out the political control of banking in Kingston).[34] By the end of the decade, in Kingston as in other New York towns, Clintonians had migrated to the Whig Party, leaving the Bucktails to control and define the party now known as Democrats. What, in the meantime, had happened to the control of Kingston's banks? In fact, every politically identifiable board member of the original Bank of Ulster County was a Whig, as were ten politically active directors of the newer Kingston Bank. There were, on the other hand, two Democrats on the latter board, and nine bank directors in Kingston (of thirty-one) whose names do not appear in any political context in the party press. Political "ownership" of the banks does seem to have been modified somewhat; yet, it is evident that politics and political affiliation still affected the banking business in Kingston in the early 1840s.

Politics did not carry over so clearly into banks in our other towns, or into other economic and communal institutions, even in Kingston. Whigs and Democrats mingled on the boards of four of Augusta's five banks, and a number of directors on each board (one-fifth in all) are not identified in the press with either political party. The Mechanics' Bank had no Democratic directors, but three of the nine board members were not politically active, and the bank's cashier was a Democrat. It is doubtful that this was a Whig institution in any purposeful way. Men from both parties (and from among the politically inactive) can be found on the boards of the Steamboat Company of Georgia, and of both banks and the local insurance company in Greenfield. In Kingston there were two public meetings called to discuss the town's interests with respect to railroad construction projects. The officers and committees appointed at these meetings were drawn nearly equally from the two parties (but not perfectly equally, which might suggest a deliberate political compromise), and at one of them more than two-thirds were drawn from men who played no visible political role in the community. Our list of Marietta Democrats is incomplete, but is just large enough to reveal the presence of men from both parties on the board of the Marietta and Newport Turnpike Company.

There is hardly any suggestion of partisanship in the leadership or membership patterns in any of the communal institutions of our towns. The Ulster County Agriculture Society, the Kingston Young Men's Association, the Greenfield Lyceum, three Augusta Masonic lodges, four militia companies in the same city—these and others reveal a seemingly random mixture of Democrats, Whigs, and the politically inactive. The only significant hint of partisanship is in the membership of the five sections of the Augusta Fire Department, which perhaps should not surprise us, given the political role that some fire companies played in the wards of larger cities. A slight majority of the 116 Augusta firemen of 1840 cannot be identified with either party through the partisan press. But among those who can, there is a decided partisan imbalance in four of the five sections of the department: ten Whigs and one Democrat in section 1, for example, and seven Democrats and one Whig in section 4. Section 2 is evenly balanced between the parties. Did these local units of the Augusta Fire Department function as political institutions? There is no mention of this in the party newspapers, and we would observe that among the politically identifiable firemen (only 47 percent of the department), most were only minimally active in party affairs. There was, in addition to the regular department, an Augusta Independent Fire Company, in which we do find a number of significant political activists, but they are almost evenly divided between the two political parties.

An Augusta city directory published in 1841 helps us go still further into the relation between partisanship and daily life.[35] We get a glimpse of how politics may have functioned in the workplace, for example, from the listing of business partnerships in the directory, and from the inclusion of employers' names in the entries of many of Augusta's commercial clerks. Thirty-three of these clerks are in our file of political participants—twenty-six Whigs and seven Democrats. Fourteen of the Whigs worked for Whig employers, three worked for Democrats, and one worked for the cross-party partnership of Stovall and Simmons, cotton factors and commission merchants. The employers of the other eight are not identified in the party papers. Of the seven Democratic clerks, four worked for men not listed in the party press, and one each worked for a Democrat, a Whig, and the partnership of Stovall and Simmons. The tendency of Whigs to hire and work for other Whigs is largely explained by the preponderance of Whigs in Augusta's commercial economy (and in our file of political participants); that is, it is not disproportionate to the extent that suggests politics played a role in the employment process. Of the 169 identifiably partisan merchants in our file, 122, or 72 percent, were Whigs. Interestingly, the most politically active Whig among our clerks—John J. Cohen, one of the most active Whigs in Augusta—was one of the few who worked for a

Democrat. Nor do commercial partnerships disclose a disproportionate political affiliation, even among party leaders. There were seven leading Whigs and two leading Democrats who were members of business partnerships. Pleasant Stovall was one of these Whigs, and we have already noted his partnership with the Democrat Granville Simmons. Stovall also maintained a partnership in a wholesale and retail grocery business with the Whig Robert Hamlen, and two other leading Whigs ran businesses with Whig partners, but four others had partners who had no identifiable political affiliation. Both leading Democrats, the hardware merchant John Bones and the physician, medical school professor, and druggist Ignatius P. Garvin, had Whigs for partners. The pattern is similar among Whigs and Democrats who were not party leaders. Did politics shape business life in the grocery and dry-goods stores of Broad Street in Augusta? Perhaps customers shopped mainly in the stores of their fellow Whigs or Democrats, and perhaps political talk suffused or supplanted discussions of goods, prices, and credit. Our participant files and the Augusta city directory do not tell us about shopping and shop talk (we will soon visit a document that does), but they do invite us to question the role of politics in the commercial employment market, and in the establishment of the most fundamental business relations.

Nor did political affiliation have much of an effect on where Augusta's merchants and clerks found room and board when the workday was done. In the cities and towns of this era there were numerous commercial men, young and not so young, single and married, who boarded in hotels, boarding houses, and private houses. One hundred and two of our Augusta political and communal participants boarded in 1840, including fifty-nine Whigs and twenty-three Democrats.[36] Nearly half lived in a half-dozen boarding hotels, only one of which reveals even a hint of partisan segregation. (It is an ambiguous hint at that: the four identifiable partisans who lived at Washington Hall were all Whigs, but all four were also grocers.) Augusta's largest boarding hotel, the Eagle and Phoenix, housed fourteen Whigs and six Democrats, and was owned and managed by a Democrat. Private boarding was equally nonpartisan. Eight Whig householders took in Whig boarders, but five gave room and board to Democrats or to a mixture of Whigs and Democrats. Two Democratic householders boarded men listed on our file; one took in Democrats, the other Whigs. There was a mixture of Democrats and Whigs in three of the seven households that had room for more than one boarder.

All of these clues are valuable because they go behind the rhetoric of partisanship that we find in the political press. But we can also find evidence bearing upon the extent of partisan enthusiasm in the press itself, in both the heat and the aftermath of the 1840 election. Partisan editors vigorously and continuously promoted their parties' electoral campaigns for months preceding the election. It is perhaps surprising, therefore, to encounter the expressions of relief written by editors and occasionally by correspondents at the conclusion of this unusually energetic campaign. These expressions were by no means peculiar to 1840; indeed, as active campaigns became regularized in ensuing elections the relieved farewell to political agitation would take on the character of a ritualized cleansing. But we can already see the themes embodied in this ritual in 1840, in editorials and letters that suggest more than empty posturing. Consider this lengthy statement by the (victorious) Whig editor of Greenfield, written immediately after the 1840 presidential election:

> We are heartily glad the contest is over. It is not very agreeable to be compelled to wallow in politics day and night, for months together. There may be some who have no higher appetite than to derive pleasure from the asperities of political controversy; who view with exultation the tattered characters of their opponents, cut in shreds by the keen weapons of party knights who endeavor to win imperishable fame by tilting with and unhorsing the champions who dare oppose them. Such persons, we hope, are not numerous. Indeed, the activity of our population forbids that they should be; for such a perverted taste can only be created, or at any rate indulged, where idleness invites to the perpetual contemplation of political measures, tricks, and chicanery, and thus renders a clatter and disturbance necessary to furnish food for a gangrened mind. The great majority of our citizens are industrious, and find it pleasanter to pursue their labors un-harassed by the excitement of politics. These are glad when the warmly contested elections are over, and they can devote their energies to their business in quietness and peace.[37]

In a matter of days the portrayal of the campaign had changed dramatically, from the necessary and principled warfare of a Cincinnatus to the unsavory scratching and gouging of the idlers of the community, those few ("such persons, we hope, are not numerous") the editor contrasts with "the great majority of our citizens" who prefer to "devote their energies to their business in quietness and peace." The latter were not so much enthused as harassed by the campaign, which, in any case, was an unnatural and even unhealthy excitement that temporarily distracted people from the more genuine business of quietly making their livings. Two themes, then, pervade this postelection statement from the victorious professional exhorter of Greenfield's quiet citizens: the superiority of private life to politics, and the separation of the community into a politically eager minority and a politically harassed majority. Only the latter were cleansed of politics in the election aftermath. The former were merely quieted.

These were by no means the only sentiments expressed at the end of the 1840 campaign. We have already observed the very different election postmortem of Kingston's Democratic editor, who urged the faithful to maintain vigilance and organization during the political off-season. We might note, too, that the posture of detachment from the fray was perhaps more freely available to the winner than to the loser. It is remarkable, however, that the Whig editor did not pronounce upon his party's principles, nor upon the redemption of the nation from Van Buren and the Democrats, nor upon the beauties of a political system that could produce so splendid a result. And we can find the same detachment expressed by people who were not party editors. Following the 1841 election, but with clear references back to the excitements of 1840, "Augusta" wrote to the *Daily Constitutionalist*:

> "Why, if party excitement is to be continually harrassing our community, let there be a general declaration! Elect upon no other principle—buy sugar and coffee upon the same—dry goods, groceries, hardware and cutlery. Have Harrison and Democratic grog shops and loads of wood—political butchers, bakers and gardeners—party clothing stores, boarding houses and livery stables—party lawyers, physicians and preachers. . . . [Now] when the sky is clearing, and social intercourse once more hallowing with its divine associations, our comminglings together, let *him* be regarded as an enemy to peace who would light again at an unseasonable time, the fires of political discord among us.[38]

Harassment again (if spelled a little differently), and here expressed in a way that helps answer the question we raised earlier about the infusion of politics into the workday world of dry goods and groceries. "Augusta" believed that "party clothing stores, boarding houses and livery stables" did *not* exist, and used the threat of such things as a comical reductio ad absurdum of the effects of partisan enthusiasm. How deranged our works and days would be if party politics disturbed "our comminglings together," especially during that quite lengthy "unseasonable time" when an election was not at hand. "Augusta" seems, indeed, to have had a more general indictment in mind, as he or she was writing at the end of a political campaign, in obvious exasperation at even a "seasonable" intrusion of politics into daily life.

Attempts such as these to mark the limits of legitimate political intrusion tell us also that such limits had been exceeded during the campaign, with the willing cooperation of large numbers of ordinary citizens. Something did impel Americans in 1840 to participate in politics to an extent never before seen in a national election. Continuing, active engagement, as we have seen, may have been somewhat less than the party editors would have us believe, but the massive vote on election day was the culmination of a campaign in which, as never before, "every man, woman, and child preferred politics to anything else."[39] Why did Americans, including at least some who professed distaste for political controversy, become so caught up in the 1840 campaign? Or, to shift this question slightly, to what extent was the evident quickening of political interest driven by substantive political questions, the pursuit of which involved a significant expansion of civic engagement and, perhaps too, a deepening of American public culture? The two parties had in fact clarified significant policy differences over such issues as banking and the management of public funds, and the economic depression that followed in the wake of the 1837 collapse made the stakes seem much higher. Was the 1840 election, then, a massive referendum on significant public issues in a time of crisis? Famously, it was not. Historians have long recognized the reductionist sloganeering of the log-cabin and hard-cider campaign as a means of stirring up popular support without engaging policy issues; indeed, by avoiding them as much as possible. The Democrats had earlier trumped their poorly organized and more circumspect opponents with simple images of Old Hickory as military hero and man of the people, and now it was the Whigs' turn with William Henry Harrison, the hero of Tippecanoe and the Thames, the ordinary farmer of North Bend. Outmaneuvered Democrats fought back mostly with charges of aristocratic hypocrisy, and, even more, with attacks on the legitimacy of Harrison's generation-old claim to military heroism. This, more than anything else, was the "issue" of the 1840 presidential election, its popular resonance nicely captured in this description of the campaign in Ohio by a correspondent to the Whig *New York Express*:

> The People out here, are not settling "Bank Questions," nor "Monopolies," but they are settling whether the retired Farmer of North Bend served his country or not,—whether Fort Meigs was gallantly defended, or honor or dishonor was won upon the Thames. . . . They sit down and form the Tippecanoe order of Battle again, in diagrams, with pieces of chalk and charcoal, and they scratch down where Harrison was, where Joe Davies fell, where the savages rushed upon the bayonet even, and thus Tippecanoe is all fought again. . . . You can enter scarcely a village, or hardly a Log Cabin: you cannot find an Old Settler, but tells you some War Story thus.[40]

Whig orators, Harrison included, referred constantly to the details of Tippecanoe and the Thames, and to Democratic slanders of Old Tip's bravery and military achievements. They contrasted Harrison's work as an ordinary farmer with Van Buren's career in politics, far removed from the common people (while conveniently ignoring such facts as Harrison's birth to a politically prominent Virginia family, Van Buren's to a small-town tavern keeper, and Harrison's career in politics and diplomacy). They muddled the substantive differences between the parties by attacking Van Buren's profligacy in office and by calling for "retrenchment." And they promoted the " 'hurrah' campaign" at every turn. Summing up the campaign, a Georgia Whig gloated to his party's state convention a year later: "[I]f we had effected a revolution on the politics of the country by means of 'coon skins, pepper pods, and log cabins,' it was to say the least a splendid humbug."[41]

A revolution and a humbug—to others who experienced it, this was a disturbing combination. Some Whig leaders were not comfortable with the new tactics of popular mobilization, and there are occasional expressions of disgust in the newspapers of our four representative communities. The papers include also editorial warnings about political excess, and humorous tales satirizing mindless partisanship: " 'Sewke?'—'Well, Jonathan?'—'I love you like pizen

and sweetmeats.' 'Dew tell! . . . Jonathan Higgins, whats your politics?' 'I'm for
Van Buren, straight.' 'Wall sir, then you can march straight home cors I wont
have nobody that aint for Harrison, thats flat.' 'Three cheers for old Tip!' sung
Jonathan. 'Thats your sort!' says Sukey, 'when shall we be married Jonathan?' "[42] All of these register at least a small measure of dissent from the Tippecanoe campaign. The 1840 election, it seems, attracted vast numbers of Americans who had been, and perhaps continued to be, only superficially interested
in politics, but it disturbed others who expected a more serious discussion of
public issues. One disgruntled New York Democrat predicted that each party
would henceforth behave "like a circus company with bands of music and
dazzling ponies, clowns with pink noses to make folks laugh & banjo singers,
a little lofty tumbling to secure votes."[43]

Was the 1840 election, then, no more than a political circus, and the expansion of popular participation merely a sham? In his full-length study of the
election, Robert Gunderson asserts that they were. "Implicit in this new Whig
strategy," writes Gunderson, "was of course a contemptuous evaluation of
the intelligence of the people."[44] Most historians do not go as far as Gunderson
in this respect, but agree instead with William Nisbet Chambers, who finds
"beneath the strategy" of campaign clubs, pole raisings, and symbol-laden parades and rallies, "an emergent political democracy" within which national
politics was becoming popular, and popular politics national.[45] Michael F. Holt
goes even further, arguing that there were significant economic issues "behind
the folderol" of the Tippecanoe campaign, and that voters responded to significant policy differences between the two parties.[46] Deliberately or acciden-
tally, Whig leaders were creating a new kind of political forum for the exercise
of a more forceful and independent citizenship, shaped, to be sure, by a more
centralized political party, but freer of the constraints and parochialism of old
local influence networks. Its initial enticements were more than a little crude,
and some traditional leaders had reason to be disturbed by its unseemliness
and triviality. They may have been even more unsettled, however, by its democratic implications.

Whether circus or forum, the new political techniques introduced in the
1840 campaign must be understood within the context of an extremely small
and limited government. Richard L. McCormick has accurately characterized
both state and national government's role in this era as "that of promoting
development by distributing resources and privileges to individuals and
groups."[47] The granting of public lands, franchises, and special privileges and
immunities, the raising or lowering of specific tariffs, the appointment and
removal of public officials—this continued to be the day-to-day business of
antebellum government, and it constituted a system that, save perhaps for the
delivery of mail, touched lightly and usually indirectly on the vast majority of
Americans who had few claims to make on their legislators or on other public
officials.[48] Recognizing this fundamental fact somewhat deflates the impact of

both Gunderson's denunciation and Chambers's and Holt's validation of the 1840 campaign. Despite its energies and enthusiasms, this was not, after all, a life-and-death struggle. Ordinary citizens who subjected themselves to the "splendid humbug" were able to enjoy the contest of spirits and wills, argue over the merits of Harrison's claims of valor, and vote as they would, knowing—even if they did concern themselves with banks, the subtreasury, and hard times—that the outcome would not have a significant impact on their lives. Nor was the 1840 election for many citizens a confrontation of nation-defining political symbols. On balance, the forum seems more important than the circus, the fact of expanded participation more important than its trivialization. But neither should be exaggerated. Americans were freer and likelier to engage, to be humbugged, and then to turn away to other things.[49]

JACK DOWNING'S DISCOVERY

Some Americans, as we have seen, invested more of themselves in the institutions that drove the 1840 campaign. "Augusta" and the Greenfield Whig editor distinguished, as has much of the preceding discussion, between an excitable but less deeply engaged mass of citizens, and a smaller cadre of political activists more fully involved in the campaign and in the ongoing party apparatus. The role of organization in the electoral revolution of 1840 appears in other ways as well. For example, several historians have discovered detailed instructions from state party leaders, in states such as Massachusetts and Illinois, concerning the organization of county and town committees, the gathering of information about local voters, and the institution of campaign and election-day voter mobilization techniques.[50] These instructions were not intended for public circulation, as each party sought to disguise the organization behind a facade of grassroots popular participation. Interestingly, the Confidential Circular of the Massachusetts Whig State Central Committee was published in Greenfield's Democratic paper as a revelation of the antidemocratic machinations of the opposite party—yet another indication of how novel and how vulnerable to the charge of "wire pulling" such instructions, and such things as county and town committees, still were.[51] But they were also forceful, even to an extent that helps explain much of the difference between 1840 and earlier national elections. William Henry Harrison, we should recall, was one of the regional Whig candidates in the 1836 presidential election, and in fact he stimulated no revolutionary voter turnout in that year in the states on whose ballots his electors appeared. On the contrary, the 5.5 percent increase of votes in these states between 1832 and 1836 was certainly smaller than the increase in the numbers of eligible voters. In 1840, in the same states, the total vote increased by 53.5 percent.[52] Organization was a big part of the difference between 1836 and 1840, probably the biggest part, and its effectiveness returns us to the question of what impelled some American men to become active within these organizations.

An important answer to this question is anticipated in a striking fiction of the preceding decade. Within a year of Andrew Jackson's first inauguration, Seba Smith, the new editor of the *Portland Courier*, began printing the "letters" of Major Jack Downing of Downingville, Maine. Smith's Jack Downing is a shrewdly innocent country bumpkin who discovers the world of politics on a trip down to the state capital to "sell my load of ax handles, and mother's cheese, and cousin Nabby's bundle of footings."[53] At first Jack has difficulty in figuring out what is going on in the state legislature, but it is one of the sights to see in the city, and he is pleased to report back to his Uncle Joshua, "for you know he is always reading newspapers and talking politics, when he can get any body to talk with him."[54] Soon, though, Jack has a revelation—politics can be a lucrative alternative to real work! The rapidity with which the legislators passed bills near the end of the term puts him in mind of those "noisy talking fellers" at a husking who "care a good deal more about what they can get to eat and drink, than they du about the corn."[55] Jack disapproves of this, and when he finds himself mentioned as a candidate for governor, one of his first reactions is to worry about his qualifications for the job. He reassures himself in an interesting way:

> Considerable part of the business I shouldn't be a mite afraid but what I could du, that is, *the turning out and putting in*. I know every crook and turn of that business; for I dont believe there's a boy in our county, though I say it myself, *that's turned out and tied up more cattle than I have*. And they say a Governor has a good deal of this sort of work to du.[56]

Perhaps Jack does not yet understand the difference between herding cattle and dispensing patronage, but as he endures a sobering political apprenticeship in the ensuing gubernatorial race his stance toward the rewards of office shifts decisively. He writes Uncle Joshua:

> I am tired of hard work, and I mean to have an office some how or other yet. Its true I and all our family got rather dished in the governor business; if I'd only got in, they should every soul of 'em had an office, down to the forty-ninth cousin. But its no use to cry for spilt milk. I've got another plan in my head; I find the United States offices are the things to make money in, and if I can get hold of a good fat one, you may appoint a day of thanksgiving up there in Downingville, and throw by your work every one of you as long as you live.[57]

Jack's plan is to run for Congress, but news from Washington gives him an even better one. "They say the President's four great Secretaries have all resigned; only think of that, uncle. And they say their salaries were *six thousand dollars a-year*; only jest think of that, uncle. Six thousand dollars a year. Why, a governor's salary is a fool to it."[58] So Jack is off to Washington and further adventures in the paradise of patronage.

Even in the earliest days of "rotation in office," in short, Seba Smith found the seam between the popular and the professional. His ordinary country boy, somewhat baffled at first, and tending toward disapproval, comes to understand the new world of politics as a better and easier way of making money than the real work of farming and peddling ax handles. This is the core of his political awakening, and it remained the sum of his motivation through his many incarnations in the years that followed. Jack Downing became the emblematic American political adventurer, and in some measure, too, an emblematic Jacksonian era entrepreneur, a Young American eager to seize upon some aspect of a quickening capitalist economy to make his fortune. Amidst the economic opportunities provided by the "market revolution," we should remember, was occupational dislocation and uncertainty as well. That the second American party system arrived as the market economy was taking off may have been more than mere coincidence, for, in addition to providing the issues that divided Democrats from Whigs, it also provided an incentive for various not entirely self-reliant entrepreneurs who might model themselves on Seba Smith's man on the make. Others might build cotton mills or bottle patent medicines; Jack's field is politics, and it never once occurs to him that there might be some other purpose in this field than the making of a good living from some kind of elective office or patronage appointment.

The currency of this emblematic figure circulated very widely through the antebellum press, and in other media, and it would be difficult to overstate its influence. In his classic 1840 memoir, *Two Years before the Mast*, Richard Henry Dana recounts an encounter in September of 1836 between his ship, which had long been absent from the United States, and another that was outbound from New York:

> We had made the mistake, on board, of supposing that a new President had been chosen the last winter, and as we filled away the captain hailed and asked who was President of the United States. They answered, Andrew Jackson; but thinking that the old General could not have been elected for a third time, we hailed again, and they answered Jack Downing, and left us to correct the mistake at our leisure.[59]

Patronage had always been an important part of the political order—the term itself grew out of long-established deferential relations and practices, as did another key term, "friendship," signifying the norm of political fidelity, protection, and reward that defined the ethos of patronage as an institutionalized system. The small governments of the age of Jackson and Harrison provided no sudden explosion of patronage jobs, although the expansion of the postal system did create postmasterships and assistant postmasterships in towns all across the United States (the number of post-office employees increased from 8,764 to 14,290 between 1831 and 1841),[60] party newspapers expanded in nearly as pronounced a way, and political reward extended as well to the selection of notaries public, military officers, West Point cadets, and a variety of state and local offices and candidacies. Still, Federal civilian employment in 1841 accounted for no more than half of one percent of the male workforce, and total public patronage, civilian and military, could not have extended at any one time to more than one or two of every hundred voters.[61] Party organization thrived on patronage, nonetheless, more often as a promised reward for continued loyalty and service, the very imbalance between positions and aspirants serving to enhance the value of political "friendship" to party activists (shall we say the 3 percent to 7 percent we found in our representative communities?). Parties organized personal aspirations, in sum, no less than they did campaigns and voter turnout, and it is in the organization of real Jack Downings in towns and counties all across America that we find one of the significant forces driving the new political system of the era of Tippecanoe.[62]

The correspondence of public officials—those with patronage appointments at their disposal—provides a fascinating perspective on this important part of the political system. Governors and other high-ranking officials had many things to do, but it was the filling of lower offices that informed the bulk of their correspondence, not only during the early days and weeks when they frequently could do little else besides deal with office-seekers, but throughout and even beyond their official tenure. The tone and content of this correspondence, moreover, is as instructive as its quantity. Consider as an example the letters that were written to Governor William C. Bouck of New York.

Bouck was elected governor in 1842 after having served for many years in the important post of canal commissioner. A Democrat who succeeded a Whig in office, his patronage opportunities were large, and the issue of who would get what from the governor's office was made at once more significant and delicate by a serious rift in the state's Democratic Party. On the other hand, Bouck was not a devoted organization man in the mold of a Martin or John Van Buren. A Schoharie County farmer, he had risen to prominence on the kinds of merits that would have made him less likely to appreciate the exercise of this kind of power, or to encourage the approach of office-seekers.[63] But approach they did, most of them in person, clutching letters of reference from prominent party men, or petitions from friends in their towns and counties, attesting to their long and faithful service to the party and to their tireless efforts during the governor's campaign. It is difficult to reconstitute this crowd of office-seekers, and we cannot eavesdrop on their interviews in Albany, but we can read the appeals of those who relied on the mail to reach the governor's sympathetic attention.

There were, first of all, quite a number of them. Bouck's correspondence file is extensive, but the vast majority of letters written to him concerned appointments, either in the form of appeals for office or as advice from friends about

the exercise of his patronage power. Most writers wanted an office, for themselves, or for a friend or relative. Sometimes any office would do (William H.
Brown wanted "a little appointment" for his friend General Fowler, who was
vain and wanted to be "properly acknowledged" for his efforts and influence),
but most often the request was quite specific. Several men offered to become
Bouck's private secretary, while others requested appointment as loan commissioner, canal superintendent, prison inspector, adjutant general, appraiser, customs inspector, police justice, or even lumber inspector. John D. Lawyer saved
postage by recommending his friend John Diefendorf as loan commissioner,
and, in the same letter, inquiring about the positions of prison chaplain at Sing
Sing for himself and prison matron for his wife. No public office was too small
to be brought before the governor; lumber inspector, for example, was a minor
local office, but William Deitz nonetheless hoped Bouck would exert his influence on behalf of Deitz's wife's relative Isaac Sternburgh, who wanted the job.
Some requests were for Federal appointments, and not within the governor's
purview, but applicants understood the close political connections among state
and Federal leaders in the small world of party politics.[64]

That small and distinct world, centered on major political figures and radiating outward to local party activists, and to canal contractors and other businessmen whose affairs required the right sort of political connection, emerges
from William Bouck's correspondence. Patronage requests sent to the governor
in Albany reveal something of the political geography that underlay the institutional pyramid linking local party activists to state leaders. Both New York
State as a physical place and the political party as an institution were too
spread out to permit the direct, personal command of state party leaders over
local activists and participants, but they were small enough in size and numbers
to permit a fairly clear and direct line of contact between the localities and the
state center. Supplicants from the counties and towns needed to write to the
governor (or to travel to Albany), and to supply written references or petitions
proving the loyalty and service that the governor could not be expected to
already know. But even small-scale performers applying for minor appointments expected a hearing at the highest levels of the party, and the references
they supplied, often written by men known in Albany, provided the short
but necessary link between even the most remote counties and the state capital. The demanding tone of some of the letters of office-seekers conveys quite
well the sense that these men had of their physical and institutional proximity
to power.

This relatively intimate political geography (which we will examine again as
an important element in the parties' efforts to maximize voter turnout on election day) served as well to facilitate the transfer of information of other kinds
from local activists to state party leaders. Alongside and often intermingled
with requests for political reward, are numerous descriptions of local political
conditions, nearly all of which focus upon those key players whose actions are

presumed to influence decisively the outcomes of local nominating conventions and elections. Thus, when John W. Edmonds reported to Bouck from the Oneida County convention at Utica, it was to name the men—Bill Russell, McCarty, Judge Snyder—who opposed the governor, "All Because they didn't Get Thare Friend appointed Suragate." George Carlyle of Palmyra warned Bouck that "Sherwood and his junto will be almost certain to control the action of a convention should one be 'got up' " in Wayne County. And E. D. Essnor, writing from Buffalo, explained the significance of continuing a Mr. Burnham in the office of turnpike inspector:

> "It is undeniable that William Scott of Black Rock Dam controls more votes in the town of Black Rock than any other man. He has become roused by the continuance of Burnham in office. Last year I had as much as I could do to keep him right telling him that Burnham would be displaced another year. Now if you had given him that little office as a token of your remembrance of him all would be right. . . . I shall go to Black Rock tomorrow & do all I can but some Germans called on me last week from the dam to say that I need not go to Scott again. He has made up his mind to stay at home this town meeting and keep all his friends there [if] he can. If I cannot reconcile him I fear we shall lose our town this spring.[65]

What needs emphasis here is not that men such as William Scott controlled significant numbers of voters in Black Rock Dam, or that Sherwood's junto could determine the outcome of a convention in Wayne County, or that the opposition of three disappointed politicians was the most important fact to report from the Utica convention. Rather, it is that correspondents such as Essnor, Carlyle, and Edmonds believed these things to be so, and that elected officials such as Bouck were expected to act on the assumption that rewards circulated properly through a small community of influential political activists were the surest means to continued electoral success. It is important to note in this connection that ordinary citizens did not write letters urging Bouck to support or oppose some public measure, or responding in more general terms to his administration. There are, indeed, only a handful of letters that address or acknowledge "the people," or public issues, and several of these advise Bouck to keep a safe distance from both. Say nothing about the proposals to improve the state canal system, advised P. J. House when Bouck ran for governor in 1842, as insiders agreed that "the man who shall come out before the publick for or against either of these schemes may as well withdraw from the canvas." Samuel Beardsley's advice was similar, but more general. Bouck "should not go to answering questions put by any individual, or to draw out an exposition for the public, of your views on political subjects." Nor, Beardsley later advised, should he address county or state conventions on issues. Bouck should convey soundness of "democratic principles in general," and leave it at that. Advice of this sort may have been particularly compelling to a Democratic candidate running only two years after Tippecanoe, a moment when campaign strategy had become more significant without necessarily having become more settled. Four years later, when Bouck was a candidate for delegate to the state constitutional convention, he was told by Demosthenes Lawyer (could there be a better name for a nineteenth-century politician?) that "public meetings are unnecessary," and that "vigilant efforts of our friends conducted secretly will effect all we can ask." The problem in this instance was not public sensitivity, but the lack of it. "Our people feel dull. They had rather make fences and ring the pigs than to go to an election at this time of the year." Whatever the electoral setting, Bouck's correspondents assumed the same thing—that work and reward among party activists was far more effective than discussions of public issues.[66]

Most of the party men who wrote to Governor Bouck in search of an appointment were careful to express devotion to Democratic principles, and every one of them sought to demonstrate their *bona fides* as partisan activists. But a surprisingly large number couched their appeals in terms of economic need. Few if any place-seekers were poor men of the working class; most were businessmen and professionals who claimed some permanent or temporary displacement. A. Keyser, for example, wrote that he lost money in business and needed the job of adjutant general. Without it, "my property must be sold and I and my family turned into the street and for ought I know become City Paupers." P. Granden, too, was out of business and needed to support a large family. "Why may I not have something?" he wrote, with an eye on the 150 Whigs who were about to be ousted from the customs house. S. L. Holmes wanted a customs-house clerkship after "struggling with unavoidable embarrassments, and urged by the claims of a large and endeared family." A. B. Hamilton had closed his law office a year ago; although he was careful to note that "for a long time previous to your election my time was wholly devoted to politics," his appeal for an appointment as appraiser came down to economics: the other applicant for the job "is rich (*I am poor*) and can well do without it."[67]

There are many such letters, but the most interesting are those written to Bouck over a number of years by John Staats of Geneva. Staats was a physician who surrendered his practice around 1840 because of poor health, and entered the office of state court clerk under the patronage of his and Bouck's friend, Judge Sutherland. Almost immediately, Staats applied unsuccessfully to President Van Buren, whom he also claimed as a friend, for appointment as secretary of the Territory of Wisconsin, and later failed to get the post of canal collector in New York. During Bouck's unsuccessful campaign for renomination in 1844, Staats wrote the usual sort of local political report, noting among other things that the "prime movers at Canandaigua whom I need not mention" have "procured the appointment of delegates of their own kidney to our County Convention." Then, after reminding Bouck of their "short acquaintance" of the previous summer, Staats gingerly (and somewhat testily) introduced the matter of patronage: "I do not *expect* any official favor, neither do I know that I shall *ask* any in the event of your re-election. I felt that I had not been generously dealt with a few years since, in not receiving the appointment of Canal Collector at this place. . . . But it is no matter of grievance now."[68]

Perhaps not, but Staats would in fact ask for "official favor," from Bouck and no doubt others, long after the governor had himself accommodated to a less distinguished appointed office. Facing the abolition of his court clerkship under the new state constitution, he wrote at length to Bouck in 1847 for his help in getting any kind of patronage job (in "a Consulate or an Indian Agency," perhaps), accompanying his request with characteristic apologies and expressions of distaste for office-seeking. Three months later he wrote again to ask Bouck to suggest to "one or two of the City delegates of the right stamp," and to "Mr. [Edwin] Croswell, who is acquainted with everybody," that Staats receive the Democratic nomination for inspector of state prisons. If "your compliance with my request might subject you to reproach," wrote Staats, "the greatest act of kindness and friendship you can do me is *not to* comply." Failure to obtain the nomination impelled another long letter, beginning and ending with abject apologies for having imposed on the former governor, but including long and bitter complaints about having been poorly treated by the party he has served for so long (there is even a bit of a jab at Bouck himself for not having spoken to Croswell about the prison inspector nomination). That old canal collectorship continued to rankle, especially since it had gone to a less deserving party man who, while poor enough, was a bachelor, while Staats had had a large family to support. Could Bouck, by the way, look into securing for Staats a position of assistant surgeon (he did not want the responsibilities of surgeon) "in some one of the regiments of volunteers going out to Mexico"?[69]

Staats wrote again for the same post two months later, but the thrust of this letter was to seek an appointment for his son as assistant purser in the navy. As the son was single, his salary could support Staats as well. In 1851, now a reluctant and overburdened editor of the *Geneva Gazette*, and expressing once again considerable distaste for office-seeking, Staats put himself forward a second time for prison inspector. He did secure some kind of connection with the Auburn prison, but in 1853 wrote to Bouck for his help in becoming canal collector. Then, in 1857, Bouck received a letter remarkable for the fact that Staats did not ask for office—indeed, for the fact that he wrote specifically not to ask. "I neither ask nor desire office," he wrote, and "as to the honor of office, I have no ambition for it." The explanation is telling. Some years earlier Staats had bought eighty acres of Wisconsin land for $160, and recently sold them for $4,000. This, in addition to rent he was receiving on some land in Michigan, finally gave him the economic security he had long sought through political patronage.[70]

A few months later, Staats reflected on his long, generally frustrating, and often conflicted career as a political activist and would-be placeman. Having had a close brush with death from bilious fever, Staats took stock of his more long-term prospects, and decided that "hardly anything has a more deadly effect on the religious feelings than an active participation in politics. I was partly obliged by the force of circumstances, not from choice, to take an active part in them," he insisted "and never lost entirely a sense of my responsibilities." He was never a "popular politician," and his conscience would never have permitted him the "intrigues and deceptions" necessary to that trade.[71]

Staats, in his own view, was no Jack Downing, and it is interesting that the most Downing-like characterization of a real-life politician in the correspondence files of William C. Bouck comes from his pen. In 1854 Staats wrote to Bouck about C. Chauncy Burr, editor of the *National Democrat.* "Necessity (for he is, or *was* poor) compelled him to shift from one thing to another and from one side to another in order to get a living." He was a Universalist minister, abolitionist lecturer, editor, lecturer on "Electric Psychology" (illustrated "with a series of humbug experiments"), and exposer of Spiritual rappings. When the last "run out," he came to the *National Democrat.* "His great *principle*," concluded Staats, "is to make *principal.*"[72] But Staats himself was not an adventurer, and neither were many others who wrote to Bouck and to other patronage-dispensing public officials for deserved and necessary political reward. Their letters take us beyond simple caricatures of cynical, office-hungry politicians to men who, in varying degrees, found in politics a sheet anchor against misfortune for themselves and their families; or, to use a more current image (more appropriately drawn from the circus than from the sea), a safety net in a most uncertain economic world. The "market revolution" had created both opportunity and dislocation, and it was the latter that was most prevalent during the economically difficult years when Bouck served as governor and when the second party system began to take shape.[73] The parties were constructed for the conduct of elections and other political affairs, but it is important to understand how they served some men as a main chance or a last chance in the struggle for well-being. Staats himself wrote of a "hardly endurable" mental depression, and of partisan editorials written "with the greatest reluctance," and in part "for the sake of mental exercise."[74] We are a long way from "Tippecanoe and Tyler, Too" here, and perhaps even from specifically political ideas and passions.

We must not exclude, however, these ideas and passions from our understanding of men such as John Staats. Staats wrote editorials for "the cause of democracy" as well as for a remedy for depression, and fought hard and no doubt with genuine feeling on behalf of the Democrats' war against Mexico, criticizing local clergy who used their pulpits to oppose the war. Most office-seekers were men who wove political interest and activity into lives that revolved primarily around wives, children, and personal success and failure in the stores, offices, farms, and workshops from which they gained their livelihoods. Some may have approached politics, like Jack Downing, merely as a way to get an easy living. Others combined political and personal interest according to well-understood rules of a game that did not insist upon a clear separation of the two. And we should not be surprised to find still others who, when circumstances required, subsumed political interest, and even a disinterested commitment to public affairs, to the survival of self and family. This does not deny the importance of politics and public issues to such men, but calls upon us to recognize the more complex lives of people we might otherwise reduce to a single dimension. Even to the most active and interested, politics was only part of life, and at that not always the most important part.

———————

We must recognize, too, the interweaving of politics and daily life—or at least build politics into the sequence of seasons of the year—among those less active citizens who were stimulated to participate in the 1840 presidential election. Perhaps it was the "circus" that attracted many of these new participants, but, as we earlier suggested, the effect of this attraction on the practice of democracy may yet have been significant. For it was a political circus, after all, to which they had been attracted, and it was a political process in which they had participated. Put another way, Americans in 1840 engaged in an incontestably public realm to which significantly large numbers had never before paid so much attention. Were there important and enduring effects of this experience, on a newly awakened electorate and on the public realm itself? Perhaps Tippecanoe did not provide so promising a start (or, if one prefers, so promising a fulfillment of the energies stirred by Andrew Jackson a dozen years earlier), but what of the future? Ronald Formisano warns us, as few historians do, about generalizing from the experience of 1840: "So much has been written about the 1840 campaign as a climax of the new political culture, and of its *representative* character, that its specialness has been lost. . . . The 1840 campaign was made possible by a political innocence and trust that would never be greater."[75] Formisano avails himself of two apt metaphors for this era, the revival and the factory, to distinguish between the politics of 1840 and the political system that would evolve during the next two decades. The campaign of 1840 had been a "revival," an organized but broadly felt and perhaps ephemeral burst of enthusiasm. The parties, though, sought to systematize its results by becoming "factories" of political commitment and enthusiasm.[76] The "factory" was already up and running in 1840, and we have seen that the "revival" of the Tippecanoe campaign was its first product. But could the production process be continued in this way? What would be the relation between citizens and politics, between the private and public realms in America, as the political parties built upon the experiences of 1840?

CHAPTER 2

The Maturing Party System: The Rude Republic and Its Discontents

WHAT PERHAPS was not clear in 1840 would soon become so. Political parties had in fact succeeded in placing themselves at the center of what Joel Silbey has called "the American political nation." And from that center, during the next decade and beyond, they would extend their presence across nearly the whole range of political activity, incorporating once-informal hierarchies and relations into party structures, organizing local elections that previously had resisted partisanship, and building a strong and seemingly stable set of institutions for carrying out the tasks of recruitment, discipline, mobilization, and reward. Henceforth, very little that would happen in American politics, especially in the routine conduct of political affairs, would occur beyond the realm of the party. "The primacy of political parties," writes Silbey, "was the dominant fact of this political era." And if the constituent elements of the partisan system were not so very stable—the Whigs would disappear within two decades, and Free Soil, American, and other parties would come and go—the system was stability itself. The various re-alignments of the 1850s, Silbey concludes, "did not fundamentally redefine the structure of the existing political nation," which was to last at least another forty years.[1]

The creation of the party system is one of the striking developments of an era that experienced changes of many kinds, including the formation and spread of institutions other than but much like political parties in their organization, appeal, and geographic reach. What we will explore in this and in subsequent chapters, therefore, are the ways that political institutions developed and functioned within larger social and cultural worlds; put another way, we wish to examine the relations between the *political* nation, as Silbey and other political historians define it, and the nation to which we attach no adjective. Among other questions, we must ask how the institutionalization of the political "factory" related to continuing evidences of popular political enthusiasm, including voter turnout that remained at very high levels. We will look first at the years following the Tippecanoe campaign, and especially at the 1850s as a decade during which a maturing party system exerted its incontestable hegemony, even while it struggled with new issues and re-alignments. Again, we will begin within local communities, where political institutions, practices, and events interacted tangibly with the comings and goings of daily life, for those more and those less caught up in political affairs.

By the 1850s the United States had expanded beyond the Mississippi River, and we have accordingly expanded the size and geographic range of our town "sample." To our eastern towns, Greenfield, Kingston, and Augusta, we add Marion, a small county seat typical of the town centers set within the general farmland of northwestern Ohio (and our substitute for Marietta, whose newspapers fail us); Clarksville, a north-central Tennessee shipping center for tobacco, pork, and flour on the Cumberland River; Dubuque, Iowa, once a distant settlement of lead miners, now a rapidly growing Mississippi River town; and, for the latter part of the decade, Opelousas, an old Cajun settlement in the bayou country of Louisiana, at once one of the oldest and one of the newest parts of the United States. Marion grew from some 2,300 inhabitants in 1850 to just over 3,000 in 1860, with fewer than two-thirds (1,864 in 1860) living in Marion Village at the center of the township. Clarksville may well have reached the 5,000 a local editor claimed for it by 1859 (typically of southern towns of this size, Clarksville is not set apart from the rest of Montgomery County on the manuscript census schedules), but the free population probably did not exceed 3,500. Dubuque was a particularly robust frontier town, quadrupling its population during the 1850s. The census marshals counted exactly 13,000 inhabitants in 1860. Opelousas, a few miles west of the Mississippi but in a different world from Dubuque, experienced nothing like the latter's growth. Its 1860 population was 787. As for our eastern towns, Kingston and Augusta were becoming significant urban centers (their 1860 populations were 16,640 and 12,493, respectively), while Greenfield grew more modestly, to 3,198. Our towns capture, therefore, not only the expanding geography but also the quickening urbanization of antebellum America.

We will examine here two election cycles of the decade preceding the Civil War. The first, 1850–52, represents the Democratic-Whig alignment of the second party system in its full maturity, and includes also one of the most ordinary of presidential elections, the 1852 contest between Franklin Pierce and Winfield Scott. The second cycle, 1858–60, presents us with a realigned third party system of Democrats and Republicans, and one of the most significant and fiercely contested presidential elections in American history. We will take note of the differences between the 1852 and 1860 campaigns, and we will find variations between north and south, east and west, as we did in the 1840–42 election cycle. Underlying these differences, however, were important similarities of political organization and life that underscore Silbey's use of the singular in defining the American political nation. One of the most interesting qualities of party development in this era is the institutional uniformity that blended with and to some extent overrode variations of regional culture and local economic and social organization, and that preserved the continuities that Silbey notes between the second and third party systems.

INITIATING THE POLITICAL PROCESS:
CAUCUSES AND CONVENTIONS

How, in fact, did the process and the people interact in our representative communities during the party battles of the 1850s? We begin at the start of the political process, with the local caucuses and nominating conventions that had been one of the significant innovations of the Harrison era, but that now had become the relatively uniform means for nominating candidates and selecting delegates to conventions higher in the nomination pyramid. Editors and other party activists pointed to the local caucus, in particular, as a crucial meeting point between the party and the people, where all who were considered adherents to the party, or who even wished to be considered members, met with a seemingly equal voice to select delegates, offer and pass resolutions, and even nominate some local candidates. Editors urged party members to attend, and were delighted to report later that the courthouse or district school had been packed with enthusiastic voters. Here, if anywhere, was Robert Wiebe's "lodge democracy," the most obvious and accessible venue for the self-motivated political participation of ordinary citizens.

Was the local caucus, then, an effective transfer of the initial stage of the process of candidate selection and campaign definition from state legislators and other leaders to the party rank and file? Did the people actually show up and express themselves when the caucus was announced, and did their participation help legitimize political parties as democratic institutions? Party editors promoted this view of the caucus, but the tenor of many of their urgings and reports suggests the contrary—that these grassroots meetings did not typically attract significant numbers of ordinary citizens. "We hardly have the face to ask it," wrote Kingston's Whig editor in 1852. "Give us a few hours. Go to your caucus meetings and come together one evening." The same editor, working seven years later under the aegis of the Republican Party, urged "the better class of citizens" to "remember their duties to their country and attend the caucus." These were not the announcements of a party organizer who expected a large turnout of enthusiastic citizens. The Whig editor of Marion, Ohio, lamented in 1850 the "disposition on the part of the Whigs to stay at home" rather than attend caucuses, while at the same time local Democrats were abandoning an experiment with local party primaries that failed to attract voters. In Dubuque, editor Alonzo P. Wood, in urging a more complete party organization upon the Whigs of the frontier town in 1851, complained of "sleepiness and inactivity" among local partisans, and, perceiving that party affiliation did not necessarily translate into active political commitment, warned that in-migrating Whigs must be met promptly upon their arrival in town and urged to become active party members before they lost all interest in politics. A year earlier, this exasperated party man had reported the failure of just such a local meeting as he was perpetually calling for: "We attended the court house on Saturday last, between the hours of 2 and 3 P.M., but there were not sufficient Whigs in the neighborhood to constitute a meeting, and we went away." Many party caucuses were not nearly so dismal, but the Greenfield Democratic editor may have told us more than he intended when he claimed that an 1851 Democratic town caucus was "more fully attended than usual."[2]

Most of these laments referred to poor attendance at party meetings convened at the county courthouse, a block or two from partisan editorial offices and at the active center of each county's political life. Outside of the county seat it was by no means certain that a town caucus would even be held. Greenfield was one of twenty-six towns in Franklin County, but on only one occasion during the six years we examined (or one in nine years, if we include the 1840–42 election cycle), did either party manage to convene more than nineteen town caucuses, and the number could fall as low as thirteen. In June of 1860 the *Franklin Democrat* described "the largest and most enthusiastic" Democratic congressional nominating convention "which has been held in this District for many years," before reporting that it consisted of delegates from only seventeen of the sixty-eight towns in the district.[3] As many as sixteen caucuses were held during these years among the eighteen towns of Kingston's Ulster County, but thirteen was a more typical number. Greenfield and Kingston invariably held their caucuses, and so too did Deerfield, Saugerties, and a few other reliable (and generally larger than average) towns in each county. But in some of the smaller and more remote towns caucuses were not to be relied upon, and in a few they were rare.

Evidence of nonparticipation can be found as well at later stages of the nominating process. Not only did town caucuses attract small numbers or even fail to meet, but in many instances delegates failed to attend the conventions to which they had been sent. Convention reports usually do not permit a precise calculation of delegate attendance, but it is clear from reported delegate and convention vote totals that many delegates were staying home. Towns ordinarily selected three or more delegates to county and district conventions in Massachusetts and New York (the days of selecting delegations of two or three hundred were past in Kingston and other New York towns), but the average number of attending delegates was frequently less than three per represented town. Franklin County's Democratic congressional convention of 1850, for example, attracted only sixty-seven delegates from the forty-three towns that had caucused to send delegates, while at an 1858 Republican state legislative convention to which twenty-three towns sent delegates, the total number of votes cast was thirty-two, little more than one per town. The thirty delegates who represented thirteen towns at an Ulster County Republican convention in 1859 constituted the high-water mark of delegate attendance in the two counties, but they still had to proceed in the absence of nine of their colleagues.[4]

Editors of party newspapers recognized this problem, and often urged town caucuses to select delegates "who will be sure to attend conventions."[5] This was not easily accomplished. Party rules were adopted authorizing delegations to fill vacancies; individual delegates were permitted to appoint substitutes for themselves; party members who happened to show up were seated as delegates even if they had not been selected in their town caucuses; and conventions were held whenever possible on court days, when large numbers of eligible men were drawn to the courthouse on other business—but still convention seats were left unfilled. At a Kingston Democratic convention in 1851, after four delegates were selected and empowered to appoint substitutes, one of the delegates was authorized to act as a substitute for each delegate *and substitute* who did not appear.[6]

These illustrations are all drawn from our northeastern towns, where party organization was most complete. Further west, and in the South, the problems of caucus and convention nonattendance were even more acute. In Marietta, in 1841, the Whig county convention had selected *every* Washington County voter as a delegate to the legislative district convention, and had resolved that "the elderly men, in particular, are earnestly solicited to attend."[7] This might have impressed us as a peculiarity of the earliest days of party formation in Ohio were it not repeated by Marion County Democrats eleven years later. Still later, at their 1859 county convention, Marion's Democrats fell back on nearly the same device, allowing "any Democratic voter" to cast the vote of his township if that township was "not represented by delegates." For its part, the younger Republican Party managed to achieve (or claimed to have achieved) full or nearly full township representation at its county conventions, but experienced difficulties higher up the pyramid. In March of 1860 the Republicans selected fourteen delegates and fourteen alternatives to their congressional district convention; yet, the convention report lists only one Marion County delegate, who appears to have cast all of Marion's fourteen votes.[8] In Dubuque, only four of seventeen townships were represented at a Republican county convention in 1858, and fully twenty-seven of the thirty-two delegates present were from Dubuque (an only slightly exaggerated pattern of overrepresentation from the county's political center). Two years later, according to the Democratic paper, the same convention attracted delegates from only three towns. There were few Democratic embarrassments of a similar magnitude, but the party's editor in Dubuque did admit that "apathy has gone so far as to leave whole precincts unrepresented in many of the [Democratic] county and district conventions."[9] It is tempting to speculate about why, on the urban frontier, those whom the Dubuque Republican editor would call "property holders and tax-payers [who] are apt to neglect primary meetings and conventions, . . . think they discharge all the duty that is required of them when they simply go to the polls at each election and vote."[10] It is often noted that migrants tend to be less involved in institutional affairs than settled residents, but the Whig editor expected newcomers to *lose* interest as they became settled, and it was to neglectful and presumably well-settled property owners that his successor addressed his complaint. Perhaps it is best simply to observe that these westerners, newcomers and older settlers alike, imported from eastern states both the forms and the defects of the party system.

Southern parties, too, experienced difficulties in stimulating attendance at either caucuses (which in the absence of townships were generally on the county level) or conventions. "There is very little chat about politics," lamented Augusta's Democratic editor in June of 1859. "Some few Democrats speak in favor of having a meeting and appointing delegates to attend the State Democratic Convention, but . . . it would be difficult to get more than a dozen or two persons to attend such a meeting." The meeting was in fact held (there was no report of attendance), but of the seventeen delegates selected by it only five attended the state convention at Milledgeville, eighty-five miles away. A week later the *Constitutionalist* was again pessimistic, this time about the chances of securing "a full representation of the counties" at a convention being proposed for the selection of delegates to a national convention. Ten of thirteen Richmond County delegates did attend two congressional district conventions that summer, but the second convention, held in Augusta, attracted only twenty-five delegates from the eleven other counties in the district. Similarly, in Clarksville, Tennessee, of seventy-two named delegates from Montgomery County to the Democratic state convention of 1860, only nine actually attended. That this was a general pattern was admitted later that year by the Clarksville Democratic editor: "Heretofore our electoral conventions have been very slimly attended, and with very slight manifestations of interest. They have been regarded as the working days of the party and not as occasions for the outpourings of Democratic feeling."[11]

To some extent, the difficulty in Clarksville seems to reflect a more embryonic organization. More than in our northwestern towns, Clarksville's experience reminds us of the experiments of the early 1840s. This is especially the case with the most southwestern of our towns, Opelousas, Louisiana. Opelousas did have two organized parties, the Democrats and the (formerly Whig) Opposition, but neither party held many caucuses or conventions during the three years we examined. The Democrats were the more active of the two parties, but even they had difficulty mobilizing voters in the nomination process. Apparently dormant through 1858, the Democrats of Saint Landry Parish selected delegates in 1859 to a judicial district convention to be held in Baton Rouge, and met occasionally thereafter. But the most striking evidence of political organization to be found in the local press refers not to either of the political parties, but to the eight nonpartisan parish vigilance committees (constituted to fight crime and track down runaway slaves), said to number some five hundred of Saint Landry's citizens. "Opelousas was thronged by representatives" of the vigilance movement in May of 1860, wrote the Democratic *Courier*, in language never used to describe a Democratic Party meeting.[12] As they did on a variety of American frontiers, the vigilance movement may have provided Saint Landry with an alternative form of government, and an alternative politics as well. We should not be surprised to find the more customary institutions of politics relatively lethargic in such a setting as this.

Why were the "working days of the party" of so little interest to so many citizens in all of our towns, even to the point where elected delegates often failed to attend nominating conventions? The absence of competition—electoral domination of a town or county by a single party, or the certainty of a party's nomination of a particular candidate—no doubt contributed to the lethargy of ordinary citizens and perhaps even some party activists in various places and times. But thin attendance at local caucuses and the absence of delegates from conventions were general patterns, and in our selected towns were as evident in close contests as in dull ones with predictable outcomes. They continued, too, despite much editorial pleading—to local party voters that the upcoming election *was* going to be close, and to delegates that their presence was necessary to provide the psychological advantage of a well-attended convention. A rather different explanation is provided in the partisan press itself, which expands upon the *Clarksville Jeffersonian*'s telling phrase with surprising clarity. Most direct, perhaps, was the *Dubuque Daily Times*, which wrote in 1859 that "the better portion" of the electorate "retire in disgust from the heat and turmoil of political strife. They leave primary meetings, and County, District and State Conventions to political gamblers and party hacks."[13] The Greenfield Democratic editor made the same point a little differently: "We hear a great deal about 'management,' about everything being 'cut and dried' beforehand—about 'wire-pullers,' 'office-holders' dictation' etc and we warn the voters to look to it in season and see that their confidence is not abused by anything of the kind."[14] That there is no denial of the close "management" of caucuses and conventions in these statements, or even the characterization of political leaders as "gamblers" and "hacks," is notable, given the fact that the local editors themselves were party insiders. Whether describing their own party or the opposition, local editors drew upon a broad understanding of politicians' control of seemingly open meetings, and frequently related this understanding to the tendency of many citizens simply to avoid what a Clarksville editor (referring to the other party) named "party despotism under a show of popular consultation."[15] Why would Kingston's Democratic delegates wish to attend congressional conventions after reading in their party's paper that the geographic pattern of congressional nominations had been set for the next ten years?[16] Augusta readers well understood the *Constitutionalist*'s advice not to attend Opposition meetings: "Such of them as may visit them, will only be spectators."[17] Quoting the *New Orleans Picayune*, the editor of the *Opelousas Courier* criticized the process in similar terms, but without sparing his own party: "Primary assemblies are a mere blind for the eyes of the masses. They seem to rule, but like the Roman Senate in the time of the first Caesars, only record the edicts of masters. . . . [H]e who dreams the people had anything to do with the result, labors under a pleasant but irrational hallucination."[18]

The newspapers provide another perspective on this phenomenon in the formal reports submitted to them by party conventions. By the 1850s, the party convention was a maturing institution, tending toward a representative system of small delegations acting on behalf of that larger body of party voters who attended, if at all, as observers rather than actors. Editorial denunciations of "party hacks" and "wire-pullers" challenge the meaning of such representation in an obvious way, but so, too, do the relatively standardized postconvention reports that unintentionally reveal the close management of most party meetings.[19] According to these reports, each meeting began with one of the assembled being called to the chair, and with another being made secretary. Then, if the meeting were to select delegates, a motion would be made and invariably carried to empower the chair to select a delegate committee. The chair immediately appointed such a committee, which would retire, often "for a few moments," before returning to propose a list of delegates.[20] In the dozens of conventions whose reports we have read this list was approved in *every* instance without discussion or dissent. If the meeting were to pass upon party resolutions, the chair would appoint another committee, which would in many instances almost immediately offer a list of resolutions long enough to occupy a column or more of newspaper space. There might be some discussion of these resolutions, and some proposed additions or changes, but most often they would be accepted without alteration or dissent.

Candidates for elected office, too, were often nominated with the same smooth harmony, and in some cases the nominee was "loudly called for" and fully prepared to give a speech. To be sure, candidacy nominations were often contested, and sometimes provided the occasion for genuine dissent, but frequently a good deal of maneuvering went on before the convention, such that the latter's role was to ratify what had already been done. An exception to prove the rule is the nomination of Greenfield's S. O. Lamb by a poorly attended Democratic state senatorial convention in 1858. Lamb won eighteen of the twenty-two votes before being declared the unanimous choice of the convention. His nomination, claimed the *Franklin Democrat*, "was entirely spontaneous, resulting from no previous consultation so far as we could ascertain, and we have good reasons for believing was entirely unexpected by him."[21] Even if this dubious claim is to be believed (Lamb, we should point out, was the publisher of the *Democrat*, and one of Greenfield's most powerful politicians), it is obvious that "previous consultation," not spontaneity, was the norm in Connecticut Valley political conventions.

We have already seen evidence of preconvention maneuvering in some of the letters written to Governor Bouck of New York in the 1840s, and there is a good deal of corroborating evidence in other sources, too, of our editors' more and less deliberate revelations about insider manipulation and management of party meetings. Some of this evidence is in the form of angry denunciation that suggests the expectation of a more democratic process, but much of it seems to assume that maneuver and control were routine in caucuses and conventions. "If the delegates from your own Town were true, you had one Town for Capital," wrote former congressman Hugh White in 1859 to a son who had just lost his own bid for nomination. "[T]he next move," the elder White advised, "would have been to secure more towns, & in order to do that you should have some friend who would go to the man who might control the primary meetings to secure your own delegates."[22] In 1840, S. G. Hathaway, Jr., wrote to his father from Elmira, New York, that "it would be well indeed highly desirable that there be the right kind of a delegation from Cortland" to the upcoming congressional convention. "If you can manage the thing right in your own way with the Cortland delegation we shall be much pleased. . . . You will of course know who of our friends (if any) at Cortland to confer with on the subject either before your Co. Convention or to operate with the delegates after their appointment." "I should not like to be made conspicuous," concluded the son, perhaps unnecessarily. Nor did the thoroughly political Hathaways learn a more open style of politics after the Tippecanoe campaign. In 1851, another of S. G. Hathaway's sons wrote his brother Cal to "attend to your next Co. Convention to appoint delegates to your Dist. Convention." The point was to secure delegates for William L. Marcy to the Democratic National Convention, as Marcy "has always been very friendly to me & remarked to me in Albany the other day he was sure he could count my Father among his friends." Cal was reminded that Marcy had gotten "John" appointed to the military academy, and that "when he first entered the Cabinet he told me if I wanted anything for myself I should have it." This was surely reason enough among Hathaways to gain control of a county convention, a practice with which they were quite familiar.[23]

These New York examples are by no means peculiar. Thomas Jeffrey cites a congressional candidate's bitter description of the convention system in North Carolina in 1847. Conventions, argued Henry Toole, were "controlled by a few second-rate politicians near the Court House and villages of the several counties, who appointed a substantial country gentleman as honorary president to provide a veneer of respectability, and make sure the secretary and members of the nominating committee are provided with resolutions 'cut and dried' for the occasion—*of course* they are adopted unanimously—*of course* they are published in the newspapers . . . as the sentiments of large masses of free and enlightened citizens." There is no evidence, argues Jeffrey, "that the convention system in North Carolina was any less democratic than the old system of self-nomination and informal selection by local notables," but Toole's attack allows us to question whether it was significantly more so, or indeed much different.[24] In his memoir of a long career in nineteenth-century politics, E. L. Dohoney describes a Democratic convention in Kentucky with more humor, but hardly less bitterness, than Toole. Threatened by the ascending Know-Nothing movement in the mid-1850s, the Democratic "wire-pullers" of Dohoney's county decided to court Whig voters who had not gone over to the Know-Nothings by nominating Captain Billy Grady, a " 'cussing' Irish Whig," for the state senate:

> The cards were shuffled and dealt by Col. Cravens and Capt. Tom Rhodes Dohoney, one of the most expert politicians in that part of Kentucky, who for his successful party work was appointed United States marshal for Kentucky by President Buchanan. On the appointed day about one dozen true blue Democrats repaired to the court house in Columbia, and after an eloquent nominating speech by Colonel Cravens, unanimously nominated Captain Grady. I will never forget the Captain's eloquent speech of acceptance and will quote it verbatim et literatim: "Fellow citizens, I never made a speech in my life, I don't know anything about politics, I don't know what the issues are; but one thing I do know: these damned Know-nothings, whatever they are for, I am agin." Tremendous applause, a general Democratic love feast, and all hands repaired to the "grocery" as liquor shops were then called.

Dohoney, then a young Democrat, was repelled by Colonel Cravens's cynical manipulations, and never again attended a Democratic convention in Kentucky. He did remain in politics, however, and attended Democratic, Greenback, Populist, and Prohibition conventions in Texas and elsewhere. "They were not as ridiculous as the Grady convention," he concludes, "but all were more or less disgusting, and none entirely satisfactory."[25]

What these various episodes tell us is that some men—local party leaders, political entrepreneurs, and their "friends"—were deeply concerned with the outcome of party caucuses and conventions, but that most ordinary citizens were much less involved or interested. "The great mass of people," wrote Samuel Love to Ezra Cornell from Ithaca, New York, in 1859, "are satisfied with the nominations. They have no feeling who shall be promoted, save qualification, whether it be this or that man—all the same to them—for they are not seeking power or *place*."[26] Does this mean that most citizens were entirely indifferent to, or even repelled by, the nomination process? Did they perceive it as just another part of the quest for power and office by party professionals? Love's qualifying phrase, "save qualification," suggests that ordinary citizens were keeping an eye on the nominating process to this extent: they wanted their party to assure them that nominees, many of whom they did not know, were qualified for office. Party leaders, on their part, had good reason to promote the idea of open and responsive caucuses and conventions, even when they did not intend to surrender control of the nominating process. By publicizing these meetings, making them accessible, and urging all to attend local caucuses, they gained the right to insist that even those party members who did not attend give faithful support to the entire ticket as a reflection of popular will and interest. At the same time, by repeatedly stressing the commitment of the party to "measures not men," they provided less active partisans with a good reason for *not* attending local caucuses or giving close attention to the outcomes of conventions. "The great mass of citizens" whom Samuel Love described as satisfied with their party's nominations were evidently more interested in having the option of participating in the nomination process than in actually doing so, and were in any case satisfied with the trade-off presented to them by party activists. The latter deferred to the people's right to choose candidates and delegates, and to formulate policy, and the people in turn deferred to the specific choices made by party activists in caucuses and conventions that they controlled or contested among themselves.

The nominating system did not always work this way, and the players did not always play their roles according to this script. Partisan editors, for example, were not always party insiders in the strictest sense—we will soon see, indeed, that several of the editors in our representative towns were restive in their role of party defender and promoter—and could express a seemingly genuine desire to increase popular participation in caucuses and conventions. Delegates who did not attend conventions were, in some cases, party men who were not needed or able to control an outcome they already perceived, but in other instances were newcomers and other outsiders who resisted an attempted recruitment by the party or one of its factions or leaders. And there were certainly party meetings that were attended by ordinary party adherents, contested rather than controlled, and productive of nominations, resolutions, and delegations that reflected the will of a majority of those present. Later, we will see in the diaries of men who were more and less involved with politics that there were some among the latter who did attend local caucuses and conventions, and that they did not seem to consider themselves "only spectators." But there is simply too much evidence of public nonparticipation and of insider control to assume that the nomination system generally manifested the workings of a broadly participatory democracy. At this initial stage of the recurring political process, "the great mass of citizens" most often accepted the partisan package of candidates and resolutions—men and measures alike—that emerged from the contests and understandings of a much smaller group of active party men.

THE CAMPAIGN

Once candidates had been selected, the political season moved into a new phase, the campaign for votes, which invariably entailed a much greater effort on the part of editors, orators, and other partisan activists to generate popular participation. Kingston's Whiggish but nonpartisan *Rondout Courier* joked, at the end of the fall campaign in 1851, about the climate of urgency fomented by party propagandists. Only four days remained "between this and the awful

day 'big with the fate of candidates and rum,' " observed the *Courier*, but editor
J. P. Hageman advised his fellow citizens to remain calm: "Don't allow your-
selves to be run away with on the strength of the assurance that the present
election is a crisis. . . . It may be a crisis to the candidates, but the constitution
ain't in danger just at present."[27] Some readers, perhaps many, might have
laughed appreciatively at Hageman's deflation of campaign rhetoric, but there
is no doubting the success of party orators and editors, and of those who
planned and carried out campaign rallies and parades, in stimulating the interest of many citizens who had stayed away from nominating caucuses and conventions. Long after the famous campaign of 1840, political contests remained
popular events in which large numbers of Americans participated, some with
just the intensity that party leaders demanded. "The great mass of people" who
cared little about which candidates carried their party's nominations for state
representative, sheriff, or town justice, seemed to care a good deal more about
the success or failure of the party itself in the coming election. Their participation in the campaign spectacle is a second dimension of American popular
democracy that deserves close examination.

In most American communities there were two political contests each year,
but the local election that typically occurred in the winter or early spring did
not usually involve a long or even visible campaign. In the nation's smaller
towns and cities, even those local elections that were formally partisan (many
preserved a fiction of nonpartisanship; some were genuinely conducted without reference to party) involved so brief a period of nominating and electing
that weekly party papers often could do little more than print the election
results, accompanied, perhaps, by a little postelection crowing or sniping. New
York's villages and towns, for example, usually held party caucuses on the
Saturday evening preceding the Tuesday election, allowing candidates only
Monday and election day to campaign for votes. Party men often took these
elections seriously, as they helped define the overall electoral balance in the
town, provided for a certain number of elected and appointed offices, and,
through these offices, reshaped the specific distribution of party roles for the
upcoming fall election. Ordinary voters were usually less deeply concerned,
and were less likely to think or behave in strictly partisan terms, especially
where formal nonpartisanship masked the parties' role in generating local
candidacies. These candidacies, moreover, could be genuinely nonpartisan,
and could on occasion reveal motives that remind us of the hard-up supplicants
to Governor Bouck. In 1850, incumbent Richmond County coroner Joshua
Walker appealed for reelection through a paid notice in the *Augusta Daily
Chronicle and Sentinel*. "I am poor and unfortunate," he announced, "and therefore it is that I am constrained thus to appeal to your generosity. . . . Snatch
from me the perquisites of this office, and you virtually doom myself and little
ones to almost certain want and poverty."[28] Walker says nothing of his partisan
affiliation; neither is there a word about how well he has performed his job.

The editor of the *Chronicle and Sentinel* took no note of his announcement, and paid little attention to the election itself. Happily for Walker and his little ones, he was reelected by sixteen votes in a light turnout.

Local elections in small cities and towns could become lively, but when they did it was usually because of some specific local issue or candidacy that carried few if any implications for larger partisan battles in state and national elections. Augusta's city election of 1860 provides an interesting example. The campaign for mayor, councilman, and other city offices in Augusta lasted about a month, long enough for parties to nominate and publicize tickets, and even to generate a good deal of back-and-forth arguing in the daily party papers over the merits of each ticket. In most years, however, there was not much of the latter, and there was no tradition of local party rallies or of organized campaigning of any sort. In 1858, a letter to the *Constitutionalist* urging support for the Democratic ticket could accurately say that municipal elections in Augusta "as a general thing, attract very little attention."[29] In 1860, however, interest was stirred by the potential candidacy of the incumbent mayor, Foster Blodget, Jr., who had made friends and enemies by pushing an aggressive agenda of local improvements, including a controversial plan for a new waterworks. Blodget had been a Whig in former times, but was now a Democrat. The two-party system had been threatened in the South by the absorption of northern Whigs and Know-Nothings into a new Republican Party that was entirely unacceptable to southerners, but it was preserved in Augusta and elsewhere by an Opposition Party that gave a political home to those who continued to oppose the Democrats. As in previous years, therefore, there were party tickets in Augusta's city election of 1860.

In high revolt against Blodget's Whiggish public activism, the Democrats dropped the mayor from their ticket in favor of Robert H. May, who himself had been a Whig (and Know-Nothing). When the Opposition put Blodget at the head of their ticket an interesting race was assured, and Augustans responded with uncharacteristic enthusiasm. "In the parlor, and in the bar room—in the counting-room and in the work-shop—at the Church door, and frequently, it is to be feared, in the Church," wrote "Augusta" to the *Chronicle and Sentinel* (could this have been the same "Augusta" who wrote in a similar tone and rhythm in 1840?), "wherever two or more assemble together, whether they be parsons or pick-pockets—men of substance or men of straw—legislators or loafers . . . there is but one subject upon which they converse, . . . and that subject is the Municipal Election."[30] The editorial war was intense, letters to the editor frequent, and the voter turnout high, with Mayor Blodget managing to keep his office by a margin of one vote!

A defeat for the Democrats, to be sure, but not in the usual sense. In fact, neither party had put forward a strictly partisan ticket (on each, there was a nearly equal number of Democrats and Oppositionists for the city council), party names were avoided—the Democrats labeled their slate the "People's

Ticket," the Opposition was the "Independent Ticket"—and each party's paper printed *both* tickets, along with a third, "The Mechanics' and Workingmen's Ticket," in its column of "Special Notices." There was also a good deal of letter writing and editorializing about the irrelevance of party differences to municipal affairs, the *Chronicle and Sentinel* concluding, a bit disingenuously, that "it was a contest entirely between individuals, mostly for the fun of the thing."[31] Most importantly, the focus of the election was entirely local, and, because of the numerous concessions the parties were forced to make to the tradition of nonpartisan localism, even party editors did not attach any larger significance to either the outcome or the unusual stirring of popular interest.

It was the fall election, in Augusta and in all our representative towns, that created the real political season and that generated the unqualified and unrestrained efforts of the political parties. In presidential years this season could be a long one, much longer than even the most exciting local election. Consider, for example, the Republican side of the 1860 campaign. It began in May, with rallies held (in northern towns) to celebrate the nomination of Abraham Lincoln. In Marion, an already organized Young Men's Republican Club marched with beating drums to the courthouse, where they and other Republicans listened to speeches, passed a resolution to ratify the Chicago nomination, and finished the evening with a bonfire in the public square. This was typical, as were subsequent events. Within a week the *Republican* was calling for a Wide-Awake marching club, and before the end of June reported a regular schedule of Thursday evening torchlight marches by the Marion Wide Awakes. These recurring events were supplemented by occasional grand rallies that drew thousands from all over the county. The pace was maintained until the very end, and even after, with two "Republican Jubilees" to celebrate the party's victory, first in Ohio (which voted for state offices in October) and later in the nation as a whole. Six months of sustained political activity, matched, we might add, by Lincoln's opponents. "ONE FIRE MORE," urged Marion's Democratic editor in announcing a procession of Douglas Invincibles on the evening before the November election.[32]

It is difficult for the historian (if we may recall the *Rondout Courier*'s advice) to avoid being "run away with" by a campaign such as this. The last of the antebellum presidential elections seems to have been just as stimulating to the American people as the Tippecanoe campaign of 1840; indeed, it produced a slightly higher turnout of voters. The conclusion seems inescapable that the energetic campaign spectacle had found a central place in American life and culture. A closer look at the wider range of elections in this era suggests, however, a number of qualifications with respect to the depth and extensiveness of popular engagement in campaign rituals. One is that presidential campaigns varied in their fervor and length, the much analyzed 1840 and 1860 elections being especially long and intense. Unlike either, the 1852 contest between Franklin Pierce and Winfield Scott was a relatively mild affair. In Greenfield, for example, a Scott and Graham Club was founded in late June, but it appears to have been dormant until early August, and the Whig paper was still calling in early September for a meeting to organize the campaign.[33] The Democrats, for their part, did not answer with a Granite Club until mid-October.[34] In Greenfield and in all our towns there were fewer campaign events than there were in 1840 or would be in 1860, and far fewer evidences of popular enthusiasm. The nonpartisan editor who complained in 1860 that "politics seem to enter into everything" could not have made that complaint in 1852.

Nor could he have done so during any off-year election. With rare exceptions, campaign clubs appeared only in presidential elections, and torchlight parades and mass rallies were smaller and much less frequent in the off years. In many nonpresidential campaigns there were no torchlight parades at all. Off-year campaigns also began later. Whig nominating conventions in 1851 for governor and other state offices were held in mid-September in Massachusetts, and Franklin County towns got around to their state legislative nominations still later, in the case of Deerfield only days before the November election.[35] In other states where nominating conventions were held as early as July, the campaign itself often began in earnest only in September or October (and in Ohio ended earlier, with the October election). As late as September 12, in 1851, the *Rondout Courier* could still head an item "Politicians Waking Up," and write that "the November conflict is near enough to arouse all the party men."[36] The reference to "party men" here reveals the *Courier*'s understanding that the voting masses were to be aroused still later. Augusta's off-year calendar was similar. On September 21, 1859, the *Constitutionalist* wrote that "Politics, up to this time have remained silent."[37] It may be fair to say, therefore, that historians of political campaigns have been guilty of a kind of "presidential synthesis," the effect of which has been to overstate the presence of the spectacle in American life.[38] Only once in every four years were Americans treated at length to a political campaign that pulled out all the stops.

Further qualifications emerge from examining the spectacle itself. One is the high degree of management in political campaigns, and the consequent disproportionate participation of party activists in campaign rallies and other events. Party leaders planned a long series of public events—from ratification bonfires, to pole raisings and torchlight parades, to postelection celebrations—and in the process drew heavily and frequently upon those partisans willing to commit substantial amounts of time and effort to the cause. Editors repeatedly stressed the importance of organization, while continuing to portray campaign events as spontaneous displays of popular enthusiasm. This description in the *Mirror* of a pole raising by Marion Democrats is no more overheated than most:

> Very little effort was put forth to attract hither a crowd beyond the bare announcement that there would be a pole raising and that the Hon. H. B. Payne would be present and address the Democracy that day; and yet . . . before 10 o'clock in the

morning delegations from the country began to pour in by thousands . . . . The Republicans stood back in perfect amazement. . . , for never was there such an uprising, such a spontaneous outburst of the popular will.[39]

This was an unusual campaign rally if so large a crowd was produced by "very little effort" on the part of party organizers. It is clear that in nearly all instances, crowds at major campaign events were swollen by the carefully arranged importation of party workers of nearby towns and counties, who, alongside those who did show up on their own initiative, enhanced the appearance of a massive and spontaneous expression of popular support for the party's candidate. Support may have been genuine, but it was seldom if ever entirely spontaneous. Editors, indeed, sometimes boasted of prearrangements. On the eve of a campaign visit by the Little Giant himself, the *Dubuque Herald* based its prediction of a massive turnout on some surprisingly precise information: "We understand that 200 are coming from Lansing, 700 from Independence, 600 from Bellevue, 1,000 from Maquoketa, . . . 500 from Galena & so on."[40] These numbers may have been exaggerated, but the *Herald* reveals here something important about the way campaign events worked. Local party leaders loaned their activists to the leaders of other towns (and in the present case another state) to help swell their rallies, expecting payment in kind when they planned their own affairs. The visual impact of the resulting crowd could be impressive in a small town, and provided local editors with evidence of jammed streets and public squares. What was left unsaid was that the same people were being counted repeatedly in one town after another.

The specific elements of party rallies were also significant. It has been observed many times that campaign events were designed to be entertaining, but what is perhaps insufficiently stressed is that by the 1850s many of the elements of the political rally had nothing to do with public issues or specific candidacies, and some of the more attractive even went beyond any sort of political symbolism. Log cabins and cider barrels may have evoked a specific (if misleading) image of William Henry Harrison in 1840, while hickory poles were associated with Andrew Jackson and his Democratic successors, but in later antebellum campaigns these images were largely replaced by less specifically connotative artifacts such as torches, liberty poles (erected by Whigs and Republicans as well as by Democrats), and even, with no little irony, hot-air balloons. Torches and liberty poles were, in fact, traditional icons of popular collective action, but editors who argued over the height of each party's pole did little to cement these associations to any particular candidacy or party platform. Balloon ascensions, which were the central attractions of some of the largest rallies, were devoid of political connotation; indeed, they were as likely to be seen at county fairs as at political rallies. But they drew the people, as did brass bands, barbecues, and even the simple prospect of a routine-interrupting big crowd in town. Party leaders well understood that speeches or even specifically political icons would not attract the masses in sufficient numbers, and readily resorted to whatever would do so. The strategy could backfire. In his memoir, the Illinois politician Gustave Koerner recalls a Chicago rally made "more attractive" by the addition to the dais of the celebrated tragedian James Murdock. After an hour of band music and singing, and just before the introduction of the political speakers, the crowd began to chant "Murdock, Murdock." Koerner cut short his speech as the chant continued, and the following speaker was forced by the crowd to yield to Murdock, who read poetry and performed a scene from *Hamlet*. "The people had come to see a show," Koerner concludes, "and evidently did not care to hear speeches."[41]

Political campaign clubs were also made attractive in apolitical ways. The young men and boys who joined the Wide-Awakes, Invincibles, and other marching clubs were sold inexpensive uniforms and taught impressive march maneuvers. In Marion the Wide-Awake uniform consisted of an oil cloth cape and cap and a red sash, which along with a lamp or torch cost $1.33. Their "worm fence march" can be imagined, as can a nice connection to Lincoln as rail splitter—a connection that does remind us of the log-cabin and hard-cider symbolism of earlier days.[42] The more important connection to be made, however, is to the "militia fever" of the 1850s. Many Americans north and south delighted in military uniforms and titles, musters and parades, and the formal balls their companies sponsored during the winter social season. Their younger brothers no doubt delighted in aping them, so far as $1.33 would allow, while their parents were provided with a means by which youthful rowdyism was, for a time, channeled into a military form of discipline. The regular campaign clubs, meanwhile, were given a different attraction. One of the first items of business, once the club was organized, was to invite "the ladies" to meetings. Many members were single young men, and the campaign occurred during a relatively slow social season following the picnics, steamboat excursions, and other outings of the summer, and preceding the balls sponsored by militia companies, fire companies, and fraternal lodges during the winter. Campaign clubs helped to extend and connect the social seasons for single young men and women, and gave both an occasion for high-spirited travel. "Coming home there was fun," wrote the Democratic editor of a Dubuque Republican club excursion to a rally in Galena. "There were frequent 'three cheers for Miss Nancy Rogers.' . . . Captain Pat Conger was the best looking man on the ground and we can only say that it is a pity he is not a Democrat."[43]

It is important to understand, too, that the reports of massive turnouts for political events were often exaggerated. Indeed, they had become formulaic, as were editors' constant reassurances, in response to or anticipation of charges of rowdiness, that party gatherings had been "respectable." Hardly less routine were descriptions of the opposite party's parade or rally as a "fizzle," the result being that in a number of instances we obtain two very different descriptions of the same event. The major Democratic mass rally in Marion in 1860 was set

PROCESSION OF THE WIDE-AWAKE CLUB OF HARTFORD, CONN., ON THURSDAY, JULY 26.—FROM A SKETCH BY OUR SPECIAL ARTIST.

2.1. Wide-Awakes in uniform and on parade. *Frank Leslie's Illustrated Newspaper*, 1860.

at eight thousand by the Democratic editor.[44] When the *Republican* claimed the same number for the "Glorious Republican Rally" a month later it insisted that the Democratic rally had been only half as large.[45] It is impossible to say how accurate these estimates were, but it can be noted that there were as many claims of meetings in half-filled rooms and of parades through nearly deserted streets as there were boasts of courthouses and streets bursting with enthusiastic partisans. Editors frequently found in the opposing party's rallies, and in the opposing editor's numerical claims, occasions for the exercise of their satirical talent. The Lincoln ratification meeting in Marion, according to the Democratic *Mirror*, "managed to muster together a crowd of about 125. . . . Dr. Fisher told a yarn . . . [and] scratched himself in the usual place."[46] The *Republican* got even after the Democrats ratified the Douglas nomination, counting "100 Douglas politicians; 75 Full dyed Black Republicans, grinning; 25 Breckinridge men; 40 Irrepressible boys; 1 dog, with the 'bark' on."[47] One week later the *Mirror* replied in kind, describing the crowd at a Republican pole raising as "the Leader and his body guard, two ladies, a little girl and boy, a pig with his tail curled up, a la snub nose, and a little poodle with the bark off."[48] And so it went. These comic lampoons told readers as little about the size of political rallies as did boasts of huge turnouts by one's own party. They did, however, add an effective satirical footnote to those opposition boasts that local readers already knew to be exaggerated.

Americans of the nineteenth century ventured out for a variety of public events, of which political rallies were but one type. The political newspapers in all our towns tell us of nonpolitical events that drew crowds as large or larger than any claimed for political rallies. The five thousand who paid to see Van Amburgh's Menagerie in Greenfield during the early days of the 1860 presidential campaign, for example, outnumbered any crowd at a free political rally, feast, or torchlight parade in the months that followed.[49] Local editors often disagreed as to whether an indoor political meeting filled the courthouse, but both Kingston editors described a courthouse crowd of more than five hundred, with hundreds more turned away, who paid to hear the *Oratorio of Esther* in early 1859.[50] Religious revivals and camp meetings could attract many hundreds of people every day for several weeks. The techniques we associate with political campaigning, moreover, were not the exclusive property of the political parties. During the New York gubernatorial election of 1858, for example, a torchlight parade was held in Kingston, not to promote one or another candidate, but to celebrate the completion of the Atlantic telegraph.[51] In both respects, political events competed for public attention and interest, and for a separable ritual space within the community's recurring and episodic calendar of public events.

Even more important to recognize, perhaps, are those events and activities that seemed to supersede politics. The county fair held each year by the Franklin County Agricultural Society, and the several cattle shows held by town

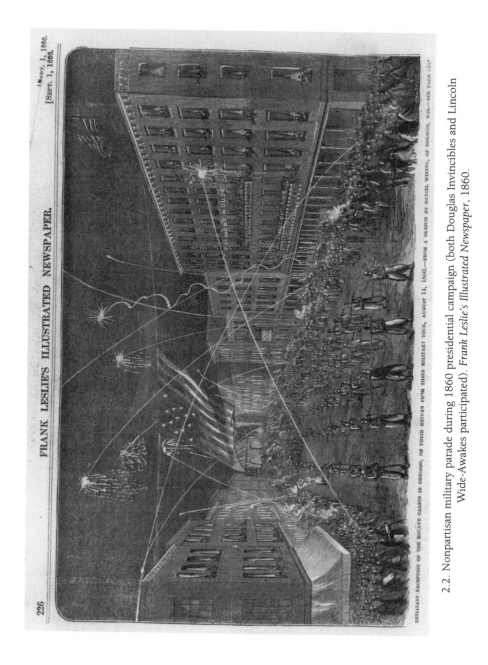

BRILLIANT RECEPTION OF THE ZOUAVE CADETS IN CHICAGO, ON THEIR RETURN FROM THEIR MILITARY TOUR, AUGUST 14, 1860.—FROM A SKETCH BY DANIEL WENTEL, OF HORICON, WIS.—SEE PAGE 232.*

2.2. Nonpartisan military parade during 1860 presidential campaign (both Douglas Invincibles and Lincoln Wide-Awakes participated). *Frank Leslie's Illustrated Newspaper*, 1860.

societies, were serious affairs in and around Greenfield, organized by dozens of committees, and attended by thousands of people. The fairs and shows were held at the very height of the fall political campaign; yet, they regularly pushed politics to the side, even during presidential elections. During the weeks leading up to them the party papers in Greenfield reported the fair and show schedules and the selection of committees alongside political notices of the same type, and during the week of the fair politics simply disappeared from the partisan press on behalf of very detailed reporting of what was clearly the major fall event for many of Franklin County's citizens.[52] A rather more frivolous event in Greenfield is equally helpful in placing politics within a broader context. In the midst of its reports on the turbulent 1860 Charleston convention of the national Democratic Party, the *Franklin Democrat* described the large crowd that collected at the railroad depot to get the news, by late train, of the "great fight" between Heenan and Sayers. The sporting paper, *Wilkes' Spirit of the Times*, was auctioned for fifteen to twenty cents each. "The rush Monday morning was also very lively and newpapers disappeared with rapidity."[53] The political news from Charleston apparently was received with greater equanimity.

The appeal of these apolitical events helps explain why politicians sought to make rallies, clubs, and other elements of the political campaign as entertaining as possible. Unlike the caucuses and nominating conventions, the campaign required the participation of the people, and the masses would not turn out time after time if only politics were involved, especially when there were other things to amuse and engage them. Hence, the campaign was different from nomination meetings at which political men indulged their taste for purely political combat and maneuver. To the "package" of candidates and resolutions offered to the public by each political party were now added party slogans and images, along with attractions that had little or nothing to do with politics— barbecues and parades, torches and uniforms, James Murdock on the dais in Chicago, Miss Nancy Rogers on the ride home from Galena. Did this improve upon the circus of 1840? In fact, political discourse was becoming more serious amidst the campaign spectacle, and men who had waited breathlessly for news about Heenan and Sayers would soon pay closer attention to the consequences of that convention in Charleston. But the events that were overtaking politics did not grow out of the spectacle itself, or in the way party leaders, already practicing "the art of the possible," shaped the larger political forum.

We should recognize, finally, an important aspect of the election campaign that was separate from the spectacle (often, indeed, separate from the party), and that did not usually find its way into local newspapers. This was the be-hind-the-scenes efforts of candidates and their "friends" to gain the backing of influential local leaders, and to reach and influence individual voters, often with incentives more private than public, and more material than ideological. Letters to E. B. Morgan, a Whig who ran for congress in central New York against Thomas Howe in 1850, tell us how this was done. Morgan's friends wrote to specify the funds that would be needed in their towns, to identify key men, and to describe what they and their opponents were doing. R. H. Duell wrote from Cortland County that "in Virgil we shall have to distribute considerable money," and that in Cortlandville Morgan's opponent "left a large sum of money which they are using freely." Some funds were needed to defray the expense of publicizing the candidates' appearances and positions, but others went to more direct means of persuasion. "How[e]'s friends have commenced operations here," wrote William Beach from Auburn. "They offered one of our voters here yesterday a cost of pair of boots if he would vote for How[e]." This sort of bribery has long been associated with election day, but it is important to understand that it was also part of the longer campaign. The amounts were not necessarily large (the "Leading Whigs" in Aurelius, reported James Lash, "think that 20 or 25 dollars can be used so that it will pay 20 per cent"), but neither were the numbers of voters in rural townships, and a candidate's local operatives were expected to reach all of the voters one way or another, persuading with cash if civic argument did not suffice. Sometimes, indeed, the line between argument and bribery is hard to draw. The promise made by Howe's men to Irish voters in Union Springs to "contribute liberally" to the construction of a Catholic church in return for their votes is easy to classify, but the handbill claiming that Howe had paid two thousand dollars to survey a railroad route from Auburn to Binghamton, and the assurance to Cayuga County farmers that, because of his backing of this route, "ploughs would be 8/ cheaper if Howe was elected," might almost pass for political economy.[54]

A recurring element of the letters to Morgan during this campaign was the identification of important men who had their own means of influencing voters. Hank Knapp, recommended by U. B. Judd as a man who "if we get him right . . . can do us a good service if not vice a versa," might have been a leader of some local coterie or merely a square-shouldered thug willing to use physical intimidation on behalf of the highest bidder, but other correspondents were clearer in their recommendations. E. R. Cobb sent a list of "prominent names in such towns [of Cayuga County] as you have not so frequently visited," itemizing forty-seven men in eleven towns. How influential these men were we cannot determine, but the listings of real property values on the United States census manuscripts of that year suggest that Cobb had identified the wealthier men of these relatively remote townships. The majority of the male householders of the eleven towns owned no real property, and the mean value of real property among all male householders was just over eight hundred dollars. Those men on Cobb's list who could be identified on the census manuscripts were significantly wealthier. Only four owned less than eight hundred dollars in real property (two of these men were physicians), and the mean for the group as a whole exceeded thirty-six hundred dollars. In what way were these well-off men useful to Morgan? Did their wealth (and in a few instances their professional standing) give them a general visibility in their communities, or did it confer more specific forms of influence? Either way, it was Cobb's assumption that the campaign in Cayuga County ought to be conducted from the top down, through the medium of local influence. Morgan and his opponent gave stump speeches, to be sure, and Morgan even issued a public letter on the Fugitive Slave Law, but it was to less democratic, less civic aspects of the campaign that Morgan's men pointed when they urged strategies for winning. Morgan's public letter, indeed, was condemned by his correspondents as a mistake that contributed significantly to his defeat. When he ran again two years later he was advised, "for God's sake banish the use of pen except to write upon the ink stand 'poison.' "[55]

Morgan's advisers were, of course, party insiders, just the sort of men who would stress the insiders' game. Needless to say, they were also the sort who would press their own patronage claims, during and after the campaign. Jacob Schoonmaker, for example, who was in the process of polling his school district, threatened to do no more unless Morgan wrote back assuring him the position of superintendent of section 8 of the Erie Canal. U. B. Judd wanted Morgan to help him get the three dollars a day that was paid to the doorkeeper of the state assembly: "It would be a small fortune for me . . . get board in Albany say 20/ p week, yes all nice." We are hearing voices here that we thought we had left behind when party conventions gave way to the popular campaign, and if they seem to reflect a narrow selfishness, we must also remember that these were men who thought they knew best how to win elections, which was the key to their own success. We must attach some significance, therefore, to the fact that not one of Morgan's correspondents mentions any aspect of the campaign spectacle. Newspaper banners and editorials, rallies and speeches—these were the things that most evidently called the people into the public sphere, and these are what suggest a heightened popular engagement in politics during the campaign season. To at least some political professionals, however, they seem hardly to have existed.[56]

ELECTION DAY—AND AFTER

The numbers of people who participated in parades, rallies, and other campaign spectacles (and in the less publicized campaign activities of the U. B. Judds and E. R. Cobbs) may be questioned, but it is certain that large numbers turned out for the political season's culminating event. The entire process pointed to the election, and it was to the election that the vast majority of eligible voters went, particularly in presidential election years, but often impressively in the off years as well. In the nation as a whole, 70 percent of eligible voters cast ballots in the 1852 presidential election, and this was the ebb tide of presidential voting in the post–Harrison era. By 1856 turnout was nearly back to the 80 percent of the Tippecanoe election, and in 1860 it was nearly 82 percent, the highest ever recorded to that date. In our selected towns, voter participation matched these national percentages, and was probably typical also for off-year elections. Local elections there (for county, township, and city or village offices) generally attracted the fewest voters, while greater numbers turned out for state and congressional races. Four elections in Marion during the 1850–52 election cycle suggest the larger pattern: approximately 42 percent voting in the village election in 1852, half in the township election in 1851, nearly two-thirds in the gubernatorial election of 1850, and some 73 percent (somewhat above the national average) in the presidential contest between Franklin Pierce and Winfield Scott.[57]

It is high voter turnout, more than anything else, that has undergirded historians' claims of an active participatory democracy during this era. By voting, citizens validated political institutions and the entire political process, as well as their own status within both. The fact that massive turnouts followed energetic campaigns has been especially impressive to historians, who have tended to find in this sequence a positive causal connection, widespread and deeply felt engagement in the campaign spectacle manifesting itself in the most natural way in the culminating act of voting. Voting, however, is a deceptively simple act. If those who failed to vote may be said to have rejected the political process by their abstention, it does not follow that those who affirmed it by their participation expressed a commitment that was uniform and straightforward. Voting itself was simple, and its quantities simple to tabulate, but its meanings are more variable, complex, and elusive. It is those complexities that we must attempt to understand before we can attach high voter turnout to the campaign spectacle as a validation of the idea of a broadly and deeply engaged antebellum electorate.[58]

The parties themselves behaved as though many in the electorate would not appear to vote, let alone participate in other political activities, in the absence of their own strenuous exertions. Their efforts to enhance voter turnout (apart, that is, from organizing the campaign spectacle) began near the end of the campaign in endlessly repeated editorial appeals to vote on election day. These could assume a tone that approached the frantic. "Let no business, no engagement, no pleasure, prevent you from exercising your right as a free citizen," urged the *Augusta Daily Chronicle and Sentinel* a week before the 1860 election. "See your neighbors, and impress the careless with the necessity of action, arouse the indifferent, implore the wanderers to come back to the right path. Put your carriages and wagons, and horses, and purses, into requisition." And on the Saturday before the election: "Go to work, then, each of you, all day Monday, all Monday night, . . . spare no moment but what is absolutely necessary for other business, till the polls close Tuesday evening." "Don't let a single vote be lost," warned the *Clarksville Chronicle*. "Give one day to the cause," implored the *Kingston Democratic Journal*. Here the partisan papers unwittingly marked the boundary between ordinary voters who were asked to "give one day" to the work of the party, and activists who were expected to work throughout the campaign. And in fact it was not individual effort but *organization* that was the overriding theme of election-day exhortations, and it was organization, on the ground, that was of greater significance than anything that appeared in the partisan press.[59]

The political parties attempted to maximize their turnout by systematic assignments of responsibility for specific lists of voters. Acting in many cases under precise instructions from state party central committees, local parties drew up poll lists according to school districts or other geographic subdivisions of the town or county, and distributed the lists to district vigilance committees or other groups of party activists.[60] These men were responsible for distributing tickets, tallying votes, challenging illegal voters brought in by the opposing party, watching out for (or performing) other election-day tricks, and above all for making sure their own party's voters got to the polling place. A small-town and rural environment made the voter tracking system work quite well across much of America, especially where the roads were good and the population not too dispersed. Voters and their places of residence were known, and the numbers and distances allowed recalcitrant voters to be called upon more than once during election day. Consider Greenfield, a township of some eight hundred voters in 1860. If each party's list ran to four hundred, then twenty election-day workers could be made responsible for only twenty voters. If only half of these men came to vote on their own initiative, the remainder could easily be called upon, exhorted, and driven to the polls. Both party instructions and editorial exhortations stressed the importance of early voting, precisely so that vigilance committees could know where to direct their forces during the final hours. Under these conditions, and considering also the visibility of each man's actions in such a community, it may well have been more bothersome not to vote than to have voted.

This characteristic configuration of organization, landscape, and community may have been more significant than has yet been recognized in explaining the high voter turnouts of the middle decades of the nineteenth century. Earlier in the century, the proportion of areas with low population densities and poor roads was significantly greater, while in the century's last decades there was a dramatic increase in the numbers of Americans living in the increasingly anonymous streets and alleys of big cities. In between lay an era in which a developed but still largely rural landscape predominated as never before or since. One of the most striking elements of the letters between campaign workers and candidates in this era is the small size, the accessibility, one might even say the intimacy of the human landscapes they describe or imply. A campaign worker named Bailey, for example, reported to E. B. Morgan just before election day in 1850 that he had seen "nearly every Whig voter" in the town of Locke, and "every one of whom there is any doubt & wherever there is a Loco that may possibly be got for a part of the ticket I have put somebody on his track." A congressional district may have been large, but each worker's baili-wick permitted the most specific reports. Honeywell is still undecided, wrote Bailey. "His wife puts in for you—she remembers the 'handsome young clerk with black eyes.' "[61] Intimacy indeed seems the right word here, but the im-portant point is not that Mrs. Honeywell knew the color of Morgan's eyes but that this world of farms and villages along good country roads may have been the ideal human landscape for maximizing voter participation.[62] "If there is a neighborhood left unattended to, there is time enough yet," wrote an anxious candidate to Calvin Hathaway after hearing warnings that Hathaway's town might not produce its usual Democratic majority. "In most of the towns, teams are employed to scour every road & bring out every democrat. . . . Teams will start from this village, from Homer, from Truxton, from Preble, from Scoto, from Virgil, . . . to bring in every voter who is not at the polls by noon." *Every* voter, known, reached, and delivered if possible. And when it was over, the still more intimate community of local politicians would gather on its own ground: "Come up Tuesday night if you can. We shall all be at the Eagle. There will be something good to eat, 'pur-haps.' "[63]

There had no doubt been "something good" for voters, too, earlier in the day. Partisan editors never admitted that their own party practiced election day "treating," but they invariably accused their opponents of attracting voters with free food and drink, and especially the latter. "Whiskey was as free as water" for illegal Irish voters during the 1859 election, complained the *Marion Republican*, "and, brutally drunk, they were led up to the polls like so many CATTLE, a Locofoco ticket put into their hands, and they COMPELLED to vote it."[64] Democrats were more notorious for treating, but it was practiced by both sides. "The one that gin the last treat, old hoss, is the fellow I go's in for," responded one Dubuque citizen to the *Times* editor's question.[65] "There is an immense quantity of liquor disposed of by what is technically called 'whipping the devil 'round the stump,' " explained one of William Bouck's correspondents, al-though the governor was surely as aware as anyone of the time-worn practice of election-day treating.[66] Temperance reformers had long since identified this tradition as a corruption of the democratic process, and in some places had succeeded to some extent in toning down election-day revelries of various sorts.[67] Temperance reform, moreover, was part of a larger force working against treating. A middle class increasingly insistent on respectable behavior, and increasingly suspicious of interclass interactions of any kind, made it more difficult for politicians with social as well as political aspirations to supervise or condone the rough traditions of an American election. Nonetheless, treating remained part of the electoral process. "Brick" Pomeroy's fond recollection of an 1858 election in Wisconsin shows us how it could be done in frontier settlements where the local tavern served as the polling place. The landlord in this instance had ten gallons of whiskey in the tavern, which Pomeroy bought at $1.50 per gallon:

> Then I brought in from the kitchen a clean washtub, poured half the whiskey into it, supplied the outfit with a tin dipper, and appointed a stout Belgian farmer to take charge of it and treat men as they came in—with Judge Larabee's compliments. . . . It was not long before the tavern was full of voters, as election day they all come out to meet each other and to vote. I asked the landlord if he could supply dinners for all, if I would pay for it. . . . Then I went into the bar room and through the man in charge of the washtub, invited all who came to have dinner with me—with the compliments of Judge Larabee. . . . We had a jolly time, and all agreed that the young man was a good one, and if all Democrats were like him they were a good lot.[68]

Capturing an election in this way was more difficult in older settlements, where voting was generally not held in taverns, and where both parties were on the ground competing for votes. But if whiskey could not always be ladled out of washtubs, treating could be accomplished in other ways, and could take the form of products other than food or whiskey. E. L. Dohoney recalls the Whigs purchasing Hawk Fletcher's vote with a pair of shoes, a practice we have already noticed in the 1850 congressional campaign in central New York. On another occasion, Fletcher was given a set of plates in return for his vote.[69] And, of course, there was cash. "Buying votes was always common in Kentucky," recalled Dohoney, "and was indulged in by both parties." Joe Finn "did not know the difference between an election and a militia muster; but always attended both in the hope that some candidate would buy his vote."[70] And in central New York, one of E. B. Morgan's campaign workers warned that the Democrats had set out from Auburn for his town, just before election day, with "a fresh supply of funds." Morgan, in turn, should "pour in the hot shot."[71] Alas, Morgan was outgunned. Among the explanations for his defeat in Cortland County, R. H. Duell mentioned a peddler named Sunderland, "extensively acquainted in Virgil & Harford," who had "scattered How[e]'s money profusely."[72]

Treating and cash bribery attracted some voters to the polls, and gambling attracted others. Betting was a widespread activity in America, and elections provided one of its most obvious and compelling venues. "Some here are sadly disappointed," wrote a woman in New York after the 1844 presidential election, "and that with reason, as they had staked *all* in *betting*."[73] The political parties were not responsible for most election betting, but there is some evidence that they encouraged it among their own voters and party workers, and partisan papers carried betting offers as paid advertisements. Party leaders

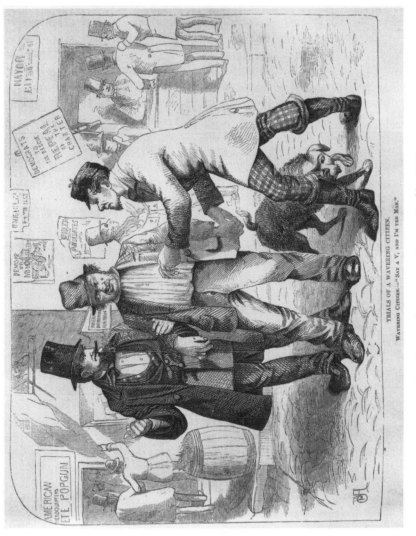

TRIALS OF A WAVERING CITIZEN.

Wavering Citizen.—"Say a V, and I'm the Man."

2.3. Election-day treating. *Harper's Weekly*, 1857.

understood that betting could motivate men to vote and perhaps to work for the party or candidate on which they had staked even small sums. As the *Boston Herald* pointed out, "a man may buy his own vote, and his own influence—much more actively exercised than it would be for the money of another—for the side which will win his stakes, without regard for what he considers to be right."[74] At a hearing held by a committee of the New York State Assembly to inquire into the disappearance of a ballot box from an election in Schenectady, one Peter Ouderkirk, who had been distributing tickets, incidentally detailed the scope of his betting on the results in the county and in various city wards: "says he, witness, . . . that he bet fifty dollars with Mr. Cob and fifty dollars with Lims Peck; says Sheriff Wemple held the stakes; . . . says he also bet with Peter Cochran ten dollars . . . ; says he made two bets on the result of the election in the second ward; . . . says he bet thirty dollars on the result of the election in the fourth ward; says it was his own money he bet."[75] John Lassells bet a beaver hat at the same election—a much smaller stake, but notable because Lassells was an election inspector. Ouderkirk and Lassells were both party men who did not come to the polls only to bet, but the gambling that swirled around the polling place was clearly an attraction to less political men, some of whom may have attended—and voted—primarily for this reason.

Finally, and apart from all these other attractions, men went to the elections to talk, to conduct some business or another, or simply to take a break, knowing that others would be doing so as well. As all that we have reviewed here demonstrates, elections were not the silent and single-purpose events that they would become in the era of secret ballots and voting machines, and voters did not attend them just to vote and depart for work or home. They came, in Pomeroy's words, "to meet each other and to vote," and in many cases to remain for hours in the first of these pursuits, availing themselves or not of the parties' inducements to cast a particular ballot.

And still the parties worried a great deal about the turnout of their own voters, and about being outhustled and outmaneuvered by activists on the other side. There were, indeed, more tricks to be played and to watch for, and these, perhaps even more than other tactics of greater and lesser legality, reveal something of the parties' perceptions of voters. In an age when ballots were printed at party newspaper offices and distributed by party workers, opportunities existed for deceptions of various sorts in the titling of ballots and the listing of candidates. In 1858, for example, the Greenfield Republican editor reminded voters that in the previous year's election the Democrats had printed ballots that imitated the type font of the Republican ballot, and that substituted some Democratic for Republican candidates.[76] This was, in fact, a common practice by local parties that were expecting defeat, and it was based on the assumption that there were sufficient numbers of inattentive or ill-informed voters on the other side to allow one or two of their own candidates to sneak into office in this way. "The tickets you have . . . had better be destroyed,"

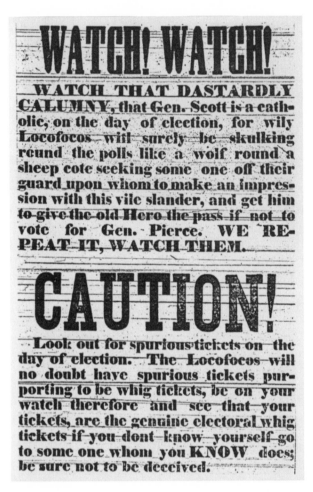

2.4. Election-day warnings in a partisan newspaper. *Marion Buckeye Eagle*, 1852.

advised F. G. Day to Morgan. "We are *fully satisfied* the Locos have our engraved head," and we have "got up" a new one. Too late, it appears. In Scott, Cortland, and perhaps elsewhere, the Democrats succeeded in distributing their "Whig" tickets with Howe's name substituted for Morgan's, and a number of them were voted.[77] Two years later, in a town near Augusta, Georgia, Whig voters were presented with all sorts of ballots headed as the People's Ticket, the Union Ticket, the Conservative Whig Ticket, and the Republican Ticket, none of which contained the names of electors pledged to Winfield Scott. "Doubtless many voted without knowing for whom they were voting," concluded the *Constitutionalist*.[78] Editors who advised their party's voters to compare the ballots they were handed with the ticket printed week after week, at the top of the editorial page of the party newspaper, clearly believed that some voters did not know who the candidates were. "DON'T VOTE FOR GEN. JACKSON! For he is dead," advised one rather jaded editor in 1858.[79]

Testimony at various New York State Assembly hearings provides an unusually close view of the way some men voted in the 1840s and 1850s, and of the role of the party workers from whom they obtained their tickets. It reveals that there were numerous voters who, in state races at least, did not know or who could not recall who they voted for, and many who never even read their ballots. Stephen Cooper "did not open and examine his tickets"; Lawrence Glover "voted at said election for [state] senators, but did not look to see their names"; Charles DuBois "does not know for whom he voted for senators"; Vincent Blackburn "did not examine the ticket he voted for senators"; Abraham Doty "did not open the ticket."[80] Ananais Carter's testimony begins with a proud statement of purposive citizenship and then gradually unravels, demonstrating that voters did know what they should have been doing when they went to the polls, even when they could not live up to expectations:

> I read my tickets over after I got them. I saw what they were. I would have been a fool to have voted without. I think I read them; I am pretty well assured I did. . . . I was informed enough to know what the tickets were. I did read those tickets before I voted. I think Joe Davis' name was on the State ticket. I did not take particular notice of other names on the State ticket. I guess I did not vote for any judge. I think I did not; I cannot positively say. I don't know as I took any notice of who were candidates for judge. . . . I cannot tell whether I had been drinking or not before I voted. It's likely I had.[81]

The scene that emerges from much of the assembly testimony is a confusing one, even for sober men who read their tickets. Most elections involved races on several different levels, and generally there was a different ticket, and a different ballot box, for each. Poll workers from both parties pressed tickets, regular or irregular (sometimes in several versions), on every voter they could reach, so that voters approached the ballot boxes with any number of pieces of paper in their possession, variously headed and variously constituted, with names printed, scratched out, and written in. Even an attentive voter could become confused, especially when poll workers were there to badger him right up to the moment he voted. A Schenectady voter named Schermerhorn voted tickets given to him five or ten seconds earlier by Jerard Anthony, according to John Lassells (the election inspector who had bet a hat); while one Ryer J. Schermerhorn attested that the tickets he had voted had been given to him by Peter Ouderkirk. Was this the same Schermerhorn? If so, did he know which tickets he gave to the inspector to be voted? Nelson Hall already had Democratic tickets with him when Samuel Irish gave him a Whig ticket for the state senate race. "Hall said he did not care for whom he voted; had always been a Jackson man."[82] How did Hall decide which tickets to hand in? (Did he write

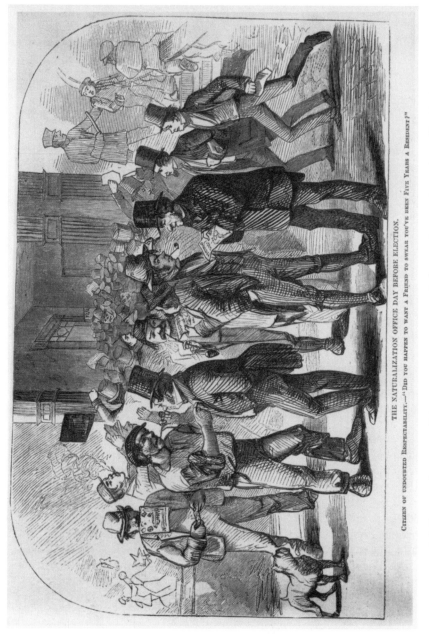

THE NATURALIZATION OFFICE DAY BEFORE ELECTION.

CITIZEN OF UNDOUBTED RESPECTABILITY.—"DID YOU HAPPEN TO WANT A FRIEND TO SWEAR YOU'VE BEEN FIVE YEARS A RESIDENT?"

2.5. Party workers naturalizing immigrant voters just before an election. *Harper's Weekly*, 1857.

in Andrew Jackson? Perhaps some voters really did need to be told when to stop voting for Old Hickory!) Why did this Jackson Democrat "not care" for whom he had voted? Matters were further complicated by personal considerations. John J. Vanhagen was given a printed ticket with the name of E. Crosby written in by hand. "I asked him if E. Crosby was the man down on the dock (Crosby is in the freighting business); he said it was; I told him that he would do, and I took the ticket and walked in and voted."[83] Alonzo Avery, a Whig voter, accepted three apparent Whig tickets that prominently substituted the Democratic for the Whig candidate for lieutenant governor, agreeing to the change because the Democratic candidate was his townsman. After voting one of these tickets, he showed another to Peter Tice, who pointed out that he had been duped, for the one explicit change had been used to disguise another—this "Whig" ticket also excluded the Whig candidate for assemblyman.[84] There are many incidents of this sort, and others that remind us that the polls could still be used to settle business of a quite personal nature. Abram Lewis, a tenant of candidate John I. DeGraff, "mentioned to DeGraff that he, witness, was poor, and if he voted for him, witness expected he would show him lenity on the rent. Mr. DeGraff replied, saying did you ever know me to distress a poor man?"[85]

Voting in antebellum America was not so simple an act after all, and high voter turnout, as all the foregoing evidence tells us, did not necessarily indicate a widespread and deep engagement in politics on the part of the American people. What it may more powerfully indicate, indeed, is the extraordinary achievement of American political parties in mobilizing voters, some of whom were ignorant of, uninterested in, skeptical about, or even averse to political affairs. Here we concur in an important sense with many political historians who have emphasized the significance of party development in the antebellum era, and reiterate the importance of understanding how the political parties functioned as institutions. Where we differ from most interpretations is in the relationship between parties and the American electorate. The parties, we argue, developed their elaborate structures and techniques for nominating candidates, devising platforms, conducting campaigns, and maximizing election-day turnout, not from the political passions of a uniformly engaged citizenry, but in response to the very variations of engagement we have been describing. They constituted the efforts of those who were deeply involved in political affairs to reach and influence those who were not. The very intensity of this "partisan imperative" suggests the magnitude of the task party activists perceived and set out to perform.

It is important to recognize the essentially transactional character of many of the means utilized by parties for reaching and mobilizing voters. Treating and bribing were the most obvious and crude of the transactions parties made with voters. More important, we believe (and quite apart from continuing, informal habits of personal influence that could resemble a crude treating for

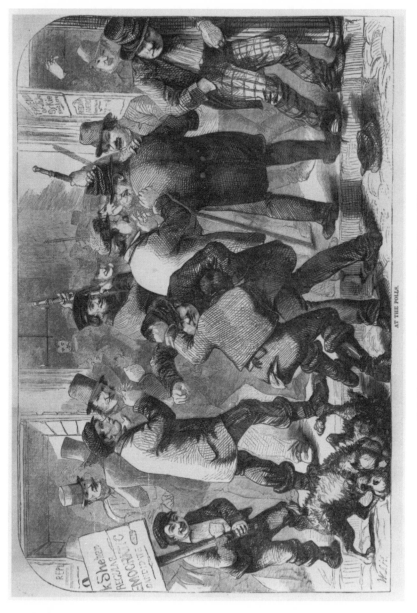

AT THE POLLS.

2.6. Election-day brawl. *Harper's Weekly*, 1857.

votes), was a different, less explicit type of transaction that derived in large part from the configuration of party institutionalization and a variably engaged electorate. We have already described the clearly labeled "package" of candidates, programs, and images that less thoughtful or less interested voters could "purchase" without difficulty, the package including even the writing of names on a printed ticket that needed only to be dropped in the ballot box (once the various tickets one was offered were sorted out, by those who cared to do so). To the parties, this was a way of reaching the lukewarm portion of the electorate, not by impelling a deeper commitment, but by recognizing and accommodating to their less intense engagement. It should be recognized in this context that parties, though similar in many ways to other institutions that were proliferating in antebellum America, were also different in one important respect: ordinary partisans were not organizational members in the usual sense. They did not pay dues, attend weekly or monthly meetings, or assume obligations for carrying out the organization's purpose; and there were no criteria for or even a process of admission. For ordinary Democrats, or Whigs, or Republicans, the party did not even exist as an accessible institution except during the political season.[86] Not membership, then, but the marketplace, defines the relation between the political party and some of the people who voted its ticket, including many of those who were not bribed with cash, food, or drink.

The very institutional development that facilitated the more widespread purchase of party packages may have deepened the distance between less engaged citizens and the political process. Consider for a moment a parallel (and nearly simultaneous) development in the governance of American cities. Through the eighteenth century and somewhat beyond, most municipal functions—policing, fire protection, poor relief, street cleaning, and the like—were performed in various ways and degrees (and with varying effectiveness) by the citizens themselves, serving the community according to the dictates of municipal legislation. During the early decades of the nineteenth century, however, this system of publicly mandated private service evolved toward a new system, and a new relation between people and government, in which residents of the city purchased municipal services, through taxation, from specialized and professional employees of the city government. City government was institutionalized, and in the process the people of cities, by purchasing what they had previously performed, stood in a new and rather more distant relation to municipal affairs.[87] They continued to participate, but at a remove that made it more difficult to comprehend and more compelling to ignore the operations of city government. The institutionalization of political parties was a somewhat different phenomenon, to be sure, but its effects may have been similar with respect to some voters' relations to the political process. As in the performance of urban services, Americans could, if they wished, leave the work to the professionals, and go about their other business. Parties, therefore, were in this sense instrumental to Americans who wished to perform, but not become absorbed in, their duties as citizens.

Could political parties have facilitated this more moderate form of political engagement, even while they developed and perpetuated the energetic campaign spectacle, and even while party workers scoured the back roads to reach all of their voters? It may be instructive at this point to consider, as we did in chapter 1, what happened in American communities after the campaign and election were over. Historians who have focused on the passions of the political campaign, and for whom the election is both climax and denouement of a stirring and universally engaging political drama, have tended to overlook an important aspect of the election aftermath; namely, the rapidity and the seeming determination with which Americans turned away from politics once the votes had been counted and the results announced. By the 1850s, if not earlier, there emerged in both the partisan and the nonpartisan press an almost ritualized invocation of relief at the end of the political season, which in party papers was often joined to an apology for the regrettable but necessary political preoccupations of the campaign, and an assurance that the paper would now return to more congenial matters. " '[T]he smoke of the battle' having been cleared away," wrote the editor of the *Clarksville Chronicle* after a state election in 1859, "we can begin to dish up a variety of items for our local department, which is more congenial to our feelings than to give the 'news from election,' or other political matters."[88] Statements of this sort were as common in northern as in southern papers, and were expressed by Democratic as well as Whig and Republican editors. They reflect the editors' understanding that some of their readers, and perhaps the greater part of them, wearied of political exhortation and vituperation after a few months, and were anxious to read of other things. The political season required containment, in part because there were aspects of daily life as well as times on the calendar into which politics ought not intrude, and in part because the message itself was suspect—that the politicians from whom voters were purchasing candidates, images, and party platforms, even within the selling season, were in many respects offering shoddy goods. It is striking how frequently the partisan press itself invoked the image of the corrupt politician who deepened the gulf of misunderstanding and distrust between the political party and ordinary voters.[89] We will return to these subjects often in the pages that follow. Here we will cite only the little tale of "Wilhelm Von Sweitzel," printed in the *Clarksville Jeffersonian* in the aftermath of the presidential election of 1860. "Von Sweitzel" was a blacksmith who had been duped by a politician into working for him during several elections in return for the false promise of large payments of money. Pressed for the cash, the politician told Wilhelm that he "might go to the bad place and eat sauerkraut," inducing a response from this newly socialized American citizen that the editor clearly intended as a broader statement about American political culture: "I makes a fire in my plaiksmit shop. I blows my own bellers again. I heat my own iron, and strikes mit mine hammer. I says to myself, 'Wilhelm Von Sweitzel, do your own blowin', and let politicians do theirs.' "[90]

If Wilhelm Von Sweitzel became disaffected from politics (and others, as we have seen, remained passive or indifferent), the simultaneous ascendancy of the political spectacle and a frequently iterated "grammar of corruption" in Jack Downing's America gave rise to yet another relation to politics, best captured, we believe, by Joshua Gamson's recent discussion of "engaged disbelief" as a mode of popular participation in celebrity culture. Gamson distinguishes among believers who uncritically accept the messages in texts about famous persons they do not personally know, believers who accept a "discernible authenticity" in the face of perceived distortions and manipulations, and skeptics who retain enough interest in the very techniques of artifice to participate in a highly qualified, ironic fashion, maintaining a core of disbelief that permits the act of apparent acquiescence—hence, "engaged disbelief."[91] The relevance of Gamson's distinctions to antebellum political culture is suggested by the role of "humbug" in nineteenth-century America. Self-interested deception had no doubt increased in this age of easily counterfeited bank notes, confidence rackets in cities and on steamboats, mesmerism, phrenology, and national advertising for cure-all patent medicines appearing in newspapers alongside editorial claims of massive turnouts for party rallies.[92] Much of this was vicious and exploitative but, as Neil Harris observes, the era's greatest artist of humbug, P. T. Barnum, understood "that American audiences did not mind the cries of trickery; in fact, they delighted in debate. Amusement and deceit could coexist; people would come to see something they suspected might be an exaggeration or even a masquerade."[93] Not only gullibility, but also skepticism—belief, but also disbelief—were the foundations of Barnum's astonishing career. That some Americans approached politics in much the same way—rising to its deceptions as they might not have to sober exposition and debate—is suggested by the many references to humbug, and to Barnum himself, in antebellum political discourse. "There is a man in Pennsylvania who was nominated for governor eight months ago and hasn't been lied about yet!" complained Kingston's *Ulster Republican*. "Where's Barnum?"[94]

This political attitude, too, is different from the enthusiastic commitment to partisan politics that suffuses most political history. Consider again the political "package." To those Americans who were attuned and attracted to humbug, the partisan spectacle was an emporium of showy goods, some overpriced and falsely advertised—or a Barnum circus to go to when it happened to be in town. That they bought some of these goods, and went to the political circus, suggests neither high purpose nor gullibility. We must recognize among some Americans a more detached involvement, and a more ironic appreciation of the Barnums of politics.

Barnum's own relations to politics, we would note, was that of the detached, disbelieving participant. A fairly frequent officeholder (he served in the Connecticut legislature, was the mayor of Bridgeport, and was nominated for Congress), he remained skeptical of politicians. Speaking at the reopening of the American Museum in the midst of the 1860 presidential campaign, Barnum observed:

> Four years ago I furnished the title for the "wooly horse candidate," and now the opposite parties are charged with having drawn on the museum for their "what is it" electoral ticket. After the election is over, I may possibly make reprisals by securing several of the defeated candidates and exhibiting them as about the smallest specimens of the dwarf genus even since my little friend Tom Thumb made his debut in this establishment. If, like Madame Tussaud of London, I had a separate apartment called "the chamber of horrors," I might perhaps engage certain greedy and corrupt office-holders and swindling lobby members, who swallow whole blocks of houses in a single gulp; but as I make it a point to reject unpleasant monstrosities, I can give them no place in the museum.[95]

Barnum's interweaving of parties and politicians with the famous curiosities of his museum expresses the popular association of politics and humbug, and underscores our argument that the connections between the campaign spectacle and voting in the antebellum era—and more generally, the behavioral and cultural patterns of political engagement—were manifold, complex, and sometimes ironic. Parties at once increased, energized, and discouraged political participation; electoral campaigns stimulated both enthusiasm and skepticism, sometimes in the same minds; American democracy found its greatest validation in the peaceful and apolitical aftermath of the strident political campaign. And there are still further ironies, not least in the serious exercise of the franchise by interested citizens who *avoided* the political circus. Consider this depiction of the early hours of an election day in New York City, in the mass-circulation weekly *Frank Leslie's Illustrated Newspaper*:

> Early in the morning the voting places . . . are thronged by crowds of well-dressed, quiet and respectable citizens, who are anxious to deposit their votes and proceed to their business at their banks, stores, offices, or wherever else they may do their respective endeavors to achieve their individual bread and butter. . . . This class of voters is made up of businessmen, who do not mix deeply in politics, but who, for the most part, leave the whole preliminary portion of the campaign—the nomination of candidates, &c.—to those professed politicians who make a living by that dirty trade, and then, on the morning of election day, these said business men march up and vote the ticket nominated by the particular party to which they may happen to be attached, and then think no more of politics till Election Day comes round again.[96]

Frank Leslie's could not have known how detached from the campaign these early-morning voters had been, but the image it sought to convey is an important one. Politics was a "dirty trade," but voting was important to respectable people who avoided the "preliminary portion of the campaign" while engaging primarily in the business of earning "their individual bread and butter." So they appeared at the polls, quietly and soberly, before the candidates, the ticket hawkers, and the "shoulder hitters," and cast presumably well-considered votes before departing for their work. They were partisans, to be sure, but they had detached themselves from the unseemly spectacle of the campaign, and had no interest in its humbugs. The author of this little magazine article was careful to demonstrate that these respectable Americans of the business class were insistent upon exercising their civic duty as self-governing citizens, and that they saw no contradiction between this commitment to the republic and the exclusion of politics from their daily lives. Perhaps we should call this "disengaged belief," and recognize, with *Frank Leslie's*, a solid core of such citizens, not only among the businessmen of the city, but among artisans, workers, and farmers whose sense of civic responsibility, more than their passion for partisan politics, brought them to polling places all across America. Perhaps, too, we should count among them many of those voters campaign publicists and workers coaxed and herded to the polls as though they were so many asses and sheep. Here, again, is the problem of seeing through the biases of the political insider, whose job it was to see people as party voters, and who was likely to overstate the importance of his own efforts to get them to behave that way. The parties, as we earlier stated, could claim a good deal of the credit for the high voter turnouts of this era, but this does not mean that they succeeded as well in transforming seven or eight of every ten eligible voters into avid partisans for whom (to cite again the words of one political historian) the political party was "a natural lens through which to view the world."[97]

All of these variant attitudes toward politics must be set alongside that of the avid partisan to understand more fully the "space" that politics occupied in American life. There is, of course, no possibility of classifying and adding up voters as though indifference, skepticism, hostility, "disengaged belief," avidity, and other postures were stable and defining attributes of specific individuals. Rather, these terms identify impulses and reactions available to all citizens, and no doubt they mingled in different and sometimes contrary or even contradictory ways in the minds of many of them. In the next two chapters we will look more closely at the community of political activists, and at the larger community to which they and their partisan work belonged, and we will examine a variety of sources generated outside the bailiwick of parties and the electoral process (including diaries and letters written by ordinary citizens), to help gain a richer sense of how politics worked in people's lives. There remains, however, a final (and related) observation about the recurring political events we have just reviewed—the caucuses, the conventions, and especially the campaigns, elections, and postelection celebrations. All of them occurred in physical places in and near which people lived and worked. Courthouses and courthouse squares, hotels, taverns, and village streets, were familiar public spaces that periodically became the sites of political activity, just as community newspapers periodically became the "sites" of political exhortation and dispute. Many of the organizers of political events were familiar as well. If politics was a circus, it was not an especially exotic one, and it is worth considering both how the spectacle may have been domesticated by the familiar, and how the familiar may have been enlivened by the spectacle. On the one hand, the setting, the personnel, and the very frequency and predictable form of their recurrence, made the events of electoral politics more humdrum than they were made to seem in the partisan press. But on the other, these events also periodically invested familiar spaces, and perhaps familiar people, too, with a larger public significance. That neighbors did not go elsewhere to be citizens may have added a significant public dimension to neighboring itself, at least for those who lived in the Greenfields, Augustas, and Dubuques that served as political centers for a still largely rural nation. To repeat the question we raised at the end of chapter 1, was a significant and enduring public realm created in such places by the recurring events of the political season? It would seem that by the 1850s the energetic politics (in Formisano's words the "revival") of 1840 had become a habit of American life, part of the townscape itself in the nation's widely scattered political centers. We must continue to ask how, to what extent, and with what consequences, this ongoing political "revival" changed human minds and hearts.

CHAPTER 3

Political Men: Patterns and Meanings of Political Activism in Antebellum America

IN THE PRECEDING CHAPTERS we have referred frequently to political-party leaders, insiders, and activists, and to "ordinary" citizens or voters to whom these labels do not apply. Our view of the political party, if not the entire process of democratic self-rule, has been essentially binary—there were those who ran the party system, and who made politics a vocation or a significant avocation; and there were those who responded to the decisions and efforts of the party's active members, "purchasing" a package of candidates, slogans, and enunciated principles and proposals. Insider and outsider, seller and buyer, perhaps even circus performer and audience. And yet we have already seen in the quite variant responses of voters to the political package, and in the kinds of appeals some men made for patronage appointments, that these dichotomies do not in themselves represent the full range of relations to political affairs. Rather, they are an important frame, an initial distinction that helps us understand how different people built politics into their lives. In this chapter we will look again, and more closely, at those men we have called leaders, insiders, and activists. We will attempt to place them within their larger communities, and to place their political activism within the larger round of community affairs. By analyzing political men in this way—as local people as well as politicians—we will, among other things, both amplify and modify our understanding of the binary relation between the insiders and outsiders of antebellum American politics.

We know beforehand that political activists were concentrated within their communities in two quite important respects—they were men, and they were white. Women could take an active interest in politics, and exert influence over political affairs (we will turn to these matters in due course), but they could not hold party positions or conduct politics in any formal sense. African-American men retained voting rights in some places, and a small number may have become party activists, but there is no evidence of the latter in any of the seven communities we have selected as representative laboratories of American political life. But what of concentrations and variations among the white male electorate? Who, in social terms, were the active partisans? To what extent were the contours of local society echoed in a political community of greater and lesser activists? These questions have been raised before by historians attentive to political life within specific communities, and it is by now well established that political leaders were drawn disproportionately from the more settled and more prosperous members of a mobile and unequal society. Kenneth Winkle's close analysis of voting in Ohio communities, for example, includes the observation that officeholders were significantly wealthier than even their well-settled neighbors.[1] Similarly, Paul Bourke and Donald DeBats have found in a frontier Oregon county that candidates, county convention delegates, and party organizers "accounted for much of the wealth, professional skill, and experience to which the county could lay claim."[2] These and other studies point to a significant difference that we wish to explore further in two distinct ways; first, by examining the social "location" of men who were more and less active in building party institutions and organizing political affairs in our seven representative communities; and second, by relating these political activities to other forms of community participation. Political men were also townsmen—Augustans as well as Democrats, Greenfielders as well as Whigs. By returning first to our records of institutional participation, and then to other, more personal evidence, we hope to explain how each of these two forms of action and identity merged with and modified the other.

A meager social record precludes such an analysis for the 1840s, but we are luckier with the decade that followed. As American historians well know, in 1850 the Federal government introduced a new method for collecting the decennial national census, one that recorded a significant set of social facts—age, race, gender, occupation, ownership of real property, place of birth—about each enumerated individual. In 1860 it added a single but quite important improvement by asking for the value of each person's personal as well as real property. The manuscript population schedules of these censuses have proved a gold mine for American historians, and we will prospect in this mine again, attentive to both its wealth and its limitations—for example, that the 1860 census is the only comprehensive record of individual wealth-holding among Americans, but that the self-reported real and personal property entries that constitute this record are only rarely perfectly accurate. As a first step, therefore, we have once again recorded all the names we have found in the newspapers of our representative towns (this time for two election cycles, 1850–52 and 1858–60), and have linked the record of each individual's political and other communal activity with the information provided about him in the manuscripts of the proximate census. We have also drawn systematic samples of adult white men from the census manuscripts for each town, for comparison to our linked activist files. The files are themselves more comparable than are those we extracted from the newspapers of four towns in 1840–42, as both the political party system and the local partisan press were more regularized in the 1850s. Except for Clarksville, for example, local parties had abandoned the naming of very large convention delegations, and in all the towns there were fewer long lists of the sort that could do as much to obscure as to reveal the contours of the active political community. Still, there are 5,745 men listed in these later files, ranging from the most active political and communal leaders to those whose visible activity was confined to signing a petition or a temperance pledge, joining a political club, or marching in a band. We were able to locate slightly more than two-thirds of these mostly anonymous Americans on the census, and to record those few but basic facts the census tells us about their lives.

THE SOCIAL STRUCTURE OF POLITICAL ACTIVISM

We begin in Augusta, where we earlier gained a glimpse of a political community of Broad Street merchants, lawyers, and clerks. On the eve of the Civil War there were approximately 3,460 white men living in and around this inland cotton-shipping center, and there were 866 men who we were able to identify in the local newspapers as local institutional participants at one time or another during the years 1858, 1859, and 1860. This suggests an overall participation rate of 25 percent, but we must recall and further elaborate on our earlier observation that such a calculation distorts the actual rate in two contrary ways. First, it does not reflect those types of participation that were not reported in the local press—most notably, church membership and leadership, but also participation in those clubs and societies that made no effort to report their activities to local editors, and, most importantly for our purposes, attendance at party caucuses by voters who played no formal role in them, membership in political clubs that reported only their officers to the press, and the exercise of backroom influence (unless, as in Kingston in the early 1840s, it was picked up and reported by the opposition paper). In all these ways, the rate of actual participation in Augusta's affairs is understated, and with respect to politics what we can claim to be measuring (and here we would assert that our information is very nearly complete) is the performance of formal roles in local political institutions.[3] Secondly, this type of calculation is systematically *overstated* by the demographics of mobile and youthful American communities. Excluded from the denominator of the fraction—in the present instance from the 3,460 white men who are reported on the 1860 census for Augusta—are those men present in Augusta during 1858, or 1859, or the first half of 1860, who died or migrated out of the community before the census was recorded in the summer of 1860, and those who came of age or who moved in during the six months that followed. This is by no means a trivial exclusion, and it probably offsets exclusions from the numerator to a considerable extent. But we cannot measure the effects of these distortions, and, as we suggested in chapter 1, the proportions of overall participation we report should be regarded as no more than guidelines for estimating the size of the active population in our communities.

Of the 866 Augustans in our file for those years, 590 were mentioned in the paper in association with some kind of political activity, but most of these had done no more than sign a petition in late 1860 urging the county's voters to send uncommitted delegates to Georgia's secession convention. Two hundred and sixty-two men (about 8 percent of the total adult white male population of 1860) were visible to us in some other way as political participants. A small majority of these men appear to have been only moderately active, offering themselves through the "Special Notices" section of the local papers as candidates for some local office, serving as election inspectors, joining a campaign club, or participating in one of the public meetings urgently called to respond to the crisis caused by Lincoln's election. One hundred and ten Richmond County men, some 3 percent of the 1860 local electorate, combined activities of this sort with more significant participation in political-party affairs, as members of the county executive committee, as officers or committee members at local party caucuses or conventions, or as delegates to conventions higher in the political pyramid. About a fourth of them (twenty-seven men), comprising less than 1 percent of the 1860 electorate, participated in three or more party conventions, and accounted for more than half of all the delegations, convention offices, and committee positions held by Richmond County men. Because political reportage at this level is very nearly complete, these proportions almost surely overstate the size of the very active political community in relation to the numbers of men who lived in Augusta during some part of the 1858–60 election cycle.

The number of formal political roles had increased in the new party era, expanding the potential for a more extensive participation of voters in partisan affairs. There were, for example, more than two hundred convention delegate slots to fill from among Richmond County voters in 1858–60, and the sum of partisan roles and official candidacies during these three years was probably two or three times that number. To some extent, participation did increase since the days of legislative caucuses and pre-party factions, reflecting this expansion of political roles. Yet, the pyramid of participation remained steep, much as it had been in the early 1840s (and early 1850s, which we will slight here for reasons of space). It was narrowly and selectively based, as well. Augusta's political activists were drawn almost entirely from the upper reaches of a quite unequal local society. We were able to locate on the census manuscripts 88 of the 110 men who played a visible role in their political party on the county level or higher. Of these, a third were professionals (twenty-five lawyers and four physicians), five-eighths were merchants, manufacturers, planters and other businessmen, and one-twentieth were clerical workers. Not one was a skilled or unskilled worker, or even an independent handworking artisan, despite the fact that more than 42 percent of the adult white male workforce in Richmond County was made up of such workers and artisans.[4] (Lawyers comprised 28 percent of the group, and 2 percent of the general workforce.) More than half reported property that placed them within the highest wealth decile in the county, and more than three-fourths placed within the highest quintile. Moreover, the few men who reported little or no property were, for the most part, young businessmen and professionals, and included several young lawyers and planters still living in the homes of their wealthy (and politically active) parents.[5]

Of the twenty-seven most active party men, we identified twenty-three on the census. These men differed from the larger group mainly in the greater concentration among them of lawyers and others with distinctly political professions. They consisted of eleven lawyers, the publishers of both party newspapers, the local postmaster, Mayor Blodget (still mayor, recall, by grace of a single vote), and eight merchants and planters in the highest quintile (four were in the highest decile) of reported wealth. Were these the "wire-pullers" who ran the political system in the presence of greater or lesser numbers of "spectators" among the wider electorate? Most likely they were, but we must be careful not to claim too much about the exercise of political influence, which could occur apart from visible and formally defined party roles. Our files do not tell us about wire-pullers. What they do tell us is that the institutionalized party system in Augusta contained an extraordinary concentration of lawyers, partisan publishers, officeholders, and rich merchants and planters at its activist core.

Georgia—Augusta included—had a long tradition of relatively aristocratic political rule on both the state and local levels of governance. Perhaps the quite pronounced concentration of political roles in the hands of Augusta's lawyers, merchants, and planters reflects this particular tradition. Greenfield was a quite different place. Its wealth was much less unequally distributed (Augustans at the ninetieth percentile of wealth were more than twice as wealthy as their counterparts in Greenfield), and its politics were grounded in the most formally democratic of American local institutions, the New England town meeting. Local governance in New England called upon householders and other men not only to attend annual public meetings, but also to fill a large number of local offices, practices that fostered civic and, quite possibly, political engagement. In fact, 310 of Greenfield's 850 white men are listed in our file for 1858–60, and 202 of them (nearly a quarter of the 1860 adult white male population) can be identified with some kind of political activity or public office. The town meeting itself, and in particular the lower-level nonpartisan offices, filled each year by the meeting—highway surveyor, constable, field driver, surveyor of lumber, sealer of leather—accounted for much of this activity. Greenfield's annual town meeting was partisan with respect to higher offices such as selectman and assessor (the lines of party conflict were usually muddled, though, by mixed tickets and the absence of a campaign during the three or four days between the party caucuses and the election), but lower officials were chosen without apparent reference to party. Fully 108 different men were appointed by their peers to serve the community in this way during these three years, and 82 of them did not appear in the local papers in any other political capacity. This means that the number of identifiable partisans in Greenfield was 120, and that the proportion of these partisans to the 1860 electorate (about 14 percent) was almost exactly the same as it was in the early 1840s. Political activity within this group, moreover, was similarly stratified. Most men appeared only once or twice in the local press as a delegate, a campaign club officer, or perhaps as a participant in the Republicans' 1860 victory celebration. We would count some twenty-five men (as in 1840–42, around 3 percent of the electorate), as very active partisans. The participation pyramid was somewhat more broadly based in Greenfield than it was in Augusta, and one in seven should be regarded as a high rate of party activism. But the slope of the pyramid from this broader base seems just as steep as it was in the southern town.

The eighty-two men who served only in nonpartisan, low-level town offices ranged in occupation and wealth from fairly well-off businessmen and farmers to propertyless farm laborers and teamsters. Nearly 40 percent of those we located in the census were laborers, skilled workers, and modestly situated independent artisans (compared to approximately 60 percent in the population as a whole), and as a group they were only moderately wealthier and better placed than the rest of their fellow townsmen. No lawyer was among them. The party men in Greenfield offer a quite different profile. Sixty percent of the lesser activists were farmers in the upper wealth quintile, professionals, or businessmen, and fewer than 20 percent were artisans or laborers (there were only three of the latter, one of whom reported twenty-three hundred dollars in real and personal property). They were a somewhat less exclusive group than their counterparts in Augusta, to be sure, but they were by no means a mirror of Greenfield society as a whole. The party leaders and other high-level activists could have exchanged places with those in Augusta. Among the twenty-three we located on the census were seven lawyers, nine businessmen, four farmers in the highest decile of reported wealth, the postmaster, the register of deeds, and the richest man in town, Henry W. Clapp, retired manufacturer, railroad director, and director also of the local bank, and gas, water power, and bridge companies, who reported $170,000 to the census marshal in 1860.

Long-standing traditions of leadership and deference within the formal democracy of New England towns may help account for this stratification of political activism in Greenfield in the 1850s. It was in eastern towns such as Greenfield and Augusta that partisan democracy was most heavily freighted with such traditions. More recently established, western communities were freer of them—such, at any rate, is the assumption of one of the most influential schools of American historical interpretation—but the greater fluidity of populations in the West was itself a source of concentration of local influence. Historians have long understood that migration into and out of specific western communities by large numbers of highly mobile Americans effectively delivered a disproportionate influence over local affairs to a settled and well-off core of the population that remained in the town for many years, accumulating property and social position while unknown newcomers came and went. This phenomenon was at work in eastern towns, too, but "repeat migration" was more prevalent in the West. Kenneth Winkle has shown, for example, that the vast majority of voters in Springfield, Illinois, during the 1850s belonged to that " 'movable column' of migrants who might vote only once or twice in a community and then move on"—indeed, did move on, more than four thousand of fewer than seven thousand Springfield voters in that decade voting only once in the town, and another thousand voting only twice. Needless to say, few of these migrants held political office in Springfield, and in general they "made little impression on the structure of power in the city," not even, we might add, settling in long enough to become followers or "friends" of an established political patron.[6] But could not the political parties provide an institutional bridge for migrating Democrats, Whigs, and Republicans that could span the communities and states of the East and West, fashioning instantaneous connections between the newcomers and established residents of western towns that could not be so quickly formed between would-be political "friends" in an informal system of influence and reward? Migrants to western towns often arrived with letters of dismissal and introduction from their former churches, which facilitated their smooth transition into churches of the same denomination in their new western homes. Quite apart from their contribution to the religious lives of individual migrants, these letters helped maintain the institutional reach of denominations across the spreading American landscape. Parties, as we have suggested, did not create ongoing membership, reinforced by year-round meetings, dues, and other obligations for ordinary adherents in the same manner as churches, lodges, temperance societies and other organizations; nor did they provide letters for migrating partisans. But they were national institutions with respect to the cultivation of political identity and loyalty within the electorate, and should have provided the material for just the kind of associational bridge that the Whig editor of Dubuque wanted to build across the Mississippi for the purpose of welcoming in-migrating Whigs, and effecting their immediate integration into Dubuque's political affairs. Perhaps, too, it would have been a more fluid political system into which these migrants were integrated, one in which established leaders could claim only a few years of precedence over interested newcomers.

Our sources do not permit analysis of the relationship between migration and partisan activism, but they do allow us to create the same kind of participation profile that we have already reviewed for Augusta and Greenfield. Was the base of the pyramid broader, and the slope less steep, in our western towns? Marion is not as far west as Dubuque, nor was it a frontier town in the 1850s, so we should perhaps not be surprised to learn that political activity there, while somewhat less steeply stratified than in Augusta, was not very different from Greenfield in its overall shape. There were some 725 white men recorded on the 1860 census of Marion. During the 1858–60 election cycle, 125 men (17 percent in relation to the 1860 electorate) played some kind of visible public or political role in the community, and a slightly smaller number can be identified with partisan activity. About one man in ten was significantly active in his political party, and perhaps one in twenty can be called a leader or high-level activist—a decidedly higher proportion than the 1 percent we found in Augusta, but only moderately higher than Greenfield's 3 percent. The social recruitment of political men was also much like that in the New England town, with significant numbers of artisans and others lacking high economic standing serving in local public offices, but far fewer ordinary folk performing visible party roles. Five artisans and three clerks were counted among the mostly young campaign club officers during the 1860 presidential campaign, alongside thirty-three others with more exalted occupations: seven lawyers, three physicians, thirteen businessmen, six farmers (five in the upper quintile of reported property), the postmaster, the superintendent of schools, and the county auditor. Convention delegates, committeemen, and officers were more exclusive, as were the thirty-two men we would specify as Marion's most active political figures. Among the latter were twelve professionals (eight of whom were lawyers), fifteen businessmen (including no fewer than five who owned and operated Marion's political press), three farmers in the highest wealth decile, a bank teller, and one artisan, a twenty-nine-year-old German-born printer named Philip Dombaugh, who almost certainly worked in the pressroom of Marion's Democratic newspaper. The twenty-seven lawyers, doctors, and businessmen that formed such a large majority of this group of thirty-two were drawn from occupations that represented less than 20 percent of the male workforce in this Ohio country town.

Dubuque, the newest of our towns, would seem at first glance to confirm the efficacy of Editor Wood's proposal to welcome newcomers as active participants in partisan affairs. There were some 3,400 white men in this rapidly growing frontier city in 1860, and 1,030 men whose names appeared in political contexts in local newspapers during the 1858–60 election cycle. As in Augusta, though, a large number of these men had done no more than sign a petition of some kind, and the proportion who may be said to have been partisan participants is 17 percent of the 1860 adult white male population, about the same level as in Marion, and only slightly higher than in Greenfield. It might be argued that such a proportion in a larger town such as Dubuque suggests a greater tendency toward political participation, as the population base expanded while the numbers of many political roles—city, town, or county central committee members, for example, or delegates to legislative, judicial, or state conventions—remained relatively fixed. As the frontier town grew into a city, however, each party quickly developed a ward-based system of caucuses, committees, and (in 1860) campaign clubs that greatly expanded political roles. Indeed, they did so in a way that made political activism more accessible to groups in the population that may have been discouraged from participating in smaller towns such as Greenfield and Marion, or in those larger, mostly southern cities such as Augusta that looked outward to the county rather than inward to city wards for their primary level of organization.[7] Dubuque had a large population of artisans and unskilled workers, most of whom were immigrants from Germany and Ireland. As in many cities, these workers clustered in relatively distinct neighborhoods that were as large as or larger than individual wards. A ward-based system of caucuses, clubs, and party committees, therefore, made it much likelier that workers, and immigrants who ran small businesses in ethnic working-class neighborhoods, would gain a foothold in political parties. The men whose names appeared in the local press at the lowest level of public activity—usually as petition signers—mirrored Dubuque's larger society almost perfectly, which means that some 60 percent of them were artisans and unskilled workers. Was this a foothold? Some of the petitions they signed were calls for the formation of ward campaign clubs, and it is possible that many of these men went on to join the clubs that were formed in their wards. We cannot tell, but the proportion of artisans and other workers we can actually identify at the lowest rung of identifiable party activity—the officers of ward clubs, members of election-day vigilance committees, and so on—was a significantly lower 28 percent. Still, this is higher than in any of our other towns, and it does appear that ward organizations increased opportunities for political participation, and did expand the party system in the direction of the working class.[8]

The 240 men we counted in Dubuque as midlevel or high-level political activists—men who participated beyond the ward level, or who held several different positions within their wards—amounted to 7 percent of the 1860 population of adult white males. There were artisans and other workers, thirteen to be exact, among the 197 activists we were able to locate on the census, but nearly 70 percent of this more general political community consisted of professionals and businessmen. Fully 20 percent were lawyers. In their proportion to the estimated 1860 electorate (3 percent), and in their numerical domination by professionals and businessmen (83 percent), those men we would identify as high-level political activists in Dubuque were much like their counterparts in Augusta, Greenfield, and Marion.

The consistencies we have found in these towns, and in the others—Kingston, Clarksville, and Opelousas—we have not reviewed here, reinforce the argument that the American political nation functioned in a similar way across a variety of regions and in communities of different sizes and types. They help validate, as well, the specific profiles of political activism we derived from newspapers and census manuscripts. In each of our representative towns a small number of professionals (lawyers especially), businessmen, and well-to-do planters or farmers occupied most of the positions of party leadership, and appear over and over again in their party papers as delegates, convention officers, members of central committees, candidates, organizers of party dinners and celebrations, and in whatever other contexts local newspaper reportage permitted us to see. Moreover, lesser party men—a sixth or a seventh of the 1860 electorate in three of the towns, 7 or 8 percent in Augusta—were frequently of the same social stamp. The political activities of party men can be differentiated, too, in temporal terms. Lower-level political activists were called upon only occasionally, some mainly on election day, others for a few weeks during most years and for a few months during the expanded spectacle of the quadrennial presidential campaign. Those higher in the party experienced a longer political season, beginning, perhaps, with the first caucuses or local conventions of the annual fall campaign, and including as well a week or two of preparations for a local election in the late winter or early spring. Party leaders were more continuously involved, and only in part because, as central committee members, their formal duties included custodianship of the party when no election was in the offing. Party leaders, we believe, were just those men for whom there was no politically "unseasonable time," but who mingled politics with law or dry goods, lodge meetings or church suppers, most days of their lives. To the extent that this was the case, it compounded the difference between political leaders and others—lesser party men and, even more, that large majority of local men who did not appear in any political post in the partisan newspapers of our representative towns.

If local party leadership was an oligarchy it was not a closed one—it did not belong only to well-placed and well-settled local men whose political responsibility was to cajole votes, year after year, from lesser neighbors and from strangers among the "moving column" of migrants. There was, in fact, a certain amount of turnover among local party leaders, not all of whom were permanently settled in one town. If we trace the sixty-three most active partisans of the 1840–42 election cycle in Augusta, Greenfield, and Kingston to the election cycle of 1850–52, we find that nineteen, or 30 percent, were still among the political leaders of their towns, while another thirteen, or 21 percent, were at least midlevel party activists. At the end of the 1850s, seven men (five of these were Augustans) were still among the leadership, and eleven were midlevel activists, these eighteen amounting to 29 percent of the original leadership group of the Tippecanoe era. Similarly, of 105 political leaders during the 1850–52 cycle in Augusta, Greenfield, Kingston, Marion, Dubuque, and Clarksville, forty, or 38 percent, were still leaders in 1858–60, and twenty-two, or 21 percent, were midlevel activists. In other words, nearly half of the leaders of 1840–42 had ceased to be party activists in their towns during the ensuing decade, and another 20 percent were lost (or removed) over the course of the 1850s. Some 40 percent of the leaders of 1850–52 election cycle were no longer very active in their local parties by the end of the same decade.

There is, however, an important difference between our eastern and western towns in the nature of this leadership turnover. In Augusta, Greenfield, and Kingston, most of the leaders of the early 1850s who did not remain active were men over the age of fifty at the start of the decade, and many of these men may have died or retired from active life by the decade's end. In Greenfield, John J. Pierce's only visible party activity in the 1858–60 election cycle was his presidency of the local Douglas Club. Pierce was sixty-seven in 1860, and it is likely that this office honored a long and completed political career. If we exclude men such as Pierce, and examine only those leaders of 1850–52 who were fifty or younger in 1850, we find a much more impressive rate of persistence, thirty-two of thirty-nine (or 82 percent) remaining active in their parties, and twenty-four (62 percent) remaining as party leaders.[9]

The situation was entirely different in the western towns. Of twenty-one leaders of the early 1850s who were no longer active in their local parties in 1858–60 in Marion, Dubuque, and Clarksville, only one was over sixty in 1860, and seventeen were under the age of fifty. Clearly, retirement and death do not explain leadership turnover in these towns. Out-migration may explain some of it, and here we must recognize that not all party and communal activists were fixed in one place while the rest of the population moved around the country in search of opportunity. Activists, and even leaders, could participate in this most American of activities. They could feel the effects, too, of another national trait: the competitiveness that could raise the lowly and bring down the mighty in a volatile market economy, and in noneconomic arenas as well. Americans of this era frequently described their society as a wheel of fortune, and the image could suit political as well as economic life; indeed, the two were related in those instances where men who had failed in business lost political influence or will. (The men who wrote out of economic need for patronage jobs were supplicants, not leaders.) These forces did not operate uniquely in the West, but their effects may have been greater there on men who had risen to local leadership, in many cases only recently, and before becoming as financially entrenched as their eastern counterparts. Whatever the explanation, this difference between East and West in the persistence of local political leadership stands out as the most striking variation in the social pattern of political life among our representative American communities.

LAWYERS, LEADERS, AND THE AMERICAN COMMUNITY

Among the consistencies that outweigh this difference is the role of lawyers in organizing the political affairs in all our communities. As historians have long recognized, lawyers were vastly over-represented among local political leaders; indeed, given their numbers in the local male workforce, they could hardly have been more so. In our smaller communities, nearly *every* lawyer was at least an activist, and most lawyers were political leaders. In Greenfield, for example, thirteen attorneys were very active in their parties during the 1850–52 election cycle, and we would count nine of them among the town's political leaders. According to the census of 1850, there were a total of fifteen attorneys living in the town. Only two, therefore, were not political activists, both were young men (F. G. Tuckerman was twenty-nine in 1850, Joel Gleason was only twenty-two) and neither remained in Greenfield until the end of the decade. During the 1858–60 election cycle thirteen of the fourteen lawyers listed on the 1860 census were among the most active partisans of Greenfield. The single exception was fifty-nine-year-old Henry Chapman, who had been politically active earlier in the decade. This very striking numerical correspondence reinforces our earlier observation about the spatial dimensions of political activism in small American communities of the antebellum era. County conventions, and the caucuses that preceded them in the county seat, were nearly always held in the courthouse around which virtually all the law offices of the county clustered. Party rallies were most often held in the courthouse square. Caucuses and town and village elections were held in other towns, and called other men to action, but the major partisan events in the county took place in this tiny space, sprinkled with law offices and, we should add, within a stone's throw of the offices of the party newspapers, and of the Main Street stores of other men who frequently joined lawyers and editors in conducting partisan affairs. Law and editorial offices, in fact, served as the "smoke-filled" back rooms of party conclaves, and as meeting places of active party men when a campaign was in progress. A fledgling lawyer in the little western New York county town of Bath (Ansel J. McCall, whose fascinating correspondence we will soon examine in greater detail), wrote a college friend just after the election of 1842: "In your quiet life [as a teacher] I suppose you dont meddle with politics but lawyers offices are like club rooms where every body meets to gable & we are thrown . . . in the very forefront of party strife. I begin to be fond of the excitement."[10]

Were lawyers "thrown" into the political forefront because their offices were such handy "club rooms" for party men? "I have become one of the noisiest brawlers you ever saw," McCall, then a law clerk, had written to the same friend in the midst of the Tippecanoe campaign two years earlier. "Cant help it. Am forced into it. Our office is half of the time a perfect bedlam."[11] Obviously, more was involved than mere proximity, and men such as Ansel McCall did not involve themselves in politics just to join the bedlam in their offices during a heated campaign. The connection between law and politics is an ancient one, and in America it had been reinforced by the early need to write constitutions, to generate new bodies of law, and to understand both in the context of a continuing common law. In antebellum America, law continued to be the only profession that prepared men for public life, and it is clear that some young men read the law with a political career in mind.[12] Beyond this, there were communal dimensions to the association between law and public influence. Lawyers were respected and deferred to within their communities as professional men of learning. Many were among that tiny minority of American men who had attended college. (Physicians in this era, we might add, were themselves fighting for professional and communal recognition, and were also heavily overrepresented among political activists.) Lawyers generally made more money than most of their neighbors, and some became quite wealthy. A fairly large number had been born to respected and well-off families. To be sure, respect could be tinged with suspicion and even with resentment, and lawyers as politicians could be sneered at as a "courthouse gang" of manipulators and office-seekers, but these attitudes were themselves concessions to the superiority that lawyers gained over the ordinary farmers, shopkeepers, and laborers of American communities. Only a farmer could "control the politics of the County," wrote the young Schenectady lawyer James M. Bouck to his father in 1834 after an uncle had advised him to improve his political prospects by returning to his native Schoharie County. "A great majority of our people are labouring men such as mechanics, Farmers, &c. and they look upon each other as members of the same great family whose interests and feelings are the same," while "everything advanced by the professional man who they say lives upon the quarrels of the community is looked upon with an eye of suspicion. . . . They think he is seeking for place and power—that he considers himself their superior in every point of view."[13] Bouck nicely accommodates deference and democracy here, with ordinary people empowering some natural leader from within the community to "control the politics of the County." This leader must express the values of the "great family whose interests and feelings are the same," and cannot be one who asserts a haughty superiority while living "upon the quarrels of the community." Many Americans, the elder Bouck included, would have found this an attractive statement of their own more traditional values, and it probably served James as a good excuse for not returning to his rural roots. Even in 1834, however, it misrepresented the facts that stand out so clearly in our towns fifteen or twenty years later. Both Boucks surely realized that the young lawyer was himself pleading a poor case. Had he returned to Schoharie in 1834, James would no doubt have been in an excellent position to achieve local political influence, and perhaps eventually to "control the politics of the County."

Statements such as James Bouck's suggest the possibility that the political power lawyers did establish in their communities was seized rather than freely conferred; that it was gained primarily through the newly established institution of the political party; and that its exercise (we might wish to add that of the political editors, too) constituted the first episode of political professionalism in America. Bouck, if confronted by opposing counsel with the facts of political leadership by lawyers, would no doubt seek refuge in such an explanation, pointing out that successful farmers, and perhaps merchants, were better placed to build and benefit from traditional networks of dependency and "friendship" that stretched away from the courthouse square. Indeed, in his letter to his father he more or less describes the process by which the ambitious farmer builds this network: "His acts, his daily intercourse with his neighbours if honorable will make him friends. He is called on to fill some town office and in that capacity . . . he is enabled to do something for a friend and for his town; and there are a thousand other ways by which he can ingratiate himself into the good graces of the people." All this is contrasted with the business of the lawyer, which "must necessarily bring him into collision with the people."[14] Bouck's remarks constitute an interesting proposition about political influence, and lead to significant questions about the relationship between political leaders and the community. Should we see lawyers as political professionals whose principal purpose was the mobilization of the local electorate for the good of the political party and their own political ambitions? Were they in this sense external to the community, a cosmopolitan force that acted upon it rather than from within?[15] Or was their political activism principally an extension of their professional role in the community—that is, as attorneys and counselors—and of the prestige that attached to that role? Did lawyers, along with the doctors and well-to-do merchants and farmers who joined them in local party leadership, perceive or seek to establish themselves as traditional community leaders and boosters rather than as party professionals? More importantly, were they perceived that way by more ordinary citizens? *What else* did lawyers and other party leaders do in their towns besides throw themselves into the bedlam of politics?

The consistent pattern across all of our representative communities is one of general community participation and leadership on the part of lawyers and other party leaders and activists. Consider Greenfield, whose newspapers provide a good record of local institutional life beyond government and the political parties. Like most American towns of this era, there were numerous local societies and clubs in Greenfield, including the Franklin County Agricultural Society (probably the most important in the town and county), the YMCA, the Greenfield Library Association, the various volunteer militia and fire companies, the Franklin County Benevolent Society, two temperance societies, a Masonic lodge, and clubs and societies devoted to horticulture, farming, books, schools, cricket, ice-skating, and the improvement of horses. There were banks, railroads, insurance companies, and other economic organizations, along with a cemetery company and a loan association, that appointed local notables to their boards of directors. Political-party leaders, lawyers included, were disproportionately active in most of these organizations, and constituted the greater part of a small group of local men who can be described as generally active in communal affairs, especially in leadership roles. Three lawyers can stand for the larger group. Whiting Griswold was a trustee of the Greenfield Library Association, a member of two committees of the Franklin County Agricultural Society, the moderator of the local fire district, a director of the Franklin County Bank, and a speaker at a special meeting of the town that was convened to consider a local subscription to the proposed Troy and Greenfield Railroad. James S. Grennell was the secretary of the local Masonic lodge, a member of the Fourth of July celebration committee, the secretary and treasurer of the Franklin County Agricultural Society and the Greenfield Farmers' Club, a director of the Greenfield Horticultural Society, the clerk and treasurer of the Massachusetts and Vermont Association for the Improvement of Horses, the assistant engineer of the local fire district, a director of the Greenfield Stock and Mutual Fire Insurance Company, and an assessor for the Green River Cemetery Company. George W. Bartlett, who was younger and politically less exalted than either Griswold or Grennell, was the secretary of the YMCA and the president of the Greenfield Skating Club.

Politicians could join local organizations as a means of extending their political influence, and it is possible that the broader participation of Greenfield's political elite was instrumental in this way. It is more likely, however, that they were simply exercising the kind of general community leadership that was available to men of their social, economic, and professional position. Political leadership was, after all, a form of civic responsibility as well as a quest for partisan advantage, and in a variety of ways political success—a large local rally, an increasing vote total in the town or county, a native son sent to the state legislature—could help confirm the growth, vitality, and importance of a particular community. It is important to note in this respect that leaders of both political parties (and of the Bell-Everett presidential ticket) mingled in nearly all of Greenfield's nonpolitical organizations, and that there is no evidence that any of the latter served as vehicles for partisan mobilization. Nor were there any discernible clusters of nonparty (or antiparty) men who might have used, say, the local benevolent society, or temperance organizations, or the YMCA, or all of these in combination, as a base for exerting an alternative community leadership. Men who were not party activists did join and even lead other community institutions, but nearly always alongside party men, and as a group they were less rather than more active in the town's nonpolitical associations, companies, and clubs. This was the case even within the stratum of wealthy townsmen that provided most of the leadership of Greenfield's political and nonpolitical institutions. Sixteen of the eighty-five men constituting Greenfield's highest wealth decile in 1860 were political leaders in the town, and of these, all but one were active in several nonpolitical local organizations. Twenty-two men of the highest decile were not active at all in partisan affairs.[16] Eight of them were absent as well from the town's other institutions, and twelve were visible to us as members of only one or two. Only two wealthy nonparty men can be described as fairly active in Greenfield's nonpolitical organizations.

The same patterns are visible in all of our towns, although in some instances inadequate newspaper coverage of nonpolitical institutions gives us a less sweeping view than the one provided by the Greenfield partisan press. However complete the picture, its shape is the same. Political leaders in Kingston, Augusta, Marion, Dubuque, Clarksville, and Opelousas were more active in communal institutions than other men, including those from the highest wealth decile. Lawyers, who everywhere were overrepresented within the political leadership, were among the most active outside of politics. Leaders of both parties joined and frequently served as officers in the same literary associations, lodges, militia companies, and Bible societies. They sat on the same bank and railroad company boards, too, although this appears to have been the area of communal life in which they were the least active—an interesting and rather surprising pattern, given the fact that these companies were the most cosmopolitan, and in some respects the most political, of local institutions outside of the parties themselves. In Kingston, once the site of a vigorous political "bank war," only four identifiable partisans (two Democrats and two Republicans, none of them party leaders) sat on the boards of the very banks their predecessors had brought into existence as vehicles and rewards of political struggle. Five more (one leading Democrat, one leading Republican, and three others from the latter party) formed a significant part of the board of one other bank that had never been a focus of political contention. Kingston's political men were more frequently to be found, indeed, on the boards of the town's churches than in the boardrooms of local banks. Lay leadership in Kingston's churches adds to the larger picture of general community participation by political leaders. The large majority of the town's church trustees, vestrymen, deacons, and class leaders—sixty-four of seventy-seven—were not identifiable partisans, but the rate of lay church leadership by political activists was higher than it was among other men. Again, within the highest wealth decile, about one in six significantly active partisans were lay church leaders, while the proportion among the politically inactive was one in twelve.[17]

What did this general institutional leadership mean with respect to the status and influence of political activists in their communities? Most obviously, it suggests that politicians were anything but isolated, and that politically active lawyers could not have been perceived as men whose only roles in the community were to bribe voters, seek office, and live off their neighbors' quarrels. Leadership of such institutions as benevolent societies, the YMCA, churches, lodges, fire and militia companies, and perhaps also local banks and railroad companies, also implies not only a high general standing in the community, but also an immediate hierarchical relation to significant numbers of lesser men who filled the ranks of these organizations, or who benefited from their largesse. To be sure, the intermingling of Democrats, Republicans, and the politically inactive in the leadership and membership of nearly all of the institutions of these small cities and towns complicated and possibly even precluded the use of such institutions as vehicles for constructing networks of political "friendship" or partisan solidarity. They were, at best, competitive fields of political influence, hardly different in this respect from the larger field of daily community life. There may also have been negative consequences of institutional leadership, in that it could have engendered in some the resentment and class feeling that James Bouck attached automatically to "professional men." Might it, too, have been less important than historians are accustomed to assuming, as much a manifestation of the propensity of some men for organized social activism—in political parties, lodges, lyceums, skating clubs, and whatever else offered itself—as of the way social worth was perceived and assigned within the community? We should reemphasize in this connection that there were many men in each of our representative communities, including men of substantial wealth, who were not active in politics, or especially active in any other local organization. Shall we automatically assign more prestige and influence to organizational activists than to those who remained apart? Might the latter have exerted in less formal ways an alternative, or even a contrary influence?

Personal, informal prestige may have counted for much in nineteenth-century towns and cities, but the growing local presence of formal institutions, and the sometimes vital role of organized, ad hoc meetings addressed to such issues as railroad subscriptions or public disorder, increased the claim of organizational activists to civic leadership. The political leaders of our representative towns were as a rule highly regarded members of their communities, and it is clear that their high communal standing and general institutional activism were essential qualifications for a political leadership that was not yet so professionalized and so responsive to extralocal institutional imperatives that it no longer resembled older modes of influence. The respected amateur or not fully professional politician may, indeed, have done much to legitimize the second party system within communities all across America. Politics and party politicians were in bad odor, but men such as Greenfield's James S. Grennell were not, even though they were the evident vehicles through which partisan politics entered the community. By means of a more general eminence and institutional leadership, and as local boosters, they elevated at least some aspects of politics, and made more credible the claim that the system was not being run by political professionals in their own narrow interests.

And yet, as we have seen in the previous chapter, political leadership was becoming problematic for some of these men, in part because of changes in political practice, and in part because society itself was changing in ways that challenged both traditions and innovations of voter mobilization. In our introduction we discussed the possible political consequences of the increasing articulation of social-class boundaries in mid-nineteenth-century America, and of the appeal of various modes of social and material refinement to a newly self-aware middle class. And in chapter 2 we observed that such traditional political practices as election-day treating, once part of the compact between greater and lesser men in a deferential society, were now condemned as corrupt by guardians of respectability—men and women who were perhaps as concerned with the social promiscuity of such arrangements as with their effects on the political process. Political leaders were themselves part of this new world of refinement and social separation; yet, they necessarily continued and improved upon the very practices their social circumstances inclined them to condemn. In his memoir of Oregon politics in the 1850s, George E. Cole tells a story that serves nicely as an emblem of this difficulty. In 1854, one Judge Pratt, "a good lawyer and a learned judge," came to Cole's county to test the waters for a run for Congress. Pratt was "very proud and very dignified," but he recognized the need to address the local men, which he did in the bar of a hotel:

> He stood before the bar, a thing he was never known to do before in Oregon. He was arrayed in a faultless suit, including a silk hat and a high shirt collar. . . . His boon companions were miners in their rough garb, ranged along the bar on both sides of him. The judge was a good talker, and he was giving them the best he had for the occasion, and they were listening with apparent interest. As soon as they caught his drift, however, they looked at each other knowingly, as they were ardent admirers of General Lane [Pratt's opponent], having met him during the Indian war of the year previous. One tall miner reached down to his boot, drew out a long knife and took the silk hat off the judge's head, saying, "This stove-pipe is too high by a j'int." Suiting the action to the word, he slashed it into two parts, and slapping the parts together, put it back on the judge's head. Pratt took this all in good part, and set up the drinks, which at this juncture was the only thing in order.

Pratt suffered other indignities, including a hug from the tall miner, who in the end promised not to "take off the top rail of his 'stake-and-ridered' collar." The would-be congressman bore all of this quite well. But when he was defeated he moved to San Francisco, where he was elected judge "and wore his stove-pipe hat in peace."[18] It is much less likely that Judge Pratt would have had to buy a new hat if he had addressed men from his own town in Oregon, or if the men he did address had not already become backers of his opponent, but the miner's attack on his "faultless" clothing was a clear enough message to Pratt that he must choose between dignity and popularity—that this was a rude, not a decorous republic. In other settings well removed from the Oregon frontier the choice was perhaps not so stark, but the reconciliation of personal dignity with popular politics was everywhere becoming more difficult. Political leaders, as we have seen, were only part of the community's prospering and increasingly refined upper and middle classes. Others did not participate in or benefit from election-day treating and bribery, or the printing of false tickets, or the setting up of drinks for men who had just destroyed their hats, and they were less likely than in former times to condone these practices or accept the social claims of those who did. That party men themselves recognized this difficulty is evident from the way that many of them wrote about politics in memoirs and in the more immediate vehicle of the partisan press.

DEALING WITH DISREPUTABILITY

It is remarkable how frequently the memoirs of political life in this era express discontent with and disapproval of politicians, political practices, and electorates. E. L. Dohoney's contemptuous descriptions of voter bribery and of a rigged county convention in Kentucky are typical of a fairly consistent genre of retrospective condemnation of politics by life-long politicians. The autobiography of another Kentucky politician, C. W. Hall, describes a congressman in his state plying "his vocation of cozzening the voters" in a whiskey shop, while Mifflin Wister Gibbs explains the attraction of the new state of California to "the unscrupulous, but active politician, having been dishonored at home," as a "new field of booty." "Brick" Pomeroy, who seems to have enjoyed the tricks and deceptions of the stump, focused his venom on Washington, where "political aspirants day by day supply men with whiskey, furnish them with money with which to play cards and continually lead professional female tempters before them." Congress, to this political editor and placeman, is "an assemblage of persons . . . who hasten to Washington from every part of the country . . . as members of a free-lunch gang rally to an oyster saloon on its opening day in the autumn." Gustave Koerner's memoir more moderately details a different set of complaints: the Chicago crowd that insisted on entertainment rather than campaign speeches; partisan editors who lied about the size and enthusiasm of political rallies; party committees that explained away failures (the circus was playing in an adjoining town, the creeks were swollen, the opposing party spread rumors of smallpox) when "the true reason generally was that there were not enough people of the right political color to make up a respectable crowd"; political processions that were "often grotesque" rather than inspiring. Koerner's tone is one of contempt born of disappointment, not so much in the cupidity of politicians as in the dishonesty of their attempts to generate the semblance of popular enthusiasm where none existed. This, too, was unseemly and disreputable.[19]

More telling, perhaps, is the frequently conflicted manner in which political autobiographers describe their own careers. Several cut short their careers, and describe their departure from politics as a blessing. Levi Leighton, for example, was a Maine schoolteacher, storekeeper, and local school committeeman and assessor, who "was foolish enough to be drawn into the whirl of politics." Soon initiated into "party tricks and corruption," Leighton was elected to the state legislature. Because he worked for his constituents rather than for party interests, however (Leighton pushed for a survey for a new railroad to his county, and tried to raise the bounty on wolves and bears), he "was left behind at the next state election," and happily confined himself thereafter to local offices that were beyond partisanship. Roger Pryor left politics, too, after a more successful career culminating in an ambassadorship to Greece. His wife's autobiography recalls an interview a few years later between her husband and a young man who had come to ask whether he should go into politics, law, or the coffee business. "The coffee business, most decidedly," Pryor answered. "I have tried the other two and have a poor opinion of both of them." Those who remained in politics were sometimes equally direct. C. W. Hall refers to his frequent efforts to gain political office as "below ambition. It was inordinate vanity and credulity." Hall's recollections suggest a continuous struggle between ambition and a better nature that resisted following "the vicious life of a politician." Hall was by no means peculiar. Nearly all of the autobiographers who continued to pursue public office express at least some ambivalence toward political life, and in several memoirs the partisan necessities of the rude republic clearly outweigh any satisfactions of personal achievement or public service. "A life spent for a party," concludes Charles Reemelin, "is a life lost."[20]

To some extent, the negative tone of these recollections reflects the jaded political mood of the post–Civil War years during which most of them were written. Some of their off-handed comments about self-seeking and besotted politicians, by "Brick" Pomeroy in particular, do seem to partake of an idiom of political corruption that their authors knew would be familiar and persuasive to Gilded Age readers. We should not simply dismiss the specific indictments that suffuse these documents, however, or understand them merely as some sort of self-justifying or expiating ritual invocation of imagined crimes or folly. They were, to some degree, self-expiating, but in ways that seem to us real and significant, and that manifest the force that "Victorian" refinement exerted on upper- and middle-class American men both before and after the Civil War. C. W. Hall's description of the politician's life as "vicious" is especially important. More than it does today, "vicious" in the nineteenth century meant "base," "vile," "low"—in social terms, "disreputable." Whatever honors might accrue to a governor, an ambassador, or any other high public servant, were threatened by disreputable political practice—by "the vicious life of the politician." Interestingly, one of the few political autobiographies we have read that fails to indict political practice directly, does so by luxuriating in its disreputable qualities. *Davy Crockett's Own Story As Written by Himself* may or may not have been a legitimate autobiography, but its antibourgeois themes are no less interesting for that. In it, Crockett is depicted as a hard-drinking, tobacco-chewing adventurer, who campaigns for office with a twist of tobacco in one pocket and a large bottle of liquor in the other. At one point he advises a small group of would-be politicians: "Treat widely and drink freely. . . . True, you may be called a drunken dog by some of the clean shirt and silk stocking gentry, but the real rough necks will style you a jovial fellow, their votes are certain, and frequently count double."[21]

The retrospective character of even the most reflective of these autobiographies requires a more immediate analog, which we find in various elements of the partisan newspapers of the 1850s. Important as these newspapers were to the conduct of local party business, there is a surprising amount of criticism of politics in them, some of it responding to what editors perceived as the limits of public toleration for political propaganda, and some of it reflecting the qualms of editors and others about the nature of political life. We have already noticed, for example, that editors often prepared their readers for the vituperation of an upcoming campaign, or apologized for it after an election was over. At the approach of the campaign season in 1850 the Dubuque Democratic editor warned his readers not to be alarmed at the "few strong political dishes" that would be served up before the election, and his counterpart in Greenfield asked patience of his less politically inclined readers two years later, reminding them that "a presidential campaign occurs only once in four years, and then lasts but a few months."[22] Occasionally, an editor could apologize for the political content of the "campaign paper" (as the partisan paper was sometimes called during the political season) while appearing to do just the opposite. Here is an editorial from the *Marion Buckeye Eagle* at the start of the same presidential campaign:

> We hope our readers will enjoy a political feast until after the election. We shall use our best endeavors to have it well spiced and as savory as possible. The wise man says there is a time for all things and the present we deem the time for politics. Our friends, so far from complaining, therefore, would censure us if we devote much of the precious room in our paper to aught else for a little season.[23]

Statements of this sort clearly reveal the partisan editors' awareness of readers to whom the "political feast" was an offense or an annoyance rather than a treat. Editors communicated their concern with this readership in other ways, too, including humorous squibs poking fun at their readers and at themselves. The *Dubuque Weekly Times* traced the "life" of a newspaper as it went from hand to hand, first to a shopkeeper who read only about "sales at auction, advertisements etc.," and then to a succession of ladies who looked for stories, poetry, and marriage notices. No one paid any attention to the political content of the paper: "a newspaper," huffed the shopkeeper, "should be devoted to prices current."[24] The rival *Herald* went further, commenting dryly on what is usually taken to be one of the partisan press's duties to a serious and informed citizenry, the printing of legislative proceedings and presidential and gubernatorial addresses: "We have devoted a large share of our space today to the getting up of the President's Message. We do this to give outsiders an insight into this the most exciting of all Printers' experiences: and because it was easier to write thus than to hunt up Dog Fights and other Local Items."[25] Two of our papers, the *Augusta Daily Constitutionalist* and the *Marion Democratic Mirror*, reprinted a humorous poem and commentary entitled "An Editor's Trials," which probably does tell us something about the partisan editor's difficulty in reconciling the different ways a newspaper was read in antebellum America. It begins with a young lady reader who laments:

> No marriages here
> I think it quite queer
> When there's ever so many
> They don't publish any.
>
> . . . .
>
> Next a grave politician, who with dignity grows
> Adjusts his gold spectacles over his nose
> Takes a huge pinch of snuff before he proceeds
> Then opens the paper and leisurely reads
> Of breaches and speeches and foreign reports
> Of Senate, of House, of Railways and courts
> And says as he read the last column of war
> What a strange kind of people these editors are
> These horrible rhymes and love stories to print
> If twould do any good I would give them a hint.

Others follow, including the "prim old maid" who reads of "Marriages, Accidents, Suicides, Deaths / the Robberies, Murders, All in a Breath," and the "angry contributor, eager for fame," who complains that the sonnet addressed to his lady has been made "a Bonnet and Dress for Baby." And the poem concludes with antipolitical sentiments that further isolate the "grave politician":

> The farmer complains that his crop is neglected
> While so much time is spent guessing who'll be elected.
> The minister says it should be more sedate
> And not so much wasted in matters of state.[26]

Editors knew they were on safer ground when they wrote pieces boosting the local community in a nonpartisan fashion, and when they piously objected to the insertion of party into institutions and events that ought to remain "above" politics. The *Marion Democratic Mirror*, for example, regularly warned against any sign of partisanship in public schools, or in sermons, or in young ladies' singing groups. "The husting is not a proper place for reputable young ladies," wrote the *Mirror*.[27] The rough-and-tumble of politics could on occasion be deemed inappropriate for boys as well. The *Dubuque Daily Times* described at length the new political club room opened by a local restaurateur, "for the use of politicians, without respect to party, free of charge." With its political and literary newspapers, and its supply of pens, ink, and writing paper, it seemed an ideal school room for political socialization. But the *Times* was aware that less intellectual, perhaps even dangerous, activities might dominate, and reassured its readers that "boys will not be admitted under any circumstances."[28] Some of these editorial concerns were not genuinely nonpartisan—the Democratic *Mirror*'s complaints were generally directed against Republican preaching or singing—but some were. When a Whig was appointed chief engineer of the Henderson Road, the Democratic *Clarksville Jeffersonian* refused to object: "We know nothing of his political sentiment, nor do we care; and it does not strike us now that politics ought to have anything to do with the Road."[29] This was a clear assertion of the primacy of nonpartisan local boosterism over party politics, as was the sharp rebuke in the Dubuque Whig paper of a local Whig who criticized Democrats at a public meeting promoting the formation of a local steamboat company. "Political issues should be discussed, and political differences settled, on political occasions," wrote the *Tribune*'s editor. "Meetings for business, such as the one last evening, ought, if possible, to be held sacred from the intrusions of political asperity."[30]

"Political asperity" was the very stock-in-trade of the political editor; yet, in myriad ways editors sought to acquit themselves of the charge of mere partisanship. Given the nearly ceaseless urging of editors to the party faithful to organize for any upcoming campaign, the amount of criticism of parties and politicians in their papers is striking indeed. Dubuque's Whig editor, Alonzo P. Wood, was especially forceful in arguing for better organization among the Whigs of this frontier town. But this did not prevent him from expressing a remarkably different attitude: " 'Party!' 'Party!' Such is the eternal cry of those hacks who live by 'party,' and we might naturally enough suppose expect to *go to party* when they die."[31] Were not Wood and all the other partisan editors "hacks who live by 'party' "? No matter, they all criticized politicians, particularly those who tried to make politics pay. Their most bitter rebukes were directed toward congressmen. "It would only seem necessary for a man to be elected to Congress in this country," wrote the *Dubuque Herald*, "in order that his character, morally and financially may become bankrupt."[32] The *Franklin Democrat*, in language reminiscent of "Brick" Pomeroy's, likened Congress to "a kennel of fighting dogs," while Kingston's *Ulster Republican* used humor to make a somewhat different charge: " 'My lad,' said a schoolmaster, 'what is a member of Congress?' 'A member of Congress is a common substantiative, agreeing with self-interest, and is governed by eight dollars a day understood.' "[33] The point of many of these attacks and jokes was, of course, to discredit one's opponents as mere office-seekers and party hacks, while suggesting that one's own activities and candidates rose above partisanship to serve a higher principle. But this was by no means their only intention or effect, and we believe it is significant that editors so often chose criticism and ridicule that was general, not partisan. Moreover, even an overtly partisan attack on political ambition or venality could be generalized to the system as a whole by readers who saw each party answer the other in kind. What we must see in the partisan press, in sum, is the material for a popular critique of the very system it was designed to promote.

Partisan editors found other ways of raising themselves, if not their political associates, above the charge of party hack. R. W. Thomas, editor of the *Clarksville Chronicle*, was one of a number of partisan editors who conveyed to readers a higher literary ambition—they were men of letters, working out of temporary necessity at the somewhat distasteful job of editing a party paper. Thomas devoted as much space as he could to literature and art, and in the political off-season frequently devoted his lead editorial to reviewing a local lecture or concert. In February 1858, he began serializing his own novel, *Ida Holmes; or, The Belle of the Fort*, and this was soon followed by a second, *Helen Berne*. Thomas could write lively political propaganda, too, but he made it clear that this was not his vocation. Although many editors were active and important partisans in their communities, and some very highly visible as political leaders, others did not seek or accept other party posts, and a few quickly moved on to other pursuits. Will Cross edited the Republican paper in Peekskill, New York, for only a few weeks in 1856. He explained to his brother that "the owner is a one-horse lawyer in NY City, has been the Gov's 'Private Secretary,' and is now one of the Harbor Masters of N.Y., a reward probably for some disreputable political or other act he has done."[34] Cross, as it happens, was a Democrat. The fact that he agreed to even a trial editorship of a Republican paper is no less eloquent an expression of his political attitude than his assumption of the disreputability of the man who had hired him.[35]

Recitals of distaste for politics are numerous in antebellum America, and are to be found even in unlikely places. Although sometimes unconvincing, especially when uttered by political men, they had real consequences, even to the point of fueling the partisan re-alignments of the mid-1850s. As historians of the antebellum era have long observed, disgust with "ambitious demagogues," "old political hacks," and the "corruptions and vices of the old parties," played an important role in the meteoric rise of the Know-Nothings in 1854 and 1855.[36] We have been arguing that the participation of politicians in this common language of disgust is best understood as an ongoing and never entirely successful attempt to reconcile political activism with the desire to become or remain socially respectable, in a society in which this was becoming more difficult to do. Indeed, the rapid decline of the Know-Nothings, who were quickly tarred with their own brush, testifies to that difficulty.

Politicians did seek more positive ways of avoiding the stigma of political viciousness. Insistence upon the principles of one's political party was one means of self-justification, and it was resorted to quite often by men who did not exult in the shady details of political life. For many it was quite genuine. It could appear in strange ways, however, as it did in the letter that Will Cross wrote to his brother, explaining his presence in and intended departure from Peekskill. "I could not remain here and wield my pen in the cause of Black

Republicanism, nor permit the use of my name to recommend its disunion doctrines to the people," he declared. "I am a Democrat. . . . I am for our whole country—the continent. The Constitution, the Laws, and the Institutions, I revere, and uphold in every particular." Cross's brother might have responded that despite this lofty affirmation of Democratic principle, wielding his pen in the name of "Black Republicanism" is exactly what Will had agreed to do. Others were more consistent, and still others found another, more general political principle that fit more easily with the nitty-gritty of politics. This was the principle of political friendship, which we propose to revisit through the correspondence of Ansel J. McCall.

ANSEL'S ANSWER

McCall was the young lawyer of Bath, New York, who light-heartedly complained to his college friend that he was being thrust into politics by the unavoidable political turmoil that spilled over from the courthouse into his office. In fact, McCall sprang from a family of active and influential Democrats, and his own interest in politics can be traced back to his boarding-school days through the letters his mother wrote to him reporting on local political affairs. At college—first Hamilton, then Union—McCall was known as an avid Van Buren supporter, and was especially active in opposing college secret societies, a stance that reflects his family's previous Anti-Masonic Party activism. His letters during and just after his college years express Democratic expansionist doctrine, too, although this quickly merged with—indeed, was supplanted by—charmingly youthful dreams of personal adventure. McCall was probably the leading spirit in the formation of a small club at Union College that was devoted to the idea of founding an independent republic on the Pacific coast, probably in Oregon, to be called the Republic of Jaurantia. This exceeded even the extravagant ideas for Oregon held by Young Americans of the Democratic Party, but McCall seems to have been quite serious about the adventure, and he prodded his "Brothers in Jaurantia," most of whom were becoming distressingly settled into professions and family life, for several years after they all left college.[37] McCall was a great dreamer of adventures in the wild, and was not entirely of the armchair variety. Twice he took as college vacation employment the wild and dangerous work of rafting logs down the Susquehanna River, and he was the only one of his college friends actually to move to the Pacific coast, which he did for a short time during the days of the California gold rush. Had he not had the care of a widowed mother on his mind, he might have made this—and possibly Jaurantia herself!—an earlier and longer-lasting adventure. His expansionism, in short, suited his temper and his very personal dreams. How convenient for young Ansel that he was born a Democrat!

But a Democrat he was, and when McCall moved back to Bath after college and had a brief stint as a schoolteacher in Wayne, New York, he quickly became very active in the local Democratic party, fighting factional wars in and around caucuses and conventions, giving stump speeches, writing for and later editing the party newspaper, exerting a growing force in patronage decisions, and running occasionally (and occasionally with success) for public office. His political life and values can be traced through the extensive correspondence he maintained with college friends and others, and especially with two "Brothers in Jaurantia," James S. McLaury, who became a doctor in his home town of Walton, New York, and James F. Chamberlain, who settled in New York City to pursue a varied career as schoolteacher, superintendent of the New York Institution for the Blind, real-estate broker and investor, and banker. Of the three men, only McCall became an active politician, although all three of these college-educated, professional men maintained an interest in public affairs. Their correspondence, which is warm and friendly (McCall and Chamberlain, especially, considered themselves very close personal friends), is filled with politics, and not entirely because McLaury and Chamberlain understood that this was their correspondent's obsession. But there is a very striking and consistent difference between the political discussion of the active politician and that of the two sympathetic outsiders—a difference touching upon the very meaning of political life to these three men.

McLaury, whose letters are the fewest, directed his political remarks almost entirely to matters of public policy. McCall had written him, at the start of his first active campaign, that McLaury must himself become involved: "I hope you are doing things up in Delaware [County]. Come now 'Mack,' buckle on your political armour & give the Democrats a lift this fall."[38] But McLaury did not become involved, then or ever, in local party battles. Instead, he wrote of distaste for the kind of party loyalty that overrode a broader patriotism, and, cleverly, resigned the field to McCall on professional grounds that by now will sound familiar to us: "I am no disputer & not at all fond of political strife[;] hence I avoid it as it is too little of my business. But it's part of your legitimate calling & you can scarce be out of it if you would."[39] More importantly, he wrote about issues—Texas and Oregon, the post office, railroads and economic development (not a strictly partisan or even public issue, but of deeper concern to this resident of a remote valley in the steep hills of central New York), and, some years later, slavery.[40] McLaury became a Free Soiler for a time, but not a party activist. He maintained an interest in public issues throughout a long life, and a consistent aversion to party politics, which he at one point conventionally described as "a scramble for the spoils & a fight about men rather than measures."[41]

Chamberlain, too, was both interested in public issues and repelled by party politics. He differed from McLaury mainly in his greater vehemence, particularly on the latter subject, and in a tendency to discuss broad principles of government rather than specific issues. In his first letter to McCall he submitted his Democratic apologia, "that business of all kinds will flourish best when left to its own regulations, and that legislative enactments having for their object the advancement or protection of trade, are in a majority of cases more injurious than beneficial."[42] Eight years later he wrote even more broadly, to the effect that Democrats and Whigs were the latest incarnation of a long struggle, dating back to the Protestant Reformation, between those who would expand and those who would limit freedom.[43] This is a quite partisan statement, modified only by criticism of Barn Burners as extremists within the Democratic Party, but Chamberlain's indictment would soon detach itself from ideology, and grow both more general and more vigorous. Just after the 1848 presidential election, in response to McCall's suggestion that he come to Bath to help edit a paper to be devoted to "Agriculture, Morals & Politics," Chamberlain found a gentle enough way of declining: "I don't quite see how morals and politics will go together. . . . That part of it which relates to the farm I like very well."[44] This was, however, just a precursor to an increasingly venomous rejection of disreputable politicians, expressed in terms no less conventional than McLaury's. In September of 1851 he wrote to McCall of his "disgust" with the "unseemly struggle for place," and for the first time directly questioned his friend's political vocation: "How you can stand it is more than I can know."[45] Three years later he described politicians as "such a miserable set of wretches that a decent man does not wish to have much to do with them," and of his "intense abhorrence" for them all, excepting, of course, McCall himself, who he maintained in a different category.[46] This tone would remain a fixture of his correspondence with McCall for the next nine years.

Chamberlain was writing from New York City, during a period when the nation's Babylon was experiencing a good deal of well-publicized political corruption, mostly by Democrats. In one letter to McCall he described a Democratic ward caucus (which he did attend) in terms of political control combined with the kind of hooliganism that we did not find documented in our smaller cities and towns. Votes in this "caucus" were taken not in a room where men could meet and give even the semblance of deliberating, but through the fan light over a barricaded front door, in the dark of night. "Everybody voted that wished to," Chamberlain wryly commented, "& as often as he wished to, provided always he was a loafer or a rowdy. No decent man could get near the door it was so beset with scoundrels."[47] The disillusioned Democrat also partly contradicted his general political indictment by participating briefly in a municipal reform movement, by testing McCall's patience with one or two approving comments about the city's Know-Nothings, and, finally, by joining the Republican Party, which at least for a time seems to have provided him with a happier political home. But Chamberlain's statements of disgust were rarely modified by either party or place. He never argued that the Know-Nothings or Republicans were morally superior to Democrats, and never suggested that McCall operated under more acceptable political rules in his little upstate village. A year before voting for Abraham Lincoln for the presidency, Chamberlain reaffirmed his rejection of politics in the most general terms possible: "Pah! how the whole thing stinks. How *can* you have anything to do with it?"[48]

McCall had been answering this question over a number of years, with a clarity and consistency that might have surprised even himself. "I wish I was fairly out of the ring & could only keep out," he had written to Chamberlain six years earlier. "But I see plainly I cant. There is always some friend to be helped & I cant stand back in his need. And then there is some plug that deserves heading & I alone will not forgive him." "I never can abandon my friends nor coldly yield them aid," he added a month later. And a month after that: "I will labour for a friend as I would hardly for myself. So I find myself in this campaign labouring for friends regardless of personal considerations."[49] McCall was not devoid of ideas about government or public issues, and in his college days was evidently more than willing to share them with anyone who would listen. As an active politician, however, his guiding principle was "friendship"; that is, unwavering loyalty to his political allies (in McCall's case, the "Hunker" or "Hard Shell" wing of the New York Democratic Party), unwavering opposition to his enemies, and unmitigated contempt for any politician who transferred his own friendship from one party or faction to another. These values constituted an organizational ethos that was very nearly unique to the political party. They can be found, perhaps, in urban volunteer fire companies (which in some cities were closely linked to parties), but political "friendship" differed from the "brotherhood" of fraternal lodges, and from less affective forms of membership in lyceums, literary societies, and other special-purpose clubs. "Friendship" appeared early in McCall's correspondence, and remained at the core of whatever he wrote about politics, to Chamberlain, McLaury, and others, for more than forty years.[50] It represented the working politician's view of what really mattered, and reflected the particularities of McCall's day-to-day absorption in the politics of Bath, Steuben County, and New York State. McCall surely did not lose touch with his broader ideas, but clearly uppermost in his mind were his more immediate circumstances and struggles, and these involved not political economy, nor Mexico, nor slavery, but men—specific men, trustworthy or traitorous, worthy or unworthy, working with McCall and his other friends or working against them. McCall hardly ever wrote about issues or about principles of government, even to his nonactivist friends, who he knew to be more interested in these things than in the skulduggery of Steuben County politics. In one particularly bitter moment (and McCall could be very bitter about politics) he chided Chamberlain for the latter's naive belief in the significance of public issues:

> Did you not know that all politicians are scamps—that it is all a game to cheat somebody—to profit one & punish another—that all talk about principle is twaddle[?] This measure is supported & that opposed from motives of interest to themselves or friends. Are you so weak as to be caught with the chaff of the Nebraska

bill? Nobody cares a boodle about it. We favour it because we can by so doing take the wind out of Pierce. The Whigs oppose it because they think the fools aint all dead & they by some possibility can gull them again. The whole thing is a humbug so Huzza for Nebraska. . . . I shall stick to my old associates always bad as they may be for there are none any better.[51]

On one occasion Chamberlain managed to get McCall on his own plane of political ideas. "My notions about state rights, squatter sovereignty & the powers of Congress under the Constitution can not be changed," McCall wrote, rather less testily, in response to one of his friend's characteristic discussions of Kansas and slavery. But in a breath he was back to his customary concerns:

I see Schell is struggling for the Collectorship. I think the chances are in his favour. The Black crew are down on him. I mean your Barn Burner friends. I hope he may succeed. What do you want? I will go for you in consideration that you once hated the B[arn] B[urners] as cordially as I did. If Schell is appointed you might get one of those sinecures that would make you comfortable for 4 years.[52]

McCall was not necessarily being facetious in this quick turn from Kansas and the Constitution to the collectorship of the port of New York. Within a few weeks he was seriously urging Chamberlain to apply to the new customs collector, and pointing out what a nice job he could have: "Those who are about the Custom House do not work more than 2 or 3 hours each day," he reported without a hint of disapproval.[53] Less than a year earlier, he had tried to convince his old friend not to turn Republican, not because of the principles involved, but because he knew that Chamberlain's old law mentor (Chamberlain had read the law briefly) had a good chance at the Democratic gubernatorial nomination, and that Chamberlain could apply to become his private secretary.[54] On other occasions, too, McCall urged patronage appointments on his friend, and once almost succeeded in arousing Chamberlain's interest.[55] The latter, in any case, understood that this was the inevitable filter through which McCall passed political events, issues, and ideas. "What is the moral of all this?" McCall asked, when the Democrats won the presidential election in 1852. Patronage opportunity, of course. "Will you be in for a slice? Pay it! and I will try & fix the ropes."[56]

Patronage was not quite so strange a "moral" to McCall as it might have been to either Chamberlain or McLaury. It was, of course, the reward for the faithful performance of political service; that is, it was an essential part of the principle of political friendship. (Chamberlain might have been able to buy an office in 1852, but only after an activist such as McCall had "fixed the ropes.") In his letters, McCall's explication of this virtue is matched only by his recital of the details of patronage expectations and appointments, and it is clear that he spent a great deal of time and effort, at home, in Albany, and once or twice in Washington, working for appointments for himself and his political friends.

3.1. Ansel J. McCall. *Landmarks of Steuben County*, 1896.

He also "cheerfully" agreed to help when Chamberlain needed assistance in getting a new savings bank approved by the state legislature, there being no problem for McCall when Chamberlain asked "whether we shall have to apply some soap to the ways before the ship will be launched." Unquestionably, answered McCall, some "greasing the wheels" would be required, although it is not clear that he helped Chamberlain do it. Chamberlain paid a high price in remorse for the "little pipe laying" he performed (or the "pecuniary appliance" he utilized—Chamberlain never could bring himself to use the word "bribe"). McCall expressed nothing more than his understanding of how the job was to be accomplished.[57]

None of this would have suggested to McCall that he was a less worthy man than any of his old college friends—not even McLaury, who apparently never bribed anyone. He worked in an unseemly political world, to be sure, and he was as ready as either Chamberlain or McLaury to denounce all sorts of political sins. But McCall found honor in a system that outsiders saw as merely corrupt. It was a system that relied upon and tested one's faithfulness to one's friends, and it gave McCall a compelling moral measure that included right as well as wrong. To Ansel McCall the honor of faithfulness was a high form of self-justification, and there is not a word in the many hundreds of letters he wrote to friends who were not part of his political world to suggest that he felt in any way their inferior. We have seen this same measure applied, moreover, in various other settings besides McCall's Steuben County—in letters to Governor Bouck, for example, explaining in the most minute detail even slight departures from the norm of faithful support. This was a general, not an idiosyncratic value, and it appears to have been at least as persuasive—and enabling—as professions of adherence to a party and all its works because of that party's superior principles of governance.

The highly personal tenor of "friendship" expressed the hybridization of amateurism and professionalism in local political leadership. As Paula Baker has written with reference to a slightly later period, "friendship was a matter of favors given and returned, a relationship that removed the taint of patronage by implying that favors sprang from a sense of mutual obligation."[58] Patronage was institutional, but favors were personal; hence, by stressing friendship McCall and other political men obscured the new institutional mechanisms of political mobilization and reward behind a traditional and compelling moral language, more suggestive of the community than of the party. The concept of friendship also accorded with communal hierarchy, even while it appealed to those who found in it more democratic, egalitarian implications. In both respects it reflected the patterns of political leadership we have reviewed in this chapter, just as the primacy of "men" over "measures" among politicians reflected the visibility of community leadership in the context of small and remote extralocal governments. This primacy, as Baker astutely observes, had yet another dimension. Honorable execution of the demands of political friendship was *manly*, and defined the very core of what Baker has called "the moral vision of men's politics." Here, too, the amateur-professional hybrid we have been observing provides the essential context, as it was "subservience to party" that posed the danger to "true manhood."[59]

Was "friendship" as a code of honor a sufficient response to those middle-class non-activists who found the political system increasingly disreputable and distasteful? Honor could reek of "honor among thieves," or at least convey the unpleasant aroma of the working-class saloon, where treating, gambling, and fisticuffs, all matters of honor within an understood social code, provided the closest analog to the corrupted polling place.[60] To the "respectable classes" of big cities, where the politics of working-class wards were merging these two codes in visible and troubling ways, this was, surely, an inadequate response. But in such places as Bath, New York, and among such college friends as

McLaury and Chamberlain, it served the likes of Ansel McCall quite well. McCall could protest his worth in the way he did because neighbors and friends who knew this college-educated lawyer and his family needed little persuading. McCall's social credentials invested his assertions of honor with a different meaning than that which might attach to a saloon brawler or an election-day "shoulder hitter." Had McCall simply defied his friends and neighbors he might have been classed a hooligan, but there was no question of that. McCall could be a politician, an office-seeker, and all the rest, and still be known and respected as a good and honorable man—not the least because that is what he said he was. In later and quieter years, some time after McCall had retired from active political work, a local historian described him in terms that could encompass both the politician and the respected neighbor: "He is a very genial and companionable gentleman, and one of those persons who never seem to grow old."[61]

McCall's solution did not, however, eradicate the boundary between the politician and the less active citizen. On the contrary, political friendship was premised on the existence of a relatively closed and continuous fraternity of like-minded and similarly active men, drawn in part from the local community and in larger part from other communities across the county and state. When McCall was doing political things, which was often, he was active within this fraternity, to which most of his neighbors did not seek or gain access. Chamberlain and McLaury had both made extensive visits to Bath (Chamberlain seems to have broken a heart or two there), but when McCall wrote to his college friends it was generally about this other and separate world of political friends, not about the local community he and they both knew. When McCall died he was buried in Bath, among his family, not his political friends, and it is not likely that he expected to "go to party" as his final reward. But during his most active years in Bath it was that separate fraternity of political activists that engaged him, and, in that engagement, set him apart from most other men.

CHAPTER 4

A World beyond Politics

CLEMENT FALCONER; *or, The Memoirs of a Young Whig* appeared in two volumes in 1838. The product of William H. Price, a Maryland Whig politician whose published works ranged from a critical biography of Martin Van Buren to reports on judicial reform in Maryland, *Clement Falconer* is a tale of youthful misadventure, a love story, and, above all, a political novel. In it, the hero of the title learns of the partisan corruptions perfected by a thinly disguised Van Buren, is persuaded by good men (and by the prospects of a softer prize) to offer himself as a virtuous, noncampaigning candidate for Congress, suffers the attacks and tricks of his unworthy opponents, and emerges victorious in both politics and love.[1] The novel is a heavy-handed, artless production, as this brief summary suggests, but it is at the same time intriguing in its merger of the newly revived world of American partisan politics with the traditions of the domestic romance. The Tippecanoe campaign would occur two years later, and two or three years after that there would begin a significant, continuing upswing in the production and consumption of American fiction—parallel events, one might say, in the development of techniques of mass circulation and persuasion. Did *Clement Falconer* forecast the bending of these events toward each other in a new American literature of political adventures and heroes? What, in fact, does the fiction of the antebellum era tell us about the reinsertion of partisan politics into American life?

We turn to fiction, and after it to other documents generated by people who were not necessarily active in politics, in order to gain the perspective that will help us set political life within larger social and cultural worlds. As we observed in our introduction, the traditional sources of political history, created for the most part from the "inside"—that is, by politicians, with reference to political matters—do not provide that perspective. We must somehow take ourselves "outside" the specifically political world, and look back upon it from some distance, and from varying angles of vision. How shall we accomplish this? Novels and stories written by Americans and set within their authors' own country and era offer one possibility. They provide a varied panorama of a nation's scenes, values, interests, and styles, and are all the more useful for being intrinsically neither hostile to nor appreciative of politics as a part of that panorama. To be sure, using fiction as historical evidence is a complicated matter, not only because the only "facts" it provides are its own representations of a fancied reality, but also because the varied representations of various novels and stories do not constitute a uniform or consistent genre. It may be possible, and useful, to identify subgenres of fiction—domestic novels, adventure stories, and the like—but it is wiser simply to keep before us the idea that novels and stories provide insights that bear a problematic relation to the real worlds they imitate with varying degrees of invention. Put another way, we examine here not a singular "American fiction," which tells us in an accurate and coherent way about the American past, but multiple fictions, which, individually and as a constructed whole, allow us to look in sometimes curious and curiously mediated ways into the quotidian worlds of a departed generation.

The novels we read (along with a few collections of short stories) were selected in ways intended to maximize the reasonableness of our extrapolations. First, we selected a large number of them, approximately two hundred for the century as a whole, of which eighty were published before 1861. Second, we selected systematically, in consideration of both the overall production of fiction and the fact that some novels and stories were read widely while others were neglected. Fifty-one of our eighty antebellum titles were drawn systematically from Lyle H. Wright's *American Fiction* microfilm collection of American imprints, while the other twenty-nine consist of every American-authored novel listed by Frank Luther Mott as a "best-seller" or "better-seller" in the United States during the period.[2] As would be expected, the best-seller list contains more books of generally acknowledged value (*The House of the Seven Gables* and *Moby-Dick* are among them), but for our purposes the general sample proved just as interesting and rich, and is even more varied as to genre and theme. We feel little need to distinguish between the two sets of titles in the discussion that follows.

FICTION: POLITICS IN THE AMERICAN PANORAMA

Clement Falconer does not foretell an age of novels about politics; indeed, the simplest and most basic point to be made from our reading of antebellum fiction is that political characters, events, and institutions constitute a very small presence in this vast panorama of American scenes. Some of our novels are domestic tales in which no political event occurs and no character expresses a political thought; others are frontier-adventure stories in which the parade of heroic and disreputable types—the hardy woodsman, the desperado, the Methodist circuit rider—does not include a politician. There are few elections in the novels, fewer still mass rallies and stump speeches, and only one or two novels other than *Clement Falconer* that can be described as significantly political. What, if anything, should we make of this omission? The absence of political themes, scenes, and characters from any given book can mean much or little, and it is difficult to discern any systematic way of accumulating the meaning of such textual phantoms. On the other hand, the larger pattern of omission does seem significant in light of the deliberate search by many authors of this era for distinctly American subjects. And, at the very least, we gain from it a rough idea of the extent to which politics failed to "enter into everything" in the imaginary worlds of American writers who were not themselves politicians.

In two ways, moreover, the absence of politics from some of their fictional representations of American life is more clearly significant. First, there are novels in which the omission appears to be more or less deliberate, and in some this seems to be part of a larger authorial strategy to present an alternative and superior male ethos grounded in religious piety, domestic refinement, and familial privacy. In numerous domestic novels, heroes are pious, learned, sensitive (and wealthy) men who express no ambition for public office, and in the few in which public office is mentioned there is little or no discussion of electioneering or other means for gaining that office. To introduce the political party and the rough world of partisan politics would contradict, it is clear, the central aim of defining the genteel piety that makes the marriage of hero and heroine the event that closes and validates the narrative. As in the eighteenth century, worthy men do not "run" for office in these novels. In a few instances they have it bestowed upon them; otherwise they remain in private life. It is fair to say, therefore, that partisan politics are not merely missing but are virtually banished from this literary genre. This banishment could, indeed, be explicit. In *Edith Allen; or, Sketches of Life in Virginia*, Laurence Neville describes, with no apparent irony, the minor character Henry Bentley:

> He had, at an early age, devoted himself to politics; and, though too young to serve, there had several years previously been "thrown away" upon him quite a large vote, in the last Congressional election in his own county, where neither of the regular candidates for the district had been very popular. Having fallen very much in love with Ellie Claiborne, however, and discovering that his political aspirations presented an insuperable barrier to his hopes, not only with her family, but with Ellie herself, he at once abandoned them. His own family had been highly gratified at this, and his father had sent his express thanks to Ellie, for her kindly influence.[3]

Secondly, many novels introduce ideas or themes that are not pursued politically, or are not connected to politics, in ways in which the omission seems worthy of note. Often, for example, patriotism is a virtue ascribed to characters who are either uninterested in, or are repelled by, political affairs. And in several novels there are concepts that suggest, but are not given, a political connotation. Timothy Shay Arthur's *Agnes; or, The Possessed. A Revelation of Mesmerism* is, as the full title suggests, a tale about a young woman who falls under the influence of an experimenting mesmerist, losing thereby her "liberty." The latter term is used throughout the book, and in each instance it refers not to her rights or abilities as a citizen, but to her capacity to make moral judgments as a Christian. Agnes regains her "liberty," indeed, by reciting the Lord's Prayer, which blocks the mesmerist's trance.[4] Similarly, in *The Curse of Clifton: A Tale of Expiation and Redemption*, one of Mrs. E. D. E. N. Southworth's early best sellers, "republicanism" is a social concept grounded in religion. The lowly-born Catherine, who loves the haughty aristocrat Archer Clifton, denies the difference in their social stations on the grounds that God makes everyone equal. Archer frequently calls his mother, who is Catherine's sponsor and tutor, a "republican," but it is to this religiously derived social egalitarianism that he invariably refers. If there are any political connotations to the term they are not made explicit. We might note in this connection that Archer betrays no political interests, and that he loses his haughtiness in direct proportion to Catherine's gaining of social graces, so that by the novel's end they are a piously genteel couple of the usual sort. In *The Curse of Clifton*, in other words, we see a merging of two kinds of political omission.[5]

The significance of such omissions is underscored by the manner in which some of our novelists do discuss political matters. Political enthusiasm appears as an element of several novels, but it is almost invariably criticized and, more importantly, contained and isolated in important ways. Consider the role of the political enthusiast in the little moral tale by Cornelius Mathews, *Chanticleer: A Thanksgiving Story of the Peabody Family*. In this Thanksgiving gift book, the family of Sylvester Peabody returns to the old homestead to celebrate the holiday with their one-hundred-year-old father, a veteran of the Revolutionary War and a man of teary-eyed patriotism. Each grown child returns with an acquired fault, which he or she learns to shed under the benign influence of the paterfamilias. The older son has become a grasping, miserly businessman, his mind always on money. The daughter is a fashion-conscious snob. And the younger son, Oliver, who returns from one of the more westerly states, is a political enthusiast. We first meet him while he is busily cheating a farmer out of compensation for the ride he has given to him and his family, but Oliver's most objectionable quality is not cunning or dishonesty but an overheated tediousness. A florid man, constantly mopping his brow with a large handkerchief bearing a printed image of the signing of the Declaration of Independence, Oliver is given to long, boring speeches, "in reference to the supply of gold in the world—whether there was enough to do business with; he also had some things to say (which he had out of a great speech in Congress) about bullion and rates of exchange, but nobody understood him."[6] At the local church, the knowing parson directs his sermon, in the form of critical questions, to each of Sylvester's erring children: "(For Mr. Oliver: who was wiping his brow with the Declaration of Independence,) [am I] eager over much for the good opinion of men, when I should be quietly serving them without report?"[7] Oliver's political preoccupation contrasts with his patriotic father's apolitical piety. At dinner, Sylvester offers grace in terms that remind us of Mark Hanley's Protestant quarrel with the American republic:

He neither solicited forgiveness for his enemies nor favors for his friends; for schools, churches, presidents or governments; neither for health, wealth, worldly welfare, nor for any single other thing; all he said, bowing his white old head, was this:

"May we all be Christian people the day we die—God bless us."[8]

Chanticleer was written in the immediate aftermath of what is now known as the Compromise of 1850, and there are several references in the book to the possible secession of southern states. The character of Oliver, moreover, identifies political overheatedness as a characteristic American fault, alongside the money-madness and vanity of his older brother and sister. But it is a fault that is isolated in Oliver, and Oliver is socially isolated because of it. This location of political passion in a single and often peculiar character in a larger social setting is to be found as well in several of our "village" novels, among whose varied casts of local characters is the village politician. In E. Z. C. Judson's *English Tom: or, The Smuggler's Secret. A Tale of Ship and Shore*, the local tavern keeper and postmaster, Nehemiah Hunt, is described as

the "news-agent" of the village. That is, he read the papers and retailed the news to all listeners; for he dearly loved to talk. Politics was one of his hobbies. He was a born democrat, he said, and he meant to die one. . . . [He took] the Bangor Whig—a paper [he] believed in so religiously, that his oath upon it would have been as good as if taken upon the Bible.[9]

Hunt is an amiable, three-hundred-pound village "character" whose passion for politics is linked to his size and loquacity as the key elements of his comic peculiarity. No other character evinces the slightest interest in politics. The same may be said of George Payson's *Totemwell*, another village tableau, only here the peculiar village politician is brutish rather than amiable. "Col." Totling, again the local postmaster, is an ambitious, posturing, and hypocritical man, who, among other failings, is the only character who falls asleep during a long recitation of the sad tale of honestly earned woe by the novel's hero, babbling as he awakes to the effect that mere happenstance had made him postmaster of Totemwell rather than secretary to the American legation in France.[10] In a long book in which warm human feeling and genuine piety triumph over greed, luxury, hypocrisy, and repressive religious cant, political hypocrisy and foolishness are minor targets which are represented entirely by the relatively insignificant and isolated character of Col. Totling. As with Oliver Peabody and Nehemiah Hunt, political enthusiasm is a singular trait, defining a type of American. In these novels it is far from defining the character of a people.

Other novels, too, note the significance of political passion in antebellum America as part of the process of criticizing and containing it. One of the most pointed critiques was penned by the Unitarian minister and sometime novelist

Sylvester Judd. *Richard Edney and the Governor's Family* is in most respects an ordinary bildungsroman, laden with moral messages, about a good young man who has come to the city of Woodylin to help his father pay off the mortgage on the family farm. On his first day at work in a sawmill, Richard, the young hero, meets the whiskey-peddling Mr. Heskill, who introduces himself as

> the Friend of the People. . . . I look after the public good: I vote for it at the polls; I canvass for it before election. . . . I am an advocate of the people: I defend their rights; I teach them their independence; I stand between them and monopoly; I take the brunt of oppression.[11]

Richard knows better, and sends the politician–whiskey peddler packing. Shortly after, we are told that Richard's good character and sense were formed by the three fundamental American institutions, "the Family, the School, and the Church,"[12] a trinity that excludes electoral politics and the political party. Richard's encounter with Heskill is instructive, but the most interesting comment Judd makes about politics appears well into the story, in a chapter that temporarily transforms the novel into a Swiftian satire. Long ago, it seems, a respectable resident of Woodylin "had his cat worried by a dog." A dispute arose, which soon divided the entire city into two factions, one of which would kill all the cats in town, the other of which would kill all the dogs. "Two parties were formed, and officered, and drilled, and propagated." Newspapers, named *The Catapult* and *The Dogbane*, were founded to give voice to each party's program. The dispute "opened various and lucrative offices. It determined the election of Mayor and Alderman." "The subject matter was ordinarily denominated 'Phumbics.' The origin of the term cannot be discovered."[13] In time, a third party, the Hydriatics, appeared on the scene to complicate "Phumbics" by arguing, in part through their local paper, the *Rinser*, that the real issue was the insufficient use of water in the town.[14]

There are several digressions in *Richard Edney*, but "Phumbics" is the only subject that turns the ordinary characters of the narrative into bizarre players on a fantasy stage. At the end of the chapter they and their town return to the domain of plausible fiction, but not before Judd makes one additional point about "Phumbics." "Let it not be implied," he writes, "that Phumbics was the sole-absorbing topic of Woodylin. It was not; and only at critical intervals— just before an election, or something of that sort—did it rage." It was excluded from the pulpit, and the local lyceum, and though "it did determine the course of trade somewhat, . . . a merchant did not ordinarily ask after the Phumbics of his customer, when a good bargain was on the threshold."[15] Judd reinforces this point, adding important elements:

> We repeat that Phumbics, except at brief periods, was not an absorbing theme, save with those who made it a profession and trade; and at the time Richard came to the city, the excitement had materially exhausted itself. The great interests of

life, the diversified occupations of human beings, the Family, the School, and the Church; trade and manufactures; the farm, the factory, and the ship-yard; wooing and marrying, preserved the balance, and exerted their supremacy.[16]

Judd is careful to describe the containment of political enthusiasm, and its ultimate subordination to other, more fundamental dimensions of American life and culture. These are detailed in a way suggestive of what we have called "vernacular liberalism," as powerful a force here as religion is in other passages. The only Woodyliners who resist this containment are those who made "Phumbics" "a profession or trade," the Heskills of the story, and in this observation Judd recognizes and insists upon the differences between a continuously engaged cadre of political professionals and an episodically inflamed community of generally peaceable citizens who are more characteristically absorbed in the "great interests of life."

In several of our novels, men "talking politics" form part of the background of a scene in a local tavern, or on a path back to town following a funeral. This motif appears frequently enough to suggest that political interest could be attached to the male persona as a plausible cliché—novelists made occasional use of the fact that men did talk about politics in taverns and other places in antebellum America. It is perhaps of equal importance, however, that we do not hear what these men are saying, and that the topic of conversation is just as likely to be crops or the weather—men's small talk, analogous as a scene-setting literary device to women's "gossiping" or trading recipes. It never forces or even enters the action of the novel; indeed, in the one instance in which such talk is noticed by the author (Timothy Shay Arthur, in *Ten Nights in a Bar-Room*) it is summarily dismissed: "I heard nothing in the least instructive; but only abuse of individuals and dogmatism on public measures."[17] The real action in these stories, even in Arthur's temperance novel, hurries past these conversations, which clearly are of no interest to the author or his central characters. Most often, they appear not to be of much greater importance to those who are engaged in them.

The barroom setting of the discussion dismissed by Timothy Shay Arthur underscores another aspect of our novelists' treatment of politics—the disreputable character of political ambition and partisan activism. The ability of Woodyliners to detach themselves from "Phumbics" is in some measure attributable to its association with rough characters such as Heskill, and it is clear that Ellie Claiborne's objection to Henry Bentley as a suitor was that his political aspirations rendered him suspect as a gentleman. Several of the novels deepen this implication by putting political discussion in the mouths of unattractively plebeian characters, and in general politics are more likely to be found in novels *about* proletarian brutishness than in novels about the upper and middle classes. George Lippard's *The Quaker City* is full of political ruffians such as Rusty Jake, skilled in "swearing native paupers and thieves into the inestimable knowledge of voting," and Buzby Poodle, editor of the *Daily Black Mail*, who shakes hands "in the manner of a stump orator, who wishes to enrapture a mass meeting, consisting of a few dirty boys, one loafer, and two small dogs."[18] More importantly, Lippard mocks policy differences between Whigs and Democrats, and popular perceptions of them, in an exchange between two proletarian characters, the "sleepy watchmen" Smeldyke and Worlyput:

> "I say Smeldyke, wots yer opinion o' the Tariff?" said the watchman in a fur cap. "Don't yo' think its cause of half the robberies a-goin?"
>
> "I don't know about that Worlyput," responded the other guardian of the night, whose distinguishing characteristic was an extremely picturesque relic of a hat. "It seems to me there ha'int been nothin' like comfort since the Nasshunal Bank was destroyed. . . . Why you may believe it or not, but the wery day the news came in that the Deposits was removed, my wife makes me a present of a pair o' boys. Now that never happened to us afore, and bein' a poor man with six growin' children it wasn't a bit funny."
>
> "What had the Nasshunal Bank to do with that?" responded the Fur Cap. "I tell you Smeldyke it's the Tariff wot makes all the mischief. . . ."[19]

The best-selling novel of the era disparaged politics and political engagement in a similar way. There is a fair amount of sniping at politicians in Harriet Beecher Stowe's *Uncle Tom's Cabin*, but it is nowhere more effective than in the portrayal of Black Sam, whose political principles are suitably expressed in plebeian dialect: "I'm persistent in wantin' to get up which any side my larder is. . . . Yes, my feller-citizens and ladies of de other sex in general, I has principles. . . ."[20] Black Sam would be a political villain if he had the means, as would the outlaw Black Donald in Mrs. Southworth's *The Hidden Hand*. "Ten thousand dollars will give me a fair start" on the road to Congress and the White House, Donald informs Colonel Le Noir. "Many a successful politician, your honor *knows*, has started on less character and less capital."[21] Mrs. Southworth's gentlemen harbor no such ambitions. Indeed, her only central male character who turns to politics is her only genteel villain, Orville Deville of *The Fatal Marriage*. Deville, despite the name, is not an evil man, but is a moral weakling, and commits bigamy because he does not have the courage to admit to his fiancée that he had impulsively married a wild and beautiful young woman (the daughter of an exiled Scottish laird), whom he had met while traveling across a remote mountain range. The wild Lionne is abandoned, and the marriage to the pious, domesticated Adelaide is, needless to say, unsuccessful. After many years (and in only seven pages near the end of some eight hundred pages of text), the guilt-ridden and embittered Deville turns to politics as a consolation: "And to a man of his high rank, ample fortune, splendid talents, and not too scrupulous honor, that path was sure to lead to preferment."[22] It does, for a while, but at the moment of triumph in Deville's scheme for elevation to the governor's chair Lionne reenters and denounces the bigamist-deserter, who drops dead in disgrace.

To be sure, there are a small number of novels in which a career in public service (but in no instance a career as a party professional or activist) represents the pinnacle of achievement for a respectable character, and there are several in which the title of governor, senator, or congressman stands as an emblem of respectability. If Heskill and "Phumbics" serve to discredit party politics in *Richard Edney and the Governor's Family*, the governor, who must have been a partisan candidate for his office, nonetheless confers the dignity of his high office upon the family into which the young hero will marry. In Augusta Jane Evans's *Beulah*, the title character cherishes the hope of an eminent public career for her childhood friend Eugene, and the author even refers to (but does not describe) Eugene's oratorical contribution to a presidential campaign.[23] The young hero of J. P. Brace's *Tales of the Devils*, overcoming obstacles even greater than Richard Edney's, achieves his final vindication and triumph in his election to Congress. But political achievement and exaltation are frequently compromised in these novels. Heskill is a far more prominent character than the governor in *Richard Edney*, and in Brace's novel (as in Price's *Clement Falconer*) the electoral process is subjected to much ridicule. Brace's young hero, for example, runs against "an aristocratic lawyer, residing at the county-town, [who] had been nominated by the junto who usually governed the county without any appeal to the voters, or even any farce of a convention." (Here and elsewhere, we should observe, Brace stresses the political control of the county seat, and the customary political deadness of more remote parts of the county.) And in the denouement, Congress itself is ridiculed in similarly conventional terms. The scene is Hell, and Satan emphasizes the need to tempt Robert Woods, Brace's new congressman. "One would suppose," whispers an attending demon, "that some of our members of Congress had enough of the devil in them without any external temptation!" And when Satan responds that Woods is an "honest, upright, religious man," the demon exclaims, "And yet a member of Congress!"[24] Less blatant qualifications of official dignity appear in other novels, perhaps with greater effect. In Rhoda E. White's *Portraits of My Married Friends*, Harry Weatherall, "a man of sterling principle and well tried integrity," is urged by his friends to run for public office after his retirement from business. He accepts the call, however, only because his children are grown and his lazy and self-indulgent wife provides him with little domestic pleasure. "What had he to lose?" asks the author, in a rather qualified endorsement of public service. The political theme in this novel turns out, in fact, to be little more than a plot device for getting Weatherall out of the house and into a fatal train wreck, so that his wife, realizing her loss, can repent of her selfish ways. Dubious in the first place, Weatherall's political adventure turns out to be, in itself, not very important.[25]

A small number of the novels on our list respond to specific political events. In Cornelius Mathews's *Chanticleer*, as we have seen, there is muted reference to events leading up to the Compromise of 1850, and we are told in an introduction that Sophia L. Little's 1852 novel, *Thrice through the Furnace: A Tale of the Times of the Iron Hoof*, was written in direct response to the Fugitive Slave Law. In the novel itself there are explicit denunciations of this law, and of the men who should not have agreed to pass it, most notably Daniel Webster. As in most antislavery novels of the 1850s, however, political actions and characters remain in the background of a story that is devoted mainly to depicting the evils of slavery.[26] Four years later, Ada M. Field drew upon the wave of Know-Nothing electoral victories to construct, in *Altha; or, Shells from the Strand*, a strange, disjointed story of adventure and romance in which, among many other things, the young heroes join a secret society of "Know Nothings" that turns out to be *pro*-Catholic and *pro*-immigrant![27] And among the several temperance novels is A. D. Milne's *Uncle Sam's Farm Fence*, written in 1854 to promote the spread of the Maine Law throughout the states. Politics and politicians are unfavorably depicted in all of these books, but figure prominently only in Milne's, where they also receive the roughest treatment. The central character of *Uncle Sam's Farm Fence* is a politician who at first seeks the least controversial way through the delicate issue of prohibition, but is then converted to a religiously inspired view of the need for the Maine Law (the efforts of several women, including the politician's wife, are crucial here), and on the basis of this and his renunciation of the corrupting influence of political ambition is elected to the state legislature. There he gives a fiery speech, concluding: "We *demand* the Maine Law because it accords with the genius of the Christian religion; and he who opposeth, opposeth not man but God."[28] Milne cleverly achieves a difficult reconciliation here between the looked-for political solution to intemperance, and a view of politicians as insensitive to the larger Christian vision that will produce it. From *Clement Falconer* to *Uncle Sam's Farm Fence*, in other words, the few political heroes in our fictional panorama triumph only through the renunciation of the customary practice of politics.

In these patterns of inclusion and exclusion, we find within our novels much to qualify prevailing notions of antebellum political engagement. There is another kind of fiction, moreover, that can be added to this ensemble of representations. As novels multiplied in number and increased in popularity during the 1840s and 1850s, so too did paintings, engravings, and lithographs of American scenes. Literary and pictorial representations were linked through the medium of illustrated magazines, but popular visual images also developed separately from literature in several modes that provide rather different perspectives on political engagement. Perhaps the most interesting are the genre paintings that have been examined many times by cultural historians, most recently by Elizabeth Johns, as stereotyped, sometimes ironically playful, and frequently anxious or hostile "representations of social orderings," images that fix upon an American "type"—the rustic Yankee, the southwestern trapper, the African American, the American woman—to serve as vehicles for exploring what Johns calls "the politics of everyday life."[29]

Johns construes "politics" in a general way, but in the career of the most successful of the American genre painters, William Sidney Mount, we find, for a few years at least, an increasing focus upon the party system. In *Bargaining for a Horse* (1835), *Farmers Nooning* (1836), and *Raffling for the Goose* (1837), "Mount critiqued the body politic at large and general economic and political behavior,"[30] but in *Boys Trapping* (1839) there are specific references to Whig electioneering and the 1841 *Cider Making*, commissioned by the Whig merchant and sometime political satirist Charles August Davis, is a complex allegory of Harrison-era Whiggery.[31] Did these paintings presage an era of increasingly political and more specifically topical genre paintings? Curiously, few other painters followed Mount down this path, and Mount himself suddenly abandoned it, returning after *Cider Making* to apolitical themes. "The high tension of the mid-1830s," Johns explains, "never returned to public life," at least in a way that could engage the interest of genre painters and their viewers.[32] Once past the "hard cider" campaign of 1840, and until genre painting itself went out of fashion toward the end of the antebellum era, American artists would probe the "politics of everyday life" through stereotypes that made little or no reference to party politics.

But weren't the most famous and most overtly political paintings yet to come when Mount abandoned his political allegories? George Caleb Bingham's election series—*The County Election* (1851–52), *Stump Speaking* (1853–54), *Verdict of the People* (1854–55)—along with at least three other canvasses—*The Stump Orator* (1847), *The County Politician* (1849), *Canvassing for a Vote* (1851–52)—provided Americans of the final antebellum decade with the most tangible and engaging images of American grass-roots democracy. They continue to do so for American historians today. Critics, including Bingham's latest biographer, have tended to emphasize the more celebratory aspects of these paintings over the drunks, gamblers, brawlers, and loungers that share space in them with eager and attentive citizens.[33] What seems most important to us, however, is not whether Bingham meant to celebrate or condemn American politics, but whether these canvases establish electoral politics as a popular theme in antebellum American visual art. In fact, and as in the case of Mount's earlier political allegories, they stand almost alone in their time, and constitute but a small portion and a brief phase of Bingham's artistic output.[34] Nor were these paintings, or the engravings made from them, among the artist's most commercially successful work. And there is one more point that seems to us significant. Bingham was, as is well known, an active politician throughout his adult life.

4.1. George Caleb Bingham, *The Verdict of the People*, first version, 1854–55. Art Collection of the Boatmen's National Bank of St. Louis.

He served in the Missouri state legislature and in various other public offices, spoke often on the stump for others as well as himself, and was occasionally mentioned as a possible candidate for governor. Antebellum America's only notable political painter, in short, was also its only notable painter-politician.

We would prefer, in any case, to direct our examination of visual fictions to a broader range of images than those produced by a handful of well-known painters. Many hundreds of American scenes painted or drawn during these years by a variety of lesser-known artists were reproduced for the popular market by scores of lithographers in the nation's major cities. How many such scenes were created in this way, and what they all looked like, are no doubt beyond recovery, but very nearly the entire output of what was surely the nation's largest and most successful lithography firm has been traced and cataloged by art historians and collectors. The most recent *catalogue raisonné* of the firm of Nathaniel Currier and his partner (from 1857) James M. Ives reaches seventy-five hundred items, of which some twenty-five hundred to three thousand were in all likelihood printed and distributed between 1835 and the Civil War.[35] "[D]esigned with an unfailing instinct for the public taste," writes one afficionado, they provide today "a matchless record of a vanished time."[36] It is a record familiar to many: of farms and city streets, racing steamboats and heroic firemen, pioneers and sportsmen, beaus and dandies, horse races and boxing matches—seemingly all the things that Americans did, and all the places in which they did them, rendered in modes ranging from realistic to sentimental to comic. There are, indeed, only two notable omissions from this American panorama. One is the unpleasant reality of working-class labor and life. Farmers gather hay and tap sugar maples in Currier & Ives prints, but slaves do not pick cotton, and Yankee girls and Irish immigrants are not seen spinning or weaving it in mechanized factories. The other is politics. Remarkably, among the many hundreds of Currier & Ives American scenes of this era, there is only *one* that may be called political. That single exception is a frontier scene by the English-born genre painter Arthur F. Tait, printed in 1855 over the title *Arguing the Point*. In it a frontier farmer at his woodpile, his ax idle with much wood remaining to be split, argues with a man who holds a newspaper while another looks on in amusement. So absorbed is our farmer that he pays no attention to the little girl who tugs at his pants leg while pointing back to her mother who stands, no doubt disapprovingly, in the doorway of their log cabin. Wife, daughter, the unsplit pile of wood, and the repairs on the cabin roof all tell us of a man who is neglecting important things in order to argue his point. Such is the political presence—the entirety of it—in the Currier & Ives catalog of American scenes. (Nor is this little scene indisputably political. Might not some viewers have imagined the argument as having arisen from the printed price of pork or potash, or the newspaper's account of another dreadful train wreck or murder trial?)

REAL LIFE: PUBLIC IMAGES AND PRIVATE RECORDS

Americans mainly of the upper and middle classes, among their families, lovers, and friends, sometimes at work, and frequently in a posture of pious devotion to God, good behavior, and country—these are the dominating images of the literary and visual fictions we have examined, and they are suggestive to us of the themes of religion, respectability, vernacular liberalism, and republicanism. They are images into which partisan politics does not often intrude, and is seldom welcomed when it does. But fiction, after all, is fiction. What of lives actually lived, and events and conditions in the world real Americans encountered outside the pages of novels and beyond the frames of painted and lithographed American scenes? Currier & Ives portrayed parts of that real world as well as the fictions of genre painters, and it is instructive to look again at their catalog to see how the lithographers may have attended to political actors and events. They did so, in fact, in three different formats. One was the election "banner," or heraldic double portrait of a presidential party ticket, suggestive of the large banners painted for display in parades and on the exteriors of party headquarters, but printed by Currier & Ives in the ordinary lithographic size for hanging on interior walls. The firm printed from one to three banners for each major party during every presidential election beginning in 1844, apparently not on commission but in response to what it perceived as public demand. One historian of Currier & Ives claims that they sold well, and were regarded by the partners as important items in election years.[37] Portraits of presidents and other American statesmen were published separately from election banners, and in greater numbers—181 by our count, as compared with 24 banners. And finally, Currier & Ives published 54 political cartoons between 1848 and the outbreak of the Civil War.

These 259 political portraits and cartoons constitute perhaps 8 to 10 percent of the different images published by Currier & Ives before the Civil War, and to them we might wish to add perhaps a third to half of the 146 mostly undated portraits of George Washington and other presidents who served before the firm was founded. The specifically political dimension of this gallery of portraits is, however, rather smaller than these figures suggest. Many of the presidents are portrayed as military leaders, and the portraits of soldier-presidents far outnumber those of presidents who came to office without a military background. There are nine portraits of Martin Van Buren, who ran three times for the presidency and served a four-year term, and sixteen of William Henry Harrison, who ran twice (once nationally) and served thirty days. General Zachary Taylor, a one-time candidate and two-year president, is portrayed twenty-four times. We should recognize, too, that portraiture was a major art form in the nineteenth century, and that notables of all sorts were made the subjects of Currier & Ives prints. There are military leaders who did not run

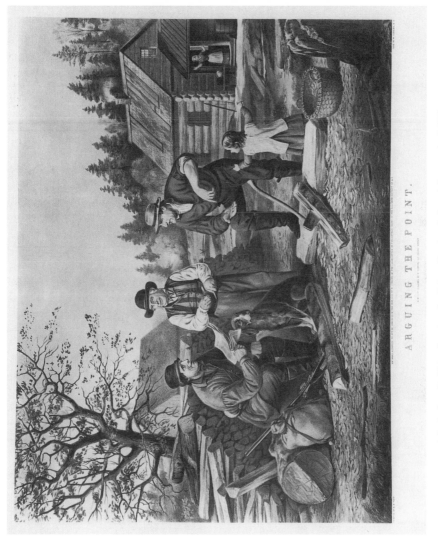

4.2. Arthur F. Tait, *Arguing the Point.* Currier & Ives lithograph, 1855.

4.3. The general as hero: Zachary Taylor one year before running for president.
Currier & Ives lithograph, 1847

for political office, actors and actresses, clergymen (and saints), sports heroes, and, within this last category, the most frequently portrayed American notables of all—race horses. Currier & Ives printed more than five hundred portraits of race horses, mostly trotters, between 1835 and 1898. As many of these portraits are undated it is difficult to say how many were printed before the Civil War, but it appears that horses well outnumbered presidents throughout the firm's history.

The election banners, nearly all the political cartoons, and many of the portraits, it is important to note, were printed in presidential election years. As we earlier observed, a good deal of the popular engagement that political historians have described as a nearly continuous phenomenon, carrying over from autumn to spring and from spring to autumn of virtually every year in this land of frequent elections, was actually squeezed into a few months of the quadrennial election for president. A significant hint of this rhythm of engagement and disengagement is provided by the Currier & Ives catalog. Only five of the fifty-four political cartoons can be dated to years in which there was not a presidential election, and one-sixth of all of the political banners, cartoons, and portraits published by Currier & Ives before the Civil War appeared in the single election year of 1860. It is clear that in the long periods between presidential election campaigns, the firm sensed little demand for political pictures.

This observation takes us into the realm of events, which are more effectively examined through pictorial journalism than through commercial lithography. Currier & Ives did respond to events, but not as regularly or sensitively as the editors of the mass-circulation pictorial magazines and newspapers of the 1850s and beyond. We have examined three of the most successful pictorial weeklies, *Gleason's* (later *Ballou's*) *Drawing Room Companion*, *Frank Leslie's Illustrated Newspaper*, and *Harper's Weekly*. The first of these was founded in Boston in May of 1851, in the midst of the considerable local excitement that attended the arrest, trial, and return of the fugitive slave Thomas Sims. *Gleason's* gave a good deal of space to this story in its first two issues. But when it concluded with the declaration "So ends the business," it in effect announced a general editorial policy, for thereafter very little attention would be paid to political affairs in the magazine beyond a small number of general editorials, a few satiric political tales, the portraits of presidential and vice-presidential candidates and a few other political notables, and the significantly more numerous portrayals of local hero Daniel Webster, including his home, his birthplace, his funeral, and various monuments erected to his memory. Political campaigns were not depicted, even in presidential years, and it is emblematic of this publication's attitude toward politics that at the very moment of the 1856 presidential election it printed a two-page engraving of the huge crowd that had gathered in Boston, not to promote a party candidate, but to witness the unveiling of the city's new statue of Benjamin Franklin.[38]

Gleason's explained its neglect of partisan politics, and in the process articulated an apolitical—even antipolitical—mode of celebrating American republican culture. As the 1852 presidential election drew near, it editorialized on "Political Warfare": "How volubly the lie is given and returned! . . . How active are the partizan editors! . . . What seas of ink are shed!" In the midst of "the noise, confusion and commotion," though, *Gleason's* itself enjoyed "the peaceful position of neutrality; seeking rather to amuse, divert and instruct the minds of our readers, than to influence and exasperate them." This was not intended, however, as a smug rejection of the public sphere. "For ourselves," *Gleason's* continued, "we have a full faith in the fortunes of our country, and the brilliancy and permanency of her institutions."[39] On several other occasions, too, *Gleason's* extolled "the firmness and stability of our institutions," which prove themselves not in partisan conflict but in the peaceful acquiescence of losers in the victory of their opponents, and in the quiet enjoyment of the blessings of American liberty away from the fulminations of candidates and partisan editors—blessings that include, for three dollars a year or six cents an issue, the weekly amusements and instruction to be found in *Gleason's Pictorial Drawing Room Companion*—during and especially after the campaign ended, when "all is once more quiet, peaceable, *American!*"[40] "To make politics a trade," the editor wrote some months later, "is a poor business."[41] The upright American loved his country, "deposited his vote in the ballot box quietly"—he *did* vote—and then went home to his family, having made his choice of candidates without paying much attention to the partisan spectacle, or worrying too much about the outcome.[42]

Gleason's comfortably assumed the pose of patriotic quietude appropriate to a parlor magazine. *Frank Leslie's* and *Harper's*, in contrast, were more deeply involved in the ebb and flow of events.[43] Unlike *Gleason's*, these two weekly newspapers did provide illustrations of major party conventions and political gatherings of various sorts, White House receptions, inaugural parades, and meetings of Congress (especially if these meetings involved something notable, such as a contested election for Speaker or a brawl on the House floor). Some of their images, moreover, strikingly capture the enthusiasm of a convention or campaign rally, as did the dramatic fold-out view of the Wide-Awake torchlight parade in New York City printed in *Frank Leslie's* at the height of the 1860 campaign (*Harper's* had a two-page engraving of the same scene).[44] More than any other source we have considered thus far in this chapter, *Frank Leslie's* and *Harper's* inserted politics into the panorama of American life. And yet, for all the drama of the occasional campaign or inauguration picture, coverage in print of illustrated conventions and campaigns was quite minimal, and the political illustrations themselves, even including the staid candidate portraits and the views of new public buildings, accounted for 5 percent or less of each publication's total. These several dozen images could convey something of the public drama to readers who were attentive to them. Even in a presidential election year, however, political scenes had to compete with other images, as they did in *Frank Leslie's* in the spring of 1860, when five illustrations pertaining to the party-splitting Democratic convention in Charleston appeared alongside more than forty illustrations and many pages of print leading up to and describing that Heenan-Sayers boxing match, coverage of which included several fold-out views and an extra edition printed in one hundred thousand copies. Later in the year the Republican convention was almost entirely squeezed out of the paper by coverage of a visit to America by Japanese dignitaries, and the postconvention campaign was ignored until mid-October, while the paper devoted page after page and some seventy illustrations to a visit by the young Prince of Wales.

Like *Gleason's*, the two illustrated newspapers described American electoral politics as the temporary surface agitation of a great calm sea of common sense and day-to-day private life. As the 1856 presidential campaign began, *Frank Leslie's* warned its readers to brace themselves for the coming fury, and at the same time assured them that all would be well in the end:

> The bitterness of partizanship, and the indulgence of sectional feelings are more rife in newspapers and in the hearts of profound politicians than in the feelings of the voters. The planter and the farmer, the merchant and the mechanic, have none of this hostility, and do not believe that the country is in danger, whoever may be elected to temporarily fill the presidential chair. The strife, the bitterness, the brawl, and the abuse, that characterize our public assemblies, disgrace our legislative halls, and that fill the columns of many of our papers, . . . are nothing but the natural results of liberty, and must and will be repressed by the good sense, and law-loving spirit of the mass of the people. Those things so justly complained of, are after all but the froth and scum which rise upon the surface of our society; below, all is just, safe and sound to the core.[45]

Public journals such as *Frank Leslie's* and *Harper's Weekly* applauded sober citizens who quietly informed themselves, voted without paying heed to the political circus, and then returned to their private affairs. We have encountered similar values in other types of publications—in the editorials and letters of postelection newspapers, and in novels such as Sylvester Judd's *Richard Edney and the Governor's Family.* The private letters and diaries of "the planter and the farmer, the merchant and the mechanic," (those ordinary Americans *Frank Leslie's* was careful to distinguish from "profound politicians") add another and possibly more authentic voice to this chorus of appreciation for the quietly and temporarily engaged citizen, while providing other perspectives on the mixture, normative and actual, of politics and daily life. But what letters, and what diaries? Examining political engagement through personal sources expands the problem, already present in any analysis of published works, of generalizing to a very large number of people from the expressions of a very few. The vast majority of nineteenth-century Americans left no record of their ideas and interests, and those that did were generally of the upper and middle classes, and were probably among the more publicly oriented citizens even within these social strata. Particularly before the Civil War (which introduced large numbers of ordinary men and women to the practice of writing letters and keeping journals), the surviving personal record is thin and biased. The letters and diaries that do survive from this era do, however, suggest something of the range and meaning of political engagement on the part of Americans who were not political insiders. Let us begin with a small group of Americans who were neither planters nor farmers, merchants nor mechanics, but women whom *Frank Leslie's* would have designated, and who might well have designated themselves, wives and mothers.

4.4. Democratic rally, New York City. *Frank Leslie's Illustrated Newspaper*, 1856.

GRAND TORCHLIGHT PARADE OF THE NEW YORK FIRE DEPARTMENT, IN HONOR OF THE PRINCE OF WALES, ON THE NIGHT OF THE 12th INST.—THE PROCESSION PASSING THE FIFTH AVENUE HOTEL IN PRESENCE OF THE PRINCE OF WALES AND FIFTY THOUSAND PEOPLE.—See Page 350.

4.5. Torchlight parade celebrating the visit of the Prince of Wales, New York City. *Frank Leslie's Illustrated Newspaper*, 1860.

Historians have frequently described the private writing of American women of this era in terms of the pious domesticity that also constitutes the pervading theme of nineteenth-century fiction. In their letters and in their diaries, women wrote mainly of family and household affairs, of love and death, and of religion. In the private records we read they wrote of these things, and also of politics, expressing many of the same political ideas, and conveying a similar range of political attitudes, as we find in the public and personal writings of men. Some wrote in a fashion much like that of *Frank Leslie's* or "Augusta." "The great question is settled," wrote Mary Bartlett to her brother after the presidential election of 1844, "and I am 'Loco' enough to hope it will be followed by tranquility and prosperity to the nation, and good fellowship and peace between friends and neighbors." Six days later she wrote again to say that she is "glad you have kept yourself free from party strife in politicks."[46] Bartlett was pleased to get beyond the political conflict involved in settling the "great question," and, with a whiff of sisterly didacticism, elevated good personal relations above partisan politics. But she was also a Democrat (and, we would add, the wife of a political activist who would later be elected to the New York state legislature), and it is clear that her pleasure partook also of the fact that the election was settled in favor of her party. Other women mentioned politics as a way of distancing themselves from it, but again in ways that belie the simple embrace of an apolitical domesticity. Ann McCall, Ansel's mother, wrote frequently to her son when he was away at boarding school and college, urging him to follow a Christian life, hoping for his conversion, and passing along family and local news. The latter often included political matters, which were invariably joined to disclaimers of personal interest or knowledge. "As for the political news," she wrote after one long recital of family events, "I expect I cannot tell you any more than you [already know]. The thruth [*sic*] is I neither know nor care much about it[.] [T]he Jackson party seem to feel quite triumphant[;] they have carried the day in the county by a considerable majority." "Nothing very special to communicate to you," she wrote during the following year, "times rather dull in every department—some political strifes & squabbles about which I take no interest in therefore do not pretend to inquire into the thruth [*sic*] of them."[47] There is, however, a ritual quality to these disclaimers, and one can sense beneath them a lively interest in the political affairs from which this pious woman so carefully distanced herself. Some years later, Elizabeth Hathaway (whose politically active father and brothers we have already met) chided her sister for not having sent a local newspaper: "I am at a vast loss. I always read the advertisements and now I don't know where you get your frocks and groceries." Was she yet another American woman who ignored the political news in pursuit of these domestic tidbits? Three weeks after Elizabeth wrote this letter her brother sent her "the only paper I can find that has the speeches of the fiery little Gov.," and her extensive family correspondence is, in fact, laced with politics. She wrote often to her father and brothers of local political news, and they wrote often to her of political affairs in Washington. There is not a hint of condescension on either side, nor is there any suggestion that Elizabeth ought to confine her interests to "frocks and groceries." Elizabeth wrote occasionally of politics to her sister, too, and could write of "my politics" with the clear understanding that this was not something only men could or should possess.[48]

Ezra Cornell's sister also wrote of "my politicks," and his niece responded at length to her uncle's request for a report on the political conditions in Rhode Island during the 1856 presidential campaign.[49] Annie Osborne also followed this campaign, and was "quite excited" to hear the results.[50] All of these women, we should note, came from political families, and it appears that their partisan engagement reflected the heightened presence of political discussion in their family circles. The most political of them, Elizabeth Hathaway, belonged to a politically voracious family, and it is hardly to be wondered at that she herself had such a large appetite for politics. Elizabeth's interests extended to the details of party (and intraparty) combat, but these women were not directly engaged in the plotting and maneuvering (or the treating and gambling), and there is a hint in their letters of a less compromised interest than among their husbands, brothers, fathers, and uncles in "measures" rather then "men." Julia Clapp, for example, asked her aunt in 1842 to tell "Mary [that] her opinions on Bankruptcy, Temperance &c correspond with my own. . . . With her I mourn for my country—but I cannot see how wearing old patched calico dresses and bonnets can rescue the United States Bank or convey other than mournful impressions to our friends."[51] In this sense, these women may have more closely approached the ideal of the interested and informed citizen than did their menfolk. But it is obvious that we cannot easily generalize from the letters of these few, atypical women. At best they help establish the dimensions—the upper limits, we might suggest—of women's political engagement in the antebellum era.[52]

Generalization from written sources is difficult for men as well as women. A selection of men's diaries of this era does suggest, however, something of the range and meaning of political engagement on the part of voting men who were not political insiders. Even more than letters between family members and friends, these personal journals allow us, in varying degrees, to follow particular Americans in their daily rounds, through and beyond political seasons, and to catch something of the meanings they invested in political affairs.[53]

John Bower, for example, was a farmer and woolen-mill worker in the little village of Pine Grove in Dutchess County, New York. His diary extends over little more than a year, but that year includes the intense presidential campaign of 1844. Bower spent an hour or two at a mass rally in August, and reports that the village was "filled with wagons & people," that two speeches were given, and that music was provided by the glee club and the Poughkeepsie band. He says nothing about the speeches, however, and neglects even to tell us which party's rally it had been. Politics then disappears from his diary until election day: "I went and voated in the afternoon[;] in the evening Uncle Rodman brought sum Buckwheat and got some coal. He brought some apples." Buckwheat, coal, and apples substitute for election results and any mention of their significance to Bower, and we do not learn whether he had voted for Polk or for Clay. Similarly, his participation in that year's local election is recorded in a single line: "Mr T C Barnes came for me to vote."[54]

Bower's diary is not so sparing with respect to other activities and interests. Bower was a religious man, who reported not only his attendance at church services and other meetings, but also something of their content and meaning. On January 26: "Sermon by Mr. White from Psalms 119 then I began to think on my ways." Five (not seven) days later: "We went to meeting in the forenoon and we had a good time of it the tears flowed copeously we felt the spirit of God was within us."[55] Bower frequently attended (and sometimes describes in detail) temperance meetings and sessions of the local singing school, and makes occasional mention of lectures on anatomy and elocution. He read several books, subscribed to *The Christian Parlor* magazine, and wrote numerous entries about gardening and bee keeping. To the extent that his diary reveals his interests, he may be said to have been a man who cared a great deal about religion, morality, and self-improvement, and much less about politics.

Philo Munn conveys a similar attitude through a longer, more reflective diary, of which three volumes (covering the middle 1830s and late 1840s) survive. Munn was a journeyman and then master shoemaker who lived in Deerfield, Massachusetts, within walking distance of Greenfield, where he went fairly often. Like John Bower, he was a religious man who attended church, almost always recorded in his diary at least the text of each week's sermon, and described as well numerous meetings of local temperance societies, the singing school, the young men's lyceum, and the fire company. He read widely in history, fiction, and in newspapers, and subscribed to a temperance journal. Munn was active and deeply reflective, but there is hardly any mention of politics in his diary, and the only political activity he recorded during these years was participation in an attempt to elect temperance men to local offices in the 1836 town meeting. (Munn describes the meeting as "very full," but does not mention the outcome.)[56]

The neglect of politics in Munn's diary is noteworthy, given his extensive descriptions of other events, some of which occurred during congressional and presidential campaigns. On October 10, 1834, he describes at length Deerfield's muster day, the town having been crowded with spectators and peddlers for what Munn clearly took to be a quite special annual event. Less than two weeks later the town was crowded with cattle drovers, and Munn's description of the scene leads to reflections upon the reasons why he has had "no calls from my old mates": perhaps "they are all engaged in husking corn or visiting the ladys .... There are some amongst them that may be at home reading some interesting book or newspaper." It did not occur to Munn that one or two of them might have been busy with the political campaign, and when election day arrived two weeks later he took no note of it. Indeed, his diary is silent during these days. His first entry following the election reflects at length on life and death, and concludes by observing that "nothing very serious hapened" since his previous entry. These were, to be sure, the early days of a reviving partisan system, and the fall election may not yet have become as interesting an event in Deerfield as it would be in the years to come. Fourteen years later, in 1848, Munn would take note of the coming presidential election, and would comment a week later that General Taylor had apparently won. But even in that year there had been no mention of politics in his diary until two days before the election, and there is no indication that this religious, intellectually active, and sociable shoemaker had become significantly more interested in political affairs. As in the case of John Bower, Munn's diary never tells us whether he was a Democrat or a Whig.[57]

As many as a third of our antebellum diaries were kept by men who express in them little or no interest in politics, and who voted with little or no comment about the election or their participation in it. Only slightly more interested, or forthcoming, was William G. Randle, an itinerant daguerrotypist whose diary records his adventures while traveling on business through a number of small Tennessee towns during the presidential-election year of 1852. Unlike Bower or Munn, Randle reveals his partisan affiliation, but it is by no means a passionate one: "I vote the Whig ticket myself yet I cannot think 'tis right for parties to be such partisans, for opinion alone and that opinion or opinions so nearly the same, indeed the distinction between whig and democrat is almost nominal." The context of this remark is Randle's report of an obviously contrived "demonstration of great joy" among the Whigs of Trenton, Tennessee, upon receipt of the news of Winfield Scott's nomination for the presidency. Houses were illuminated, a small howitzer was fired, and firecrackers ("cracker matches") were "thrown about in the street in whole bunches." Randle wryly notes that the same thing had occurred a few nights earlier, when the Whigs of Trenton had received a false report that Webster had been nominated. The diarist, in any case, would have none of this. He does report political events (there is also a description of a local Democratic convention), but he distances himself from them, and expresses no political ideas or hopes of his own during this presidential election year. His mind was on other things as he traveled about. The sound of village bells induced a somber reflection on life and death, and Randle was one of a number of diarists who recounted the substance or text of each Sunday's sermon. Just as frequent as these religious reflections and reports, and a good deal more frequent than Randle's descriptions of political events, are entries focused on respectable sociability, and on his own attempts to acquire the habits and appearance of a gentleman. "I am particularly interested with the young Gentlemen of Trenton," he wrote on June 15, "they *all* seem to be neat Gentlemen particularly polite and fashionable, but not too much so to be quite kind to strangers." Lexington's young men did not please him, as they indulged in "low vulgarity and wicked profanity," even while passing themselves off as gentlemen to the ladies. For his part, Randle vowed to give up chewing tobacco ("'tis a filthy thing . . . and the commonest decency should forbid it among ladies"), and to join the Sons of Temperance, which to him was as much a matter of religion and decency as of sobriety, as he does not seem to have been a heavy drinker. The local events he describes in his journal also help place political conventions and celebrations in a larger context. Randle attended school commencements in Lexington and Perryville, and gives these important communal events more space and attention than he does any political event. The story of a runaway horse occupies more lines in the diary than the same day's description of the Whig celebration of Scott's nomination. Politics, like the circus—like Randle himself—passed through the town, and through Randle's sight, leaving a fainter trace on the glass plate of this itinerant daguerrotypist's consciousness than the faces of young ladies, the language of young men, and the text and meaning of each Sunday's sermon.[58]

Having been on the road during the presidential campaign of 1852, William Randle could not have participated in his party's affairs even if he had wanted to. Much more firmly rooted was Julius C. Robbins, a West Deerfield farmer who appears never to have left the Connecticut River Valley, and rarely ventured from Franklin County, during the thirty-five years in which he recorded his daily experiences. Robbins's diary begins in 1840, and includes three references to the epochal campaign of that year. In May he attended the Whig mass rally we described in chapter 1, commenting on the log cabin and especially on the cider, ham, and other treats. On July 4 he went to an Independence Day celebration held by the Democrats, and on election day he reported: "[W]ent to town meeting polyticks rage verry high."[59] It does not appear to have raged very high in Robbins's own mind, however, and like many of our diarists this young farmer does not comment on his own vote, or on the outcome of the election locally or in the state or nation. His diary is not a reflective one, and most of his entries are relatively terse, but Robbins does describe a variety of experiences and local events—exhibitions, lyceum and singing school meetings, house raisings, the circus—that establish the broader context in which we can place his few comments about politics. And on occasion Robbins did write at length about events that mattered deeply to him, such as the death and funeral of his minister.[60] Recalling the words of the Greenfield Whig editor at the close of the Tippecanoe campaign, we think it reasonable to place this young diarist among that "great majority [who] find it pleasanter to pursue their labors un-harassed by the excitement of politics."[61]

Robbins's participation in public affairs would gradually increase, however, and his diary entries reflect a growing political attentiveness. In March of 1844 he was elected town wood measurer, his first local office, and in September recorded having "had a fine time" at the Democratic convention in Greenfield. Two years later he became town surveyor, and began the practice of reporting in greater detail the results of town elections. His comments on the 1848 and 1852 presidential races express some interest in the outcome, and in 1849 he commented for the first time on the inauguration of a new president. In 1851 he attended the first of many state legislative nominating conventions (Whiting Griswold was the nominee of this one), and two years later was elected to the first of a number of terms as town assessor. In 1854 he was elected as well to the school committee. Robbins's political activity remained at this level—one or two nonpartisan local offices, attendance at the state representative nominating convention—for the rest of the decade, but in 1860 it moved up another notch. Having become a Republican, he attended three nominating conventions in that year, and commented in his diary on the outcome of a fourth.[62]

And yet, even while his political participation expanded, Robbins's political horizon appears to have remained as circumscribed as his movements. Despite his occasional mention of a presidential or gubernatorial candidate or race, Robbins's attention stayed fixed on the state representative race that followed up the only political convention he attended with any regularity. Even in presidential election years (including 1860) the only results he reported in his post-election entry were those for state representative. More importantly, the enthusiasm Robbins expresses in his diary is directed primarily at other things, the most frequent recipient being the annual cattle shows of the town and the county that were held, recall, at the height of the political season. Like so many of his neighbors, Robbins unfailingly attended these shows, and his reports upon them sometimes glow with pleasure. On one occasion it does so in more than a figurative sense—in 1855, Robbins surrounded the words "Deerfield Cattle Show" with little radiating lines representing rays of light. In his long diary he did nothing of the kind for any political event.[63]

Other diarists reveal an interest in political affairs that may have been, for at least a short time, somewhat deeper. Robert Brown Fiddis was a farmer and metal worker (probably a blacksmith) in Owego, New York, whose brief diary contains a number of entries indicating active engagement in the 1842 state and congressional election. Fiddis talked politics with a number of men that autumn, and appears to have worked for the Whigs before and on election day, recording in his diary his efforts to bring a number of reluctant voters to the polls. After the election Fiddis was discouraged by more than the Democratic victory, however, and resolved "that I shall never vote for either of the parties again as they now exist."[64] His diary does not extend to another political season, and we cannot tell whether he kept his vow, but our glimpse of his private thoughts reveals a man of political ideas and interests who was also capable of turning away in disgust from the emerging second party system. Edward Jenner Carpenter, a young journeyman cabinetmaker in Greenfield, paid a good deal of attention to the 1844 campaign and election. More than most diarists, Carpenter recorded descriptions of the political spectacle, and there is an astute analysis by this young Whig of the extent to which a late September "Loco Foco mass meeting" was sustained by artillery companies and brass bands whose membership was mostly Whig. (This is an excellent point: not only did party members travel from town to town to swell the size of local rallies; parties also rented or borrowed the services of some of those rally participants who made the most impressive show and the most stirring sounds—including some who were indifferent or opposed to the party's success. Here was one type of humbug that invited cynicism and "engaged disbelief.") Carpenter recorded the election results as they became known, read President Tyler's last message to Congress, and, still filled with political thoughts in the election's immediate aftermath, nicely reported two local couples who "have come out for Annexation." A few more days, however, turned his mind to other things. Carpenter did take note of the presidential transition in March, but there is no mention in his diary of the town meeting or anything else of a political or public nature until the diary ends in late June.[65]

Maintained for less than three years during the mid-1850s, Samuel A. Mariner's diary is a record of a young man's farm work (Mariner lived and worked on his uncle's farm near the village of Penn Yan, New York), of the weather, of church services and lyceum lectures, and, to a greater extent than most, of the details of local and state elections, and of a range of state, national, and world affairs. The latter reflect Mariner's assiduous reading of the *New York Tribune* and other newspapers, as well as his penchant for writing down in his diary things that other diarists did not think to put into a personal record— battle news from the Crimea, the passage of a "Maine Law" by the state legislature. These entries reveal a young mind alive to the world beyond the farm fence, just as his comments on local and state elections suggest a high degree of political engagement. Of the latter, however, we cannot be certain. Mariner certainly kept abreast of political events, and he twice attended Republican caucuses that nominated candidates for local offices. Thus it is surprising to read his entry for election day in the autumn of 1855: "Election day. 3 tickets in the field. Some considerable excitement but as Uncle and I were very busy and don't figure much in Political matters we did not go up to vote. We picked up our Harrison apples today; had 6 loads of them."[66] Mariner's diary entries become sporadic just as the 1856 presidential campaign was taking shape, and end the following spring. We never learn whether and how this curious self-perception shaped his political behavior in 1856, or in the years that followed.[67]

We arrive, finally, at a small number of diaries that reveal, with considerably less ambiguity, a lifelong engagement in political affairs. We are told in a brief memoir that Samuel Beach Bradley "first took an interest in politics" in 1804, when he was eight years old, and we can still find him writing about his party's electoral prospects in a letter to his son in 1876. The diary he maintained for sixty years (1816–76), and his memoir, tell us of a man active and interested in many things, and who might at one point in his life have exchanged a career in medicine for one in politics. In 1822, having already served as postmaster, and having "dipped into politics" by writing for a local political paper, Bradley was unexpectedly nominated for and elected to the New York State Assembly, where he served one term. "I was somewhat disappointed," he writes, to have been defeated at the next election, but hindsight gave him a different perspective: "I was getting a taste for public life & was pursuing a bubble, an ignis fatuus. The bubble burst, to my great benefit & peace of mind in the long run."[68] Never again a candidate for state office, Bradley nonetheless remained politically active, attending caucuses and conventions and holding local offices—town supervisor, assessor, and inspector, commissioner, or supervisor of common schools—in the several towns in which he lived. Much of this activity took place before and during the earliest years of the second party system, and it is likely that Bradley's easy movement into positions of public authority reflected the deference his small-town neighbors were willing to pay to this college-educated doctor and clergyman's son. As the party system took shape, and as he entered middle age, he gradually became less active in party caucuses and conventions, although he continued to vote in the spring and fall of each year, and he continued to write about elections and other political matters in his diary. Perhaps we should count him among the party activists, but we prefer to emphasize the continuing, nonactivist engagement of his later years. Bradley, as we have noted, was interested in many things, among them botany, literature, languages (he could read in seven), religion (he read the Bible over and over again in English, several times in French, and at least once in Spanish), fraternal lodges, and politics. He remained absorbed in all of these, including the last, throughout his long life.[69]

So, too, did William B. Pratt of Prattsburgh, New York, who, for a longer time than Samuel Beach Bradley, straddled the permeable boundary between the professional politician and the engaged private citizen. Pratt was nineteen years old when he began entering his thoughts, moods, and daily activities in a fascinating diary that would continue with only one significant interruption for the next fifty years. Some of his first entries reveal a deep interest in politics, and an equally deep devotion to crossing swords in verbal argument. Still short of twenty, he reports attending the polls in the fall of 1842: "In the PM I attended election and with friend Wilber had an animating confab with Eddy. It lasted about an hour and a half and without making myself liable to the charge of Egotism I can say that we effectually 'used him up.' " Eight days later Pratt was drafting a constitution and bylaws for a Young Men's debating society (grandly named the Prattsburgh Literary Association), and soon after that was reading a biography of Henry Clay. Quite apart from the fact that he was the grandson of the founder of Prattsburgh, and the son of this remote little village's most prosperous farmer, the young firebrand was obviously good material for the local Whig party, and he was put to work less than three months after he reached his majority as a founding member and recording secretary of the local Clay Club. Pratt was active in this campaign club throughout the months leading up to the election, helped to draw up voter lists, and worked on election day to bring in voters: "[G]ot as many such in as I could—such pulling, hauling, scratching, grabbing for votes, o, dear." He also continued to indulge his penchant for dispute: "At the village in the eve, & had an animated discussion with Artemus Smith touching Mr. Clay's moral character, the duties of men, &c &c." "I fear I am somewhat saucy," Pratt admitted to his diary after another such encounter.[70]

Pratt's political apprenticeship in the 1844 campaign soon led to higher duties in the Whig Party. By 1846 he was regularly selected as a delegate to conventions beyond Prattsburgh, and in October of that year was chosen secretary of the senatorial nominating convention. More importantly, he was made a member of the Whig county committee. Several diary entries, moreover, report conversations suggestive of a growing political influence: "Was spoken to by Mr. Canada of Wheeler on the subject of the election next week. He thinks a union of Whigs and Hunkers can be effected—but I hardly relish his terms. . . . Called at Judge [now state legislator] V[an] V[alkenberg]'s in the eve."[71] Pratt clearly relished his rapid political ascendancy, and it is likely (although he never states this in his diary) that he looked forward to a political career that included local leadership and election to the state legislature and other significant offices. Yet, for reasons worth exploring, this never happened. Pratt's diary breaks off for nearly five years in 1847, and when it resumes there is already evidence of a significantly different relation to the party and to political affairs. There were fewer conventions in 1852 and 1853, no important party offices, and no nominations to confirm a rising career. There is also an occasional note of political independence, edged with bitterness: "Town meeting. Rather interesting. Voted just as I pleased."[72] In 1854 and 1855 the issue of whether or not to dissolve the Whigs in favor of the new Republican Party reenergized Pratt, and he did attend a number of political meetings, vigorously supporting the dissolution. Its eventual success, however, did not gain Pratt a significant place among the Republicans. He was nominated by them for town supervisor in 1857, but claims in his diary that this meant little to him, and when he was defeated by two votes concluded: "Guess my political race is run."[73] He was nearly correct. His political life in the late 1850s is notable mainly for a series of bitter newspaper exchanges with the editor of the Republican *Corning Journal* over slavery (with pointed references to Pratt's political disappointments), and for his sudden switch to the Democratic Party in 1860, an event that with the benefit of hindsight (and access to Pratt's diary) is a good deal less surprising to us than it was to his contemporaries.[74]

Pratt's well-known temper, and his independent spirit, help explain why he did not advance further and more smoothly within the political party system. A self-declared "off ox," Pratt was described by one of his newspaper adversaries as "a gentleman of unusual intelligence and ability, whose misfortune consists in possessing an ardent temper which involves him frequently in trouble."[75] But there was more to it than that; indeed, there are good reasons for considering Pratt something more than a failed politician. One is that he frequently expressed, even during the heady days of the Clay campaign and his own political ascendancy, a critical distancing from partisan politics and from the Whig Party itself. Following a successful mass rally that he had helped to plan and carry off, he wrote at length of the evils of "political excitement," and of how much better it was "to gain information by reading candidly & thinking soberly, alone." The reading he had in mind was not party propaganda, either, as he turned away from a Whig paper that "contains of partisan matter an amount sufficient to nauseate one almost." In 1846, the year in which his prospects within the Whig Party were brightest, he wrote again of how trivial the political spectacle was, and of the blame the Whigs must accept for the debasement of campaign practices.[76]

Even devoted politicians could express disgust with the political circus, but Pratt's diary expresses more—and less—than we would expect from a political insider. Throughout his long and reflective diary, and in all the pages he devotes to politics, Pratt never articulates the ideal of political "friendship," or suggests his willingness to serve his party, or his particular political friends, as a matter of honor. There is much mention of political meetings, and of talks with men we know to have been politicians, but Pratt does not convey any sense of solidarity or obligation in his brief discussions of them. The term "friends" does not appear in these entries; to the contrary, by the mid-1850s, even in the context of his new commitment to the Republican Party, Pratt began to use "politicians" to identify the men he had worked and argued with for some years, and did so in a way to suggest that this was a group to which he did not belong. "Was with politicians in the AM and had some fun," he wrote shortly before the 1854 fall election.[77] "Fun," too, was a distancing word for Pratt, even though politicians themselves sometimes used it to refer ironically to serious political conflict. Pratt used it frequently during the years when his political prospects were waning, and suffused it with a different kind of irony—one that expressed isolation (and, certainly, disappointment) rather than commitment.

Most importantly, Pratt was interested in the issues, of which there was really only one—slavery. We will soon turn to a closer consideration of how this issue complicated and energized political engagement in the years leading up to America's greatest civil crisis, but here we will observe only that this one American citizen increasingly subordinated party matters to a profound and extensive grappling with slavery, approaching the problem as did so many others through the Bible and his understanding of the dictates of Christianity. Pratt was an active member of his church, considered himself a sincere Christian, and recorded in his diary nearly as many arguments at the village store over religious doctrine as over politics. By early 1860 he was turning his sharp mind and temper to public and private debates over Christianity and slavery that increasingly distanced him from his Republican colleagues. The latter were, at the least, baffled by this formerly outspoken critic of the "slave power" who now could find no biblical justification for a national assault on slavery. Did Pratt's contentiousness result, as his critics suggested, from a combination of political disappointment and bad temper? However much these may have contributed, we believe that his political independence was morally and intellectually grounded, not only in 1860, but from the very beginning of his political life. A religiously based morality and sense of social respectability contributed to the devaluation of politics among several of our diarists, and to Pratt, too, these were competing forces that required continuous evaluation and reconciliation. When this became more difficult, he could do and say things that to the thoroughgoing politician seemed merely irrational. Pratt's political independence should also be understood in the context of his many other interests. He was an avid and progressive farmer who contributed frequent articles about farming and animal husbandry to the *Rural New Yorker* and other agricultural publications. He was also involved—again, not without controversy—in the Prattsburgh Academy and other local institutions. His political ambition may have been strong, but neither it nor the insiders' culture of political friendship overrode these other imperatives and interests. Pratt's hierarchy of values, more than his "ardent temper," may have been the "misfortune" that precluded the realization of his political dreams.

We should note that Pratt did not fail utterly in the political world, and that he did not entirely succeed in declaring himself an outsider. As a Democrat, he was elected to six consecutive terms as town supervisor, beginning in 1863, and some years after that was given the state legislative nomination he apparently looked for as a young man. He also attended Democratic caucuses and conventions through and after the war. But none of these induced him to consider himself a serious politician, not even the state senatorial nomination, which he did not seek, and which he clearly understood as an offer to become cannon fodder in a hopeless race (during which he did not bother to campaign.) Pratt remained interested and involved, and his offices and other activities might even suggest the fulfillment of a political career. But like Samuel Beach Bradley, Pratt's stance toward the political world was ultimately that of the interested and informed citizen, not that of the political professional.

Both men were exceptional among our diarists, and we might almost say that Pratt was regarded by his contemporaries as idiosyncratic, and something of a crank, precisely because he approached so closely the ideal of the seriously engaged citizen. Personal peculiarities aside, these men shared another attribute—with each other, with James F. Chamberlain, James S. McLaury, and one or two other interested citizens we have met, and with many of the political leaders we have surveyed—they were well-educated and well-placed members of their local communities. John Bower, Philo Munn, and other diarists who did not reveal so strong an interest in politics were more humbly placed, and resembled in their work, their education, their material resources, and their social status a far larger number of Americans than did any of these men. We have not heard from the vast majority of ordinary Americans, and do not wish to extrapolate too boldly from the personal documents we have been able to read, however rich and suggestive they may be. We will say, however, that these documents dispel simple notions of a uniformly engaged electorate, as do the novels, the lithographs, and the illustrated magazines that sought and sometimes found mass domestic markets. All of these sources from the world beyond politics tell us of variations by group and of rhythms across time, of alternative and competing sensibilities, and of a multiplicity of private and communal worlds occasionally and imperfectly mobilized by the institutions of political persuasion and conflict.

They show us, too, how several definable elements of American society and culture complicated the claims that politically active men, working through political parties and an established set of partisan practices, made upon the attention and commitment of the American people. We have specified four such elements, using the terms religion, social respectability, "vernacular liberalism," and republicanism to identify what we believe were important constellations of thought, feeling, and action shaping Americans' responses to the partisan "political nation." In various ways, these elements, or constellations—which we isolate somewhat artificially from each other, and from the wholeness of people's lives—contributed to a kind of contest between the attractions of a rude republic and those of what many would have claimed to have been a higher set of sensibilities. In the novels, the visual images, and the diaries and letters we have reviewed here we can often sense and sometimes vividly see this contest between piety, decorum, domestic privacy, and public virtue on the one hand, and a rough, promiscuous, and base world of politics on the other. We do not claim that this contest defines the entire relation of Americans to politics, or that it was in some way won or lost by one side or the other. We assert, rather, that popular political engagement was shaped and limited by impulses that were in some respects contrary to partisan goals and methods, and that politics occupied a "space" in American society and culture that was not boundless or even secure. If, occasionally, "politics seemed to enter into everything," this was not the prevailing condition in antebellum America. Nor does this well-known phrase, emblematic of so much political history, identify the only direction of force.

CHAPTER 5.

Civil Crisis and the Developing State

IN 1863, JAMES F. CHAMBERLAIN made a curious announcement to Ansel J. McCall, his close friend of more than twenty-five years. During the previous half-dozen years Chamberlain's many letters to McCall had focused increasingly on the growing political difference between them, and on Chamberlain's own reflections on political corruption, the arrogance of southern slave owners, and the future of the republic. McCall generally deflected these comments, writing mostly of family matters, but with occasional reference to the Republican threat to individual freedoms and, characteristically, the money that politicians and contractors would make by fomenting civil war. In June of 1862 Chamberlain turned down McCall's invitation for a visit to Bath on grounds that "our views of public affairs are not sufficiently coincident," and that the quarrels they would have would damage a friendship that was still dear to him ("There is *one* union at least which 'must and shall be preserved,'" he had written a month after the war began). Now, in 1863, Chamberlain carried this notion to its conclusion. To preserve their friendship, *all* contact between them must cease! And he meant it. In June of 1865 McCall wrote a brief, friendly note observing that "the war is over," sending regards to "Mrs. C.," and proposing an expedition of the sort the two old friends used to make together. Chamberlain did not answer. His next letter to McCall, written in a weak, shaky hand, arrived twenty-one years later. In it he assured McCall that he still cherished their friendship, reiterated his claim that the civil crisis made contact between them—then, and even now—impossible, bid his old friend good-bye, and informed him that all of his carefully preserved letters would be returned after Chamberlain's imminent death. Chamberlain was wrong about his health, and lived on for another six years. But this was the last communication between them.[1]

THE PECULIAR ISSUE

Chamberlain was a strange man, but the trajectory of his political feelings was, if not typical, at least emblematic of a genuine disturbance deep within the "great calm sea" of private life in America. The conflict over slavery, and over the constitutional issues spawned by it, brought political matters far closer to people's lives, and brought people into the forum of public debate, as nothing had done before. Chamberlain and McCall were by no means the only friends to part company over it, and William B. Pratt was not the only American voter whose deep concern sent him to the Bible for guidance. Pratt's diary, being more continuous, is a better record than Chamberlain's letters of the rhythm of preoccupation with the slavery issue, and of its crescendo (and transformation into despair or exhilaration over secession and war) in the months following Lincoln's election. It was a preoccupation that responded mainly to events, distant and local—Kansas, the caning of Charles Sumner, a Sunday antislavery sermon—and it was most evident during election years. In Pratt's diary, for example, 1857 and 1859 are years in which all political questions fade to a distant background of farming, family life, and village events, the transition to a new pastor in the latter year invoking much more concern than the national crisis. Quite the reverse is true of 1860 and the months leading up to Fort Sumter. Prattsburgh, New York, was, and still is, as rustically isolated as one could find in an old northern state. It lies a good deal closer to Canada than to South Carolina. But to this most sensitive of its citizens, the culminating sectional crisis was immediate, and almost personal. "The catastrophe is upon us!" he wrote, when news arrived of South Carolina's decision to withdraw from the Union.[2]

In some ways, the conflict over slavery complemented if it did not actually deepen the distrust of some Americans toward a political system already tarnished by wire pullers, office seekers, and the unseemly political circus. Writing in the summer of 1856, in the contexts of "bleeding Kansas" and yet another unpromising presidential race, Walt Whitman fulminated, in a style all his own, against the American partisan system: "At present, the personnel of the government of these thirty millions . . . is drawn from limber-tongued lawyers, very fluent but empty, feeble old men, professional politicians, dandies, dyspeptics, and so forth. . . . [N]ot one in a thousand has been chosen by any spontaneous movement of the people; all have been nominated and put through by great or small caucuses of the politicians, . . . and all consign themselves to personal and party interests." Warming to the task, Whitman condemned the "nominating dictators" who would saddle the people with a Buchanan or a Fillmore. Issuing from "lawyers' offices, secret lodges, . . . barrooms, . . . gambling hells, . . . the jail, the venereal hospital, . . . the tumors and abscesses of the land," they are, among other things, "robbers, pimps, . . . conspirators, murderers, . . . body snatchers, bawlers, bribers, . . . sponges, ruined sports, expelled gamblers, . . . duelists, carriers of concealed weapons, blind men, deaf men, pimpled men, scarred inside with the vile disorder, . . . crawling, serpentine men, the lousy combings and born freedom sellers of the earth." "Where is the real America?" Whitman asked in anguish. "It does not appear in the government."[3]

In truth, the parties were even then undergoing an extraordinary re-alignment, largely in response to the very conflict that Whitman accused them of ignoring. But long-standing negative attitudes toward politicians and parties were not easily effaced, and an additional four years did not always make a difference. James F. Chamberlain himself experienced no immediate uplift by casting his lot with the Republicans in the 1860 election, and as the secession crisis mounted his response to political bad news was the same as it had been for some time: to blame the parties. Americans, he wrote McCall three weeks after Lincoln's inauguration, had sacrificed "the dearest interests of our country to the triumphs of party. *Party spirit has annihilated patriotism*" (his emphasis).[4] Even apart from the partisan re-alignment, this was a curious charge to make, as the crisis—the substance of it—was not of the parties' making. As many historians have shown, politicians of the second party era had for many years done everything they could to contain and deflate the slavery issue, correctly perceiving its sectional character as the greatest single threat to the construction and maintenance of political parties as national institutions. Chamberlain might with better reason have complained that patriotism (in its two sectional versions) had annihilated party spirit, and with it the prospects of the continuing union of all the states. His complaint, though, was not another one of his idiosyncrasies. Many Americans, frustrated and worried over the prospects of national disintegration and civil war, blamed party politicians for having created a political world of partisan combat and spoils, of "friendship" rather than statesmanship. They blamed the parties—even in the new circumstances of 1860 and 1861—not for creating the sectional crisis, but for being irrelevant to it.[5]

The presence of slavery on the national political agenda can in fact be attributed to forces beyond the parties—to antislavery reformers; to national expansion; to changing popular sensibilities bred by evangelicalism and, as some have argued, by a capitalist economy; to the fact that slavery was not withering away, but becoming increasingly imbedded in southern economic and social life. Like alcoholic drink, the other great and continuing popular issue to have boiled over into politics, slavery was not in itself a matter of national policy. But while temperance remained a state and local issue (on the local level sometimes pitting "No-License" or "People's" or "Independent" tickets against each other in ways that did not invoke or create easily followed footprints into the party system), slavery could not be kept out of national politics. The Federal government did not own slaves, and there was no Federal agency or mandate for regulating the slave systems of the various states. But it delivered mail, which raised the national issue of whether antislavery literature mailed to southern states could and should be seized as seditious. It directly governed a tiny piece of American soil that happened not to have been free. Its legislative branch was constitutionally required to receive petitions from its citizens, including those who objected to slavery and the slave trade in the District of Columbia. And most of all, it conquered, purchased, and otherwise claimed vast amounts of land to the west of existing states, and supervised the process by which

American citizens who moved on to this land formed themselves into new states. Here was a force far more powerful and insistent than any abolitionist petition drive could have been. Once the question of freedom and slavery in new states was made significant, as it was again after the Missouri Compromise had functioned for a time, the issue of slavery would be continuously present on the national level.

Slavery—the fact of human bondage—was a powerful issue in its own right, and it gradually bred others, some of which arose in a specifically American context. The question of the right of any state to reject national legislation or executive action, to control institutions within its boundaries, or even to secede from the Union, reflected the peculiarly federal national compact and the unsettled issue of how much sovereignty the states had surrendered to the nation under the 1787 Constitution. Popular (or "squatter") sovereignty arose from westward expansion, and the perception of a slaveholder conspiracy or slave power manifested American sensitivity to the overriding of majority sentiment by the power of a wealthy minority. Andrew Jackson's bank war, too, had spilled over into issues of this sort, but mostly by calculation, and popular feeling over conflicting proposals for a national bank and an independent treasury grew weaker, not stronger, over time, the creation of an enduring independent treasury in 1846 causing hardly a ripple among the electorate. The slavery issue, by contrast, was fueled by repetition. From Texas onward, each potential new state or cluster of states raised the conflict anew, and in Kansas there was the foretaste of civil war itself. Nor was relentless frontier expansion the only fuel. Historians have rightly stressed the significance of the slavery extension issue, and of the large numbers of northerners (James F. Chamberlain was among them) who claimed to oppose slavery only in the territories and new states and not in states where it already existed. But antislavery sentiment would have grown even if the nation's boundaries had been fixed, and the conflict would have grown with it. There would still have been an *Uncle Tom's Cabin*, and cotton cultivated by slaves would have remained the nation's largest export. There were many dimensions to this irrepressible conflict.

One of these was the injection of energy into the very political system that many Americans, and antislavery reformers in particular, were quick to disparage as corrupt and irrelevant. Biblical and moral arguments against slavery, and political arguments against the "slave power," had persuaded many northerners while infuriating most southerners, inflaming a sectional standoff that could only be resolved through national political action. This placed ultimate responsibility in the hands of presidents, senators, and congressmen who were also party politicians. As historians have long recognized, skeptical and disillusioned citizens, including those who focused their concerns about slavery through churches, antislavery societies, and other extrapolitical institutions, had little choice but to turn to politics to accomplish their goals in the sectional conflict.[6] James F. Chamberlain may have detested parties and politicians, but he voted a party ticket, and followed political events with intense interest. Paradoxically, the sectional conflict aroused and focused the political energies of men who ordinarily perceived the political system as little more than the feeding trough of ambitious politicians. The party system was in this sense rescued and rejuvenated by the issue that also threatened its existence.

This point can be reinforced by a quite large contrafactual proposition. Let us suppose that slavery had not existed in the American south—no deep violation of human freedom, no Missouri controversy, no gag rule, no dispute over the annexation of Texas, no Fugitive Slave Law, no "bleeding Kansas," no Dred Scott, no John Brown's raid at Harper's Ferry. What then would have been the character of American national politics? The parties, we suppose, would have developed as they did, and so too the political spectacle. The issues embraced by the parties might well have been the same. What would the popular response have been, though, in the absence of this one issue that the parties did not embrace, but that was forced upon them by unfortunate historical and geographic circumstance? Perhaps something would have provided an ongoing tension and energy, but it is difficult to see what it would have been. Banks and treasuries? Tariffs? The delivery of mail? Absent slavery, and the air seems to go out of the circus balloon of American (no longer antebellum!) politics; indeed, a sharp increase in apathy and cynicism is just what Michael Holt has found in the early 1850s, when in the wake of a series of compromises that averted the immediate threat of southern secession the two major parties failed to articulate any compelling issues or persuasively contrasting images.[7] To return to Ronald Formisano's metaphor, the political "factory" continued to produce its customary goods—campaign clubs, torchlight parades, editorial exhortation, election-day rides and treats—but the partisan "revival" had cooled, a scant dozen years after the great Tippecanoe campaign. The passions that remained were in the hearts of those who cared most about slavery and who, unlike the Whig and Democratic platforms, refused to accept the Compromise of 1850. Other voices would be heard during the next few years, most notably those of nativists, whose sudden and ephemeral electoral strength was based as much on disgust with the regular parties as it was on appeals to anti-immigrant and anti-Catholic bigotry.[8] But when the revival was rekindled, it was in response to those who preached antislavery and proslavery gospels, from pulpits inside and outside the political system.

The "peculiar institution," we must conclude, was also the "peculiar issue," unlike any other in its force, and, we might note, extrinsic to the economic and physical development of the young nation. To be sure, the conflict over slavery did not overcome all tendencies to turn away from politics, or to engage in the political campaign circus in playful disbelief. Even in 1860, the results of a heavyweight boxing match could be far more interesting than the collapse of a major party's convention under the weight of the sectional crisis. And even at the close of that year's national election, a political editor could invoke

Wilhelm Von Sweitzel's vow to himself to do his "own blowin', and let politicians do theirs." But the "peculiar issue" was making such postures increasingly difficult to sustain. It was forcing the serious attention of increasing numbers of Americans, including many of those who ordinarily were glad to turn away from politics once the political season had again run its course. It was, indeed, the only force capable of overriding the political calendar, as it did uniquely in the fall and winter of 1860–61, keeping the sectional crisis in the news and in people's minds long past the election, and in effect extending the election into the greater conflict that followed. No journalist described America as a "great calm sea" in the aftermath of Lincoln's election, and none had any question as to why he could not do so.

SECESSION AND WAR

If slavery had injected new passion into American politics, the rebellion and war to which it led provided an utterly novel and compelling focus to public affairs. These were issues more "peculiar" than slavery itself, and of more immediate and profound significance to far greater numbers of people. Who, indeed, could avoid responding to their implications? How could anyone now abstain? Americans who ordinarily allowed themselves to be mobilized by political parties now mobilized themselves, not to vote, but to pay attention, to argue and discuss, and in many cases to go off to war. Diarists and letter writers—those who previously might have taken little note of public affairs—now wrote earnestly of secession, of the firing on Fort Sumter, of Lincoln's call for volunteers, of the reports of early battles, and of how they felt about this long-anticipated crisis, which at last had been joined. "The monstrous iniquity of this rebellion overpowers all," wrote former congressman Hugh White. "We exclaim and marvel, & run hither & thither, shouting & haloing, looking for some sort of weapon to repel the rebel." "I would get up a company as soon as possible," he wrote his son.[9] Less professional political enthusiasts such as William B. Pratt now wrote incessantly about public affairs, and about the war in particular. Pratt's 1861 diary contains almost daily entries about the war, and shows us as well its author's renewed energy for verbal political combat. "Self at town making the war republicans mad as usual," he wrote at the end of July, and three weeks later he was "at town in PM, doing usual amount of blowing." The next day he wrote that he could "talk or think of little else than the . . . Revolution which the once United States are now experiencing."[10]

Now a Democrat, Pratt opposed the war, but he was no traitor. He referred to Union soldiers as "our Army" and to the South as "rebels," and as town supervisor from 1863 he worked hard and successfully to see that Prattsburgh met its military quota of ninety-two men.[11] This was not unusual. Even while it energized partisan feeling in the North, the war invoked a patriotism that was to some extent separable from politics. Wars typically do, but we must recognize the particular preparation for this feeling on the part of the Civil War generation. For one thing, these Americans were born into a century that did not qualify its celebration of military valor. War might be understood by some as a terrible thing (although this, too, was less widely felt so early in the age of mechanized warfare), but the idea that a great evil could be perpetuated by honoring the warrior was alien to them. For another, they had been taught since childhood that their nation was founded on the blood of Revolutionary martyrs, and that the most reliable public virtue and purest patriotism—the virtue and patriotism of Sylvester Peabody in Cornelius Mathews's *Chanticleer*, for example—were those of the soldier who had risked all for his country. School texts, as we noted earlier, did much to impart this military cast to the national foundation myth. They carried American history only as far as the Revolution, and focused upon the war, rather than the political struggle for independence, as the culminating event in American history. In these texts it was Washington's military leadership, not his presidency, that made him the father of his country. The lesson continued after school as well. For as long as survivors could be found, Revolutionary War veterans were given a place of honor in public rituals, especially on the Fourth of July, and the partisan and nonpartisan press alike continued to pay homage to their presumed virtues. Americans had fought in two wars since that time, but the Civil War was the first since the Revolution that had at its core the very meaning of American citizenship, and was a far larger and more immediate enterprise than the other war that this generation had experienced, the war against Mexico, which had not been fought on American soil. In a real sense, the Civil War gave Americans the opportunity to cloak themselves in the kind of glory they had learned to associate uniquely with the Revolutionary founders of the nation, and it is clear that many saw and were impressed by this connection.

When the Democrat William B. Pratt referred to the current "Revolution" (the capitalization is his) in August of 1861, he certainly did not intend to associate the glory of the nation's founders with a war he deeply regretted. Perhaps, though, it helped him perform his duty to make even an unconscious connection of this sort. Northern Republicans did so with less ambiguity. For them—and in a slightly different way, for seceding southerners, too—politics and the patriotism taught by the Revolutionary Founders coincided, and invested their support of the war with a significance identical with that which they had been taught to revere in Washington and his men. The language of the school texts was particularly available to Republican soldiers. "As long as I have breath I shall remain true to that flag which shd & will forever hang," wrote Charles McCarthy from Virginia in the summer of 1861.[12] Two years later, Henry D. Locke wrote in his diary that "this was the hardest march I ever had but it is all for my Country." Several more hard marches took him to Gettysburg. Recovering from the minor wound he received there, he repeated the language he had used a month earlier: "[I]t is all for my country."[13] Patriotism, as James McPherson informs us in his close study of the diaries and letters of both Union and Confederate soldiers, is "what they fought for"; more accurately, it was a sentiment expressed by two-thirds of McPherson's large sample, a significantly smaller proportion discussing specific ideological issues. Union soldiers frequently compared their sacrifice to those of the men of 1776, and at least one, an Ohio lieutenant, not only made the connection between the Revolution and the Civil War (he had fought for "the rights garanteed to us in the Declaration of Independence"), but looked ahead to the time when the latter war would be incorporated into the foundation myth: "I have children growing up that will be worthy of the rights that I trust will be left to them."[14]

Such high-sounding affirmations of the war were, needless to say, far from universal among the men who fought it. Julius Skelton wrote his young wife after returning to the battlefield after a furlough at home, "[M]y duties to my country are of more importance now than my duty to you for the reason that without a country [and] without a home we cannot enjoy each other['s] love."[15] This is a lovely little statement, and has the ring of patriotism, but at the same time it begins to turn the notion of duty in a rather personal, instrumental direction. George Collins went further: "I love my country very much," he wrote his wife in 1863, "but I love my wife & mother better. I love my country because it protects my loved ones, not of any intrinsic value in itself outside of that. It is not natural that a man should like his house better than his family, which it shelters." Collins had been in the field for some time, and in other letters expressed bitterness about many aspects of the war, focusing in particular on greedy contractors and others "anxious . . . that I shall stay here and expose myself that they may stay at home in security and make money during high prices." Patriotism rubbed him both ways at once. "My country" and "the patriot duty I came here to perform" recur in his letters as serious expressions of purpose, but he sometimes felt like a "Dam Fool," and assured his mother that "those flowery speeches (I believe they call them patriotic speeches) sound a little different when read down here."[16] The perils and discomforts of war eroded fine sentiments in many men, and there were no doubt many who had arrived in the field without them. John T. Andrews neither expressed nor disparaged patriotism in his letters home from Petersburg in 1864, but was unambiguous in his advice to his younger brother: "Homer, don't become a soldier. . . . [I]t is a hard, disagreeable, slavish, nasty life. . . . If more men are needed let them be got by a draft. . . . And if there should be a high bounty paid for volunteers don't let *any sum* tempt you to enlist." Nearly a year later, still near Petersburg, he offered the same advice with even more urgency: "If necessary let father pay out every cent he is worth to exempt you. Homer I would rather hear that your right leg had been taken off than to hear that you had enlisted."[17]

   The war and their participation in it surely made some soldiers more interested in politics than they would have been had the nation remained at peace.
Expressions of patriotism in their diaries and letters are more common than
comments about specific political issues or events, but the young men who
went to war participated in the general expansion of political engagement. The
war itself, of course, was the all-absorbing political issue in the nation as a
whole, and it affected these men in the most immediate way. Soldiers read the
papers that had been sent to them from home, and they sometimes wrote
letters home in response to what they read, commenting on the war and its
politics, not on local affairs. Their absorption in politics—even the politics of
war—should not, however, be exaggerated. Shortly before the 1864 presidential election General Meade wrote to his wife of "the indifference to politics on
the part of officers and men," and in most of the soldiers' diaries and letters
we read, references to politics were less frequent than they were in similar
documents written by young civilians.[18] Paradoxically, the war itself was again
a key factor. If on the one hand it gave soldiers a political stake, on the other
it removed them from the civilian world in which political discourse and combat took place. The effect of the latter on soldiers' political consciousness was
expressed quite well by J. W. Fitzpatrick, who wrote from Georgia in 1864: "I
do not agree or disagree with you in your political views. I am rarely non
commital on any subject but I have no information on public affairs beyond
my own sphere now and frankly I care but very little. . . . [T]he military man
has less to do with the management of affairs than the alien and there is no
use in saying anything about it."[19] Other soldiers would have disagreed with
this, but Fitzpatrick identifies a force that worked upon them all. The life of the
camp was isolating from the world that nurtured a rounded civic participation.
   Most men remained in the civilian world, following military events, and
participating in varying degrees in the continuing cycle of political caucuses,
conventions, campaigns, and elections. Apart from men beyond the age of
military service, they included young Copperheads and other northern Democrats ambivalent about the war, and northern Republicans (and pro-secession
southerners) to whom military honor and the patriotism of spilled blood did
not exert a decisive appeal. Two of our young diarists who had marched in
their local Lincoln Wide-Awake clubs during the 1860 presidential campaign
failed to enlist, and later bought their way out of the draft even while continuing to express considerable support for the war effort. William G. Markham
nearly did go. He considered forming a company when the war broke out, and
revived the idea a year later. "Got the warr fever pretty thoroughly. . . . talked
it over with Father & Mother," he recorded in July of 1862. The next month
was devoted in large part to discussions with various people about raising a
company, but again it did not come to fruition. His diary next refers to his
possible military service the following August, when he was drafted. At first
prepared to go, he eventually paid $330 for a substitute, recording this infor-

mation in his diary without comment. "Had a gay old season coming home from Geneseo," he wrote two days later in reference to a trip he made with his baseball club.[20] W. W. Hayden never got the "warr fever," but when he was drafted he confided to his diary that he was "some inclined to go to war." Within a week, however, he was looking for a substitute. His election-day entry that year is interesting: "I voted the Union ticket the policy of which is to sustain the government in the suppression of the rebellion and the restoration of the Union. Paid today at the bank my note of $300, which I gave for money to relieve myself from draft."[21]

If Markham and Hayden suffered pangs of conscience over their avoidance of military service they did not record them in their diaries. They did record an active concern over the war and the Union, and a fair amount of informal and formal political activity. Markham attended some Republican caucuses and conventions and an occasional mass rally, although it must also be noted that he had been more active politically in 1860 than he was during the war. Hayden's political activities appear to have been mostly informal. It is clear, in any case, that neither man would have countenanced the idea that he was not devoted to the cause. Ten days after paying his way out of the draft Hayden spent an enjoyable evening "singing several patriotic [and] sacred pieces. I very much like," he continued in his diary, "the sentiment of the one 'Rally Round the Flag Boys!' The tune is exhilarating."[22]

It is interesting to observe that James F. Chamberlain, who also did not fight (he was in his mid-forties when the war began), became much more positive toward politics during the course of the war, and remained a devoted Republican at the war's end; indeed, he seems to have become as prickly in its support as he was in his earlier disparagement of all parties. "Your friend Chamberlain has become so much tinctured with Republicanism," wrote a mutual friend to McCall six months after the war ended, "that he feels quite disposed to quarrel with every body who does not agree with him."[23] Before their break, Chamberlain had written enthusiastically of the war effort, linking it specifically to the Revolution as a morally cleansing civic event. "I believe there has not been a period since the Revolution," he exclaimed in April of 1862, "when the American People occupied so high a moral position as they do now. Five hundred thousand bayonets, the greater portion with brains behind them, have *volunteered* to stake life upon a principle; & forty times that number of pockets are willing to pay for it." Anticipating McCall's surly response, he warned him not to suggest that the bayonets were merely hired, and that patriotism was mingled with corruption. "Discount as much as you please for these things, there will still remain enough to be proud of."[24]

Chamberlain, Markham, Hayden, Pratt, and other men we have been using as a window into political consciousness during the era of the Civil War, were members of the respectable classes, and their political engagement was atypically high even before the war began. Similarly, the women whose letters and diaries we have read were interested in politics to a degree that may have been typical of only a narrow stratum of the population. It is evident, however, that in several ways the war increased the civic participation of women in a variety of social circumstances. Some women nursed wounded and sick soldiers, or worked for Sanitary Commission fairs, while greater numbers sewed bandages for military hospitals. Still greater numbers of women whose husbands and kinsmen went off to war shared its risks, and immediately assumed greater responsibilities at home. This led in many cases to an increased attentiveness to political affairs, including those not immediately connected to the war. Some women, George Collins's mother Mary Ann, for example, wrote extensively about politics to their men in the field, and it is likely that a significant number of these women schooled themselves in public affairs for that purpose.[25] And for women no less than for men, the war was a shocking, absorbing event that had spilled far and powerfully beyond the boundaries of politics-as-usual, calling into question the very meaning of *their* citizenship. When Jacob Camp went off to look for a clerkship in the first Republican administration (the war had not yet begun), his wife Lizzie wrote to him, "I don't like to share you with politicians, they are worse than newspapers." Some months later, with the war in full swing and Jacob still away, she distanced herself from public affairs in a more conventional, and yet more interesting way: "It requires all my effort to keep in order the small share of the republic which falls to my jurisdiction. When I attain to perfection there I will regulate the nation if possible." Lizzie was in fact alert to the republic beyond her domestic threshold, and corresponded with Jacob and with other women about politics.[26] John T. Andrews's wife, Em, wrote constantly to her husband about political events, and frequently noted her own participation in them. Particularly during the 1864 presidential campaign, she provided firsthand descriptions of rallies by both parties, and wrote on October 20 that she was on her way to a Republican rally in another town.[27] In a pocket of Henry Locke's Civil War diary is a letter from his cousin Jennie, dated January 1, 1863, expressing sympathy with the South and defending her right to disagree with this Republican soldier: "Henry don't be offended at what I have written. I have a right to my own opinion the same as you."[28] There must have been many thousands of letters of this kind—with or without the explicit assertion of the right to be heard—and American women of all social strata, neither away from nor formally incorporated into the civic world, surely formed a sizable portion of the awakened citizenry of the Civil War years.

And what of their men, in particular the small farmers, mechanics, and laborers whose personal imprint on the historical record is so small? Jacob Camp, in Washington in search of his clerkship (he would eventually become an army paymaster), wrote to Lizzie on June 8, 1861, reflecting on the war's effect on popular political consciousness. "No man is now so insignificant as not to feel himself an integral part of the nation," he declared. "This is good, the people should cease to regard the Govt as a machine to be run for them, they must run it themselves."[29] The people may not have come much closer to running the government themselves (Democrats would soon be claiming the very opposite), but this statement expresses perfectly our own sense of what had been, and what came to be, the political feelings of ordinary Americans during this unique national crisis. Detachment and "engaged disbelief" had been reduced, at least temporarily, by secession and war. By some considerable if immeasurable amount, the men and women of the American republic were now more seriously attentive to public affairs.

WAR AND THE COMMUNITY: FOUR NORTHERN TOWNS

We have probed this attentiveness thus far through the personal writings of individual men and women. The heightened political consciousness of the Civil War years affected as well the way politics functioned in the larger communities in which diarists and correspondents lived. To understand this more public and collective dimension of rising wartime passions, we turn again to our representative, northern communities—Greenfield, Kingston, Marion, and Dubuque—where a two-party system remained in place, and where the civic home front was well removed from the arena of war. Again, our chronological focus is upon a three-year period, 1864–66, which in this instance provides us not only with a complete round of elections (including the vitally important presidential contest of 1864), but also the record of these four communities' political transition from war to peace.

The newspapers of our towns amply reflect, from their traditionally partisan points of view, the urgency of the war and of elections critical to its conduct. By 1864, each party's brief against the other was well rehearsed, perhaps even formulaic. But even after more than three years of war, editorial combat remained undiminished in force. "The vile sympathizers with rebellion," warned the *Dubuque Daily Times* in May of 1864, "who discourage enlistments and encourage desertions, who . . . chuckle with ill-disguised delight over 'confederate' victories, . . . these pests of society all claim to be loyal." They are "only manly enough to incite the ignorant and vicious to resist law and then leave them to suffer the consequences."[30] The mission of the Democrats, countered the *Dubuque Herald*, was to secure to all states control of their domestic institutions, protect the prerogatives of free speech and a free press, and "carry out the designs of the fathers and maintain this as a white man's government." If the Republicans retained power, "we shall have four more years of war, with its desolations, crimes and miseries. . . . This the country could not stand and survive."[31] Urgent partisan rhetoric had long been a staple of the political press, but in the context of the Civil War statements such as these no longer seemed overblown. "The constitution ain't in danger just at present," joked the editor of the nonpartisan *Rondout Courier* in 1851 at the expense of his Whig and Democratic counterparts. Now it was.

In at least three different ways, the local papers manifest the heightened tensions of war. One is in their reporting of personal and collective political conflicts that were not orchestrated by the parties. The *Kingston Argus*, for example, reported that two women of Kingston's "best circle" ended a friendship of many years when one persisted in calling Lincoln "a vulgar man."[32] This was tame enough, but it was the sort of story (nearly identical to the one we have told about James Chamberlain and Ansel McCall) that could now work its way into the partisan press as a suggestion of how deeply the conflict cut through the fabric of daily life. Rather more vivid was a successful physical attack on "abolitionists" in Dubuque's Main Street, seized upon and approved by the Democratic *Herald*: "The very common and just conclusion was reached that Abe Lincoln is too ugly in phiz, too weak in intellect, and too tyrannical in the exercise of power to be allowed to 'run the machine' another four years." A year later, in the aftermath of the war and the assassination, the rival *Times* made similar partisan use of another such event. One night, a "Celtic gent" in the section of town called Dublin told a small crowd that Jeff Davis was "a betthur man" than President Lincoln. Another Irishman, "who had worn 'the blue' met this affirmation by a slight tug on the Jeffite's nag, which he followed with numerous others, until the representative of secession concluded the argument was against him." The soldier then asked any other advocates of this position to step forward, "but strange to say," none did. "It is possible the soldier's logic was overwhelming and that they became suddenly convinced that the late President *was* the better man." Lighthearted on the surface, these accounts had a darker undercurrent, which became a little more evident in the report of the Reverend Mr. Bonte's having remarked to "an excited crowd" in Dubuque that soldiers "ought to clean out" the offices of the Democratic newspaper.[33]

The war changed as well the seasonal ebb and flow of politics in the community. Because the Democrats continued to make the war a political issue—it was, indeed, *the* political issue throughout its duration—there was no longer so easily defined an "unseasonable" time for political discourse and dispute. War news came in at any time, frequently in spring and early summer, and sometimes in winter (Fredericksburg, for example, was fought in December, Murfreesboro in December and early January, of 1862–63). These were parts of the communal calendar that formerly had been relatively free from politics. But now, each report of victory or defeat raised anew the fundamental issue dividing the parties, not merely in the local press, but in daily conversation as well. Nominations and campaigns adhered to the old schedule, and the customary rhythm of electoral politics remained intact. But now there was an overlay of popular engagement that kept partisan differences alive in the community throughout much of the year, and in no easily defined pattern.

Perhaps most importantly of all, dispute over the war breached the carefully constructed boundary between politics and other communal institutions—the church, the school, the lyceum, the nonpartisan citizens' meeting. In Greenfield, where the Republican paper could boast that "there is but one party, practically," this invasion of politics into nonpartisan institutions amounted to what might well be called the Republicanization of communal life.[34] The Greenfield Literary Society, for example, invited a succession of speakers during these years who not only lectured on political issues, but who also made no effort to disguise their partisan sentiments. In January of 1865 Washington Hall was filled to overflowing for an address by Anna Dickinson on "The Meaning of the Election" of 1864. Frederick Douglass followed two months later with "Equality of the Black Man before the Law," and soon after Frances E. W. Harper, a black woman, offered "The Mission of the War and Negro Suffrage." When Douglass was refused dinner at the Mansion House the *Gazette and Courier* danced around the issue of racism in Greenfield, chiding as "foolish" those who would "refuse to allow a man to eat at their public table, who had once been a guest of Queen Victoria and the nobility of England, and of the President of the United States."[35]

The pulpit as well as the lecture platform was Republicanized in Greenfield. In 1864, the Thanksgiving Day sermon of D. H. Rogan, pastor of the First Congregational Society of Greenfield, began with the assurance that no one would be invited to "rejoice in any party triumphs here today." He then proceeded to do just that, celebrating Lincoln's re-election in unmistakably partisan terms. For the people "to come to the ballot box" and by an overwhelming majority "stand up for the defense of their country," was "an act of devotion to the right, grand and sublime beyond parallel," Rogan told his listeners. Had the Democrats been elected, we would have suffered "eternal war and blood, . . . weakness and decay, and a mighty slave oligarchy reared out of our ruins." Like a stump speaker, Rogan ridiculed every plank of the Democratic platform. "Heavy taxes," and even a "vast debt," were worth paying, for "respect in our own sight and the sight of the world." The "dictatorship at Washington," moreover, had done virtually nothing while scores of newspapers and "ten thousand snakey tongues" hissed "slander and abuse and vituperation" on the government and its leaders. When the presses advocated "open treason, or aid and comfort to the enemy," Reverend Rogan had no doubt the Administration had a right and responsibility "to impose silence upon them." He rejoiced that "God had inspired the people" to keep the government out of the hands of the "Chicago politicians," who would have surrendered it to the rebels. Instead, he concluded, the vote on November 8 was a "distinct, unmistakable, full declaration that the curse of slavery shall be hurled from us forever," because the people "*well knew*" that emancipation was the policy of the Lincoln administration: "Pause here in awe! . . . and adore our God for guiding the people to it."[36] It is significant that no criticism of the mixing of religion and politics appeared in the *Gazette and Courier* after this performance. In the fall of 1865, in fact, the newspaper insisted that "To introduce religion into politics is to purify politics." To be sure, the editor acknowledged that when politics are carried into religion, the two are put "into false relations," with religion likely to be subordinated and even corrupted. But, he argued, any effort to harmonize laws with Christian ideas and principles is appropriate, just, and necessary, when secular institutions like slavery conflict with Gospel principles.[37]

There were some Democrats in Greenfield, we hasten to add, but since they did not constitute "the respectable minority" that Joel Silbey has identified in so many cities and towns in the North and the West during the Civil War,[38] they could do little, for the moment, to stop the spread of partisanship into religious and civic institutions. Occasionally, they could add a small Democratic presence to Republican-dominated civic events. At the mass meeting held in Greenfield to celebrate the passage of the Thirteenth Amendment to the Constitution, for example, Charles Munn proclaimed that he "wished it understood that he had always been a democrat and an anti-slavery man,"[39] implying that these were not contradictions, and that Democrats participated in the (somewhat forced) local consensus on race and Union policy. This was, perhaps, a strategic concession, intended to keep the Democratic Party alive in Greenfield in anticipation of a possible postwar restoration of the two-party system. In the meantime, it kept the Republicans from claiming the celebration as entirely their own. This, and no more, is what Democrats could accomplish in Greenfield during the Civil War.

Kingston, Marion, and Dubuque had more Democrats than Greenfield, and consequently more genuine forms of political contention. In these towns, Republicans' efforts to fashion a politics for all seasons and associations met stiff resistance from Democrats, who responded with two contradictory strategies. Wherever possible, they opposed the intrusion of politics into schools, churches, literary societies, and municipal elections. If defeated in this, they formed their own equally partisan organizations. In either case, partisan identity was strengthened, as the ideological polarization encouraged by the issues of slavery and war were expressed in the ordering of a wide variety of communal affairs.

The Democrats of Dubuque, drawing upon a large Irish population to maintain majorities into the 1860s, fought a rhetorical civil war with Republicans over who should rule at home. The *Herald* was vigilant against attempts to extend politics into civil discourse and civic institutions. When "abolition" papers announced the arrest of two "copperhead horse thieves," the *Herald* editor responded: "[H]ow would it look if we should announce a Republican Highwayman and Horse Thief was arrested in this City on Friday last?" Such a statement, he added, as he ate his cake while having it too (many readers knew who had been arrested and others would now find out), was "nothing but the truth; but we think that neither the Democratic nor the Republican

Party are responsible for the acts of individuals done on their own responsibility."[40] Politics in the schools, however, posed more than a rhetorical threat. The school-board elections in the spring of 1864 appeared to begin quietly enough, in accordance with the view that party considerations impair "the efficiency and usefulness of our school system." Consequently, Republicans and Democrats agreed on a single ticket. Some Copperheads, however, finding candidate Christian Wullweber "especially obnoxious," wrote in the Democrat F. A. Gniffke. Since Wullweber prevailed, 478 votes to 273, the Republicans could make light of the affair: "We were pleased to see that John Brown is growing in popularity as he got two votes, while Jeff Davis got but one, for President of the School Board," wrote the *Times*. "If it had been generally known that they were candidates, both would have had more." Although neither Brown nor Davis reappeared on school-board ballots, their surrogates did. As late as 1866, Democrats at their city convention refused to endorse a five-man slate for school-board directors (two Republicans and three Democrats), insisting that the party's central committee did not have the authority to commit to any candidates who were not Democrats.[41]

Dubuque Democrats had reasons to suspect that Iowa public schools were being Republicanized. In the summer of 1864 the state's teachers association greeted "with joy the time" when slavery would be "utterly destroyed." Even more ominously, the members proclaimed that because "it is the duty of all teachers to sustain our Government in its struggle for existence," certification should be revoked "from all persons who show, by act or word, sympathy with the designs of rebels and traitors." Where Democrats were in the majority, turnabout was often deemed fair play. In Muscatine, Iowa, the *Dubuque Daily Times* warned, several little girls who left school with their parents' permission, "at the proper time," to work for the soldiers at the Sanitary Commission fair, were suspended by the "meanest type of a Copperhead" director.[42]

And so it went. With war "the all absorbing business of our time," and with political activists organizing draft meetings, peace gatherings, and Sanitary Commission fairs, it seemed natural that politics should spill over into nonpartisan institutions and events. Indeed, those that resisted ran the risk of irrelevance. In 1864, the Dubuque Agricultural Fair, which in the past had outdrawn caucuses, conventions, and party rallies, was deemed a "partial failure" for this reason.[43] More interesting was the fate of the traditionally nonpartisan celebration of the Fourth of July, which became the venue for alternative partisan agendas. In 1864, Republicans chided the Democrats for caring so little for the principles of the Declaration of Independence that they would withdraw from the celebration of the Fourth, "the day which gave it promulgation, unless perchance some nigger stealer and woman whipper bid them parade in honor of slavery and the Confederacy, curse Abraham Lincoln, and deify Jeff Davis as they did last year." When the Independence Day celebration for 1865 was organized at Tivoli Gardens "under the auspices of negro suffrage advocates" (the program included a reading of the Emancipation Proclamation), the Democrats organized a series of excursions and picnics, "irrespective of politics." The public fast day called by the governor to honor the memory of President Lincoln apparently fell victim to the same kind of conflict. Dubuque Democrats, remembering "the disgusting spectacle of a week ago, when a solemn occasion turned into a bitter partisan affair," refused to participate. As the city officers were all Democrats, the *Herald* assumed no assembly would convene, and there is no evidence that one did.[44]

In Kingston, as in Dubuque, Democrats heightened and reinforced partisan consciousness by fighting off the attempts by the Republicans to control public space and discourse. When the "Lincolnites" celebrated Sherman's capture of Atlanta, the McClellan Democrats took back the streets with a thirty-four-gun salute of their own, calculated to show that the Republicans did not have "a patent right to the victories of the army."[45] Democrats also protested the Republicanization of the pulpit. When the minister of the First Episcopal Church announced the time and location of Lincoln campaign meetings in church each Sunday, the *Argus* remarked that all that remained to transform it into a political club room was a portrait of the president over the pulpit "and a score of office-holding claquers beneath to give the cues for applause." Rev. McKown seemed to imply, the editor concluded, "that he could do a little better than the Deity was likely to do on election day, by ordaining that all the votes be cast for the immaculate Lincoln!"[46]

To the dismay of Kingston Democrats, clergymen also ventured outside their churches to deliver political messages. In March 1864, the Reverend Dr. Storrs addressed the Kingston Literary Association. "A great Humbug of the first water," according to the *Argus*, Storrs applauded the outpouring of patriotism that had grown out of the war, and suggested that American citizens should pay their taxes without complaint. In what was by then a familiar refrain, the *Argus*'s editor complained that ministers "dabbling with politics" invariably set back Christian progress. Since every hamlet and village had a church of "some denomination or other, where politics are not discussed on the Sabbath," he suggested that worshippers should attend it instead of refraining from attending services at all, "as some and too many are apt to adopt as the rule." The Democratic editor, moreover, was beginning to tire of lectures by "book learned men, with no practical experience whatever." At their best, he acknowledged, literary lectures improve the mind, but when the speaker "undertakes to instruct the people politically," they lose all value.[47]

The Kingston culture wars escalated shortly after the 1864 election, in former times a period when communities turned away from political conflict. The *Argus* strained to defend, and to reconcile with the traditionally apolitical election aftermath, a speaking invitation to Fernando Wood, Peace Democrat and former mayor of New York City. Not at all the "associate of rowdies," Wood, in reality, "was a polished gentleman of extensive acquirements on other than political rights" who would banish from the platform "party spirit." That Wood's topic, the character of Andrew Jackson, might belie the *Argus*'s editorial stance, was left for readers to decide.[48] Significantly, Wood's lecture does not appear to have been sponsored by the Kingston Literary Association. At the end of 1864, the partisan split was in fact institutionalized and made permanent with the formation of the Rondout Literary Association. A "counter-organization" was necessary, opined the *Argus*, because public lectures in Kingston were "so offensive in their partisanship" that "conservative men" could not listen to them "without feeling insulted and outraged. . . . As in the church, so in literary associations, it is a lamentable fact that the antagonisms of party are rapidly undermining their powers for good." Beneath this epidermal antipartisan rhetoric, however, was thick-skinned party passion. The roster of lecturers for the new association, with one or two exceptions, was an all-star lineup of Democratic politicians, editors and writers: Horatio Seymour, Samuel Sunset Cox, John Van Buren, Artemus Ward, Manton Marble, and, for an encore performance, Fernando Wood.[49]

That antiparty rhetoric continued to be expressed during these years, even as a faint counterpoint to the partisanship that was invading so many arenas of community life, is evidence of its cultural resonance and relevance. In February of 1865 the *Argus* again drew upon this tradition in advising its readers to "absent themselves" when George William Curtis appeared before the Kingston Literary Association: "What would be offensive in the last degree in the persons of Fernando Wood or A. Oakey Hall surely is none the less so in Anna Dickinson, George William Curtis, [or] Bayard Taylor, even though sugar-coated with the specious 'loyal' cant uniformly offered in justification." Taylor's lecture, delivered some weeks earlier under the title "Ourselves and Our Relations," was full of "unjust aspersions upon conservative men and views, which if presented in the undisguised character of a political advocate would have been heard with patient interest, but which, in the sphere of a lecturer, becomes an imposition not to be borne except by those who are content to lick the hand that smites them."[50] Within a month, the *Argus* would be encouraging Kingstonians to listen to A. Oakey Hall, a Democrat who, "it is to be hoped . . . will give no evidence of the fact in his lecture."[51] It was, of course, the disingenuous strategy of the minority-party editor to disparage partisanship wherever it was used to buttress the majority party's advantage, and in Kingston it was clearly the Republicans who benefited from the political invasion of the church and lecture hall. But this posture was a sensible one, drawing as it did on old communal values that had been but recently eclipsed by the exigencies of the national crisis.

Even before the crisis reached its apparent resolution at Appomattox, these older values appear to have become more pervasive. In Marion, which also had its battles over political preachers and Independence Day,[52] they may be glimpsed in a somewhat curious way through the complaint of the local Democratic editor that the party faithful were not attending sufficiently to party—more accurately, party newspaper—business. Many local Democrats, it appears, were hiring "Abolition lawyers" to carry out estate sales and other legal business, and were not sufficiently diligent about seeing to it that their legal notices were published in the *Democratic Mirror* rather than in the Republican *Independent*.[53] Understandably concerned about his paper's revenues, the editor inadvertently revealed an area of local life into which partisanship was not or no longer intruding, and, somewhat surprisingly, offered no objection to Democrats' doing business with Republican attorneys. By the fall of 1865, the *Democratic Mirror* itself began to demobilize, and to reconstruct traditional partisan limits. After the first postwar election the paper turned its attention to "the development of the local interests of our town," while pointing out to his readers that the *Independent's* editor continued to concentrate on politics. "He complains that we had not a word to say about the New York and New Jersey elections," which, of course, the Republicans won. "Perhaps not; but we had one whole column devoted to the business interests of and local improvements in our town." The people, he argued, care more about "the latter."[54]

This postwar reassertion of the primacy of the community, and of the proper limits of partisan conflict, is evident in all of our towns. In the spring of 1866 the *Dubuque Daily Times* noted with equanimity the mayoral contest that pitted a Republican against a Democrat, both of whom happened to be officers of the First National Bank. "The First National," he wrote, "is bound to come out ahead—and the city is bound to have a financier at the head of her affairs." *Which* financier won the election did not seem to matter a great deal to this party editor, who in other ways conveyed the idea that politics no longer held center stage in Dubuque. If a newspaper "contains too much political matter," he admitted, "people won't have it." He knew that the *Times's* second page, which contained national and state political news, was neglected by "many persons," and that even election news was less compelling. The rival *Herald*, for its part, published the ditty "Take the Paper," by N. P. Willis: "Why don't you take the paper? / They're the life of our delight / Except about election time / And then I read for spite." The nation had much unfinished business relating to reunification and the civil status of the former slaves, but politics was withdrawing back into its customary channels. In Republican Greenfield, despite half-fare trains from Athol and the fame of the speaker, Henry Ward Beecher's public lecture on Reconstruction failed to fill half the hall.[55]

Was the wartime politicization of the community's streets, calendar, and religious and civic institutions merely a temporary aberration, then? Or did it leave behind important traces in the peacetime years that followed? In fact, politics continued to withdraw to its traditional sphere in these and other towns, despite the deeper partisan commitment of some citizens—a commitment that looked back to the war years and to the kind of political conflict that had justified the breaching of old civic barriers by political parties. The recreation and long-term maintenance of those barriers helps us understand the depth and character of post–Civil War political engagement, a subject we will soon explore in a variety of ways. For the moment, though, we must return to the war and its immediate aftermath, to examine the incontestably political institutions to which partisan combat had traditionally been confined.

THE POLITICAL PROCESS

The survival of older, antipolitical values through the heat of the Civil War years, and the various manifestations of partisan sentiment that occurred outside the aegis of the political parties, raise the question of how the parties and the electoral process functioned in northern communities during and immediately after the war. The system of nominating caucuses and conventions, campaign clubs and rallies, pre-election canvassing and election-day treating was not disrupted by the war, and we have already seen that partisan editorial exhortation continued unabated. The latter, indeed, reached new levels of vituperation, justified by the urgency of the civil crisis. Democrats were now a traitorous opposition, in league with "bushwackers and guerrillas" determined to destroy the Union. Republicans were the usurpers of liberties once promised by a trampled Constitution.[56] We have already suggested that these editorial postures were by no means ludicrous—that many civilians would have found in them a reasonable call to political combat. How, in fact, did they respond?

Curiously, this heightened partisan rhetoric did not bring more delegates to party caucuses or conventions in our four northern communities. The war had invigorated the public forum in many ways, but its effect on the candidate nomination process was negligible. It is understandable, perhaps, that in Republican-dominated Greenfield only two dozen Democrats attended a county convention in the fall of 1865, but turnout was not significantly higher at Republican conventions. A year earlier, in the midst of war and the presidential campaign, only fifty-three Republicans had appeared to nominate candidates for local office.[57] In Marion, the *Democratic Mirror* claimed that only one township other than Marion itself was fully represented at the Republican county convention of August 1865, while three townships failed to send a single delegate.[58] This kind of underrepresentation was common before the war, but in Dubuque the nominating process had visibly atrophied, even among the majority Democrats. In 1864, the Dubuque County Democratic Committee was "so dilatory" in responding to instructions from the state committee that the party's congressional nominating convention had to be delayed. A year later, the same delegates were used for both township and county conventions in order to "save the trouble of new primary meetings," and so few delegates showed up at the latter that the convention resolved that "each person present [be] allowed to participate in the deliberations."[59] Candidacies were still sought and contested, but, clearly, wartime political energies had not made this part of the political process more interesting to party activists.

Nor, we might note, did the war stimulate significant attendance at various ad hoc citizens' meetings that lay, formally at least, outside the political process. Diarists such as William B. Pratt and William G. Markham report having attended "war meetings" in their towns in 1861 and 1862, and it is likely that these meetings, which were held all across the Union, were well attended during the urgencies of the war's early stages.[60] There are no such entries in their diaries after 1862, however, and in our towns the meetings held in 1864 and 1865 were very poorly attended, even when their purpose was to authorize the raising and allocation of funds. In Greenfield, for example, a meeting was held in the summer of 1864, in part to raise six thousand dollars for activities related to filling the town's quota for troops. Only thirteen men and two women were present when the meeting started and when it reached its last agenda item, a proposal to provide five hundred dollars for the benefit of the wives of two drafted men, the vote was two in favor and one against.[61] Shortly after the war ended, Kingston's citizens met to authorize the raising of one thousand dollars in taxes to apply to the corporation's debt. The meeting, according to the *Kingston Argus*, "did not command much attention, there being only about 80 votes taken, of which all but 16 were against the proposition."[62] Public meetings of this sort were in decline all across America, and in the years to come they would play only a small role in civic affairs. What is perhaps surprising is that this kind of public forum was only temporarily reinvigorated by the outbreak of the Civil War. The certainty of outcomes may have discouraged interest and attendance in some places. In any case, by the war's end the citizens' meeting was attracting very little public participation.

Delegates may have neglected even more than formerly their parties' nominating conventions, and citizens may have been harder to attract to nonpartisan public meetings, but people continued to attend partisan campaign rallies. This was particularly evident in the presidential contest of 1864, which galvanized so much feeling about the war itself. No less than in 1860, this election was focused on and driven by the one great issue, which the previous four years had made much more tangible and personal for many American families. Em Andrews was one of many soldiers' wives who attended rallies in support of their absent husbands, and many brought their children as well. Before the war, the presence of women and children at party rallies had provided opposing editors with the opportunity of deflating claims of massive turnouts of voting citizens; now it was taken as evidence of broad popular support for one's own party on the great issue of war and peace. In 1864, Kingston's Democrats formed a juvenile McClellan Club for boys between twelve and sixteen, and the Dubuque Republican paper would boast that "hundreds of ladies were present" among the large crowd that gave three cheers for "the cause, the country, the Government, the President."[63] A visiting French aristocrat, Ernest Duvergier de Hauranne (who, unlike his more famous predecessor, Alexis de Tocqueville, actually witnessed an American election), was struck by the size, the energy, and even the duration of American political rallies. In his published notes and reflections, Duvergier de Hauranne describes in detail several mass rallies. The Louisville audience of a Democratic orator "shivered with pleasure" at his robust and, to the Frenchman, vulgar performance. "After the meeting there was prolonged cheering. . . . A number of smaller meetings were being held in the streets. Speeches were made beside the bonfires, and the whole city resounded all night long with cheers for McClellan." At a massive Unionist rally in New York, the crowds of people who could not get into Cooper Union to hear the official speeches cheered "loudly and continually" at a dozen volunteer speakers who addressed them from stands erected in the square. This was the Republicans' response to the "giant Democratic meeting in Union Square" held a week earlier.[64] Editors could still claim that their opponents' rallies had "fizzled," but the 1864 presidential campaign appears to have attracted crowds as large—and as intense—as any previous election, even with so many young men away at war.

Having questioned the meaning of the campaign spectacle in earlier elections, we can and should question it here as well, even in the grimmer context of a long and bloody civil war. We can note, for example, that some rallies did appear to "fizzle," and that campaign clubs did not always create or sustain enthusiasm. William B. Pratt, for example, wrote frequently in his diary of unsuccessful McClellan Club meetings ("McClellan Club was not spirited in the evening," "McClellan Club didn't amount to much," "McClellan Club pretty dull") in his predominantly Democratic town.[65] In his broader account of the 1864 election, Duvergier de Hauranne made a different point, stressing the shallowness of American political engagement and the mere theatricality of mass rallies. "The great evil of American democracy," he had written in the context of the precampaign nominating conventions, "is the apathy of the general public." "It is a well-known fact," he continued, "and one acknowledged by the Americans themselves, that one leaves politics to the intriguers and underlings, and people make a boast, almost a virtue, of not getting involved," the politics of the republic thereby falling into the hands of those "who make a career out of it."[66] This judgment was reinforced by later observations of the campaign rallies, which consisted largely of fireworks, hired bands and marching units, and vulgar, simplistic, and inflammatory speeches only loosely connected to public policy and designed primarily to entertain a plebeian crowd. "If you are loyal," shouted the speaker (Richard James Oglesby, who was about to be elected governor of Illinois!) to a rally in Galena, "do as I do, go straight to the Copperheads, to the traitors, and tell them: 'Sir, you are a miserable creature, a knave, a wretch, and a damned thief!' As for myself, I say to their face: 'Yes sir, I hope you will be hanged!' If these creatures try to enter the voting booth, we will shoot them!"[67] "[T]he American people, especially

here in the West, love these raw, bloody slabs of butcher's meat," observed
Duvergier de Hauranne, who understood such performances as a relatively
harmless game, Americans knowing well "how to behave peaceably while ut-
tering bloodthirsty words."[68] Unfortunately, it made politics into a game, too,
for the rallies were unaccompanied by more serious events or reflections.
"When one has attended two or three meetings of each party," he wrote, "one
has examined the nation's politics as deeply as most of its citizens have done."[69]

Duvergier de Hauranne himself seriously analyzed the election and its relation to the prospects for war, peace, and the postwar shape of the American
republic. Did he imagine himself to be the only person in America to do so?
This insightful French visitor could perceive much of the American elephant,
but understandably focused his description on those parts of the beast that
were most novel to him and his European readers. Earlier we argued that there
were many different forms and degrees of political engagement, and this no
doubt remained true of the Civil War years. What Duvergier de Hauranne
missed, or chose not to emphasize, were more serious understandings of the
election, on the part of those who did not shout themselves hoarse or drink
themselves silly at mass political rallies, and, indeed, on the part of some of
those who did. These understandings did not need to be complex to be deeply
felt. Our argument here is that Americans continued to approach (and stand
apart from) politics in very different ways, but that the great civil crisis of the
1860s intensified political feelings among many who might otherwise have
participated lightly, thoughtlessly, or not at all. Em Andrews obviously had
fun at Republican rallies. She also knew that the 1864 election bore a serious
relation to her husband's life, her future, and the future of her country.

We can gain additional perspective on the war's effects on political engagement by turning again (and not for the last time) to testimony recorded by
state legislatures with respect to disputed elections. There were many such
elections during the war years in many states, and legislative committees sometimes examined hundreds of voters in a single election district, asking questions and recording responses that take us closer to the minds of ordinary
citizens as they approached the polls and cast their ballots. The circumstances
could be unusual, but the voters who were examined included many who we
should take to have been typical of those who voted in elections, disputed or
not, all across the country. Most strikingly, these interviews reveal something
of the passion aroused by the war and turned toward partisan conflict. They
also reveal variations in political engagement, and of the reasons why criticisms
of the American electorate such as Duvergier de Hauranne's cannot be simply
dismissed.

In border and frontier states, elections were sometimes disputed because of
the intervention of Union soldiers, some of whom expressed their partisan
commitment in brutally explicit ways. In Kentucky, for example, a Madison
County election judge named L. G. Witt testified to having been approached

by Union officers with a list of seventy names of men who should not be allowed to vote. Any who did, he was told, "would be a dead man or [Witt] himself would be hauled to town a dead man." The soldiers stayed at the polling place to make sure their orders were obeyed. William Willis may or may not have been on the list, but when he heard the soldiers "damning and cursing all persons who had voted [the Democratic] ticket," he returned home without having voted. In Pendleton and other counties voters were interrogated and sometimes prevented from casting ballots: T. M. Arnold was told "I had better-go-a-fishing"; John Arnold complained, "I was never at an election before where they had muskets and bayonets."[70] There were troops at the polls in California, too. Jesse Stark was a cattleman who sold beef to the army in Tulare County. When he declined to vote on grounds that he was not a resident, he was instructed to do so by Sergeant J. H. Gordon, who also was an election inspector. Gordon added a civics lesson: "You are a hell of a man; don't want to vote to sustain the laws and Constitution of the United States, and getting rich off the Government. We'll sell you out of this business, and buy beef from some man that will vote." Under intense questioning from the legislative committee, Gordon acknowledged that he had also said something about killing Stark's cattle if he did not vote: "Yes, Sir, but it was all said in a jocular way."[71] There may well have been more posturing than substance in all these threats (there is no indication, though, that Stark had laughed at Gordon's joke), but the presence of armed and highly partisan soldiers at American polling places was a new kind of menace, and one we cannot understand without reference to feelings stirred by the war. It was an experience that voters remembered for the rest of their lives.

No troops patrolled the polls in New York State during the Civil War. Nonetheless, elections there were occasions for the display of partisan conviction and contempt for the "enemy" that was not manifested in earlier contests. A state senatorial election in 1863 in Sullivan County, for example, brought to the surface a secretive Loyal League, whose members had pledged to support only candidates who were zealous Unionists. The Loyal League did not bring muskets and bayonets to the polls, but some members were war veterans who were quite vocal about what was at stake even in this state election. Charles Gordon, a Democrat before the war, had returned from the army and "would see all the democrats in hell before he would vote for one of them." Edward Hubert, "a black republican," was "almost always talking about politics," according to his neighbor's testimony, "and when he gets to talking with anybody, he goes to quarreling." When someone reminded Thomas Sheridan that he had not been naturalized as a citizen and could not vote, he shot back, "yes, I am, going in the army made me one." The Democrats of Sullivan County were no less hesitant to be heard. John Utter approached the polls, "damning the abolitionists strongly" as he walked. William Sullivan was heard at the polls exclaiming that he was "getting tired of living under this damned black republican administration." Earlier, he had refused the offer of Republican tick-ets from his former employer, Peter Miller, who also described Sullivan as a man who "talked a good deal on politics, more than I want a man to talk who is working for me."[72]

Nor was the army the only source of organized partisan intimidation. In the third election district of the ninth ward of the city of Albany, David Griffin, a twenty-seven-year-old grocer and Democratic election inspector, appointed Eugene Sweeney, James Fahey, George Searls, James Bemis, and Michael McAuliff, all Irish Americans, Democrats, and butchers, as "special constables" to keep order at the 1864 election. The order they kept was of a particular kind. According to Republican witnesses, the "greasy butchers" and several dozen confederates formed a wedge every time someone with a white (Union) ticket approached the polls. Jacob Vogle, a tailor, tried to get through this wedge two or three times in the morning, and his employer urged him to try again in the afternoon, this time by hiding his ballot inside a yellow (Demo-cratic) ticket. When he did so, one of the butchers came up to him, opened the ballot, "tore it up, threw it in the dirt, [and] gave me another yellow ticket." Vogle was "afraid they would cut me in pieces," and went home without voting. "I thought I had got enough," he concluded. An elderly man named Rull had much the same experience. Escorted to the polls by John McGoan, Rull was spattered with mud from head to foot by "that damned crew of bloody, greasy, butchers." Unable to get through to vote, Rull returned home, and McGoan "had to go away, just as I came, and have had a sore heart ever since."[73]

In their testimony to the legislative committee, the ninth-ward Democrats remained defiant at what they had done, shrugging off the riot that eventually brought Mayor Perry and the police to the district in a futile (and possibly half-hearted) effort to open the polls. Did Griffin appoint the butchers under the "common law of the ninth ward?" asked the Republican counsel. "Uncommon law if you choose to call it so," Griffin responded, "it is claimed by some of our particular friends that we have uncommon laws here." James Fahey, when his term came to testify, denied having struck a Republican voter with a club, but admitted having hit him with his fist, "ten times, more or less." This inci-dent had occurred while he was on "parole" from his duties as a special consta-ble to get a drink. "Q: You wanted a drink of water? A: I don't know whether I drank water or anything else . . . as long as I pay for it, I can drink what I have a mind to." Fahey, who admitted to a record of arrests for assault and burglary, beat up this same would-be voter for trying to have him arrested. "Q: Who paroled you this time? A: Myself, as usual. Q: How long were you paroled? A: I guess I was paroled a couple of hours then; I was peddling tickets through the crowd."[74]

Party thugs had for some time been a fixture of American elections, particu-larly in cities, and still more so in working-class city wards characterized by the close proximity of different ethnic groups. It was no coincidence that Fahey's target was a German; indeed, the Irish butchers frequently yelled, "Take that Dutch son of a bitch and pull him out of the window," as some voters, having somehow evaded the wedge, leaned in to deposit their ballots. This was all quite traditional. But just as some of the Civil War–era partisan editors in our representative towns applauded politically motivated scuffles in the streets, as they had not done before and would not do again, so too did Albany's ninth-ward Democrats feel emboldened, and even legitimized, by the national crisis, and most especially by the Republican threat to white men's rule. Not only did they "hurrah for Little Mac," but they railed against anyone who endorsed the Emancipation Proclamation, directly or by his vote. When James Parrott, a twenty-nine-year-old merchant tried to vote, and to hand in eleven Union ballots from soldiers in the field, the butchers made their wedge and blocked him three times, calling out, "Kill the black son of a bitch." Their harangue against the "black Republicans" and the "negurs" continued all day. When Mayor Perry arrived, the butchers warned him to "remember, we have Seymour for governor, yet, and you had better be careful."[75]

The war and its issues are laced through this election-day testimony. Although all elections, from the 1830s through the 1890s, manifested acerbic and even violent partisan conflict, at no other time does the election testimony we have read give such clear evidence of voters speaking out in substantive—if crude and simple—terms about what they and their parties stood for. And yet this same Civil War–era testimony also provides evidence of indifference to party tickets and platforms. For some partisan voters the party "package" was enough, and did not necessitate much thought or knowledge of candidates or of specific issues or events. Samuel Cunningham of New York probably spoke for many Republicans: "I am Union; don't know anything about anything but Union; I am all Union from head to foot. . . . I am down on copperheads as anybody ought to be." Leonard Fisher, a forty-six-year-old cabinetmaker, was asked for whom he had wished to vote. "Lincoln was my man," Fisher replied. "Q: Did you want to vote for anybody else? A: No, sir. . . . Q: What names were on those tickets? A: Well, you ask me a hard question, for I cannot read English." When asked who he had wished to vote for in the state assembly race, the cabinetmaker, who had gotten his tickets from a blacksmith named Henry Fink and knew they "were all right," answered with his own version of the presidential synthesis, "Well, I was for Lincoln." John Boss also knew that Lincoln was his candidate, and could add no other information about his Union ticket. Democrats, too, in no small number combined fervent partisanship with ignorance of party tickets. Joseph Aresles did not open his ticket. Dennis Madigan knew that McClellan and Pendleton were his men (Madigan, unlike Boss, knew the name of his party's vice-presidential candidate) and rested content, as had Leonard Fisher, that a "reliable" gentleman had given him a straight Democratic ballot."[76]

The Civil War brought energy and ultimately a kind of stability to the American political system. The Manichaean partisan worldview fostered by the war persisted for many years after the return of peace, and it is clear that the long and bitter civil crisis had deepened the Republican and Democratic allegiance of many Americans. It did so, however, in a way that fostered the reassertion of traditional boundaries between political, religious, and civic institutions in American communities, and that encouraged a less passionate and even less attentive political engagement on the part of individual citizens. Political scientists have used the term "retrospective voting" to describe a process by which voters respond less to new issues, policy proposals, and party tickets than to widely shared understandings of each party's past performance—its established policy orientation and track record—as they decide among candidates and form partisan allegiances.[77] Obviously, this is a process that tends toward stable party affiliation and, a little less obviously, that frees voters from active engagement in ongoing political debate. Their important evaluations and decisions having already been made, voters of this sort need not spend much time and effort informing themselves about the circumstances peculiar to any current election. The "package" offered by nineteenth-century political parties in an age of small government encouraged retrospective voting; indeed, we would argue that it offered a particularly appealing, folkloric form of retrospection, based as much on the rhetoric and symbols as on the substantive past performance of each party. And to rhetoric and symbols already in place the Civil War added its own remarkably compelling ones: beginning soon after the war, Republicans missed few opportunities to "wave the bloody shirt," northern Democrats to affirm liberty and white man's rule, southern Democrats to bemoan oppression and "the lost cause." Will you give "bushwhackers and guerrillas your votes?" asked the *Marion Independent* as the 1865 election approached. The *Dubuque Daily Times* defined "The Issue" in a similar way in 1866: "The political strife of today presents itself based on precisely the same general principles upon which we fought at the ballot box in the fall of 1860. . . . The issue is plain and simple—shall treason be made odious? On this issue prepare your ballots."[78] Appeals of this sort continued long after the threat of treason had been erased. Memory was becoming a principal mode of political mobilization, a condition most strikingly illustrated by the invention of the term "Grand Old Party" in 1876 to describe an institution just twenty-two years old. Clearly intended to associate the Republican Party with the Grand Army of the Republic, it also invited voters to continue to look backward to the party's great achievement, and to invest the GOP with a spurious antiquity that itself could become a focus of veneration. Under such conditions as the memory of the war provided, there was no better strategy for maintaining voter allegiance. It is an interesting contrast to later attempts by political parties who could no longer draw upon this memory to attract voters to a New Freedom, a New Deal, or a New Frontier.

The established postures of each party, we would reemphasize, demanded little of their loyal voters besides voting itself. In Philadelphia, John Chatham fought his way through Democratic shoulder hitters to deposit his Republican ballot in 1869. "For whom did you intend to vote for Senator?" he was asked during a later hearing. "I wanted to vote the whole ticket through; the Union ticket." "Q: You mean the Republican ticket? A: Yes, sir. . . . Q: Who was on it for Senator? A: I cannot remember that. . . . I have given it no attention since."[79] Chatham was certainly a committed Republican voter, but he was not, and in his mind did not need to be, an actively informed one. It was enough, four years after Appomattox, to vote the "Union" ticket. Nearly twenty years after that Joseph Eisenhower voted "the black Republican straight ticket," and Thomas Bringhurst, who identified himself as "a soldier and a Republican," voted the Republican ticket "as a good soldier would do, always."[80] Were no postwar issues involved in their decisions? The Union had long since been secured. But by saving it again and again at the polls, Chatham, Eisenhower, Bringhurst, and many voters like them justified a significant withdrawal from the continuing political issues of the postwar world.

THE DEVELOPING STATE

We do not wish to say that post–Civil War voters looked only to the past. There were challenges to retrospective voting in the Gilded Age, and the most important was the appearance of new and urgent public issues. Most obvious among them in the immediate aftermath of the war were national reintegration and the civil status of freemen, but even before these were settled (or, perhaps more accurately, removed from the national policy arena), Americans had to deal with the more enduring issues of taxation and debt. Along with the bigger government, expanding patronage, and deeper corruption that frequently accompanied them, taxation and debt directed the attention of citizens to the present and future, to the sins of the party in power, and to the outcries of the opposition. And unlike Reconstruction and the new amendments to the Constitution, the expenses and debt incurred during the war threatened the identification Republicans wished to secure to themselves as the party of Union and the custodians of glorious memory. The "three thousand million" that had to be paid back with interest of 5 or 6 percent, along with a government and an army of unprecedented size, gave new force to the "grammar of corruption" that had qualified the allegiance of many voters even in the days when the government spent most of its time and money delivering the mail. If Republicans wished to retain power they would have to address the new issues of taxation and debt, and the reinvigorated older issue of public corruption. All of these raised the danger of dislodging voters, and middle-class voters in particular, from their loyal adherence to the "Grand Old Party."

The potential of these issues for destabilizing the parties was understood even during the war by Republicans and Democrats alike. For northern Democrats it was an opportunity, and they pitched their appeal to both middle-class and working-class voters. Raising great sums of money, the *Dubuque Herald* editor recognized, "is comparatively a new question with the American people," and would result inevitably in "the reckless extravagance which pervades every department of the Federal Government." Democratic newspapers missed no opportunities, large or small, to provide details of departments of government "rotten with corruption," government officials "hauled up for robbing the 'people's Treasury,' " and "heaps of tax collectors" as busy as bees.[81] To make the point that the "people—the working men and taxpayers"—footed the bills, editors cited the unimaginable proportions the national debt had reached, and also the myriad ways in which it would touch the average citizen. In 1864, the *Kingston Argus* gave space to a submission by "A Workingman," entitled "Lincoln Taxation," which began with a list: "Taxes on my bread, Taxes on my butter / Taxes on my salt, Taxes on my supper / Taxes on my tea, Taxes on my coffee / Taxes on molasses, Taxes on my barley . . ." For twenty-six lines "A Workingman" continued his enumeration, reminding readers of the *Argus* that "the corrupt shoddy band" of Republicans taxed all who would "take snuff, have a puff, wear boots, drawers or coats, use a scissors or a shaving brush." The *Dubuque Herald* used the same approach. The editor called attention to yet another revenue bill in June 1864, this one imposing a one-cent tax on every box containing one hundred matches: "What a delightful country this will be to live in, after a while. A manufactory that turns out several thousand boxes of matches a day will have to employ an extra force of hands to stick on revenue stamps."[82]

The consequences of such taxes "to a free people," who "heretofore have not known anything about taxation," were not only high costs, but tyranny (the *Argus* estimated that the poor and middle class paid one quarter or a third of all they earned to support the Government: "How long can they do this?").[83] Tax-gatherers with "inquisitorial powers" might well invade businesses and homes to make their own estimate of what each person owned and owed. Given the propensity of the Lincoln administration to suspend civil liberties, what recourse would a citizen have against these "odious persons"?[84]

When the war ended, Democrats stepped up the pace. The *Marion Democratic Mirror* selected as the title of an article about the finances of the national government "Can We Bear More Debt?" The *Kingston Argus* asked taxpayers to remember the legacy of the Radical Republican Congress of 1866: "Freedmen's Bureau $7,000,000; National Bank Interest $30,000,000; Increased Revenue $8,000,000; Education Bureau $5,000,000; Mississippi and Yazoo job $50,000,000; and Northern Pacific Railroad subsidy $60,000,000." The bloated government, moreover, was attracting to Washington hordes of job seekers and, more ominously, a new and odious creature, the lobbyist. The Treasury Department, reported the *Dubuque Herald*, had on file thirty thousand applications for clerkships, with another three hundred arriving each week. And the "Lobbying Business" was becoming the most lucrative trade in the capital, promising cynical men who were willing to bribe congressmen an income of ten thousand dollars a year or more. Unless these tendencies were soon checked, Democrats warned, the Leviathan would destroy liberty as it made a mockery of democracy.[85]

During the war, Republicans were able to deflect these attacks by emphasizing that the revenues that were raised were spent to save the Union. Nations should avoid debt, if possible, the *Greenfield Gazette and Courier* editor wrote, "but there are much greater calamities," in this case the triumph of the great evils of disunion and slavery. Kingston's Republican paper was equally forceful: taxpayers should pay their assessments without complaint because they know that others had given not only "their services and means, but also their lives" to keep the nation together. A permanent Union, after all, was a "jewel above all price and cheap at any cost." A soldier stationed in Virginia was allowed the definitive characterization of those who would rob the government (and its fighting men) of the means of defending themselves and the United States against secessionists. The soldier wrote in the *Gazette and Courier* shortly before the election of 1864 that he could not bear to listen to "men who have staid at home, filled their pockets with greenback profits of the war, and paid paltry taxes. . . . I could shoot such men with a calmer conscience than I could fire upon an avowed rebel."[86]

Republicans also argued that the war could be financed without significant sacrifice by most Americans.[87] Through most of the war, as Heather Cox Richardson has recently shown, the Lincoln administration financed the government largely by borrowing money (with several bond issues) and by using tariff revenues.[88] By deferring the payments, our Republican editors argued, the secretary of the treasury has drastically diminished (and perhaps eliminated) the pain, for when the rebellion is crushed "our country will develop in material power more rapidly than ever before . . . and the treasures spent in [the war's] prosecution will return to us with interest." Given an increasing rate of population, and national capital growing more than four-and-a-half times as fast as the debt, it will take "but a fraction of our property" to eliminate within a few years all the funds that had been borrowed.[89] Dismissing "fainthearted patriotism, . . . inexcusable ignorance or wanton misrepresentation," the editor of the *Kingston Democratic Journal* wrote for all of his Republican colleagues: "We can pay every dollar we spend."[90] When the war ended the refrain remained the same. Legitimately incurred, the debt "involves no burdens and imposes no legacy on the masses." The duties were equitable, and reached "no man's domicile, no widow's cottage, no son or daughter of toil in field or worship."[91] The Republicans were stretching the truth here, but they were essentially correct. Much as they had promised, tariffs and economic growth did make it relatively easy to extinguish the debt.

Even while defending their aggressive wartime fiscal program, the Republicans took pains to present themselves as champions of economy in government, low taxes, and fiscal responsibility. Indeed, Republican editors made strenuous efforts to lay blame for the war debt at the door of the Democrats. The complicity of northern Copperheads with the rebels, the *Kingston Democratic Journal* explained, "has added millions unnecessarily" to the debt, forcing Republicans "to stay this waste of wealth and carnival of blood." After the war was over, the editor of the *Journal* announced that "there is no prospect that the debt will be further increased." The Democrats, he observed, were responsible for a bill to increase the salary of congressmen by two thousand dollars a year. Nearly every Republican in the body, the editor assured his readers, had declined to avail himself of the pay. In a strategy that would become widespread in the 1870s, the *Journal* shrewdly provided evidence of the extravagance of Democrats who controlled county, city, and state offices. An unprecedented thirteen-part series that ran from November 1865 to March 1866 documented the responsibility of the Democratic "Ring" in the board of supervisors for the Ulster County debt. Other editors followed suit, drawing heavily, when the opportunity presented itself, on the Democratic Tweed Ring scandal in New York City. Strategies of this sort allowed Republicans to vie with Democrats for the mantle of "reform and retrenchment."[92]

Addressing the charges of extravagance and big-government tyranny in this way also permitted Republicans to keep their voters focused on the Civil War and the rescue of the Union from rebels and northern Copperheads. But so, too, and quite brilliantly, did a new Federal spending program, the granting of pensions to Civil War veterans and their families. As Theda Skocpol has shown, the pension program, first instituted by Congress in 1862 for soldiers disabled or killed as a direct consequence of military duty, became in the ensuing decades a rather generous old-age pension program available to one million Americans. From 1880 to 1910 the national government devoted over one-quarter of its expenditures to pensions, granting them to virtually any soldier's family willing to make a claim. Surpluses from tariffs covered most of the costs.[93] The pension programs were at once a striking innovation and an inducement to retrospective voting, enlarging the role of the national government in an entirely new way, but also keeping the Civil War sharply in focus for four decades.

No new taxes were levied to pay for the pensions, and their administration did not add appreciably to the size of the government bureaucracy; yet, they too were subjected to withering attacks from "good government" reformers who documented cases of incompetence, cronyism, and dishonesty in the granting of awards, and who challenged even the modest growth of an arrogant

Federal bureaucracy. Skocpol links disgust with this system to the removal of social welfare from politics in the late nineteenth century. No less than the issues of public debt and taxation, soldiers' pensions reveal the Civil War's dual political legacy. On the one hand, the war froze the vast majority of voters in place as adherents to the party that had saved the Union, or to the one that had protected freedom, liberty, and white men's rule. On the other it impelled the development of a new kind of government that could unsettle voters and give them reason to do more than cast predictable, reflexive votes. How would the parties, and the people, respond to this mixture of memory and modern times?

CHAPTER 6.

People and Politics: The Urbanization of Political Consciousness

LET US AGAIN put down our political newspaper and take up a good novel. Rather, let us take up a large number of novels, good and bad, along with other sources of the type we turned to in an earlier chapter in order to gain access to the larger world beyond politics. Can we obtain from them a useful perspective on popular attitudes toward politics and public life during the years following the war? Do novels, diaries, and other "nonpolitical" sources help us understand the force of "memory" and of "modern times" on the political consciousness of ordinary American citizens? The Civil War, as we have seen, did not change the partisan institutions and practices that had been organizing electoral campaigns since the age of Tippecanoe. What it did change was the feeling Americans brought to the polls and to public discourse. How durable was that change? And how might it have been reinforced (or otherwise affected) by the new national programs that gave the Federal government a somewhat larger presence in people's lives?

POLITICIZING THE AMERICAN PANORAMA

Civil War and postwar fictions point in several ways to a significant and enduring expansion of political consciousness in America. Most obvious, perhaps, is the increasing number and weight (within our sample of a vast literature) of novels that are essentially and even entirely political. We encountered only a small number of political novels before the war, and very few indeed if we exclude novels about slavery or intemperance that make little reference to parties, politicians, and the political process. During and after the war, and particularly after 1880 or so, books that focus on public issues *and* politics are much more easily located. Among our best- and better-sellers, and in our sample of imprints, are, for example: Albion Turgee's widely read *A Fool's Errand* (1880), a fictional assessment of Reconstruction and of the politics that underlay its failures; George Koehler's *Nick Putzel; or, Arthur Gurney's Ruin* (1881), which attacks saloon keepers and other corrupting forces in American politics; John Hay's *The Bread-Winners: A Social Study* (1884), a story involving the defeat of labor reform by dishonest politicians and a neglectful citizenry; Edward P. Roe's *An Original Belle* (1885), a romantic novel set within the context of the

Civil War and the New York City draft riots of 1863; Thomas Norwood's *Plutocracy; or, American White Slavery* (1888), a populist tract within the shell of a novel; Edward Bellamy's *Looking Backward, 2000–1887* (1888), the extraordinarily influential socialist Utopian novel (like Norwood's book, a tract wrapped in a story); Lewis H. Watson's *Not to the Swift: A Tale of Two Continents* (1891), a delightfully preposterous tale of Jesuit intrigue in American politics (the Jesuits cause the Civil War!); and David Ross Locke's *The Demagogue: A Political Novel* (1891), which delivers the attack on political ambition and demagoguery promised in the title. All of these follow upon, and a few appear to have been inspired by, the satirical work that gave this era its lasting name and image, Mark Twain and Charles Dudley Warner's 1873 novel of greed, deceit, and political corruption, *The Gilded Age*.[1]

The appearance of a new or newly expanded fictional genre of political novels is, however, only part of the story. Even in novels that we would not describe as political, there is a more frequent occurrence than in earlier years of references to political matters. Some of them, to be sure, are fleeting or light, such as the mention of the silver issue in Robert Lee Tyler's western-adventure story, *A Yale Man*. "I had paid no attention to the silver agitation in public affairs," confesses the protagonist, Ned Minturn, before heading west to see what he can make of an apparently worthless silver mine he had inherited.[2] This is the only political reference in a long and typically complicated tale, and we might well be justified in dismissing it entirely were it not for the fact that the novel appeared in 1896, a year in which the "silver agitation" was in the forefront of political affairs. Similarly, Charles W. Jay's tales of life in northern Michigan begins by telling his readers that the book is worth less than the price they paid for it, "But I've got your money, and what are you going to do about it?"[3] Jay's book was published in 1874, and the author assumed that most of his readers would understand and laugh at the reference to the famous line put in Boss Tweed's mouth by the cartoonist Thomas Nast a few years earlier. Topicality of this sort appears in several apolitical novels, as do references to ward politicians, elections, and occasionally even a party caucus. The latter occurs, for example, in a recounting by two local residents of the previous year's events in their New England town (the novel is Edward Everett Hale's *Mr. Tangier's Vacation*), and is placed within the communal calendar in a manner that will be familiar to us: "They told of the political caucus in the fall, when General Logan spoke to the whole county. They told of the cattle show in the autumn; and this seemed to be, on the whole, the great social event of the year."[4]

The thread of politics is visible in more serious fiction, too, and we may take *The Rise of Silas Lapham* as an excellent example of how post–Civil War writers were inclined to draw upon public affairs in novels that were not about politics. There are no politicians in William Dean Howells's story of class ambition and moral choice, but on one or two occasions men "talk politics" in the foreground rather than in the background, and, unlike the several antebellum novels in which these kinds of conversations occur, we do hear what they are saying. At the dinner Bromfield Corey gives for Silas Lapham, for example, the conversation turns to heroism, and the absence of any current occasion for its exercise. "But why shouldn't civil service reform, and the resumption of specie payment, and a tariff for revenue only, inspire heroes?" asks Corey. The question is facetious, and Corey is ignored, but Silas, a war veteran, follows it up with a comment on wartime heroism itself, noting that motives for enlisting in the Civil War armies were not always admirable. Earlier, he had bored Tom Corey by expressing disappointment that the Republican Party could do no more than wave the bloody shirt ("Seems to me if our party hain't got any other stock in trade, we better shut up shop altogether"), and by discoursing on a variety of political matters as he scanned the newspaper. Howells is careful to give Lapham and the other men and women of the novel an apolitical cast. Silas reads the paper, for example, as part of his daily strategy to get "a complete rest from business," and to "give his mind a rest."[5] Political questions do not enter the action of the novel in any way. But civil service reform, and the tariff, and the lingering meanings of the war are there, if only for well-to-do and potentially powerful characters to make less of than their author and his readers might wish. Topical political details, however few and fleeting, give a slightly different tone and meaning to the characters' private preoccupations.

The more frequent occurrence of both topical political references and sustained political discourse in Civil War and post–Civil War fiction suggests that American writers perceived an increased attentiveness to political affairs among their readership in the decades that followed the firing on Fort Sumter. The relation between what appeared in novels and stories and what occurred in popular political consciousness is, however, not a simple one, and comparisons between the fictions of different time periods are further complicated by changes in literary fashion and authorial attitudes and styles. It is respect for these complications that prevents us from making precise quantitative comparisons between the two eras, or from making bolder claims about the meaning of the patterns we do describe. Apart from these considerations, we must qualify the apparent shift toward a more politicized American fiction with several closer observations about the Civil War and postwar novels and stories. We should note, for example, that some retrospective references to the war and its politics convey a falling-off of political ideas, energies, and commitment since the resolution of the great crisis. In *The Rise of Silas Lapham*, as we have seen, Bromfield Corey mocks contemporary issues as unheroic, while Silas himself longs to get beyond the waving of the bloody shirt. In *Chimes from a Jester's Bells*, Robert Burdette describes a "very pleasant evening" spent by Mustapha, a Republican of "the deepest dye," and Ben, a "hickory Democrat," who amused themselves talking about politics that would have bitterly divided them when, years earlier, Mustapha had been an abolitionist and Ben a slave owner.[6] We should note also that many fictional treatments of the Civil War and its era focus upon the war itself and not on political issues. This is most famously the case with the best of the nineteenth-century Civil War novels, Stephen Crane's *The Red Badge of Courage*, in which the war is hardly a public event at all, but the private testing-field of a single young soldier who loses and finds himself amidst its hardships and dangers.[7] Crane's novel is exceptional, but its subordination of the political dimensions of the conflict to the more purely military—and of the public to the private—is not. It can be found, for example, in Edward P. Roe's *An Original Belle*, the heroine of which is stimulated by the challenge of the war to find a more serious purpose than the conventions of genteel social life in New York City. That purpose is not a political one; indeed, it seems to consist of little more than holding her suitor to a high standard of personal heroism, a standard this young civilian has a great deal of trouble meeting until the draft riots of 1863 give him his opportunity to display a selfless valor. The war and the riots are excellent vehicles for the playing out of this domestic drama, but they are little more than that.[8]

The continuing presence of the Civil War in American fiction, therefore, did not in itself contribute to, nor did it necessarily reflect, a heightened awareness of public issues—just as retrospective voting did not encourage continuing political engagement beyond the reliable casting of a partisan vote. We should note in this connection that the privatization of the war by Crane, Roe, and other authors corresponds to a shift within our sample of novels in the role of public service as a background motif signifying success or high social standing. Several of our antebellum novels include references to a seat in Congress or in the governor's mansion as the capstone of a successful career (for men we do not see running for or serving in office), but in later years this motif quietly disappears, Public Man fading even from the background of novels of bourgeois private life, despite the many real-life instances of Civil War veterans who used their participation in the great crisis as springboards to a public career. Silas Lapham is a Union veteran whose worldly rise is and clearly would have remained entirely within the business world, and even his occasional political comments (the memory of war is Republican Party "stock in trade," and the party itself a "shop" to be closed if no better product can be found) are cast in the terms of the private money maker. These terms do not resemble—indeed, they are pointedly distant from—those of the orator-statesman. The war may have molded men's character, or occasioned their self-discovery, but the ensuing stories of success or failure are confined to the private spheres of business and family life.

And if there were retrospective novels of the Civil War era that did not reach a political level, there were novels of the present and future that went beyond it. In some respects there is no more political novel on our list than Edward Bellamy's futuristic fable, *Looking Backward*. Set in motion by the hero's reading in the newspaper of a strike that threatens the scheduling of his wedding (and by the consequent overdose of animal magnetism that puts him to sleep for 113 years), Bellamy's book becomes an essay demonstrating how continuing economic centralization, thus far a source of injustice and violent confrontation, can be made to perfect the economic, social, and political order in America. Many readers were attracted by Bellamy's ideas (and perhaps, too, by the charmingly conventional Victorian romance that accompanied them), but to what extent were they guided by this book through contemporary politics of economic centralization and labor-capital relations? It is perhaps too often forgotten that Bellamy sweeps aside the Constitution and all the political institutions of his own, primitive United States, in order to reach his "Nationalist" utopia of the year 2000. There is no Congress in the latter year, no state governments, no Republican and Democratic parties, no continuing political debate; nothing, in fact, except a vague and hasty historical sketch on how Dr. Leete's world emerged from Julian West's to connect Nationalism to the real politics of the late 1880s. "With the exception of this fundamental law, which is indeed merely a codification of the law of nature," explains Dr. Leete, "our system depends in no particular upon legislation."[9] It does depend upon voting, but not in domains that nineteenth-century readers would have recognized as political—Americans of the year 2000 voted to award red ribbons to outstanding authors, artists, engineers, physicians, and inventors; to elect newspaper editors (who would provide them with news of their "locality, trade, or profession"); and to urge the production of specific consumer goods.[10] Intelligent readers could, if they wished, find beneath Bellamy's fantasy a set of usable ideas about late-nineteenth-century economic concentration, and along with them a justly famous metaphoric representation of inequality in American society. But *Looking Backward* is a political novel in only an indirect sense, and the same can be said of the many other utopias and pointed fantasies of the era (such as Howells's *Traveler from Altruria*, Ignatius Donnelly's *Caesar's Column*, and L. Frank Baum's *The Wizard of Oz*); they are at once political and beyond politics.[11]

Perhaps most importantly, many of the political episodes and references in Civil War and post–Civil War novels and stories are sharply critical of politics. We observed earlier that the "grammar of corruption," already widely understood and employed in the antebellum era, acquired new force in the postwar world of public debt, higher taxes, and new Federal programs. Government was still not a great force in many people's lives, but it was larger, more visible, and more consequential than it had been before, and there were well publicized scandals—Crédit Mobilier, the Tweed Ring, and others—to confirm an ever widening cynicism toward politicians at all levels, and to legitimize a growing movement on the national, state, and municipal levels for civil-service reform.[12] This cynicism is as visible in the fiction of the era as it is in the numerous discussions of patronage and venality by those who led the movement against the spoils system. It is the very mode of *The Gilded Age, Plutocracy, The Dema-*

gogue, Nick Putzel, and other political novels, and it shapes many of the political references in other works. Benjamin Perley Poore's *The West Point Cadet*, a simple adventure-romance, contains only one political statement, and it is by the villain of the piece, who announces that "I'm going to Tammany Hall, for I find that by getting into the Board of Aldermen, I can have streets opened through my up-town lots."[13]

Poore's reference to city politics, which is but one of many in our post–Civil War novels, seems to us an especially important development. Aldermen, ward leaders, saloonkeepers, and other city politicians were relatively new targets for political satirists, and they were hit fairly often by American authors. In Burdette's *Chimes from a Jester's Bells* there is a "great American bird show," which includes the City Robin, a tenacious creature who "builds his nest in the state capitol, the council chamber and other safe places, lines it with other birds' notes, and holds on to the combination with both claws."[14] Thomas Hayden Hawkins's satirical novel *Drifting* includes a "Fourth Ward politician," whose role is to embody political baseness, opportunism, and deception: "Bob aspired to great things and almost anything that there was money in." He is "the choice of the boys of his ward for governor," and dreams of the presidency. "No one knows he is assistant to Pat" at a hospital dissecting room, "or that he is the hangman at the Tombs."[15] In Hale's *Mr. Tangier's Vacation*, the protagonist is asked if New York City aldermen are "apostles of the new civilization?" "Unconscious apostles, yes," is the answer, "for even Satan serves the servants of the Lord."[16]

These are mere passing shots, but there were novels that sustained the attack on city politicians. John Hay's *The Bread-Winners* is set in a "city of two hundred thousand people, [where] two or three dozen politicians continued as before to govern it, to assess and to spend its taxes, to use it as their property and their chattel."[17] Operating a ward-based political machine for their own benefit, they are central villains of this story of thwarted reform. A number of Horatio Alger's widely read novels for boys are set in even larger cities, including New York, which Alger conventionally portrays as a threat to traditional small-town virtues of all sorts, including political ones. His first and most famous novel, *Ragged Dick*, is peppered with satiric references to New York City politics. Claiming friendship with the mayor is Dick's running joke throughout the story, and when he is invited to dinner by the kindly businessman whose son had befriended Dick, the poor bootblack is as astonished "as if he had really been invited by the Mayor to dine with him and the Board of Aldermen." There is little bite in references such as these, but Alger also wrote more darkly of city politics, linking the political process to less attractive characters such as the young tough, Micky Maguire (the foil of the tenderhearted hero). Had Maguire been fifteen years older, and had "a trifle more education, he would have interested himself in politics, and been prominent in ward meetings, and a terror to respectable voters on election day." Politics is by no means the theme of this rags-to-respectability novel, but the city is a major element, and city politics is an understood component of Ragged Dick's challenging urban world.[18] It is much more than that in George Koehler's *Nick Putzel*, in which political corruption is inextricably linked to the city saloon as its site and its source of base values. Irishman Mike O'Brien, who "smelled of liquor" and had "more the countenance of a brute than a human," ascended from railroad worker to saloonkeeper and prize-fighter before declaring his ambition for "political distinction and power" and becoming a candidate for sheriff. The title character, a German immigrant, is also a saloonkeeper, and is more important to the story in that he leads the innocent and altruistic Arthur Gurney to ruin by introducing him to a political world in which high ideals necessarily give way to intrigue, corruption, and drink. Nick, who had been a fireman, a policeman, and a city marshal, understands the method and purpose of politics in simple terms: "[I]f dem mans want to git der office, dey must shell out. . . . [D]ey can make it again ven dey gets der office." Arthur accepts Nick's method, if not his purpose, but the former is sufficient to doom him to failure and a drunkard's death.[19]

Aldermen and saloonkeepers (occasionally one and the same) made dubious apostles, as Edward Everett Hale suggested, but for many Americans they did represent the "new civilization" of growing and increasingly heterogeneous cities. Pre–Civil War urbanization had been rapid and significant, and the sins of city aldermen were even then not unknown, but continuing population concentration after the war reached thresholds that made urban politics a more compelling subject in and beyond the city, and a more persuasive emblem of the future of American democracy. Between 1860 and 1900 the proportion of urban dwellers in the American population increased from 20 percent to 40 percent, the number of cities and towns in the nation nearly quadrupled, cities with populations larger than one hundred thousand increased from nine to thirty-eight, and there appeared for the first time on the American landscape several giant metropolitan centers of a million and more inhabitants. Moreover, cities of all sizes and in all regions had become highly visible concentration points of ethnic subcommunities, many of which followed the Irish and Germans in using ward politics as a means of group and self-promotion. And, as important as ethnic groupings, were closely related class divisions, fears, and animosities, the largely native-born middle class of each city setting itself apart in a variety of ways, in sentiment and in daily life, from the predominantly and increasingly immigrant working class. As Jon Teaford has shown, the widely shared perception of municipal corruption in this era derived in part from the functional sorting out of classes and ethnic groups within city government— upper- and middle-class men continuing to occupy the mayor's chair, the leadership of various administrative departments and commissions, and a variety of professional and technical positions (engineers, teachers, librarians, and the like), while aldermen reflected the ethnic and class composition of their individual wards, most of them home to the city's working-class (and often non-Anglo-Saxon) majority. Middle-class mayors, commissioners, and functionaries, ever more imbued with Victorian notions of respectability, found it increasingly troublesome to work with ward-based politicians, and their revulsion was shared by the respectable classes outside of city government.[20] Indeed, it was shared with the world outside the city, as an urban-based national publication industry disseminated news and opinion about city life, institutions, culture—and aldermen—far and wide through books, newspapers, and magazines. What was perhaps most troubling was that it was the aldermen, usually more than the mayor, and invariably more than commissioners and civil engineers supervising parks and schools and designing roads and sewer systems, who represented the fruits of partisan electoral democracy. They and their allies ran the political parties in the wards, where elections were organized and the votes were cast. This was an American democracy whose grass roots had to push through the sidewalk cracks in places like Albany's ninth ward; or worse, in New York's "bloody ould sixth," infamous zones of poverty, vice, and alien values. Middle-class Americans were disturbed by the mere presence of these squalid wards—their power to elect city legislators threatened the political as well as the social order.[21]

The emergence of the city politician as a type or motif in writing critical of Gilded Age politics can be traced in American political humor as well as in novels. Seba Smith did not want for successors, among whom the best known were Charles Farrar Browne ("Artemus Ward"), Robert Henry Newell ("Orpheus C. Kerr"), Henry W. Shaw ("Josh Billings"), and Finley Peter Dunne ("Mr. Dooley"). Smith had focused on the spoils system and its implications, and his vehicle was the shrewdly innocent country bumpkin Jack Downing. Jack had discovered the rewards of political life on a trip to his state's capital city, but it was state and then national politics that attracted his attention, and it was in large part his unselfconscious Down East rusticity that made his political ambitions so humorously endearing. This kind of comic persona would gradually change in the age of cities and immigrants. Civil War–era and postwar humorists did not at first change the scene of their comic political sketches, or shake the countryside out of most of their characters, even while widening the range of their attacks to include city politics. It is on a Civil War battlefield, for example, that Newell comes across an ordinary, ethnically indistinct soldier who is weeping over a hollowed-out coconut shell. The soldier explains: "I took it for the skull of my brother, the Boston Alderman—it's so hard and thick."[22] There was, of course, a long tradition of comic ethnic (and racial) parody in the political press and in other media, and ethnic types were occasionally located specifically in an urban setting. But it was only toward the end of the century that Finley Peter Dunne established an enduringly popular Irish comic hero, firmly rooted behind the bar of his Chicago saloon, and deeply aware of if only occasionally implicated in the niceties of ward politics in this

Mr. Dooley, drawing by W. A. Rogers (from *Harper's Weekly*).

6.1. Mr. Dooley. Drawing by W. A. Rogers.

major American city. "I'm an honest man," Mr. Dooley contends. "I pay me taxes, when Tim Ryan isn't assessor with Grogan's boy on th' books." On the other hand, if he were elected alderman, and offered fifty thousand dollars for his vote to betray the interests of Chicago, "I'd go to Father Kelly an' ask th' prayers iv th' congregation."[23]

Dunne's Irish-American urban political world is a parochial one, responsive to the details of political friendship far more than to larger public issues. In a characteristic sketch, Mr. Dooley recalls the time when O'Brien ran for alderman, and was called on by a taxpayers' committee to ask his views on the tariff, the currency question, pensions, and the Interstate Commerce Act. O'Brien replied that his only issue "was whether little Mike Kelly will have th' bridge or not." As for the minor issues:

Anny information I possess I'll keep tucked away in this large an' commodjious mind cage, an' not be dealin' it out to th' likes iv ye. . . . What business have you got comin' roun' to my house and pryin' into my domestic affairs. . . . Tis th' intherstate commerce act now, but th' nex' thing'll be where I got th' pianny.[24]

One wonders whether it is O'Brien or the taxpayers' committee that gets the worst of this exchange, and whether the political humorists did not foster the "engaged disbelief" that permitted voters—indeed, encouraged them—to participate in political affairs. We should note in this connection that Dunne frequently satirized ordinary citizens, as "pathrites" (patriots), partisans, and voters. "Which wan iv th' distinguished bunko steerers got ye'er invalu'ble suffrage?" Mr. Dooley asks Hennessey, who responds that he has voted for Charter Haitch in the last six elections. Dooley observes that Haitch was assassinated three years earlier. "Ah, well," answers Hennessey, "he's lived that down be this time. He was a good man." Alderman O'Brien explains that hundreds of thousands of Chicago's citizens "have on'y two pleasures in life, to wur-ruk an' to vote, both of which they do at th' uniform rate iv wan dollar an' a half a day." Voters have no interest in speeches or national issues, and do not know whether O'Brien has "th' inthrests iv the toilin' masses at hear-rt or whether he wint to mass at all, at all." In the sixth ward, at least, voters "love th' eagle on th' back iv a dollar."[25]

Attacking city politicians and voters was a new and telling literary fashion, but congressmen, partisan editors, and other more traditional political figures were not spared in post–Civil War fiction and humor. Charles Jay, whose *My New Home in Northern Michigan* is peppered with insults of politicians at all levels, even amends his copyright page to get in an extra dig at Congress: "Entered according to act of Congress (before Congressional virtue had festered into *Crédit Mobilier* villainy and back pay theft) in the year 1874, by Charles W. Jay, in the office of the Librarian of Congress, at Washington."[26] Artemus Ward's father berates his son for writing for a political newspaper because he will lose his "character for trooth and verrasserty." Ward himself ponders further political ambitions, and wonders whether he will "ever accumulate sufficient muscle, impudence and taste for bad liquor to go to Congress."[27] Newell writes of a congressman "who is a friend to the human race, and charges the Administration with imbecility and mileage," and reflects that "there is naught so fallen in humanity but it may become still more depraved. I have known members of State Legislatures," he continues, "to be finally elected Congressmen."[28] Thomas Norwood's *Plutocracy* identifies congressmen as servants of rich businessmen—another forceful new theme in Gilded Age fiction. In the words of one plutocrat they are "the fellows we keep in Congress to legislate for our pockets."[29]

The political process is attacked in numerous satires of the era, most famously and effectively in Twain and Warner's demystification of piously cloaked congressional corruption in *The Gilded Age*, but also in a variety of accounts that focus primarily upon electioneering. In David Ross Locke's *The Demagogue*, Caleb Mason's candidacy for the state legislature is promoted by an announcement in the local Democratic paper, signed by "Many Citizens."

"The 'many citizens' were Squire Harvey, who wrote, paid for and inserted the announcement." Mason professes no interest in the position, but agrees to answer the call of duty, devoting his candidacy to "the development of the resources of the Northwest." The key issue of the campaign, however, is the location of the county seat, and Mason, after dodging the issue at a mass meeting, throws his support to the town that has the most votes, and is nominated and elected.[30] John Carboy's *Kicked into Good Luck* contains a delightful send-up of a mass meeting of the Outs at the Cooper Institute, advertised by a ludicrous poster promising "No More Tyrannical Taxation! No More Infernal Revenue!" and also "fireworks, Blowhard's Brass Band, a Quartet Club, and other attractions," not least of which is the speech of the popular General Swashbuckle, which the crowd hears and participates in as a particular form of popular entertainment:

> "Fellow Outs, I feel that a crisis is coming!"
> "Let her come!" bawled an enthusiastic Out.
> "Silence!" roared a dozen voices.
> "I feel," continued Swashbuckle, "that we all have a great stake—"
> "Sirloin or chuck?" bawled an inebriated butcher, who was immediately silenced by some one smashing his hat over his eyes.
> "That we all have a great stake in the coming canvass—"
> "Sew it up," yelled a little sailmaker near the platform.
> "Silence!"
> "The Ins, headed by the bloated despot who sits enthroned in the Capitol, . . . must be hurled from power, or we are lost—and then where will we be?"
> "Advertised in the *Herald*—forty cents a line"—interrupted a shrill voice.
> "Put him out!" roared the crowd.[31]

Fictional scenes of this sort, and even the passing comments of more restrained authors, suggest the wide currency of political cynicism in the Gilded Age. There are many of them in our novels and stories, as well as in the sketches of political humorists, but rather than multiply insults it may be more useful to observe the presence and effects of antipolitical themes in a novel that also attempts to celebrate grass-roots American democracy. Ellis Horton's 1888 novel, *The Hoosier Practitioner*, is a quite simple political morality tale, set in the Indiana heartland, where "at local elections, every inch of ground is stubbornly contested, and during State and National campaigns the whole community is a blaze of enthusiasm." In this environment of widespread political engagement, the average voter is well informed, and the leading political figures are "often men of a high order, both intellectually and morally." The political spectacle, too, is an occasion for affirming, not ridiculing, participatory democracy:

There is something rather fascinating about a good old-fashioned, wide awake campaign. The charming tones of the orator ringing out on the pleasant summer air; the notes of martial music stirring the hearts of the lads and lassies, and the marching and countermarching of the lamp plumed phalanx, have a peculiar charm to all classes of Hoosierdom.[32]

The dark side of Indiana politics is represented by the novel's protagonist, Dr. Ringdon, the "Hoosier practitioner" who combines politics with his extensive daily medical rounds, stirring up support for his candidacy as county treasurer. This would have been perfectly acceptable in the author's estimation had Ringdon not been a petty tyrant, cultivating backers by means of threats and intimidation rather than respectful persuasion. Despite these means, or rather because of them, he does not prevail at the county convention. "By his domineering methods he managed to secure part of the delegation from his own township," but received not one vote from other townships, and lost the nomination and, in time, much of his medical practice to boot.[33] So, after all, for Horton, genuine Hoosier democracy prevails, and it does so through established political institutions. And yet, Dr. Ringdon's presence may have troubled some readers. He is the politician of the book and its dominating presence, and he is made to represent (even through his name) many of the sins a Gilded Age audience would have recognized as prevalent and successful in the politics of the nation and, perhaps, of their own towns and counties. Many readers would have dismissed Ringdon's easy defeat as a wishful fantasy, and would have read Horton's description of "a good old-fashioned wide awake campaign" as a more or less self-confessed anachronism, invoking a past they no longer inhabited. An equally old-fashioned (one might also say idealized) Hoosier heartland is the setting of the book, and Dr. Ringdon brings to it the disturbing reminder of the growing (and real) city over the horizon. In spite of himself, Ellis Horton paints a problematic portrait of politics in late-nineteenth-century America.

Political wrongs are righted in other books with even less effect. At the very end of Koehler's *Nick Putzel*, the villainous Nick's saloon is destroyed by lightning and Nick himself perishes in the fire. Here is a rather clumsy deus ex machina that provides a postmortem vengeance of sorts for Nick's misguided victim, Arthur Gurney, but it does little to brighten this dark tale of drunkenness and political corruption.[34] It is difficult to imagine any reader taking away from it any reassurance that corrupt saloonkeepers might hereafter have less to do with American politics. Lewis H. Bond's *One Year in Briartown* is a lighter satire of political wheeling and dealing in which Socrates Snipes, newly elected to Congress, promises a position as veterinary surgeon in the army to one Doctor Cackle before throwing his support to Doctor Tweezer Heaves. Cackle makes this betrayal known at the next election, and Snipes is "elected by a large majority—to remain at home. As an awful example to politicians of the slippery persuasion," Bond moralizes, "we insert this incident."[35] All is righted, but all remains wrong. Bond's lighthearted tale, no less than Koehler's angry one, gives the reader reasons for serious reflection on a real world in which neither lightning nor the voters can be relied upon to eradicate political evils.

So, too, does Mr. Dooley, in a pronouncement to Hennessey on the meaning of the 1900 presidential election, in which a bitter cynicism overpowers his usually more gentle humor:

> Ayther th' counthry is rooned or its rooned. An' it ain't, anyhow. . . . An' what th' divvle diff'rence does it make, me boy? Th' mornin' afther iliction, 'tis Hinnisy to th' slag pile an' Dooley to th' beer pump an' Jawn D. Rockefeller to th' ile can, an th' ol' flag floatin' over all iv us if th' wind is good an' th' man in charge has got up in time to hist it. Foolish man, th' fun'rals don't stop f'r ilictions, or the chris-tenins or the weddins. . . . Don't ye expict Hinnissy that anny throop iv angels will dhrop fr'm Hivin to chop ye'er wood on th' mornin' iv th' siventh iv Novimber if Bryan is ilicted, an' don't ye lave Jawnny McKenna think that if th' raypublicans gets in, he'll have to put a sthrip iv ile-cloth on th' sill to keep pluthycrats fr'm shovin' threasury notes undher th' dure. No, sir, I used to think that was so—wanst, in th' days whin I pathronized a lothry. Now I know diff'rent.[36]

This comment on a national election is not uncharacteristic of Finley Peter Dunne's fictional saloonkeeper of Chicago's sixth ward; indeed, Dunne's sketches were frequently aimed at national events and issues. The political world surrounding Mr. Dooley's saloon may have been parochial, but Dunne uses it as a microcosm of American politics—its charm lay in its broguish humor, but its significance stretched beyond the sixth ward and beyond Chicago to the larger events and patterns of American democracy. By the end of the nineteenth century this was still funny, but it was no longer far-fetched. In Alderman O'Brien Americans could find a representative of American politicians at all levels; in Hennessey they could find themselves.

What, then, shall we make of the politicization of American fiction (and humor) in the Gilded Age? Politics commands a greater space in Civil War and post–Civil War imaginative writing, but the content of that space is mostly negative. Antebellum authors excluded politics on behalf of a higher set of principles and practices. Civil War and Gilded Age authors included politics, but most often continued to base their political characters, episodes, and references on the judgment that public life in America was unseemly and corrupt. Middle-class readers in particular were given further grounds for believing that politicians served themselves by catering to wealthy plutocrats and to the unsavory poor, the former accumulating alarming amounts of legislative influence, the latter accumulating equally alarming electoral strength in the immigrant ghettoes of the nation's cities. This belief no doubt underlay the bypassing of politics by Edward Bellamy and other American authors (including Henry

George and other writers of nonfiction) who grappled during this period with the problems of wealth, power, poverty, and civic cohesion. The popularity of these authors may, in fact, have owed something to the fact that they did not propose ordinary political solutions. Did the political skepticism they reflected and helped to foster also counteract the stimulus of a larger and more consequential government to active political participation on the part of an apparently troubled middle class? We earlier suggested that the deadening effects of political retrospection could have been overcome in some citizens by the appeal of new issues within an expanding public sector. However, long-established skeptical attitudes toward politics and politicians, fueled by new scandals that were themselves magnified by the increasing size of public treasuries, no doubt refracted that appeal to some extent—encouraging in some, perhaps, that ironic form of political participation we earlier called "engaged disbelief"; more surely discouraging others from any kind of political interest or commitment beyond voting. How extensive, then, and how deeply felt, was political skepticism in Gilded Age America? How shall we comprehend its effects? These are difficult questions, and we must not place too heavy a burden upon imaginative writing alone in attempting to answer them. Let us turn again to public images and private documents, searching as we have before for meaningful correspondences among differing sources.

PICTURING POLITICS: CURRIER & IVES AND THE ILLUSTRATED MAGAZINES

A similar pattern of expanding attention and criticism can be found in the visual images published during and after the war in illustrated mass-circulation magazines. We must note first, however, that this is not the case with the other major source of popular illustration we examined earlier, the lithographs of Currier & Ives. Between four and five thousand different scenes, portraits, cartoons, and other images were published by this legendary firm between 1861 and 1898. Some two hundred of these are Civil War scenes—battles, camp life, regiments on the march, fond farewells at the local train station— but there are no political scenes, and the firm's traditional forms of representing politics and political figures declined rather than increased over the years. Portraits of presidents continued to be published, but there were fewer of them, and a large majority depicted the two presidents most easily represented as Civil War heroes, Lincoln and Grant.[37] Portraits of governors, senators, cabinet secretaries, and other political figures declined by more than half relative to antebellum production, and election banners declined too, disappearing entirely after the 1880 presidential election. (Mr. Dooley, incidentally, gives us a nice clue as to the market for these banners, and an interesting detail concerning the connection between politics and saloon keeping in this era, when he recalls "stickin' up the lithygrafts iv both th' distinguished lithygrafters that was r-runnin' fr office in me front window."[38]) Political cartoons did not at first decline in number—three dozen were published during the Civil War, and twenty-two more appeared, mostly in election years, between 1866 and 1872. After the 1872 election, however, these too were phased out of Currier & Ives's production. Only three were published after 1880. That was the year Nathaniel Currier retired, and we should note that the firm was itself in decline, the victim, in part, of photography and new print technologies. Currier & Ives produced its last new illustration in 1898, and closed its doors in 1907.

Political imagery, and the political cartoon in particular, lived on in the illustrated magazines (and later in the daily newspapers of big cities). Indeed, the political cartoon was entering a new era of popularity and influence, led by *Harper's Weekly* and the most important of its cartoon-drawing staff artists, Thomas Nast. Nast, who had once worked for *Frank Leslie's*, went to work for *Harper's* around the start of the Civil War. Along with Winslow Homer, he submitted a number of battlefield and army-camp sketches, but unlike Homer he found his métier in allegorical drawings and satirical political cartoons, gaining a considerable reputation during the war, and enhancing it still further after 1869 when he first leveled his pen at Boss Tweed and the Tammany Tiger. His three-year attack on corruption in New York City government undoubtedly did more than any treatise or any comparable run of editorials (and more than any novel or collection of comic literary sketches) to interest Americans in the evils of city politics, and it remains the most memorable of his many and varied contributions to *Harper's*. The coverage of politics by *Harper's* extended to text and to other illustrations, but for years it remained centered on the cartoons of Thomas Nast, whose work was instrumental in making this magazine one of the most popular and influential publications of the nineteenth century. To follow the trajectory of this coverage, and to place it in the context of the magazine's entire pictorial output, is to assess one of the principal forces in and reflections of American popular culture.[39]

Political illustration did not increase markedly in *Harper's* during the Civil War, although Nast's and Homer's war-zone images, and Nast's allegories, did help enlarge the public dimension of the magazine. In publishing, as in private life, the great issue of secession and war made neutrality nearly impossible, and *Harper's* embraced a pro-Union stance that remained after the war in the form of vigorous support for the Republican Party. By no means did it transform itself from a general-interest to a political magazine. Particularly in the immediate postwar years, and despite the more forceful assertion of its partisan identity, *Harper's* relegated political coverage to only a small portion of each issue, often including no more than a back-page cartoon and a column or two of text. Politics was given significantly more space and attention, however, during and after Nast's assault on Tammany Hall. His anti-Tweed cartoons continued through the early months of 1872, and then were turned to the coverage of the developing presidential race, with comic attacks on Horace Greeley, Carl Schurz, and other Liberal Republicans beginning even before Greeley's nomination in early May. A brisk pace of political cartooning and commentary was maintained until the election, and for the year as a whole approximately 20 percent of *Harper's* illustrations, including many that were printed on the front page, were devoted to some aspect of politics. A similar acceleration of political coverage had occurred, we should note, in *Frank Leslie's Illustrated*, which for a time remained as popular and as successful as *Harper's*. Pro-Union during the war and Republican after it, *Frank Leslie's* endorsed Greeley and the Liberal Republicans, attacking Grant in 1872 as frequently, and perhaps more vigorously—its lead cartoonist was the unsung Matt Morgan—than Nast and *Harper's* attacked Greeley. By 1872, in short, these two mass-circulation, general-interest magazines had become players in the partisan game, and politics had become a more important part of their attempt to amuse and instruct the American public.

Political coverage retreated to its usual space (5–10 percent of the magazine's total) in the off-years, but expanded once again during presidential elections, at least through 1880. In that year, *Harper's* again devoted about 20 percent of its pictorial content to politics, most of it in the form of satirical cartoons representing Democratic Party corruption (Tweed, who had died two years earlier, was again pressed into service), reliance on southern votes, and other sins. Democratic candidate Winfield Scott Hancock appeared weekly in some sort of compromising muddle. Republican candidate James A. Garfield appeared hardly at all, except in dignified portraits just after his nomination and his election. This was by now a fairly standard pattern, but the following year brought something we did not see in the previous off years we examined: the maintenance of a level of political illustration and discussion nearly equal to that of the presidential election year. This can be explained in part by the attention *Harper's* paid to Garfield's assassination. Newsworthy on its own account, the assassination was seized upon by *Harper's* as a tragic manifestation of the evil growing out of the spoils system and politics-as-usual.[40] Corruption and political spoils were pursued as themes through much of the year, even without reference to Garfield's assassin, and other political issues appeared from time to time. Was *Harper's* now building a larger, ongoing political dimension into its structure as a general-interest magazine? In fact, it was not. *Harper's* nearly doubled the number of illustrations per issue during the course of the 1880s, yet its political coverage was significantly reduced, the overall proportion of political illustration dropping back to antebellum levels—5 percent or a little more during presidential election years, decidedly less at other times. Thomas Nast's departure from *Harper's* might have had something to do with this decline, and the appearance in big-city dailies of the work of such "second generation" political cartoonists as Frederick Burr Opper and Homer Davenport may also have caused editors at *Harper's* to once again redefine the

GENERAL ORDERS.
General Dix. "If any Man attempts to haul down the American Flag, Shoot him on the Spot!"

6.2. Greeley and Tammany threaten the flag. *Harper's Weekly*, 1872.

role of the illustrated weekly magazine. Whatever the reasons, *Harper's* did reassess its role and its market, and the result was a significant reduction of political content.[41]

The volume and weight of political coverage in the illustrated magazines (*Frank Leslie's* as well as *Harper's*) during the 1870s and early 1880s are impressive, however, and demand a closer look at the character of Nast's and Morgan's caricatures, allegories, and other drawings during these years. The illustrations that compel our attention are those that carried forward an electoral campaign, or addressed a public issue or scandal. Many of these were a page or half-page in size, were prominently placed in the magazine, and, in the course of a campaign or a sustained attack on a particular foe or scandal, could accumulate impressively in the minds of regular readers. That cumulative impression was for the most part negative, for the cartoonist's primary responsibility was to focus upon the enemy, using the tools of visual satire to make him appear ridiculous, dangerous, or both. It is a sinister-looking Horace Greeley who, with the likes of Boss Tweed, threatens to replace an American flag with one covered with "Tammany corruption," "white supremacy," and other Democratic Party epithets, in one of Nast's 1872 campaign cartoons. And it is a ridiculous Greeley, right foot planted in a bucket of whitewash, who appears in another, this one depicting Greeley and his supporters busily whitewashing, perfuming, and papering over (with Liberal Republican and Democratic newspapers) the remains of Tammany Hall.[42] Greeley's image appeared most often during that year in the pages of pro-Grant publications such as *Harper's*, just as Grant's appeared most often in pro-Greeley magazines such as *Frank Leslie's*. Apart from the appearance of these images, the candidates and their allies were made to suffer from frequent verbal attack built into and surrounding the artists' drawings. Rooted in the satirical cartoons of Nast and Morgan, the political discussion in *Harper's* and in *Frank Leslie's* during that and other election years was mostly about the sins and deficiencies of the other side—Greeley's inexperience, unwarranted ambition for office, and unholy accommodation with Democrats; the corruptions of the Grant administration.

Cartoonists did portray their own candidates, sometimes in dignified portraiture, and sometimes in a caricatural form that was intended to amuse without damning. However, the effects of these images were not always positive; indeed, they often occurred in a context that invoked someone else's political sins. Shortly after Greeley's nomination by the Liberal Republicans, Morgan portrayed Greeley reading the service at the burial of a skeleton labeled "corruption." Carl Schurz has dug the grave, but it is Grant and his followers who weep at the graveside, a particularly distressed Grant staring at the skeleton, the upstretched arms of which carry the words "one term." It is this horrific skeleton, and a snarling bulldog emblematic of Grant (there is another, rather more comical bulldog weeping among the mourners) that dominates this scene, the figure of Greeley giving it no more than comic relief.[43] (It would have been difficult for Morgan, we must say, to have been other than comic in his depiction of Greeley, who was in fact a strange-looking man—and a caricaturist's delight.) The skeleton and the emblematic beast were customary cartoon devices during these years, as were more positive emblems such as the American flag, Uncle Sam, and a classically robed Columbia. Several of these combine with portraiture and text in a Nast drawing of Grant that is at once sympathetic and horrible. A very sad Grant perspires and bends forward under

"OUT, DAMNED SPOT! OUT, I SAY!"—Shakespear.

Here's the Smell of Corruption still! All the Perfumes of the Cincinnati-Baltimore Platform and the "Reform" Press will not sweeten this corrupt Hall.

6.3. Greeley whitewashes Tammany Hall. *Harper's Weekly*, 1872.

THE FUNERAL AT CINCINNATI MAY 3n, 1872.

6.4. Greeley buries political corruption. *Frank Leslie's Illustrated Newspaper*, 1872.

the weight of a huge orb labeled "a world of care and responsibility," to which a large number of specific labels (they appear to be legal briefs) are nailed: "HARD TIMES," "CUSTOM HOUSE FRAUDS," "A WAR OF RACES," "CORRUPT CARPET BAG-GERS," "WHAT CONGRESS DOES AND DOES NOT," and others. A "COPPERHEAD" snake coils around Grant's leg, and he is menaced by a large pack of barking dogs, each wearing a collar bearing the name of an opposing newspaper, while vultures labeled "office seekers" hover above. In the background, Columbia turns

6.5. Grant staggers under the burden of the presidency. *Harper's Weekly*, 1874.

away and weeps.[44] The reader might weep, too, not necessarily for the belea-
guered president, but for the presence of all these evils in the American political
system. It is not a pretty sight.

Negative images accompanied attacks on various aspects of the political system outside of presidential campaigns. These images and attacks were usually,
but were not always or obviously, of a partisan nature. In 1881, as we have

THE SENATE IS IN SESSION.

6.6. Congressional spoils. *Harper's Weekly*, 1881.

noted, *Harper's* published numerous cartoons aimed at congressional corruption and the spoils system. The focus was on the evenly divided Senate rather than the Republican-controlled House of Representatives, but the imagery was not overtly partisan, and it encouraged cynicism toward the political system as a whole. In April, a Nast cartoon entitled "The Senate Is in Session" depicted a fasces, traditionally bound with the words *E Pluribus Unum*, but mounted by an eagle and wreath with a more troubling message. "What do we come for?" is unfurled below the eagle, and, within the wreath, the answer is in large letters: $POIL$. The blade of the ax bound in the fasces is badly nicked, and bears the words, "TO GRIND." There are no people in this cartoon, but a suited arm extends from beyond its border to hold the fasces erect. It wears a cuff link bearing the initials "U.S."[45] A month later, we see "Citizen Beaver" toiling while "Statesman Sloth" lies on his back.[46]

This latter image is notable for its inclusion of an ordinary citizen into a visual world generally restricted to political figures. Nast, Morgan, and other cartoonists did do this from time to time, but the vast majority of their political cartoons depicted only identifiable political leaders, accompanied occasionally by figures emblematic of the American people or the republic. Most often these emblematic figures were Uncle Sam and Columbia, not generalized representations of real-world people such as "Citizen Beaver." In Nast's 1872 cartoon of the flag-threatening Greeley, for example, it is Uncle Sam, not a common soldier, who is given the order by General Dix to guard the Stars and Stripes. Rarely are there even onlookers to scenes such as this, and the overall picture obtained by the regular reader is not of an American panorama, but of a distinct world of politics, easily separated by tone and content from the many other worlds, domestic and foreign, that were depicted throughout each weekly issue of the magazine. (A very close look at the last mentioned cartoon does reveal two armed and disguised men lurking in the bushes, each wearing a hat bearing the initials KKK—not the onlookers Nast would have used to represent the general citizenry.) Scenes that do incorporate ordinary citizens, moreover, do little to connect politics with American life in a positive or even neutral fashion. Citizens appear as voters, for example, but, as in earlier decades, mainly as victims of or as willing participants in election-day outrages. Nast's 1882 cartoon of a voter being led to the polling place—a thinly disguised cheap saloon—by two Tammany operatives (one has the facial features of the cartoonist's stereotypical Irishman), is cynically captioned, "IT IS A DUTY AND A PLEASURE TO VOTE."[47] We point, finally, to a rare Nast depiction of an American husband and wife at their own dinner table. The grotesque husband glares across the table while he informs his wife that the crusade against whiskey is costing the government so much revenue that the next tax will have to be on tea. The startled, ludicrous wife loses control of her teacup at the unhappy news. An empty bottle of whiskey lies on a shelf above the husband's head.[48] It is not likely that the middle-class readers of *Harper's Weekly* were expected to recognize themselves and their own dinner tables in this sketch.

There is, in sum, a significant correspondence among the various print media of the Civil War and post–Civil War eras with respect to the representation of politics. The timing may have varied somewhat, but politics achieved a larger presence in different types of novels and stories, in published humor, and in mass-circulation pictorial magazines. The character and tone of that presence, however, were most frequently negative, and if these media give any evidence of popular meanings attached to the national crisis and the ensuing expansion of government it is to suggest that suspicion of politics and politicians, and a sense of the separation of politics from the more valued realms of private life, continued to run deeply through American culture. Perhaps they were felt more deeply than ever. Reinforcing traditional suspicions and hostilities were new scandals, and a new focus upon city politicians, the latter being all the more troubling because of the prospect that ever-increasing numbers of

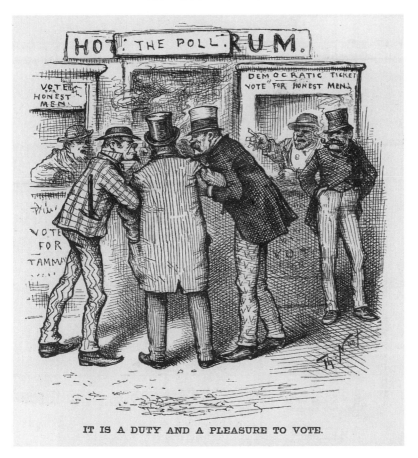

IT IS A DUTY AND A PLEASURE TO VOTE.

6.7. Escorting a voter to the polls. *Harper's Weekly*, 1882.

voters (including those whom middle-class citizens found most disturbing) would find themselves subject to the "uncommon laws" of the politics of city wards. Literary descriptions of corrupt or ignorant aldermen, and Thomas Nast's unrelenting depictions of a grotesque Boss Tweed, made it more difficult to celebrate even grass-roots democracy in this urbanizing nation.

As we have frequently emphasized, there were elements of fun in many of the satirical representations of aldermen, party hacks, and other unsavory political types, and in this sense politics was probably made more attractive to some people. Shortly after the end of the war, *Harper's Weekly* responded to legislative cries for abolishing the increasingly corrupt government of New York City. "The taste for strong excitement is not extinct with the rebellion," it warned its readers, "and the purveyors of sensational politics will still hope to startle the nerves of distant readers. Let those readers remember that there are political BARNUMS also, and not hastily imagine that every cod's tail sewed to a dried

REVENGE IS SWEET.

"My dear, since the Government is losing so much Revenue on account of the 'Crusade on Whisky,' they are going to make it up on Tea."

6.8. Politics reaches into the home. *Harper's Weekly*, 1874.

monkey makes a living mermaid."[49] Within a few years *Harper's* itself would be making a sensation of the issue of New York's municipal corruption. Was it, too, pandering to a taste for "strong excitement," and perhaps stitching a few cods' tails of its own, just in case that taste might prove unreliable? How reliable it may have been, and how politically engaged Americans may have become in this and in less sensational ways, ought finally to be addressed through the records of private thoughts and lives.

REAL LIFE AGAIN: THE PUBLIC LIVES OF POST–CIVIL WAR DIARISTS

Diaries do not always, or even frequently, tell us what their authors read, or how they reacted to novels, political humor, or magazine illustrations and essays. What they give us is personalized and often idiosyncratic accounts of daily life, and sometimes, too, the ideas and values, the likes and dislikes, of those who wrote these accounts. We have seen something of the more intense political engagement of Civil War–era diarists and correspondents. We have also suggested that postwar consciousness of politics and public affairs may have been affected in various ways by the memory of rebellion and war, by expanding public programs, taxation, and debt, and by scandals and trends that added new elements to the grammar of corruption. A sample of thirty diaries from this era helps us trace real Americans from war to peace, and into the age of Grant and Tweed. Despite rapid and significant urbanization, a large majority of Americans remained in small towns and on farms—60 percent at the end of the century—and all of our diarists were old-stock rural and small-town Americans. These were people who had relatively little direct experience with some of the pressures our writers and artists identify, and whose knowledge of aldermen and city bosses derived in large part from newspapers and from print media of the sorts we have just reviewed. None of these diaries was written by a professional politician. What, then, do these Gilded Age personal records tell us about the role politics actually played in the lives of ordinary citizens—"distant readers," perhaps, of Edward Bellamy, "Mr. Dooley," or *Harper's Weekly*?

Most of them, as we shall see, say little or nothing about politics, but we will focus here on those that do, and on the variations in political engagement they reveal among visible partisans. Three of our diarists began their private journals before the Civil War, and we have met and described each as an actively engaged citizen. All remained engaged, but in interestingly different ways, after the war. Samuel Beach Bradley, the doctor who as a young man served one term in the state legislature, remained attentive to politics long past the time when he had any political role to play even on the local level. His votes in the latter 1860s and the 1870s are recorded in his diary more as personal benchmarks than as political or civic actions—his forty-fifth town meeting, his forty-eighth fall election—but comments on the outcomes of presidential elections, in his diary and in letters to his son, suggest a continuing interest in national affairs until his death at eighty in 1876.[50] Bradley's diary, unfortunately, is less expansive or reflective during these years of his old age, and it is difficult to measure the effects of new political conditions upon this man of long-settled interests and habits. William B. Pratt's is more forthcoming. During and after the war, as we have seen, Pratt was an active Democrat and an office-holder, and for a time appeared to be on his way toward the kind of party leadership that would have qualified him as a full-fledged politician. However, the cantankerous independence of Prattsburgh's "off ox," and his passionate engagement with old and new issues, precluded any subordination to party and political "friends." In 1871 and 1872 Pratt's interest in free trade and taxes, pursued in part through some sort of association with the Free Trade League and the Tax Payers' Union, weakened rather than strengthened his relation to the Democratic Party. And in the following year he engaged in one of his political rebellions, this time over the failure of his party (and of the local

Republicans) to nominate farmers for public office. Pratt was himself a lifelong farmer, and for a number of years had been sending more articles and letters to agricultural journals than to the political newspapers. Now, in 1873, he was attracted to the Granger movement and in the following year found himself nominated once again for town supervisor, not as a Democrat but on a "People's or 'Granger's' ticket."[51] This rebellion did not last long, although Pratt would continue to chide the Democrats for nominating lawyers instead of farmers, and in 1884 he would vote for Benjamin F. Butler, nominee of the National Greenback Labor Party—the eleventh straight time Pratt had managed to vote for a losing presidential candidate![52] Prohibition and antimonopoly had by then become other interests of Pratt's, but in 1888 he voted for Cleveland (again the losing candidate), and his diary ends in 1891, before telling us whether or not he was to become a Populist.

Pratt's long and informative diary tells us that the Civil War was a powerful and continuing force in his life. In 1877, reflecting on twenty-five years of marriage to his third wife, he turned suddenly from the private to the public: "The accursed civil war & the absorbing interest in questions which caused it *shortened* the quarter of a century that has passed."[53] That is a remarkable statement, especially given the private context in which it appears. Yet, it is clear even from our brief review of his postwar politics that the evolving challenges of a growing government, not the memory of the war and its peculiar politics, shaped the voting and other political activities of this deeply engaged citizen. Pratt was anything but a retrospective voter. At the same time, we must observe that his continuing interest in political issues resided in his mind alongside a contempt for the customary practice of politics that seems stronger than it had been before, and that incorporated new elements. At the height of his Granger rebellion, Pratt nicely encapsulated his attitude toward professional politicians in a comment about the independence of farmers. Only a few farmers, he predicted, "will make politics a trade, and bet and fret, and cheat and 'treat,' to get themselves into office."[54] Pratt had never before articulated this contrast between farmers and politicians. Now, as a Granger and as a man sensitive to changes beyond the horizon of his rural world, he was impelled to claim political virtue as the particular property of those who, in an urbanizing society, remained on the land.

William G. Markham, our former Lincoln Wide-Awake who later suffered a brief and decidedly nonfatal bout of "warr fever," was one farmer who in most respects confirmed this judgment; indeed, his political interests were significantly less varied and intense than Pratt's, and there was little chance that he would become a political professional. A regular attendee at Republican nominating caucuses for town offices, in 1874 Markham unexpectedly found himself called to the chair and, in the course of the meeting, nominated for town supervisor over his earnest protest. Refusing to campaign, he voted against himself and was relieved to report his loss in the election.[55] For the next five years he was careful not to attend the annual town caucus, and was never again put forward for public office. Yet, Markham did gain and for a number of years maintained a professional relation to politics that, in a very different manner from Pratt's highly charged private citizenship, reveals the force of postwar change in American society and politics. Markham became a lobbyist.

Like William B. Pratt, Markham was a town founder's grandson who made his lifelong home on the ancestral farm. Unlike Pratt, Markham combined farming with a variety of other business interests, from which he seems to have made a considerable amount of money. These interests frequently took him away from home, as did the consequences of his notable successes on the farm itself, for Markham had turned early to sophisticated animal breeding, first in Durham cattle and then in Merino sheep. Beginning in early 1874, at almost exactly the time of his unhappy encounter with political authority and promotion in the Republican town caucus, Markham's diary records a very active involvement with several organizations of farmers, stock raisers, wool growers, and horticulturists, and in 1876 and 1877 he was elected secretary of the national and president of the New York State wool growers' associations.[56] It was in these capacities that he began lobbying in Washington to retain the high tariff on wool, beginning in December of 1877. Markham lobbied intensively for several months, and returned to Washington frequently in subsequent years to do the same, not only for the wool growers' associations, but also for a brewers' equipment manufacturing company in which he had an interest. There is nothing remarkable about his descriptions of these activities—there is no mention of "greasing the ways" through bribery or any other such inducement, even in these Gilded Age congresses—but official lobbying is itself a notable development in post–Civil War politics, when newly formed corporations and special-interest associations were beginning to make a science of presenting themselves to a government that had more to give and, potentially, more power to take away. Markham was, therefore, a quite up-to-date political player, often at the center of public affairs. His activities and political relations even had a global dimension. In 1879, having become president of a new American Merino Sheep Breeders Association, he brought two hundred thoroughbred Merinos to the Japanese government, and while in Japan discussed at length with another American traveler, former President Grant, his scheme for introducing Merinos to China.[57]

None of this made Markham a professional politician, or more than an interested private citizen. A consistent straight-ticket Republican voter, Markham served occasionally as a convention delegate, but this was mostly before he became active in Washington on behalf of the wool growers' associations, and neither in Washington nor anywhere else does he seem to have made friends (in the political or the conventional sense of the term) of the politicians he met. Nor does he appear to have relished the political world of deals and strategies, triumphs and defeats. He did attend several mass rallies in Rochester, not far from his rural home, but he seems to have enjoyed these mainly as family entertainment, much as he did the circus.[58] Markham was a man of wealth, prominence, talent, and energy, who needed only to have nodded his assent to have gained political office and influence, in his town and county surely, and probably at higher levels as well. His primary interests clearly lay elsewhere, and the public life he did lead was a matter of business, not of electoral politics.

Among our thirty post–Civil War diaries, no other reveals a passion for politics as intense as William B. Pratt's, and there is nothing else resembling the Washington lobbying of William G. Markham. On the other hand, approximately half of the men and women who recorded their daily activities and reflections in these diaries indicate in one way or another an interest in public affairs that might be said to have equaled that of Samuel Beach Bradley. Several, like Bradley, followed national elections, or made other comments suggestive of a significant level of informed interest. Others combined these comments with entries indicating some level of local political activity, such as attending caucuses, serving occasionally as a convention delegate, or running for a public office. J. W. Hobbs was fairly active for a time in the Democratic Party in Broome County, New York, more so than his son George, who recorded only having served once as an election inspector. Interestingly, the diaries of both father and son reveal a tendency to spend decreasing amounts of time at the polling place through the 1870s and 1880s, even before taking note of the novel experience (in the early 1890s) of voting "in the Booths." Both men, however, continued to comment as interested partisans on elections and other political news. The younger Hobbs had a "political talk" with an acquaintance shortly after the election of 1884; the elder recorded having written to his brother about his views of the President's message in 1887.[59]

A little more difficult to interpret are those men who were locally active in politics, but who expressed very little interest in political affairs in their diaries. Edward D. Lyons, a farmer and part-time veterinarian in Pike, New York, maintained a diary for nearly twenty years, in which we can see the gradual escalation of his political activity, from a few Republican caucuses, to occasional election-day work for the party, to election to a term as town supervisor. Despite these activities, the political discussion in Lyons's diary rarely goes beyond the noting of local candidates and elections, and his own vote for president, and the only nonlocal event that earned any space there was the assassination of President Garfield. Political issues, ideas, hopes, and fears are entirely excluded.[60] Is this just a peculiarity of the way he kept his diary, or does it suggest that politics did not make significant claims on Lyons's life and mind, even while he built a certain amount of partisan and public activity into an active daily round? Let us stress the actions rather than the words, and count Lyons among the politically engaged. We will do the same with Isaac Purdy, who

attended caucuses fairly regularly and served three or four times as a delegate
to his county convention, but who recorded only one political conversation in
ten years, never commented on the outcome of an election or responded to a
political issue or event (there is a brief mention of the hanging of Garfield's
assassin), and never wrote down a political thought.[61] Lyons and Purdy represent the lower range of political expressiveness among the activist half of our
diary sample, but, with the exception of Pratt, even those in the upper range
appear to have taken politics in season, more in response to recurring partisan
efforts at electoral mobilization than to actions of the Federal or state government, or to the continuing presence (and continuing publicity, through the
print media we reviewed above) of political issues.

Interestingly, one of the strongest expressions on a contemporary political
issue is to be found in the hand of one of those diarists we would be more
reluctant to describe as politically engaged. Washington Marsh returned from
the war to Richford, New York, in August of 1865. An introspective and frequently gloomy man, Marsh was also something of a loner. He did not belong
to or attend a church, did not become involved in lodges or other organizations, and found what seems to have been suitably isolating work logging on
a small parcel of land he had bought from his brother. Marsh's few recorded
connections to the community during the immediate postwar years did include
elections, for he was a Democrat, and he usually voted in the autumn if not
the spring. (His first fall election back home, though, produced the following
entry: "Snowed some. Went to election—didn't vote.")[62] "I think I ought not
to be alone so much," he wrote in August of 1867, but, despite an improving
state of mind, marriage, and visits with his brother and among a small circle
of friends, he remained largely detached from the community and showed
no signs of increasing political interest or activity until 1873, when he began
attending spring elections.[63] In 1876 he went to a Democratic Party meeting,
and two years later attended the spring caucus and a Greenback meeting in
the fall. (Marsh did not mention the fall election, however, did not vote in the
spring of 1879, and after that year's fall election wrote only: "Went to election—stood around inhaling wisdom and tobacco smoke untill I got up a respectable headache.")[64] An occasional attendee of Democratic Party caucuses
thereafter, Marsh was appointed (in his absence) town auditor at the spring
town meeting in 1882, and in the following year was nominated for town
supervisor. This was as surprising to him as it is to us: "I confess this takes me
off my feet somewhat and I accepted rather to please others than myself. I shall
surely worry off no fat struggling for election."[65] In fact, he did not, and was
not elected.

The nomination of this politically inactive man to the highest local office
can probably be explained as a strategic move by the minority Democrats.
Marsh was a war veteran, and had at some time joined the Grand Army of the
Republic. He may have been one of the few Democrats in town with credentials

of the sort that could induce crossovers from the Republican majority and, in fact, he ran ahead of his ticket, losing by only eight votes. In any case, this sudden elevation to local political visibility initiated a brief period of political activity on Marsh's part. He was nominated again for supervisor the following year, lost again, and concluded that he was "done with politics."[66] He wasn't, quite. The presidential election of that year was the first that he discussed in his diary, and the following year he spent the entire day at the polls. After that, however, he really did withdraw again, reporting almost nothing about politics or his own political activity save for a regretted term as district school clerk, a turn or two at election inspector, a bitter response to the rumor in 1889 that he was to be nominated for road commissioner ("God damn it, *No*"), and a milder but still negative response a year later to a report that he had been nominated again for supervisor.[67] Marsh appears to have done well over the years as a logger and farmer and probably had earned respect from his Richford neighbors, but it is clear that he spent more time and energy avoiding than engaging in politics during the quarter of a century since he had come home from the war. What, then, of his strong statement about political issues? This occurred a little later, and it focused, as we might easily have guessed, on the subject of soldiers' pensions. Marsh had voted with some reluctance for Cleveland in 1884, and though he wrote no comments about Cleveland's various pension vetoes, his response to the 1888 election was a pithy, "Harrison is elected president so I shall have to work no more."[68] Having resigned from the GAR some years earlier, Marsh rejoined in August of 1892, wrote occasionally in his diary about his attempts to get his pension increased, and commented each fall on the election's relation to the pension issue. In 1896 he wrote about the silver controversy as well, but he made it clear that it was pensions—more specifically, *his* pension—he was thinking of. "I don't want my pension cut into by being paid in bad money," he wrote shortly before that year's presidential election.[69] This personalization of two national issues nicely illustrates the penetration of post–Civil War government into some people's lives, and the strong reaction that national policy proposals could evoke even in Richford, New York, and even among militant loners like Washington Marsh. Marsh probably voted for McKinley that year (he had voted Republican at least once before, for General Grant in 1868), and in any case the issue of soldiers' pensions was unquestionably the impetus behind his rediscovered political interest. It was an interest, we must emphasize, that weakened his commitment to his political party, and that cannot be confused with enthusiasm for the political process as a whole. Marsh's political engagement was driven by and largely confined to one public program in which he had an important personal stake, and his diary entries suggest the likelihood that this kind of stake in government could lead to disappointment and a more general alienation. It was not politics that interested Marsh, but survival. When he wrote of pensions and of silver he was ill, in pain, and had retired from active work. He died four months after McKinley's election, at the age of fifty-six.[70]

"Went to election," Marsh had frequently written as his only political comment in various years of apparent detachment, and a number of other diarists contented themselves with this same phrase, or close variations of it. "Butchered & went to lection," wrote William Seward Brooks in 1876. "Went to the Hill to Election in the afternoon," wrote John C. Berry in 1889. "I went down to Uncle Jim & came back & went to Election," reported C. A. Cullings in 1892.[71] This phrase obscures much—the act of voting; the candidates and party for which one's votes were cast; the other things that might have been sought, or might have happened, at the polls; the depth of feeling and understanding about the election and its outcome. Perhaps, though, in its very terseness and form it reveals something of the latter. In the years before the Civil War, "went to election" was frequently written by men who spent much of the day at and near the polls, many of them engaging for hours in the political talk, the treating, the gambling, and the eager waiting for returns, and some taking an active part in the canvas itself. After the war it was most often written by men who, in common with increasing numbers of Gilded Age voters, attended the polls for only a brief period of time, and who did not engage in political activity in their communities. The phrase seems to have expressed a general detachment from political affairs on the part of men who saw no more need to comment on the election than to describe the hogs that had been butchered before going, or to tell their diaries more about the state of affairs at Uncle Jim's. Some of these men were equally terse on all subjects, but others did make more extensive comments about other things. In any case, the numbers of diarists who expressed little or no attachment to political affairs (whether they "went to election," "voted," or simply stayed home) may actually have increased in the post–Civil War era, even while politics expanded as a theme or motif in American novels, and even while (or shall we say because?) Thomas Nast contributed to the growing circulation of *Harper's Weekly* with graphic depictions of Boss Tweed's corruption and the absurdity of Horace Greeley's presidential campaign.

It is difficult to assess the meaning of this apparent increase of political detachment, or to interpret its relation to the growth of government and the emergence of politically attentive print media. It may, of course, reflect little more than the expansion of diary writing among the sorts of people who ordinarily did not keep diaries before the Civil War—less affluent people, for the most part, who began to write in little books to help ease the loneliness, boredom, and fear of the military camp and the husbandless home, and who continued to write in these books after the war had ended. It may reflect, too, the wide postwar circulation by American publishers of inexpensive annual pocket diaries, which is just the form in which many of our diaries were found. If this is what happened, it should keep us from making any firm judgments about the

increase or decrease of American political engagement on the basis of apparent
temporal changes within our sample, which, despite the thousands of remarkable pages of personal writing it gave us, remains a very small one for so large
a nation. Yet the "downward" expansion of that sample in the post–Civil War
era also helps establish an important point—that diaries were most often written, even after the Civil War, by people who were better situated and more
inclined than most to learn about, reflect upon, and participate in political
affairs.[72] We still have not heard from the masses of people who did not write
in such books, and we will try to reach them in other ways in the next chapter.
Meanwhile, we must conclude that those we have reached give us a somewhat
mixed message. Some of our diarists express interest in the new public issues
of the Gilded Age, and one at least, the veteran Washington Marsh, reveals
how pertinent these new issues could be to daily life and one's personal well-
being. Nearly all make their partisan affiliations clear, and it is possible—but
in no case certain—that some of these affiliations were forged or strengthened
by the great civil crisis. No diarist suggests, however, that the political system
itself had changed, certainly not for the better. In fact, it had changed, but not
in a way that would weaken or obscure the boundary between insiders and
outsiders, politicians and the people. The increased but generally negative at-
tentions of our novelists, humorists, and pictorial journalists suggest, indeed,
a shoring up of that boundary in the years following the war. This is the subject
to which we must now return, to understand better why politics and the people
were still not one.

CHAPTER 7

Leviathan: Parties and Political Life in Post–Civil War America

IN REMARKABLE WAYS, the two-party American political nation remained intact through and beyond the great domestic upheaval. No party re-alignment occurred during or in the wake of the turbulent years of secession and war. Indeed, for many in the post–Civil War era partisan commitment was stabilized by sacred memory, and it would take other pressures to wean even very small numbers of party adherents from the Democrats and Republicans to upstart Greenback, Prohibition, People's, or other parties.[1] Party institutions and practices also survived, as did the practice by voters of turning out in very high numbers for major elections. Parties continued to organize to the point of utterly dominating the political process, and the 80 percent voter turnout first achieved in 1840 remained the norm in presidential elections through 1888.[2] Even the South, in its way, contributed to the continuity of national politics. White southerners, who had removed themselves from American party politics during the years of the Confederacy, hastened to join or rejoin—and in the process to rebuild—the Democratic Party, while a smaller number of black citizens perpetuated the Republican Party in southern states. The result in most parts of the South was not a two-party system in any meaningful sense, but it is notable that even so distorted an institutional reintegration occurred, and that it occurred so quickly. In all these ways, the partisan political system may be said to have survived the civil crisis, and even to have thrived.

Even apart from the evolving one-party South, however, the party system was changing, mainly in response to new conditions, but perhaps also as a natural playing out of old strategies and techniques. Directly and indirectly, as Michael McGerr has shown, the larger and less remote governments of the post–Civil War era influenced national political leaders to call for a more substantive, "educational" form of campaigning, based on the national distribution of issue-oriented treatises and published speeches rather than on torchlight parades and other forms of spectacle.[3] The issues themselves—public debt and taxation, pensions, currency and civil-service reform—seemed more pressing, and so too did the charges of corruption and ineffectiveness to which a larger government gave new force. Attacks on self-serving politics were made still more compelling, especially but not exclusively to Republican Party leaders, when they came from the mouths and pens of men such as E. L. Godkin, George William Curtis, Carl Schurz, and Charles Francis

Adams—men who retained visibility and influence long after their Liberal Republican insurgency of 1872. These and other well-placed and well-polished "best men" of both parties expressed reservations of various kinds about American electoral democracy—about voters as well as politicians—and McGerr sees in the "educational campaign" the first phase of what he calls "the decline of popular politics."

Was this the essence of political change in the decades following the war? We have differed from McGerr with respect to the "popular politics" from which this decline might have occurred; hence, his interpretation of the trajectory of post–Civil War political change is not available to us. We do not disagree, however, that changes occurred, and that they affected the relations between political parties and the people. The changes we would emphasize, however, were of a different sort—shifts in party personnel and campaign technique that underscored what we have called the urbanization of political consciousness, and a more evident willingness, even on the part of partisan editors, to demystify political institutions. We would recognize important continuities as well, in the basic practices of electoral politics and popular responses to them. We again propose to examine these changes and continuities where they occurred—in the local communities where citizens read their newspapers (and perhaps the new treatises of the "educational campaign"), attended campaign events, talked about politics, and voted.

PARTIES AND THE POLITICAL PROCESS
IN POST–CIVIL WAR AMERICA: SEVEN TOWNS

The continuing westward and cityward migration of the American population forces upon us another adjustment to our selection of representative communities, which we choose this time for a close look at institutions and activism during a brief but typical period of post–Civil War politics, the 1880–82 cycle of elections. By 1880 the trans-Mississippi West was the most rapidly developing region in the country, and to give it voice we have added two western towns to our sample—Graham, Texas, the seat of Young County, and a farming and cattle-raising town of some twenty-five hundred inhabitants in 1880; and Auburn, California, the commercial and political center of Placer County below the peaks of the Sierra Nevada, and a community of just over two thousand. These towns replace Clarksville and Opelousas in our analysis. Augusta and Dubuque each grew to a city of some twenty-two thousand inhabitants by 1880, but to further incorporate the effects of post–Civil War urbanization we have substituted for Kingston the larger city of Syracuse, New York, where the population exceeded fifty thousand in 1880. We must, of course, continue to examine the experiences of the large number of Americans who moved neither to the west nor to cities. Our two other towns, Greenfield, Massachusetts, and

Marion, Ohio, grew only modestly to approximately four thousand and five thousand, respectively, and continue to represent small-town politics and communal life in the Northeast and the old Midwest.

How do these seven cities and towns manifest political change in the post–Civil War era? Let us look first at the start of the political season, when parties began preparations for local, district, state, and national campaigns. Save for the introduction of party primaries in one or two instances we will presently describe, the nomination process itself did not change in any formal sense. In most places, candidate selection still began with local caucuses announced by party central committees through partisan newspapers, and advanced through the traditional pyramid of county, district, state, and national conventions. Resolutions were still prepared by committees and passed by assembled delegates. But did the call by national leaders for a more substantive form of electoral politics breathe new life and meaning into this system by turning it toward issue-oriented discussion or indoctrination? Did the "education campaign" broaden the appeal of these meetings? There is, in fact, no evidence from any of our representative communities that caucuses and conventions were more fully attended than they had been before the war, or that party leaders made any attempt to increase the participation of ordinary citizens in them. The process of drafting and approving resolutions clearly remained a formality to which most voters and probably most delegates paid little attention. The most evident change, indeed, was the abandonment by most party editors of the pretense of broad and enthusiastic participation.

Editors of the 1880s rarely braved their rivals' ridicule in their reports of party caucuses and conventions. On the contrary, the consistent theme in the papers of all our communities is failure bred of professional control and public apathy and disgust. In only a few instances did we find claims of large party meetings, and in fewer still were these claims not compromised in some way. In the spring of 1880, for example, Patrick Walsh, editor of the *Augusta Daily Chronicle and Constitutionalist* (the rival papers had been merged in a city that Democrats now completely dominated), wrote that the county convention was "one of the largest we have ever seen in Richmond County." Expansive (if a bit ambiguous) at the outset, Walsh proceeded to whittle down his claim, referring to the convention a second time as having been "as large and creditable a one as the county furnishes on similar occasions," and then, in response to charges that it had been "packed" and "cut and dried" by Augusta's party leaders, simply shrugged: "If more people were not present, it is not the fault of this paper."[4] We emphasize that this was one of the bolder claims of popular participation, and that it occurred during the year of a presidential campaign, when editors were most likely to exaggerate. More typical was the Greenfield Republican editor's complaint of "meager attendance" at party caucuses, and a general "indifference about political matters" among Greenfield's citizens, in 1881 and 1882.[5] The same indifference was noted by the Republican editor of Syracuse, and by the Democratic editor of Dubuque, who also reported in 1881 that the county conventions of both parties lacked delegations from a large majority of Dubuque County's seventeen townships: only four townships had caucused to elect delegates to the Democratic convention, five had sent delegations only to the Republican convention, and only one (along with the city of Dubuque) was represented at both. Seven townships left themselves entirely outside the nominating process in 1881. The presidential race had provoked a better result, for the Democrats at least, a year earlier. But even then the *Herald*'s editor had to admit that "for years we have not had as full a representation from the different townships."[6]

As in earlier decades, local parties adopted measures to prop up the nominating system. To help produce a creditable turnout at their county convention in 1882, for example, Graham Democrats scheduled the meeting on a day when two other events, an election on local option and the installation of Masonic officers, were sure to bring large numbers of men to town.[7] Hearkening back to the earliest days of the party system, some local meetings (Marion's Democratic county convention of 1881, for example) made delegates of any and all party members who would take the trouble of traveling to the next convention on the pyramid.[8] And wherever specific delegates were appointed, they were also allowed to appoint substitutes, and to vote by proxy for other delegates and even entire delegations. (Don't surrender representation "to the first plausible stranger that comes along," pleaded the *Greenfield Gazette and Courier*.)[9] All of these tactics were evident in the party newspaper reports of the 1840s and 1850s. New to the post–Civil War era, as we have suggested, was greater candor on the part of both editors and party officials about the system's failure to attract more attention from voters, and editors occasionally reported qualified engagement by the party's more active members. In 1882, Walsh took his readers inside the meeting of the executive committee of Georgia's eighth congressional district. Fourteen of sixteen counties were represented (ten by proxy), and the committee proceeded to discuss a convenient place to hold the nominating convention. Walsh did not hesitate to report the response of one member when another suggested that delegates had a moral obligation to go wherever they were sent: "Moral obligations do not pay railroad fare."[10]

Party officials, for their part, sometimes made adjustments to the system that went beyond any we observed before the war. In Graham, a correspondent to the Democratic paper warned that a call for caucuses in the county's various precincts would probably not be heeded, "as no organization exists in any of said precincts, and no one authorized to call them together at any place." It would be better in any case, he advised, to wait until farmers and stock men had finished their busy season, and then simply to call a county convention where any Democrat (that is, any white man in the county) could vote. This warning about the probable failure of an untimely or overly elaborate demand on Young County voters' energy appears to have been heeded. There was further tinkering of this sort before the county convention met, the *Leader* reporting an effort to use the same meeting, whose purpose was to select delegates to a congressional and (possible) judicial convention, to nominate candidates for county office.[11] In Auburn, during this same year, both party central committees found reasons for simply bypassing their party memberships in selecting delegates to help set in motion the process of presidential nomination. After first considering a primary to choose county delegates, the Republican committee "agreed to dispense with such election—it being perfectly well known that the Republicans of Placer County are overwhelmingly in favor of Mr. Blaine and it was decided to be more direct, inexpensive and satisfactory, all in all" if the committee simply appointed the delegates themselves. The Democrats did the same thing, consulting first with "representative men" who assured the committee that "as nearly as could be ascertained this was the evident sentiment of the mass of the party."[12] Graham and Auburn were newer towns with less settled political institutions, but a similar abrogation of the traditional nominating process could occur in older places as well. In Marion, Democrats cited the "busy season" in doing away with a convention to appoint delegates to the state convention of 1880, empowering any Marion Democrat present at the convention to cast the county's vote.[13] Had there never before been a "busy season"? Clearly, the party organization in Marion was responding to indifference or resistance to conventions among Marion's Democratic activists.

One other type of tinkering with the nomination process seems, in some settings at least, to have responded to a different problem. In one-party Georgia, nomination to any office by the Democratic Party was tantamount to election; hence, the convention system deprived many voters of a meaningful election-day vote, especially when it came to those higher, nonlocal offices for which candidates had been nominated by delegates rather than local meetings of all interested party voters.[14] In 1880, the state executive committee of the Democratic Party decided to replace local conventions with a party primary for the selection of delegates to the state convention. The evident context of this decision was a significant challenge to the re-election of Governor Alfred H. Colquitt, which, presumably, party leaders thought best to place before the party as a whole, in essence creating a July gubernatorial election before the formality that would ensue in the fall. In explaining this innovation, however, the committee emphasized that local conventions empowered with delegate selection "have been so meagerly attended," which means that here, too, the motive was in part the shoring up of the neglected party nomination process, and not merely the substitution of the party for the state as the guarantor of democratic elections for white men. A firm backer of Governor Colquitt, editor Walsh vigorously disagreed with the executive committee's decision, pointing over and over to the weaknesses of "scrub races," which, by encouraging candidacies undisciplined by party, produced a cozening of voters more corrupting than "a thousand machines." Significantly, however, Walsh did not find language for defending conventions. The best he could do was to lay the blame for their failure on voter apathy, "the chief fault of American politics," and aver that no meeting "could be packed did the honest and intelligent voters assert their opinion and protect their rights."[15] Who could disagree? But who could disagree also with the implication that this kind of voter activism did not characterize local conventions in Georgia?

As it happened, Governor Colquitt won the primary, making a partial convert of Patrick Walsh, who denied that "the issues were not thoroughly understood by the people." During the next two years he gave the primary system a qualified endorsement, insisting that they be made compatible with "the preservation of county organizations." The turnout of Democratic voters in Augusta had been high in July of 1880, and it was high again two years later in a primary for nominees for the state legislature. But statewide turnout was not high, and concerns remained among politicians about the role of the local party under the new system. After the successful primary in September of 1882 the Democratic executive committee of Richmond County decided not to hold a primary to nominate men for county offices. One member spoke for his colleagues: "The people are tired of elections."[16] Did he speak for anyone else? It is worth noting that primaries were used selectively in other settings besides the one-party South, in ways that a party organization man such as Patrick Walsh would have heartily approved, and to which few others seem to have objected. The Republicans of Syracuse, for example, used primaries to select ward officers and delegates, opening the polls in each ward for *one hour*, from noon to one. A proposal was in fact made to extend the balloting to three hours, a modest enough concession to party democracy, but when it was tabled by the county executive committee no protest was entered in the *Syracuse Morning Standard*.[17]

Occasionally, readers of local party papers did object when leaders altered the nomination process. When the Placer County Republican executive committee eliminated the nominating caucus in 1880, the *Weekly Argus* published a letter asking if the committee "owned" the party, or simply treated it "as a thing to be used or disposed of at their own free will."[18] Such complaints, however, were rare. Far more frequent in the political pages of the local press were editorial discussions of the reasons for and results of public apathy. Greenfield's Republican editor, for example, distinguished between "the caucus theoretical" and "the caucus practical." Every citizen, he wrote, knew of caucuses controlled by a half-dozen men, caucuses convened without public notification, and caucuses that had been fixed before they began. None of these undemocratic practices would change until voters attended meetings and saw to it "that corrupt men are thrown aside before they have the vantage ground of being the regular candidates." This was, however, at best a desultory call to action, followed as it was by the gloomy conclusion that the "present generation will not see that reform."[19]

Apathy was as much effect as cause of "the caucus practical." Editors were still party spokesmen, and generally were party insiders, but they wrote insistently of the alienating effects of wire-pulling at caucuses and conventions. To be sure, their most vivid examples were often drawn from the other party. The Syracuse Republican paper, for example, asked a Democratic politician opposed to Samuel Tilden whether delegates to his party's national convention had been purchased by bribes. "Purchase?" he responded. "Why should we purchase? . . . We don't generally buy what we have in our fists." The rival *Courier*, for its part, reported that two assemblymen and U.S. Senator Thomas Platt had "fixed" the Republican nominations for state senator and supreme court judge in central New York in 1881. As for assemblyman, the *Courier* quoted a Republican authority: "You may put it down that whoever [J. J.] Belden supports will be nominated." The *Dubuque Daily Times* told its Republican readers that at their county convention the Democrats "reported a long list of names entitled to seats in the Convention, the majority of whom never saw Dubuque."[20] But editors could chastise their own parties in exactly the same way. The *Greenfield Gazette and Courier* explained poor attendance at the Republican county convention of 1882, not by bad weather or the "busy season," but by widespread awareness that the slate of delegates to the state convention had been agreed upon by party insiders long before the local convention was called to order. And in Graham, the Democratic *Leader* responded to charges that the Democratic state convention had been filled with "politicians and office-seekers." When, the *Leader* asked, was there a convention "not in the main composed of just those two classes"? Three weeks later he was more direct: "Heretofore our state conventions have been manipulated by a very few politicians, and we presume that the one to meet this summer will be a repetition of those that have gone on before."[21]

The metaphor of politics as circus, every act orchestrated by an impresario, was more commonly applied by postwar than prewar editors to the nomination phase of the political season. The *Dubuque Daily Times*, for example, mocked the Democratic "annex of Barnum's show exhibited at the Court House yesterday. . . . Ex-Alderman McCann stirred the animals to action and had things fixed to suit himself." Again, the image and its message could be turned on one's own party. A popular parable entitled "How They Voted," which circulated through many papers, seems to have been aimed at Republicans (it appears to have originated in the Democratic *Burlington Hawkeye*). But in our towns, the two papers that published it were the Democratic *Dubuque Herald* and the Republican *Placer Weekly Argus*. In it, the animals in a menagerie are asked their preferences for president by the (Republican?) elephant, who is the judge of election. The animals "didn't know a great deal about politics in their cages; but that, you know, children is no bar to talking politics." As he polls the giraffe, tiger, tortoise, turkey, gopher, and wild ass, the elephant shows his contempt not only for their choices (Republicans Blaine and Sherman, Democrats Tilden and Seymour) but also for their understanding. "Who do you go for?" he asks the tiger. "Any man that comes close to my cage" is the answer. After the monkey (a probable stand-in for African Americans) is shouted down before he can state his preference, the elephant decrees the polls closed and proceeds to count the ballots. "Grant, 54" he announces. To the animals' query, "[H]ow does that come?" he responds, "[I]t comes all the same and don't you forget it. Don't I weigh more than all this menagerie put together? What do you animals know about politics anyhow?" To this depiction of the arrogant, wire-pulling professional the story adds a striking image of animals so malleable in their ignorance as to be incapable of outrage, let alone action: "The animals were all pleased to think that they were allowed to vote, anyhow, and they were delighted that the election was over and their man elected, so they gave three cheers for Grant, and rolled around in the straw to dress for the evening's performance."[22]

It is significant that the circus metaphor attached ignorance and bestiality to lesser political performers. Readers of "How They Voted" and of other satires and attacks were invited to distinguish themselves from animals who rolled in the straw and from "the loafers, the vicious and idle bummers," whose language was "not fit for ears polite," and who packed political meetings.[23] Although he condemned the "excessive refinement" of professional men who did not wish to mix with "the vulgar crowd," the *Greenfield Gazette and Courier* editor acknowledged that this revulsion toward the social promiscuity of political meetings is what persuaded many of the community's most respectable citizens to stay at home.[24] Even when they focused only upon the caucuses or conventions of the opposite party, accounts of verbal and physical violence at political meetings further validated the withdrawal of these men. In its description of the Democratic county convention in the fall of 1880, the Republican *Dubuque Daily Times* reported that delegates "stamped, yelled, cursed, hissed, threw spit balls, chews of tobacco, and damned and re-damned the speaker until the very air was streaked with curses and cuss-words."[25] What respectable person would wish to associate himself with that? Two years later the *Augusta Daily Chronicle and Constitutionalist* reported with malicious delight that "pandemonium reigned" at the Republican county convention, as delegates and spectators assaulted one another, breaking chairs, carrying a table back and forth "helter skelter, knocking men over like nine pins." At least one delegate was knocked in the head, "a large gash being made in the scalp and an artery cut," while a knife was drawn on another. Some sought safety in flight, preferring the risk of a twenty-foot drop from the window to the bedlam within. Only when the chief of police instructed the janitor to turn off the gas, and with it the lights, did the mob and its fury disappear.[26]

We have met complaints and descriptions of all these types before; indeed, the party editors of the 1880s added few if any new reasons for distancing oneself from political party meetings. What is new in the Gilded Age, again, is the near-absence from political papers of offsetting claims of large, enthusiastic, harmonious, and effective caucuses and conventions—claims that were part of the editorial arsenal during the antebellum era. Editors, as we earlier stated, were expected to convey the appearance of openness and a thriving party democracy without necessarily encouraging the reality. Now even the pretense was largely surrendered, at least with respect to the nomination phase of the political campaign. Party leaders did usually—but not always, as we have seen—maintain formally democratic processes of candidate selection. But it was ever more clear, and less frequently denied in the party press, that it was a very small part of the electorate that set the political season into motion.

WHO LOVES A PARADE?

For the vast majority of voters in our communities, political participation began long after the candidates were selected. As the *Greenfield Gazette and Courier* noted, there were "No Politics in the Crops." While politicians warned that "the fate of the nation rested on the Republican and Democratic conventions," the "fruit grew ripe and mellow / And the wheat was nicely growing / While the farmer in his garden / Bout his turnips went on hoeing."[27] The vernacular liberals described in this poem, moreover, may have welcomed, if they even noticed, the decline in the number and intensity of rallies and torchlight processions in the presidential contest of 1880 and the two off-year elections that followed. This decline was just what some party leaders intended as they contemplated the shift from the spectacular to the educational campaign. But the virtually issueless race between Civil War generals Garfield and Hancock, and the coverage of this and other elections in the partisan newspapers of our seven cities and towns, offer little evidence that they even tried to substitute substance for show. Such tactical changes as did occur, we believe, were born of the recognition by party activists that fewer citizens were curious about the "operational aesthetic" that moved the machinery of the spectacular campaign. Convinced that bonfires and torchlight parades did little to get voters to the ballot box, local party leaders concentrated more of their time and resources on refining an "organizational aesthetic" that would do just that. Building on a broad base of retrospective voters, party men devised strategies for turning apathy and even cynicism about politics into a tool for reinforcing party regularity. In some places they did so in part by creating political clubs that fused partisan allegiance with powerful ethnic and other group loyalties. In many places they offered a partisan commitment that demanded less, rather than more, of ordinary voters' time, energy, and feeling.

The decline of spectacular campaigns was noticed by several of our editors and lamented by few. They assumed that, after forty years, torches and brass bands, parades and poles, were no longer successful in warming political passions. Although on other matters editors asserted that the people were gullible, they concluded that most citizens were not to be humbugged by a political procession. In describing the kind of person who still was, the *Dubuque Daily Times* made clear he was a relatively rare and not at all a respectable specimen. A Pittsburgher "in good spirits," the *Times* reported, met a political procession on his way home from the circus and conflated the two, declaring himself in favor of the entire county and state ticket: "clean sweep for Jarnum and Bumbo—hic!—have every confidence in Jarnum and Bumbo."[28] In Augusta, editor Walsh chose a curious moment to dismiss the politics of pole-raising and torch-bearing. Even while exhorting "the boys" to "turn out strong" and with torches ablaze for the election of 1882, Walsh opined that "political processions are all wrong. It should be the candidates who are made to march in the streets. The women and children could then see who wants offices and there would be plenty of room on the sidewalks."[29] Within days of the election he added: "Brass bands and torches are not being used much in the campaign this year. States can be saved without them."[30] That many Americans now merely laughed at spectacular campaigns is suggested by the popularity of the play *Our Candidate*. Performed throughout the country in 1880 by Richmond and Van Boyle's comedy company, *Our Candidate* presented politicians, "repeaters, egg-men, delegates and other peculiar people shown in a torchlight procession."[31]

Claims that processions or rallies emerged spontaneously were made much less frequently in the 1880s. Editors sensed that their readers knew the workings of the machines that manufactured crowds. In the fall of 1880, the *Marion Democratic Mirror* derided the Republican parade by referring offhandedly to its sponsorship. Consisting of 522 torch-bearing footmen, 39 horsemen, and 4 marching bands, the Republican procession was not worth the $140 a businessman had paid: the "general illumination was very good" but, the *Mirror* implied, the political impact was negligible. For the Democrats' procession, editor G. B. Christian hoped for favorable weather and promised "no hireling men from abroad, no free-tickets coaxed and drummed up outsiders to make a show." The *Mirror* would also make no claims about attendance. A year later, like his counterparts in Dubuque and Augusta, Christian concluded that "Brass bands, street parades, torchlight processions and other expensive and unnecessary paraphernalia of a campaign have had their day.—They never did influence a vote and they never will."[32]

In our communities there is little evidence that spectacular campaigns were replaced by educational campaigns. Acknowledging that politics deserved "deep, conscientious reflection," editors asserted that such reflection was not to be looked for in the "reason and conscience" of most men, and implied strongly that this was a permanent condition. It was, after all, not the issues but "the babble, the continual discussion in the press and in the spots where men congregate, of 'deals' and 'bargains,' the conjectures as to what this boss or that ward worker will do, the quarrels, accusations, needless personal strifes that disgust or excite and weary."[33] It is significant, we believe, that editors often lumped together party platforms with political processions as components of the artifice parties designed to divert attention from the real business of deals and bargains. The *Syracuse Morning Standard* waxed cynical about the promises of the Republican Party it supported: "[A] platform, Julie, is one preamble and twenty resolutions, strong in non-essentials, vague in essentials; round the bush on the tariff and rough as thunder on the Mormons; clamorous for civil service reform with a reserved definition of civil service reform; down on corruption, loud in its praise of purity and determined to have it if it takes every cent the party can raise." When the campaign is over, it is "stored away in the cellar or garret."[34] The *Graham Leader* was still more explicit in equating the spectacular with the educational campaign as it borrowed some of the language used by the Syracuse paper. A party platform, according to the *Leader*, "goes along with the banners, transparencies and torches, and when the campaign is over—well, it is stored in the cellar or garret, along with the rest of the uniforms and torches. A campaign platform is very much like the campaign torch in deed; it gives out a great deal in smell and smoke with a very uncertain flickering light."[35]

It is difficult to avoid the conclusion that displeasure with platforms and processions was part of a more general dissatisfaction with politics in the 1880s. Blaming the politicians, the people, or both, all of our editors expressed weariness with elections that, as the *Placer Herald* put it, "presented few questions of difference" between candidates or parties.[36] In contrasting a dreary present with the heroic eras of American politics, the War of Independence and the struggle over slavery, the editor of the *Syracuse Morning Standard* found "little to break the monotony save the snarling of political jackals over the bones the larger beasts have left to them."[37] Little wonder, then, that when candidates campaigned they could be said to be "boring the dear people with unusual persistency."[38] Or that, according to the *Daily Times*, there were no more than ten men in all of Dubuque willing to read the annual message of the president of the United States.[39]

While partisan editors allowed themselves these moments of candor, party professionals worked to turn out voters on election day, assuming more and more that public events were a distraction and a drain on resources. Democrat A. N. Luddington, for example, wanted "every cent raised for the parade in Syracuse" to be spent instead on committees in every election district to get out the vote.[40] In response to this organizational imperative activists in our communities relied less on enthusiasm-building events and, in several, more on ward or town-wide committees and clubs that focused their energies on voter turnout and polling-place vigilance rather than on the campaign spectacle. Greenfield provides a good example of the shift from spectacle to canvas. After a quiet campaign in 1880, with three rallies scheduled by each party and no editorial claims about attendance at any of them, the election brought 821 of the 953 men eligible to vote to the polls—a turnout of 86 percent. "We doubt if the town has ever been more thoroughly canvassed," concluded the *Gazette and Courier*.[41] In 1882, a gubernatorial year, the Democrats held no rallies and the Republicans only one, with a band serenading listeners in front of Washington Hall before the speeches began. The most the *Gazette and Courier* could claim was attendance "larger than usual for a meeting of this sort." Again, though, the parties were at work to get out the vote. Noting a pervasive apathy, the Republican editor threatened the citizens of Greenfield: vote within the first two hours or you will "make it necessary to have the attention of the [Rallying] Committee directed to your delinquency." On their own or with assistance, 757 men made it to the polls.[42]

In one-party Augusta the primary race in 1880 between Governor Colquitt and his challenger, Thomas Norwood, stimulated the organization of campaign clubs and rallies. But the presidential contest had no clubs, pole-raisings, or torchlight parades, and only one speech, which was not printed in the *Daily Chronicle and Constitutionalist*. Nonetheless, more Augustans turned out for the latter than the former (which was held a month earlier). Why? In an editorial entitled "Organization," written two years later, Patrick Walsh indicated that retrospective voting was still at work in Augusta: "It ought to fire the soul of every white man in the county with indignation and compel every Democrat who loves his wife, daughter, mother, and sister to rally to the banner of his race."[43] This powerfully racist appeal was obviously relevant only to general elections, and was especially so to national elections, even though the Republican Party was no longer a credible threat to gain Georgia's electoral votes. Walsh well understood, though, that an unshakable partisan identity of this sort did not pertain to primaries that pitted one white Democrat against another, and that it did not automatically translate into votes even in some general elections. Here and elsewhere he stressed the need to organize voters by means of ward-based clubs, and he was usually the principal speaker at the organizational meetings of whatever clubs could be coaxed into existence. In 1882, another gubernatorial year, the *Daily Chronicle and Constitutionalist* fought an uphill battle against apathy, observing as late as September that "the people are now intent upon gathering their crops. They will wake up politically later on." Thousands, the editor complained, fail to pay their poll tax; "thousands more take no interest whatever in political affairs."[44] Ward-based clubs were difficult to organize because even would-be activists were indifferent or complacent about a Democratic triumph. "Start the ward club, boys / There will be no more apathy," Walsh wrote less than a month before election day, and two weeks later he was still pleading for (Alexander) Stephens clubs in the first and third wards of the city. The clubs still had a role to play in what remained of the political spectacle, and Walsh was pleased to report that the second- and fourth-ward clubs were well represented at a successful mass rally on the eve of the election. This was, however, the same election during which Walsh scoffed at brass bands and torchlight parades, and it is clear that he had other work in mind for club members. Walsh and other party leaders may, indeed, have sustained aspects of the campaign spectacle as a way of fostering party organization, rather than the other way around. In any case, the final pre-election plea of the Augusta editor to his readers reveals anxiety about a source of voter disengagement that neither parades nor canvassing could be expected to overcome: "It is a mistake for a man to believe himself to be more respectable than others because he does not register and vote. The opposite is the truth. To be a good citizen one must do what he can to keep objectionable men out of office."[45]

As in Augusta, Marion Democrats experienced difficulty organizing and sustaining campaign clubs, even in the context of close and competitive contests. In this smaller town, however, party leaders seem not to have considered clubs important for mobilizing voters. Clubs, and rallies too, were by no means entirely abandoned in Marion (at the Hancock ratification rally at the end of June "the streets were thronged with people," according to the *Democratic Mirror*), but by late August the Hancock and English Club in Green Camp township was still the only such institution in the county. A club with 101 members was organized in Marion's second ward in mid-September, and meetings called for the other three wards; yet, save for activity by Hancock Guards in two rallies there is no evidence in the *Mirror* of club meetings of any kind. The vote on election day was high, however, and Marion was reputed to have "the best county organization in the state." It was an organization that obviously found other means besides rallies and clubs for maximizing voter turnout.[46]

The Republicans of Marion made more of an effort to create campaign clubs, which also assumed a rather different form. Once midsummer harvests were gathered, George Crawford, editor of the *Independent*, called on activists to organize clubs and raise funds so they could "run this campaign on their own hook." Apparently failing in the effort to form ward-level clubs, probably because a critical mass could not be found within the tiny wards of this small town, Republicans organized a town-wide Garfield and Arthur Club on September 6. To attract more men they also organized "the Buzz Club," a ladies' Republican club, with twenty-six members and the hope of enlisting two dozen more. Along with the Young Ladies' Republican Club (many women probably joined both organizations), the women entertained Republican men with suppers and balls. There is a tantalizing hint that the women tried to introduce substantive matters as well. As they hosted eighty Garfield and Arthur cadets for an oyster supper in late October, the ladies presented a tableau, "Justice throwing off the chains of slavery from the Negro," with Miss Ida Krause as

Justice. We do not know whether the Republican Ladies of Marion were calling on their party to rededicate itself to civil rights or simply waving the bloody shirt, and no response by the young men was recorded. What we do know is that events such as these took place in relatively confined, almost private spaces, and were not intended to impress or amuse the masses in a public spectacle. Were these clubs, then, mostly social in nature? Did they contribute to getting out the vote? Perhaps they did so indirectly, by serving as vehicles (as editor Crawford suggested) for raising the funds that could be put to use by party operatives on election day. Again, our newspapers do not answer—but they do reveal that neither Republicans nor Democrats organized any kind of campaign club in Marion in 1881 or 1882.[47]

Far to the west, in Graham, Texas and Auburn, California, elections came and went with very few campaign activities, and with little organization of the sort we have just described. Indeed in these two "frontier" towns public events of any kind were rare. The Fourth of July passed "without anything worthy of note being done in Graham," which sent some of its young men to Rock Creek for a baseball game. In Auburn, Independence Day and Decoration Day passed "without causing the slightest ripple" in the community.[48] The unwillingness of vernacular liberals in these communities to develop a civic culture clearly extended to political campaigns. In Graham's Young County, where all but twenty-five men voted for Hancock, the only campaign event in 1880 was a speech to a "large audience" at the courthouse by a Democratic candidate for the electoral college. On the same day candidates for county offices appeared as well. Businesses closed to afford all citizens an opportunity to attend, and the Leader could not resist a touch of sarcasm in anticipation of the event: "Let every man in the county come up and select his own stock." In a town small enough for each candidate or his representatives to "pump-handle" all "the dear people," parades and rallies (and clubs, too) seemed beside the point. A notice placed in the Leader in the spring of 1880, ostensibly reporting on a meeting of Graham citizens to organize a fish fry, suggests that many saw political events as self-serving. The meeting resolved, according to "Marshal and Superintendent" R. N. Price, that "the candidates are expected to contribute funds sufficient to purchase bread and pickles." No one who did not announce as a candidate in time to make this contribution, moreover, "shall be voted for in the election next November." A week later, after some candidates rose to the bait, Price absolved the Leader from responsibility for the joke, remarking that few people present at the fish fry would feel on that day "much interest" in the candidates, who might come or not as they pleased. Although few of the men of Graham involved themselves in campaigns, the Leader nonetheless concluded that even the modest activity associated with the fall election was too much: Texans needed a rest from "political discussions by the press and stump speakers; we need farmers who will raise wheat and hogs."[49]

In Auburn, where Democrats and Republicans were fairly evenly matched, a campaign was only slightly more in evidence. The Democrats ratified the nomination of Hancock in June 1880 with a hundred-gun salute and the *Placer Herald* reported two well-attended campaign events, a rally for congressional candidate J. B. Glascock, and a speech by Jo Hamilton, who was running for the state legislature. Editor J. A. Filcher, however, minced no words about political engagement in his town. Democrats of Placer County, he noted, "have never been distinguished for their efforts in the matter of organizing clubs." Apparently 1880 was no different: the *Herald* provides no evidence of a Hancock Club in Auburn. In describing the audience for Glascock as "surprisingly grand," moreover, Filcher moved quickly to qualify: "in view of the fact that this is conceded to be one of the worst places in the county to get up a creditable demonstration."[50] After pleading for months with his fellow Republicans in Auburn to be "up and doing" by founding a Garfield and Arthur Club in Auburn, Henry Fenton, editor of the *Placer Weekly Argus*, announced the opening of the campaign on September 11 with a speech by a former assemblyman. The arrival of a campaign songbook, "serviceable some of these fine days or evenings," might, he thought, provide the catalyst for the formation of a Republican club: "By the way, why this apathy?" Despite appeals to civic pride and competitiveness through jibes that smaller towns "are getting ahead of us in this matter," the *Argus* gave no indication that a campaign club was organized. Fenton characterized the only other Republican campaign meeting as an "unusually large gathering." Two other rallies that fall, one to "try to prevent retaliation by the Chinese for the recent demolition of meetings belonging to them," the other a temperance rally, may well have had a partisan character. But Auburnites, like the men of Graham, viewed campaigns as something less than necessary. They were partisans to be sure, and they would vote, at a remarkable rate of 90 percent. But if Fenton's remarks following the elections of 1882 are any indication, they may not have taken the campaign, and even victory or defeat, all that seriously: "We are sincerely glad that the campaign is over. Now all the mud machines will be retired from active service . . . and affairs will go on smoothly because, in any case, the country is safe. The grass will keep on growing all the same, the rain falling, the sun shining, and the farmer preparing for his harvest."[51]

In Dubuque and Syracuse there were more clubs and a somewhat more visible campaign spectacle. With larger, more concentrated, but also more anonymous populations, they had the critical mass to support clubs and vigilance committees, which served to identify potential voters, naturalize foreigners, and get out the vote, the tasks that party leaders were most keen to accomplish. Campaign clubs also supported public rallies and parades, although, in Dubuque at least, events of this sort began later and were fewer in number than in former times. Dubuque Democrats, for example, did not rally to ratify the nomination of Hancock, but opened the campaign in early August with the quieter act of adopting a constitution for a city-wide Hancock Club. Attempts to organize clubs in each ward were generally unsuccessful, despite a sufficient population base. The men of the first ward responded well enough, holding meetings twice a month and raising $51.50, probably for uniforms and torches, but in October the *Herald* could still only hope that "every other ward would brace up its loins for the presidential fray."[52] This did not happen. What did occur was the organization of more than three hundred of Dubuque's Democrats into ward vigilance committees, formal arms of the party that ordinarily were not recruited by or publicized in the party newspaper. Focused primarily on election-day voter mobilization and poll watching (sometimes in conformance to the "uncommon laws" of places like Albany's ninth ward), the vigilance committees' significant presence in Dubuque is emblematic of the turning away from the campaign spectacle and toward a more pronounced concentration on ward-level organization and the direct canvassing of voters. As for the spectacle itself, we should note that local Democrats did work hard to attract voters to party events, offering invitations to the ladies and plugs of Hancock and English chewing tobacco to the men. Against claims of "well-filled" halls, however, were, in accordance with time-honored tradition, Republican descriptions of a "fair crowd" and "a congregation of about six Democratic county officers and a dozen candidates for the Post Office."[53] After the election (in which voter turnout was a bit below 80 percent) the *Herald* provided a postscript focusing on the campaign clubs, which in tone as well as substance reveals much about partisan engagement in post–Civil War Dubuque. Those "whose memories are not burdened with too many more weighty matters," wrote editors M. M. Ham and D. D. W. Carver, "will remember that there were some clubs in existence . . . which are now among the things of the past." Although Hancock and English were "slightly slaughtered we saw looming up like an oasis in the desert of disappointment" a Democratic dividend in the form of surplus funds in the campaign club treasury. It could have been spent "for the good of the party" or for a "first class funeral procession." Instead, club officials had decided to distribute the surplus among the members. Clearly, Democrats in Dubuque had little interest in departing from the traditional disbanding of party institutions during the political off-season.[54]

The Republicans of Dubuque did not attempt to organize clubs in the wards. As an alternative, the city-wide Garfield and Arthur Club organized in August named a vice president and member of the finance committee from each ward, almost certainly to encourage participation. There were also ward-based vigilance committees, although these appear to have had far fewer members than their Democratic counterparts. The *Daily Times* attributed poor attendance at meetings and rallies to stormy weather, but claimed that the torchlight parade at the end of the campaign was the largest ever held in the city, with over eight hundred in the procession and thousands of spectators. When Garfield's victory was announced, editor M. W. Woodruff reported that the streets were crowded until midnight.[55] There were few such events, however, and as in earlier decades editorial claims of rallies this large were possible only in presidential campaigns. Two years later Republicans would hold only one public meeting during the entire campaign, and Woodruff would say little about its size.[56]

Of all of our communities Syracuse was the most thoroughly and successfully organized for a sustained campaign. Democrats established a city-wide Hancock and English Club as well as political clubs in each ward, torchlight clubs, Hancock Light Guards, and Escort clubs. Pole-raisings, rallies, and torchlight processions purportedly attracted thousands. Republicans did them one better. Their Young Republicans' Club was already meeting every Friday in January, and clubs were organized in the wards by June. Fortunate to have former President Grant and James A. Garfield, the candidate himself, appear at separate mass rallies, Syracuse Republicans claimed thousands in attendance for their processions and hundreds turned away from meeting halls. Here in the largest of our towns, the traditional campaign spectacle seems to have remained most intact. Behind the impressive show, however, were indications of difficulty in stimulating and sustaining participation. In the constitution of the city-wide Hancock and English Club, for example, was a provision allowing ten members to constitute a quorum. Did this number, far lower even than the number of officers of the organization, suggest that few Syracusans were expected to attend? Moreover, the organization of a Fat Man's Hancock Club, for which no one below two hundred pounds was eligible, may have given new meaning to the term "spectacular campaigning," but its gimmickry suggests that citizens were more likely to attend partisan events when the subject was not political.[57] So, perhaps, did the Republican glee club formed in January. Republicans' attempts to organize meetings around addresses and debates on issues such as women's suffrage and an amendment to the Constitution limiting any president to two terms did not increase club membership. And in August the Morning Standard complained that Garfield clubs had many members "who work with one arm and walk with one leg."

Most significantly, Syracuse Republicans went far beyond those in any of our other communities in the formation of clubs according to ethnic- and interest-group identities. There were clubs of veterans and of Boys in Blue, who continued to respond to the waving of the bloody shirt. Clubs were founded as well for Germans, for "colored citizens," and even for those Irish citizens willing to affirm loyalty to the GOP.[58] Appeals to ethnicity, of course, were as old as the American political nation, and to some extent these special-identity clubs, ethnic and otherwise, were founded upon Republican hopes to capitalize upon stronger forms of solidarity than the political parties could provide on their own. The clubs appear to have been more than sentimental. Also involved, we believe, and perhaps more profoundly so, were understandings of the more tangible benefits—public offices, jobs, favors of various sorts—that would flow to the group in return for the votes of men not otherwise interested in the affairs of party.[59]

It is significant that Syracuse was the most urban of our representative communities. Earlier, we described the developed rural and small-town world of mid-nineteenth-century America as the ideal social landscape for mobilizing voters on election day. Syracuse (and to a lesser extent Dubuque and Augusta) belies this claim in the sense that its parties, too, were able to turn out four of every five voters in the 1880 presidential election (somewhat below, in fact, but not far below, the turnout in our smaller towns). But the techniques for reaching these more frequently anonymous voters were necessarily different—more elaborate, more frequently decentralized to the ward level, more frequently filtered through ethnic and other subgroup identities, and more instrumental. The old political "package," as Mr. Dooley would later explain with considerable eloquence, would no longer do; now it must include—and the parties must as institutions provide—more specific and tangible benefits. As our earlier review of the 1850 congressional campaign of E. B. Morgan reminds us, these tangible benefits were not invented by urban parties. In Syracuse and in other cities, however, they were being built into party institutions in ways that were changing and would continue to change the formal practice of electoral politics, with consequences that would be felt in years to come, especially as cities would become still larger, more decentralized, and more omnipresent. The patterns of campaigning in our widely varying towns, in sum, underscore the force of urbanization that is evident also in the novels, political humor, and popular illustrated magazines we reviewed in the previous chapter.

And yet there is one curious fact about the campaigns in our representative cities and towns that this observation does not seem to explain—the old-fashioned political spectacle was most fully preserved in our largest city, and least evident in our smallest towns. Was Syracuse, then, really a throwback to former times? The retention of a more elaborate array of large rallies and parades in larger cities was actually a small (but quite interesting) part of the larger story of concentration of pageantry, entertainment, and many other things in the nation's "central places"—itself a manifestation of deeper patterns of urban-centered wealth generation and the growing dominance of cities within increasingly articulated and transport-connected urban regions. Torchlight parades and massive rallies, once a common sight in smaller towns during political campaigns, were becoming another urban attraction, not merely for partisans but for anyone in search of an entertaining occasion to visit the city. Recall that it was to Rochester that the diarist William G. Markham, a resident of the rural town of Rush, took his children to see a political parade, and that it was the pageantry itself, not its political purpose, that he commented on. Syracuse, Rochester, and other cities held large rallies, and smaller towns did not, precisely because the spectacle was in retreat, shrinking away from smaller places and toward the only places that could afford them and continue to make them accessible. In this way, and also in the way this pattern further reduced the content of the spectacle— merging it more completely with other kinds of entertainment—the city was not a relic but a portent.

We should observe that as political and communal institutions our partisan newspapers, too, were changing. The evolution of newspapers in the late nineteenth century from organs of party to enterprises responsible to advertisers is well known.[60] We believe that this transition should be attributed in some measure to the growing conviction that political fare did not interest many readers. Nine out of ten defunct newspapers of this era died of "too much politics," argued the *Cincinnati Commercial*,[61] and in our cities and towns two themes, corruption and apathy, dominated coverage during and after the political seasons of the early 1880s. Typical were the assertions of the *Syracuse Morning Standard* that the "new fruit for political shortcake" was "bri-berry," that just about every congressman could be "bought for a song," and that anyone who assumed that politics absorbed the attention of most people does not "understand the popular mind. . . . During the hottest political conflicts only a small proportion of people are particularly interested in them."[62] Editors, as we have seen, could further undermine their official party role by taking aim at their own parties. It was the *Dubuque Herald* that singled out a Democratic aspirant for office who bought votes by "setting them up" for the boys in his brewery, and, more strikingly, it was the same Democratic paper that explained loyalty to his party as the habit of the indifferent (retrospective) voter who unthinkingly responds to the "limited ritual" reminder that Republicans are corrupt: "Tired with the struggle for liberty he sinks back into slavery and votes the regular ticket."[63] For its part, the rival *Daily Times* reprinted an article about a Republican activist who paid someone five dollars to vote in the names of dead men, only to learn that the Democrats were doing the same thing: "Then the boys said everything was lovely and we took a drink and called it square."[64]

Advertisers themselves helped the transition along by participating in the ridicule of politics, and in particular by wishing "good-bye and good riddance" to elections.[65] During election week, a Dubuque dry-goods firm lamented, tongue in cheek, that "business was neglected to 'save the country.'" Fortunately, jobbers could now anticipate "a large and increasing business." Bronner's in Syracuse was more sanguine, certain that most Americans knew even in the midst of campaigns that no matter what the candidates said, the country was in no danger: "Who is to be President compares very lightly with the weightier matter of whether our wives' and daughters' millinery is fully up to the latest and best styles of headwear." Clearly Mr. Proctor, the Syracuse furniture salesman who could do "more hard work, and with a tongue hung in the middle, can talk more goods and cheaper prices into a customer than any man of his profession," was the man for all political seasons (or parties) in the 1880s. "Imbued with considerable Republicanism, Proctor was "quite Democratic in his habits." He was "willing to accommodate the Greenbackers" and "supply the Temperance folks."[66]

Editors never dared criticize these jocular advertisers, but they did sometimes bite the partisan hand that still helped feed them. Henry Fenton of the *Placer Weekly Argus* made it clear why he was interested in listing the names of Republican candidates for local office. "Send us your name . . . together with $5—this is the most important part of the item to us." Anyone who didn't would surely lose, as "a very great many people are too indifferent or too lazy to bother themselves about the candidates for such minor offices."[67] The *Graham Leader* was more militant in its assertion of pecuniary over political principles. The newspaper announced in 1880 that henceforth all communications from candidates would be charged as local advertisements. The ticket, moreover, would not appear on the masthead because "we don't suppose anyone must have it thrust in his face every time he looks at the paper to keep him from forgetting to which party he belongs." Men who run for office are motivated by "the money there is in it"; why, therefore, should newspapers who do so much party work for no pay, making enemies in the process, not be allowed to operate on business principles as well? A year later the *Leader* was still complaining, "It is the business of a newspaper to puff a candidate for nothing, print his slips for the same, and do nine-tenths of the work of electing him for a cent." In 1882 the editor bluntly informed candidates to "whack up the lucre. If you wait for the *Leader* to make mention of your candidacy before we have received the money you are sadly 'off your chunk.' "[68]

Comments of this sort foretell the disappearance of the party newspaper from American journalism, and suggest, as do concurrent modifications of the local political spectacle, a significant shift in popular consciousness and feeling. Undoubtedly, the tactical and institutional changes we have probed here through our representative cities and towns both responded to and impelled changes in public sentiment, but we should be careful not to exaggerate the extent of the latter. Even in the early days, as we have seen, editors wrote critically of politics, apologized for the tactical hysteria of the campaign paper, and found various ways of emphasizing their newspapers' more general (and apolitical) service to the community. Local citizens, for their part, read the party paper and participated in the campaign spectacle in a variety of different ways, including those we have described as skeptical or hostile, and there were some who ignored both the paper and the parades. Interest in the political circus was flagging by the latter decades of the century, primarily, it seems, because it had come to town too many times with an act that was not overwhelmingly convincing when it was new. That political men felt the need for a change seems reasonable enough—and the changes they made seem more moderate than revolutionary—given the longer history of qualified popular participation.

INSIDE LOCAL PARTIES: ACTIVISM
IN THE GILDED AGE

Our narrative of Gilded Age electoral politics points to other changes involving the size and nature of the politically active community, and the relations between political and other forms of organized collective action. It suggests, for example, the possible expansion of the numbers of active party men in cities, resulting from the multiplication of specialized campaign clubs and other vote-getting institutions and roles, and perhaps a contraction of the numbers of partisan activists in smaller towns, in conjunction with the reduced size and frequency—and the transfer to cities—of the campaign spectacle. The same changes may also have produced a downward spread of political activism through the social structure, in cities if not in smaller towns. And the greater focus on practical, vote-yielding organization suggests a greater degree of political professionalization at the higher levels of the local party. Perhaps, too, it suggests a greater separation of political from other forms of community leadership, a phenomenon that might have been further encouraged by the withdrawal from politics of some traditional leaders—doctors and possibly even some lawyers—in conjunction with the expansion of professional societies and the exclusivist ethos of the learned professions.[69]

Taken together, these changes, if verifiable, would amount to a quite different pattern of relations between politics and society in the towns and cities of Gilded Age America. In fact, when we turn again to the analysis of political and other communal activists we find some of these changes, but by no means all of them; indeed, we are struck by several remarkable continuities between the 1850s and the 1880s in what we earlier called the social structure of political activism. For example, the relative size of the politically identifiable population in the four cities and towns that are represented in the community samples of both periods is almost identical in each case: in Dubuque it was 30 percent of the adult male population in both 1858–60 and 1880–82; in Augusta 7 percent or 8 percent in each period; in Marion 17 percent in the earlier election cycle and 18 percent in the later one; and in Greenfield (leaving aside low-level, nonpartisan officials appointed by the town meeting) 14 percent and 13 percent. The profile of different levels of political activism is also much the same for each town, although in the two smaller communities one can observe a (nearly identical) narrowing of the proportion of high- and midlevel activists—from 12 percent (of the 1860 adult male population) to 7 percent (of the 1880 adult male population) in the two Greenfield files, and from 11 percent to 7 percent in Marion—and a consequent modest broadening of the proportion of lower-level activists. This is a very striking picture of stability in the overall size and shape of the political community that, we believe, accurately reflects the pattern of politics "on the ground."[70]

Continuities are found within these broad outlines as well, particularly in the smaller towns. In both Greenfield and Marion, lawyers and businessmen still dominated the higher levels of political activity, and the community's political leaders were still significantly more active than other men of equivalent occupational standing in the nonpolitical institutions of the community. In Greenfield all but one attorney listed on the 1880 census, and in Marion all but two, were politically active at some level, and most often they were quite active. These were the basic patterns of local political leadership in the 1850s, and it is evident that they carried over into and beyond the war years, preserving much of the social structure of political activism through a period of crisis and change in the nation, and through the various re-alignments and tactical shifts that affected the conduct of politics on the local level.

The evidence from our representative towns and cities suggests, moreover, that political men were no less likely than in earlier times to engage in other community activities, including those that were unambiguously reputable. The data from Graham and Auburn are too thin to interpret with confidence, but in each of our other five localities there remained a strong positive association between political and other forms of community activism among both professionals and businessmen. In each town or city, small or large, high-level political activists were, as a group, the most likely to appear on the boards of benevolent and reform societies, churches, clubs, lodges, local companies, and whatever else was offered by the many voluntary organizations of post–Civil War America to men with a desire to join or lead. Midlevel political activists were the second most active group within nonpolitical institutions, and they were followed by low-level party men and then by the large body of men who did not join in party affairs in any way visible to us. Although we hesitate to attach numerical values to these differences of kind as well as degree, the pattern seems to us a very clear one, no less so than the one we discerned among our antebellum towns. Perhaps there is some sign of a less pronounced association between political and other types of communal participation among the lawyers and other professionals of Syracuse, but this association was quite strong among the city's businessmen. Consider just one example of the latter, J. J. Belden, the man whom we encountered earlier in this chapter as the dictator of the Republican nomination for state assemblyman, and who is further described in the local press as the man who "runs things" in the city's Republican Party. Belden, who was president of a bank and two iron companies in Syracuse, was also vice president of the Bureau of Labor and Charities; a member of the executive committee of the Hospital Aid Society; a trustee of the First Presbyterian Church; a member of the subscriptions committee for St. Joseph's Hospital; a member of the advisory committee of the YMCA; a director of the Society for the Prevention of Cruelty to Children; a member of the Civil Service Reform Association; a committeeman for the Greenway Guards' Grand Ball in 1880 and a Charity Ball in 1881; a signatory to the announcement of a

Grand Music Festival in 1882; and a board member of three local banks, the water works, the gaslight company, and the Syracuse and Ontario Railroad. This is quite a long and varied list; indeed, Belden may have "run" many things in Syracuse beyond the Republican Party. Certainly he was active in as many local organizations as any of our antebellum political leaders. His example lies at one extreme—a clearly identified "wire-puller," perhaps even a party "boss," who was also extremely active outside of politics—but it is not beyond the range of generally active political leaders in our several towns. The conduct of politics may have become more professionalized, but party leaders such as J. J. Belden were not separating themselves from other community institutions. Neither were less powerful party men—the real professionals, perhaps, who organized the political life of individual wards—less likely in the 1880s than they were in the 1850s to involve themselves in lodges, clubs, and other community institutions that were outside of politics.

This is not to say that there were no changes of the sort we have hypothesized. There were some, even in these small and traditional American towns. In both Greenfield and Marion there is a visible downward diffusion of political activism, particularly at nonleadership levels, within the social-class structure. In Greenfield, the proportion of midlevel activists working in clerical jobs increased from 5 percent to 16 percent, while the proportion of skilled and unskilled manual workers increased more modestly from 16 percent to 20 percent. In Marion, a similar shift of this sort among midlevel party men (the proportion in clerical jobs increased from 2 percent to 11 percent; in manual jobs from 20 percent to 25 percent) was joined to a more pronounced shift among low-level activists, clerical workers increasing from 7 percent to 13 percent and manual workers increasing from 25 percent to 37 percent. The latter were still somewhat underrepresented even at the lowest level of party activism in Marion (manual workers constituted about 54 percent of Marion's adult male workforce in 1880), and were particularly so in Greenfield, where farm laborers and manual workers in the town's cutleries, baby-carriage factories, and other workshops made up nearly 60 percent of the male workforce. Clerical workers in both towns, however, were now somewhat overrepresented among mid- and low-level activists, and there was in general a modest but unmistakable shift in both towns away from numerical dominance at nonleadership levels by professionals, businessmen, and farmers. We must bear in mind that this shift occurred in the context of an expansion of lower-level political roles within a stable-sized community of political activists. There was no political earthquake in Greenfield or Marion—simply a small structural and social downward shift within that minority of men (a 13 percent minority in one town, 18 percent in the other) we can identify as active in some way in political life.

Greenfield was a very old town, and Marion too a long-settled one, by the early 1880s. Graham and Auburn were newer, and, as we have seen, had less well-developed and less elaborate political institutions, including a delegate nominating process that could be swept away when certain people did not feel the need for it. Near-frontier towns of the cattle-raising and gold-mining West, Graham and Auburn were among the least politicized of our communities, at least in terms of participation in organized public and political institutions. We have already seen how dismissive of politics even the party editors of these towns could be, and the degree of political cynicism and apathy they regularly ascribed to the local citizenry. There was a corresponding level of institutional disengagement in the two towns. In Graham's Young County, only some 10 percent of the adult male population are identifiable as visible partisans at any level, and a significant number of these (about four in ten) had done nothing more in organized local politics during the years 1880–82 than sign a petition asking the county's unrivaled political leader, Oscar E. Finlay, to run for the state legislature. (He did.) Finlay was a lawyer, as were three others of the seven men we counted as political leaders in Young County, a tiny group that also included the county clerk, a cattle raiser, and a farmer. (The 1880 census, unfortunately, does not provide data relating to real or personal wealth, so we cannot take a finer measure of the material or social circumstances of these or other men in our samples.) Perhaps because this leadership group was so small, we find for the first time that a number of local attorneys were not included at the higher levels of party activism. Besides the four we have just mentioned, there was a fifth Young County lawyer at the middle level of party activity, three who were only minimally active, one who did no more than sign the Finlay petition, and five who seem to have done nothing at all. In Auburn we find a similar pattern: within an identifiable political community amounting to 11 percent of the adult male population, a small leadership group of ten men, including three lawyers, the editor of the Democratic paper (J. A. Filcher, whom we met earlier as a candidate for the state legislature), the director of the water works, the county school superintendent, a farmer, a druggist, an undertaker, and a civil engineer. All but one of Auburn's lawyers are in our file, but two were midlevel and six were but low-level party activists. The political communities of both these towns are too small to bear a more detailed analysis. We can at least say, however, that in these towns so far and so different from older farming and commercial centers of the East and Midwest (and so far and different from each other), we find many echoes of the established and still largely intact pattern of local political dominance and activity.

Our larger towns bear closer scrutiny, and we begin with Augusta, now a city of twenty-two thousand, growing as a commercial and industrial center within the recovering landscape of inland Georgia. Augusta was not exceptional as a southern city, but it diverged fundamentally from our northern and western towns and cities in the absorption into its Democratic Party of nearly the entire white voting population. It differed, too, from the small southern town of Graham, in that African Americans in Augusta were able to maintain a functioning Republican Party. That the latter was not a threat to Democratic dominance in the "Redeemed" city—that Augusta maintained two race-specific, one-party systems rather than the two-party systems we find in northern and western towns of an equivalent size—reflects in obvious ways the racial division and white dominance of the post-Reconstruction South. Less obvious, perhaps, is the manner in which Augusta's inegalitarian political traditions were preserved within the all-white Democratic Party.

There was little if any downward diffusion of political activism among Augusta's Democrats. Of the twenty-seven men we would identify as party leaders in 1880–82, thirteen were lawyers, an equal number were businessmen (mostly merchants, bankers, and manufacturers), and one was a factory overseer.[71] These men performed much the same party roles as the similarly sized leadership groups of earlier decades, and engrossed similar amounts of political authority. A small number—Robert H. May, M. A. Stovall, William F. Eve, Charles A. Harper—were the same men, or men from the same families, who had dominated Augusta's politics in the 1850s and even the 1840s. New men were among them, to be sure, but in social and economic terms the top of the political ladder in white Augusta seems hardly to have changed in thirty or even forty years. Nor was there significant change at lower levels of party activity. Professionals (including another thirteen lawyers) and businessmen constituted fully 82 percent of identifiable midlevel activists, a group that also included a small number of clerks and skilled tradesmen. Skilled and unskilled workers constituted only 12 percent of a larger group of low-level party activists, two-thirds of whom were professionals and businessmen (the latter including, though, a number of apparently smaller, neighborhood-serving, retail store owners). Only among petition signers and others at the most minimal level of public activity do we find a significant number of manual workers, and even here the proportion (24 percent) falls well short of the proportion of such workers in the white male workforce as a whole (46 percent). Many things had changed in Augusta's politics since the 1850s, but the social structure of political activism among white men was not one of them.

This was not true, of course, among the city's African-American men, who had no place in the political system before the Civil War, and who retained the hope of regaining an effective political voice through the Republican Party during these post-Reconstruction years.[72] The party was almost entirely controlled by black Augustans. Among the twenty men we would count as party leaders was only one white man, Charles Prince, whose job as postmaster was an unhappy reminder to local Democrats of both Reconstruction and the continuing Republican control of the national administration. Alongside Prince in the party's leadership were two other Federal employees (a postal clerk and a gauger with Internal Revenue), a clergyman (William J. White, pastor of Harmony Baptist Church), a saloonkeeper, two teachers, six tradesmen (a barber, a tailor, a carpenter, and three bricklayers), a railroad worker, and a laborer.[73]

Twenty-one skilled and unskilled workers, but only six proprietors, officials, and clerks, are identifiable among midlevel activists, and at the lowest level of party activity we can identify ten manual workers and one post office clerk. All of these midlevel and low-level party men were African American. Here was a quite different community of party activists, reflective not only of racial separation in Augusta, but also of the relegation of most black men to the lower rungs on the occupational ladder (more than half of Augusta's African-American men were laborers, porters, and other unskilled workers, and some 94 percent were manual workers of some kind). It is difficult to speak of either elitism or downward diffusion under these circumstances. Hints of each may be found, but these seem less significant than the mere fact of a black-led, post-Reconstruction political opposition. What is notable is not that patterns of activism in the Republican Party did or did not echo those of the Democrats, but that the party functioned, isolated from power and from state and local patronage, within a community with few resources to support it, and within a larger environment of white hostility. Republican Party activism was a different phenomenon in Augusta, offering different rewards and impelled by different hopes. The forms were much the same—conventions, executive committees, and the like—but the circumstance of exclusion overrode customary political relations and meanings. This circumstance; that is, the separate one-party systems of white and black men, is by far the most significant change in Augusta's politics since the antebellum era.

Augusta may have been typical of southern cities, but patterns of political activism differed in regions outside the South, even among similarly sized cities with recurring Democratic majorities. Dubuque was such a city, and its political experience diverged in many ways from Augusta's, related to but going beyond the obvious fact that Dubuque maintained a competitive two-party system. A significant difference is that in Dubuque there were changes in the social structure of political activism that accord with our narrative of post–Civil War political practice. In both of Dubuque's parties a distinct downward diffusion of political activism is visible in two ways. One is in the greater number and proportion of clerical and manual workers among midlevel and low-level party activists. Again using the 1858–60 election cycle as our point of comparison, clerks and other white-collar employees increased from 4 percent to 11 percent, and skilled and unskilled manual workers from 9 percent to 22 percent, among midlevel party activists. Among low-level activists (we include here the many partisans who served only as members of ward-based vigilance committees) the increases were from 10 percent to 19 percent for clerks, and from 29 percent to 39 percent for manual workers. Put another way, by the early 1880s a third of Dubuque's midlevel political activists, and a significant majority of its low-level party men, were clerks, tradesmen, and unskilled workers, these proportions constituting a significant displacement of those professionals and businessmen who previously had been numerically dominant at all levels of partisan activity. There were differences between the two parties in the more precise patterns of this downward spread of political activity, in that Republicans experienced a somewhat greater increase in white-collar, and Democrats in blue-collar, activism, but these differences were not great. What is more striking is the more general diffusion of political activism within both parties.

A second form of downward diffusion, though modest in scale, is perhaps more interesting, especially in light of our discussions of political action and consciousness in this and the previous chapter. In Dubuque (but not in our smaller towns, and only at lower levels of political activity in Augusta), we can see a shift in the types of businessmen who were active in party affairs, especially at higher levels of partisan activity, and a shift in the types of professionals active at each level. At first glance, we see little diffusion of political leadership in Dubuque—professionals and businessmen accounted for 84 percent of those we deemed party leaders in the early 1880s, a proportion only modestly lower than the 88 percent we calculated for the late 1850s. A closer look, though, reveals a noticeable shift among high-level activists toward businessmen of the sort that historians have long associated with the nitty-gritty of ward politics—saloonkeepers; liquor dealers; contractors; real estate, insurance, and loan brokers—men, frequently from working-class and immigrant wards, who were well situated to offer jobs, loans, information, and other resources that could be exchanged for political loyalty.[74] Frequently, men from these and similar occupations became city aldermen, securing for themselves not only a position in city government, but also, as we have seen, a less remunerative and unlooked-for sliver of the national consciousness. In Dubuque, the proportion of political leaders who followed "ward politician" occupations of this sort expanded from about 17 percent in the late 1850s to about 29 percent in the early 1880s—an increase that is highly suggestive of the direction of change in political practice. There was only a very small increase of such men—from about 17 percent to approximately 21 percent—among the businessmen at the middle levels of partisan activism, and none at all at the lowest levels. What we are observing, it seems, is the ascendancy within the parties of small numbers of neighborhood-oriented businessmen whose political activities would have been more limited in an earlier era, and whose increasing presence did so much to discredit Gilded Age politics. Again, this was a pattern visible in both parties, but with small but interesting differences. For example, saloonkeepers and brokers of real estate, insurance, and loans were present in equal numbers among the leadership of both political parties. At the middle level of partisan activity, though, there was a partisan difference—twelve of seventeen saloonkeepers were Democrats (and two of the five Republican saloonkeepers switched to the Democratic Party in 1882), while eight of ten real estate, insurance, and loan brokers were Republicans.

Also suggestive is a change in the proportions of lawyers and physicians among party men at various levels of activism. Earlier, we described at length the political access that professional standing seems to have given to both lawyers and doctors, and the status that such men imparted to politics. Lawyers were always more numerous, but in the antebellum era there were significant numbers of physicians, too, among local party leaders. This was clearly changing in the Gilded Age. In 1858–60, there were twenty-one lawyers and six doctors among Dubuque's party leaders. In 1880–82, there were thirty-three lawyers and only one doctor. Physicians remained politically active in Dubuque, but only at lower levels, where they in fact outnumbered lawyers thirteen to seven. Moreover, a majority of Dubuque's physicians were entirely absent from our file. Were doctors withdrawing into a separate professional world? Did the advancing practice of ward politics offer fewer places or attractions to such men? Interestingly, nearly all of the thirteen low-activist physicians were members of the city-wide Garfield and Arthur Club, an organization that had little or no role in organizing the campaign and the voters in each ward. Not one was a member of a ward vigilance committee. Let us observe, too, that in this larger town, there were many lawyers who did not actively involve themselves in political affairs. Lawyers were still quite visible in Dubuque's politics, especially at the highest levels of party activity. But in cities such as Dubuque there were many paths to and through a legal career, and some of these did not involve politics. In contrast to our smaller towns, a clear majority of Dubuque's lawyers were not identifiable as political activists. In this way, too—that is, in the partial withdrawal from political activism of men in the learned professions—we glimpse the changing world of post–Civil War urban politics, differing in degree and perhaps in kind from what had come before, and from what still prevailed in smaller places.

That urban political world was most fully developed in Syracuse, the largest of our representative communities. When we look behind the rallies and special interest clubs to the shape and character of the politically active population in this city of fifty thousand, we find, however, only one significant difference from Dubuque. Syracuse was more than twice as large as Dubuque, but the active party men identified in the city's two partisan daily newspapers were no more numerous—indeed, they were slightly less so; 1,757, compared to Dubuque's 1,774—than those in the smaller city. This may reflect a peculiarity of Dubuque's; namely, that its identifiable political community was proportionately much larger than those of any of our other cities and towns. This had been the case in the late 1850s as well, although not to the same degree. A large number of men found a place in our earlier Dubuque file through no more than the signing of a petition, and if these are excluded the visible community of party men shrinks to approximately the same proportion as those of most of our other towns. In the 1880s, on the other hand, the elimination of petition signers and other minimal activists reduces the Dubuque file to 25 percent, still a much higher proportion than any other city or town in our sample. Why should this have been so? The specific patterns of activism we have just reviewed reinforce our belief that Dubuque had crossed a critical urban threshold in its political affairs. More than in Greenfield, Marion, or our other small towns, it could support a larger array of mostly ward-based political roles; yet, having merely crossed that threshold, its population base was small in relation to these roles. Put another way, Dubuque had reached a point where its population could expand without an equivalent expansion of political activism in the city and its individual wards. This, we believe, is just what had happened in Syracuse, its company of 1,757 election inspectors, vigilance committee members, campaign club officers, convention delegates, and ward and city committeemen apparently bringing the political engine to the fire just as quickly as did a similar number in the smaller city of Dubuque. In any case, let us observe that the identifiable population of political activists in Syracuse amounted to 13 percent of the city's men, and to 11 percent if we eliminate petition signers and other minimal activists—the same proportion, curiously, as in Auburn, the smallest of our towns.

In all other respects, the social structure of political activism closely resembled that of Dubuque. The pyramid of activism within the parties was very much the same, almost exactly the same numbers of men being found at higher, middling, and lower levels of partisan engagement. This means that in larger Syracuse the numbers of high-level party activists amounted to less than 1 percent of the adult male population of the city, that midlevel party men amounted to 3 percent, and that low-level participants constituted 7 percent—the same steep slope we have found in all of our towns, and smaller proportions than in most. The concentration and diffusion of political activity in and through the social structure was also very similar in Syracuse and Dubuque. In Syracuse, at least 81 percent of the small group of party leaders (we counted ninety-nine) were professionals and businessmen. All but one of the professionals were lawyers (one of these lawyers was also president of the *Courier*), and although there were large numbers of bankers and large-scale manufacturers among the party-leading businessmen, about one-quarter of this group was made up of men who followed those "ward politician" occupations we described in relation to Dubuque, where the proportion of them among high-level party activists was much the same. The profile of midlevel activists was almost identical in the two cities—66 percent in each were professionals and businessmen, and the distribution of the other third among white- and blue-collar workers differed only slightly. Almost the same proportion of businessmen at this level of political activity—21 percent in Dubuque, 22 percent in Syracuse, were saloonkeepers, liquor store owners, brokers, and other men in "ward politician" occupations. There was slightly less downward diffusion among low-level party men in Syracuse, but again the proportion within the business class of "ward politician" occupations was nearly the same. We find in Syracuse, as well, similar signs of political withdrawal among professional men. Only one physician is found among the leaders of the two parties, and

only five each at middling and lower levels of political activity, a clear majority—and a majority of lawyers, too—absenting themselves from organized political affairs. Syracuse, we might note, is and was a university city, but only
three professors are identifiable as political activists, all at low levels, and none
within ward organizations.

This apparent withdrawal of many professional men from active political
participation, viewed in conjunction with the tactical shift by the political parties away from the "communal" spectacle and toward more complex and complete forms of voter canvassing, suggests that politics was itself becoming more
professionalized, and perhaps more isolated, despite the continuing participation of party activists in other community institutions. The amateur-professional hybrid we found earlier in our antebellum communities was by no
means eliminated, but Gilded Age "politicians" were increasingly recognized as
a distinct and generally unsavory social type. In his autobiography, Theodore
Roosevelt recounts with amusement the prelude to his first foray into politics.
Not knowing the location of the Republican association in his New York City
ward (which is interesting in itself), Roosevelt asked his friends. The men he
knew best, the "big businessmen and lawyers—laughed at me, and told me
that politics were 'low'; that the organizations were run by saloon-keepers,
horse-car conductors, and the like, and not by men with any of whom I would
come into contact outside; and, moreover, they assured me that the men I met
would be rough and brutal and unpleasant to deal with." The club, when
Roosevelt finally found it, was in fact a "large, barn-like room over a saloon,"
furnished with "dingy benches, spittoons," and other objects that seemed to
confirm the ridicule of his genteel friends.[75] Roosevelt did, of course, go into
politics, as did other respectable men of the upper and middle classes, many
of whom remained active in a wide range of reputable communal institutions.
These men (we should no doubt include Syracuse's J. J. Belden) may not have
expected to associate for long with "saloon-keepers, horse-car conductors,"
and other such disreputable people on the ward level of their parties, or they
may have relished the rough camaraderie and combat of political life. Others
were not so attracted, or so willing to risk the unpleasantness of "low" associations. Their withdrawal was at once cause and effect of this era's sharper delin-
eation of the professional politician.

INSIDERS: POLITICS BEHIND THE SCENES AND ON THE GROUND

The continuing involvement of political activists in nonpolitical institutions
was not incompatible with the intense pursuit of politics by these men, or with
the continuing or increasing distinctiveness of a political culture that decades
earlier etched a fairly clear line between those who were inside and those who
were outside the world of party politics. The previous section of this chapter

addresses institutions, programs, and general social patterns of political organization and action, but it does not look behind the scenes to the deals and disputes, to the bribes and bets, to patronage and the pursuit of political friendship that we earlier characterized as animating the distinct world of antebellum political men. A brief look at documents analogous to those we discussed earlier at some length demonstrates that this world, despite the challenge posed by civil service and other political reformers, was for the moment still very much intact. Indeed, it may have been growing even more distinct, as so many Gilded Age writers, humorists, and political cartoonists (to say nothing of Theodore Roosevelt's upper-class friends) would have us believe.

As clerk of the New York State Democratic Central Committee, and as chief clerk of the New York Department of State, Daniel Lamont was at the epicenter of one state's party politics during the 1870s and 1880s.[76] His offices, indeed, were important collecting points of party business, and Lamont received countless letters from active Democrats all across the state, most of them devoted to one or another of three subjects: the control of caucuses and conventions, the recruitment and financing of election-day workers and operations, and the distribution of patronage to political friends. We have encountered all of these things before, and will offer here only a brief second taste. Two letters written to Lamont on the same day in 1876, for example, suffice to convey not only the fact but the assumption of insiders' control of caucuses and nominating conventions. Diedrich Willers, Jr., wrote from the town of Varick to assure Lamont, based on "conversations with Mr. Flanagan & Stowell, Judge Franklin & others," "that everything is to be all right" at his upcoming county convention. William W. Gordon wrote from Delhi at greater length of laxity that permitted "a great deal of tampering" with delegates by "outside parties," in particular by A. J. Parker, a former resident who "at one time was the political leader in this county. He now flatters himself," Gordon continued, "that his old friends are still willing to do his bidding." The current leadership of the county had been shamefully negligent, but with a little help from the state committee they would still be in control of the delegation. The only question was a delegate named Maynard, who should be questioned by Mr. Williams, "one of your clerks in the Census department from here. . . . If Maynard is not sound we will make him get out and substitute one that is all right."[77] One convention that "is to be all right," another slightly mismanaged and requiring a little postconvention doctoring to excise the influence of a former local boss. Where were the people in all this? Willers, Gordon, and Lamont would probably wonder at the question.

These were the kinds of letters Lamont received during the candidate nominating season. Closer to the election, concerns naturally turned to organizing and financing the canvas, processes now made more complicated by the heightened scrutiny of political reformers. One letter to Lamont from A. T. Ney warned of Republican efforts to arrest him for "any undue effort on my part to secure a vote that looks like bribery." For this reason, perhaps, Ney did not ask for money, but he did ask for a quick gubernatorial pardon for one George Warner, who "is all right," and will need to be made a citizen within a few days. John Rankine acknowledged receipt of thirty-three railroad tickets to bring party workers (or were they illegal voters?) from Elmira to Binghamton. Months after the election, D. Magone wrote to Lamont to report that he gave "our friend W. W. Gordon [Lamont's Delaware County confidant] $700 from our funds to help defray the expense that you and I know he incurred with our approval. It is an item that should not go into the record."[78]

It hardly needs saying that most of Lamont's mail following the election concerned patronage—appoint me, appoint my friend, don't appoint my enemy. These letters are much the same as those that troubled Governor Bouck thirty and forty years earlier, including even the pleas of economic need. "Can't you and Nelson manage to get a position for Dan Baker somewhere[?]" asked B. B. Jones of Cortland. "He is poor and is unable to do anything at his trade. Couldn't you smuggle him into the Assembly as one of the doorkeepers or in some position where he could earn enough to keep himself and family through the winter[?]" Two letters from John Courtney, Jr., combine patronage requests with statements about political control. In August of 1883 Courtney reported that Matt Van Hous of Preble is offended at not getting an appointment. "He & his family control almost absolutely his town." A month later he asked Lamont for a return letter indicating "that if I want to assure one of the 'Emerald Hose' boys here a position in Albany you will see that it is given to him in [the] immediate future. They are the crowd that carried caucus here last year for Hill & are now with us but this would make them all go to work and we would win."[79]

Letters such as these remind us of the politics and the incentives for activism that underlay the conventions, committees, clubs, and campaign events that were reported in the partisan press. They must be added to our review of the institutions and formal processes of local politics, and to our analysis of the social structure of political activism, in order to assess more fully the distinctiveness of the world of political insiders. Helpful also is the testimony solicited by state legislative committees charged with investigating disputed elections, much of which addresses the "on the ground" politics of party workers and voters as election day arrived. This inquiry, too, can be brief, as the testimony of party workers (we refer here to some three dozen cases involving state legislative races in New York, Pennsylvania, Connecticut, and California between 1865 and 1890) again reinforces patterns we have already seen. Most familiar to us, and most striking, were the careful and sometimes creative efforts of party men to bring in and control every possible vote. After distributing thirty Democratic ballots to voters during the 1872 election, James Pauley, a Philadelphia policemen, "saw every one to the window." "I am pretty sharp," Edwin Messler boasted to a New York committee a few years earlier. "I don't let my voters get away from me. . . . I take them around and see that they vote my-self."[80] This was standard and quite simple polling-place work, requiring little more than a certain amount of diligent aggressiveness. More clever and elabo-rate was Mike Grogan's arrangement with the deputy superintendent of the almshouse of Albany County to pay twenty-five cents to every inmate who would take the train to West Troy and, with Grogan at his side, hand in a ballot. When asked by the investigating committee if he knew he was voting for the Democrats, inmate James Simmons replied, reasonably if inaccurately, "I understood I was voting for Grogan." M. A. Smith, chief turnkey at San Quentin Prison, had a different way of using custodianship for partisan advan-tage. He had twenty-seven inmates write to their relatives to vote for Republi-can W. O. Banks for state senator.[81] These arrangements were illegal, as were bribes to individual voters, some of whom made a tidy profit from repeat voting. Promised fifteen dollars and a job as a conductor on the cars, Thomas Carroll voted several times in a New York City election in 1869. John Dillon, who was not yet twenty-one, voted twice in 1889 (he did not know for whom), receiving two dollars for each ballot from an Albany County precinct politician. Laurance Ball, who had lost the job he had gained "through political influence and nothing else" on the Third Avenue Railroad in Philadelphia, was recruited in a lager-beer saloon to vote in a state senate race. Paid twenty-five dollars, Ball cast eleven ballots.[82]

Parties and party men could make extraordinary efforts to garner a single vote. In the fall of 1867, a young man named Frederick Dowd became a clerk in the store of Kimberly and Scranton in Branford, Connecticut. As Dowd continued to live with his parents in the town of Madison, neither town's Republican committee was sure where he would vote in the 1868 election. One of the Branford candidates entered Dowd's name on the voter registry as an "intended applicant," and then enlisted the help of the young clerk's em-ployer, who in a state "quite vexed, some might call it mad perhaps," instructed Dowd he must vote in Branford so that the store would not be understaffed on election day. Dowd agreed to ride to Madison to get a certificate transferring his registration to Branford. When he did so, however, he alerted Madison's Republicans, who argued that he had a duty to vote in his home town, and arranged to have a former clerk of Kimberly and Scranton replace him in the store on election day. An exhausted and worried Dowd returned the certificate and rode back to Branford to tell his employer he would not be transferring his registration.[83]

Efforts such as these could be quite intimidating. The battle between local Republican parties for Frederick Dowd's vote gave the young man a ticklish situation at work. Prisoners at San Quentin were in a poor position to refuse to write letters on behalf of the Republican senatorial candidate. And the more ordinary election-day hustling for votes could exert enormous pressure on individual voters. "I was forced almost to go to the polls," testified Philadelphian James Imhof after the 1888 election. Democratic electioneers "kept coming to the house all the time for me to come to the polls and vote that ticket. . . . They came all day." Going to the polls was, of course, insufficient; one had to vote the right way. In Queens County, New York, Philip Hipp voted the Democratic ticket "the man gave me" because he "was afraid they hang me up there. . . . It is bad people up there sir."[84] To be sure, party workers probably spent more time and energy treating and glad-handing voters than they did brow-beating them, and in immigrant neighborhoods there may have been considerable appreciation for the efforts party men made to get new arrivals naturalized before an election. During September and October of 1868 Henry Lyle helped between six hundred and a thousand immigrants become voting citizens in New York City, serving often as a witness to men he barely knew.[85] No less than those born in the United States, immigrants appreciated the more material rewards that flowed from the hands of party workers in the form of treats or cash bribes, or from candidates and officials who wished to recruit still more workers. W. O. Banks, the state senatorial candidate who benefited from San Quentin's epistolary program, spread money around San Francisco's Italian neighborhood in this way. He made the coffee and tea salesman Louis Pistolisi an "alternate inspector of elections" at a salary of six dollars, hired the bootblack Stephano De Martini to peddle tickets for ten dollars, and paid another ten to a grocer named Mascerini to get out the vote.[86] All of these techniques of mobilization, carrots and sticks alike, were part of the vote-getting process, and it is clear that parties and candidates regarded them as important strategic elements of the culminating campaign. Political men carried them out with impunity, despite the cries of foul by political reformers.

What the postelection testimony of party workers and voters tells us, in short, is that Gilded Age political parties maintained an unpublicized second track for augmenting their vote on election day, parallel to and probably as significant as the "official" campaign of rallies, clubs, and published speeches. As in the antebellum era, the political engine advanced on both of these tracks, but there was a shift in emphasis in political organization that belies the new conceit of an "educational campaign" as the defining element of the road away from Tippecanoe. National party leaders were serious in their efforts to improve upon the campaign circus, but it was not the issue-oriented published treatise that occupied party men with specific vote columns to fill. If local parties were moving away from the old spectacle, and from the pretense of an engaged electorate rising spontaneously to save the country, state, or county through the party and its latest list of candidates, it was in the direction of more careful organizing, through groups and with individual voters, in the open and behind the scenes, by means fair and foul, for the purpose of reaching the highest possible party vote. "Educational" partisan reformers may have expected more time and intellectual effort from voters, but politicians "on the ground" expected less—a quick trip to the polls on election day, and the right kind of vote, whether or not it was responsive to issues, to the memory of the great or lost cause, to some other source of "ritual partisan loyalty," or to a two-dollar bribe.[87] "Educational" reformers may have hoped to weaken the distinction between the party politician and the politically engaged private citizen, but the practice of politics reinforced this distinction as one of the defining features of the Gilded Age.

An Excess and a Dearth of Democracy: Patronage, Voting, and Political Engagement in the Gilded Age and Beyond

WHILE SOME national party leaders attempted to elevate the substance and tone of the political campaign, other influential men (including many closely attached to their parties) attacked from the outside, challenging settled political practices by changing the legal and institutional environments in which parties worked. The increasingly visible body of political reformers of this era focused on vital sources of partisan influence, one of which was the patronage system that, in their eyes, distorted the very purpose of elections and of public life by providing a mercenary motive for activism. Civil-service reform was one of the recurring themes of this era, rising in response to well-publicized political scandals, and to the growing perception of patronage-fueled "rings" and "machines." Popular pressure for reform was difficult to mount or sustain, as the effect of cynicism toward politicians and self-serving political practices was most often to turn people away from politics. But civil-service reformers were given an outstanding if unlooked-for opportunity to influence public opinion in the summer of 1881 by the assassination of President James A. Garfield by a man widely perceived (then and now) as a "disappointed office seeker." Charles Guiteau might easily have been dismissed as the madman that his defense attorney portrayed him to be, but there was too little opportunity for vengeance in that, too clear a connection between the shooting and Guiteau's political words and actions (arguably insane, he *was* a disappointed office seeker), and, for reformers, too ripe a chance to convert this tragedy into a victory over the patronage system and corrupt political practices in general. As historians have frequently observed, Guiteau's assassination of Garfield provided the impetus for passage of the Pendleton Act of 1883, establishing at long last a merit system of appointment and promotion for at least a part of the Federal bureaucracy.

There is a convincing connection between these events, but historians who pass quickly from "the disappointed office seeker" to the Pendleton Act miss an opportunity to probe the political culture that gave civil-service reformers their breakthrough as well as their continuing challenge. Before his condemnation and execution, and before the breaking of the civil-service logjam in Congress, Charles Guiteau was subjected to a long criminal trial, the transcript of which speaks to both the brittleness and the continuing force of patronage and other traditions in American politics. Guiteau, we should first note, was a strange man who had followed a varied career as a lawyer, an Oneida perfectionist, a religious lecturer, and a bill collector. Failing in all of these, he decided around 1880 to make his way in politics, specifically by offering campaign services intended to earn him a patronage appointment by the Republican Party. He wrote a speech (initially in support of former President Grant, and then rather clumsily amended to support Garfield after the latter won the Republican nomination), and offered to deliver it on the campaign trail, visiting the headquarters of the New York State Republican Party on dozens of occasions to make and repeat his proposal. Having no standing in the party, however, or in any community, Guiteau's offer was not accepted, save for one occasion on which he appears to have been allowed to present a portion of his speech to an African-American audience in New York City's fourth ward. And yet, Guiteau was not simply dismissed as a political oddball or opportunist by those who controlled and staffed the campaign. His presence at party offices was accepted by party workers and leaders, who had seen many such men come and go with entreaties and proposals no more convincing than Guiteau's. In the small world of party politics bit players and pretenders were still not walled off from even the highest-level leaders. Chester A. Arthur, the man who was placed in the presidency by Guiteau's bullets, testified that he had seen the defendant "at least ten times, and possibly as often as twenty times" at state party headquarters in the fall of 1880. Arthur was the most important man at state party headquarters; yet, he took note of Guiteau's presence, returned "the ordinary salutations of the day," and "once or twice" personally answered his requests to be employed in the campaign.[1]

Nor was Guiteau's speech rejected on substantive grounds, despite its author's minimal credentials. The speech is, indeed, an interesting example of political rhetoric of the era, and the responses to it at Guiteau's trial constitute a telling commentary on American political culture in the early 1880s. The speech begins by invoking the Civil War, waves the bloody shirt throughout, and casts the 1880 election (which, at the presidential level, was a contest between two former Union generals) entirely in terms of a continuing sectional conflict that would surely erupt into another rebellion and war if the Democrats were to win. "In 1861 this nation was convulsed by one of the most gigantic wars on record," Guiteau begins, immediately setting in train the customary associations between Republicanism and the Union, Democracy and rebellion, military heroism and party loyalty, election and crisis. His audience would have heard this countless times before, and would have known at once that they were about to hear again of the slave power and Jeff Davis, of the rising Republican Party and Abraham Lincoln, of General Grant and glorious victory, and, once the presidential nominating convention had done its work and Guiteau had amended his speech, of General Garfield as the latest bearer of the Union banner. They would have understood Guiteau's deflection of Democratic charges of Republican profligacy and debt, even though this required the speaker to reach all the way back to the alleged corruption of the last elected Democratic president, James Buchanan. "The Democratic party are panting for the National Treasury," Guiteau warns. "They have been starving since Buchanan retired in 1861, and they are dreadfully hungry." The capture of the government by "ex-rebels and their northern friends" (Guiteau moves easily and cleverly between disloyalty and corruption as though the latter were a natural consequence of the former) would certainly require another civil war. "Ye men whose sons perished in the war, what say you to this issue? Shall we have another war? Shall our National Treasury be controlled by ex-rebels and their Northern allies?" Guiteau is rising toward a concluding crescendo here, invoking a chorus of "No!" from his imagined audience after each sentence, before a final comparison of the bankruptcy and war that will follow the election of Hancock, and the prosperity and peace that will result from the election of Garfield—the man Guiteau himself would soon shoot down.[2]

Taken by itself, Guiteau's campaign speech simply adds to the impression we have gained from other evidence that retrospective voting was still quite strong in 1880, fifteen years after the end of the Civil War. On the other hand, we have also seen that other forces were gaining ground (historians would add movements toward sectional reconciliation to the substantive issues we have discussed), and it is important to understand just how this speech was used and responded to in Guiteau's trial. The speech was entered into the trial record by the prosecution in order to help portray the assassin as a political opportunist who well understood the customary rhetorical devices for arousing Republican campaign audiences, and who artfully employed these devices to further his prospects for a political appointment. Guiteau's own lawyer turned this evidence in a quite different direction, pointing to its absurdities as proof that it could have been composed only by a fool or a madman.[3] What is important is that neither the prosecution nor the defense took seriously Guiteau's warning of a renewed civil war, or of his overheated retrospective rhetoric. One saw in them a customary political cynicism, while the other saw mere foolishness or lunacy, and in both of these reactions we can ourselves see a political culture at an important moment of transition, when the late civil crisis was beginning to lose its force in shaping political strategy and response.

It was not unreasonable, however, for Guiteau to believe that this speech would find favor among political managers. Nor was he foolish to expect that political appointment would follow from the kind of political service he proposed. To be sure, Guiteau vastly overreached, and his application for a consulship to Vienna or Paris on the basis of a single speech delivered once in one city ward was a good sign of his mental instability. But here, too, Guiteau's actions were grounded in an understanding of how politics and "political friendship" had heretofore worked. Guiteau's testimony (and that of Secretary of State Blaine and others called as witnesses to Guiteau's behavior) reveals, for example, that the most important executive departments, and even the White House and the president (no less, perhaps, than state party headquarters), were still accessible to crowds of office seekers, and that even so dubious a claimant as Charles Guiteau could receive personal attention from important Washington politicians. Guiteau met at length with Congressman John A. Logan and with Senator Benjamin Harrison, both of whom were national leaders in the Republican Party. He joined the daily throng at the State Department, speaking frequently if briefly to Secretary Blaine about his consulship application, and persisting until Blaine finally told him, without "any special harshness" (these are Blaine's words) that he had no chance for the position.[4] At the White House, he passed notes to the president through a doorkeeper he knew, receiving polite if formulaic responses.[5] And he met other important men on the streets of Washington, in restaurants, and in the parlors of political boardinghouses, where he received personal greetings and possibly even some words that an eager and somewhat deranged supplicant might have interpreted as encouragement.[6]

Guiteau commented on political friendship in ways that would have been familiar to Ansel McCall and countless other visible partisans of this and previous generations. "Was Mr. Evarts your personal and political friend?" asked the prosecutor. "He was a political friend. Every Republican is my political friend, ain't they? It is not necessary that I should be a bed-fellow of a man." Again, with reference to Blaine: "He was not your political friend?—A. He was a Republican, and in that sense he was my political friend." Both Guiteau and the prosecuting attorney were careful to distinguish between personal and political friendship, and if Guiteau here applies the latter concept too broadly, his subsequent remarks emphasize its more particular and instrumental meaning. Responding to the prosecutor's scornful observation that he had promised support in the 1884 election to both Garfield and Blaine, Guiteau noted simply that he meant to support the man responsible for getting him a job. "This is the way politics are run; understand that. You tickle me and I tickle you."[7]

What Guiteau evidently did not understand, but what stands out in reactions to his testimony, and also in testimony by Blaine, Logan, and others, is that patronage and "friendship" were increasingly ridiculed, even by men at the heart of the political system. For Blaine the office holder, the dozens of office seekers who crowded his rooms every day, and the Guiteaus who would not cease clamoring for offices they clearly did not deserve, were an annoyance of very little political value. When asked how many times he had seen the defendant, Blaine at first estimated that Guiteau had visited the State Department twenty or twenty-five times, and then quickly added that it might have been only eight or ten, "but eight or ten visits that are of that kind are apt to make the impression of twenty-five or thirty." A little later Blaine observed that forty or so office seekers visited him every day. "And all alike in the forty substantially?" asked the prosecutor. "All alike in desire, and pretty nearly all alike in

8.1. Charles J. Guiteau, office seeker. *Puck*, 1881.

disappointment," Blaine wearily responded.[8] The prosecutor, for his part, heaped scorn upon Guiteau's somewhat smug definitions of political friendship. "You tickle me and I tickle you," explained Guiteau. "Did you try to tickle President Garfield?" was the prosecutor's sharp reply. With one eye on the jury and perhaps another on the public media, the prosecutor was condemning more than the assassin who sat in the prisoner's dock.

The trial of Charles Guiteau ended in a death sentence for the defendant, and delivered as well a heavy but not mortal blow to political patronage. To be sure, the Pendleton Act was in some respects a quite limited victory, for in its initial application only 14,000 of 131,000 federal positions were placed under the merit system. But in other respects it was more significant than these numbers suggest, and not merely because the new civil service would grow to 95,000 by the end of the century, holding the number of patronage appointments steady despite the continuing growth of government. It was the nature of the opposition that made the victory so notable. "It cannot be overemphasized how important patronage was to nineteenth-century parties," Michael Schudson has written; yet, politicians themselves, sensing the nation's mood in the aftermath of Garfield's assassination, voted to circumscribe the patronage system.[9] Over time, civil-service reform changed the political landscape. It allowed congressmen, senators, and secretaries of state to give less time to office seekers; in turn, visible partisans became less inclined to seek or expect access. For some Americans an incentive for political activism had been removed.[10] Moreover, the Pendleton Act, however fortuitous and exceptional an event, was a victory that emboldened reformers to extend their assault into other areas of politics, and to other political actors. Most significantly, they turned to elections, and to the voters themselves.

To many reformers of the Gilded Age the fundamental cause of political debasement lay not in the patronage system of dispensing public jobs but in an electorate far removed from the more and less deluded pleadings for office. It lay, too, in the political parties' continuing exploitation of ignorance and venality among voters, especially in the squalid neighborhoods of growing, ethnically diverse cities. Convinced that America suffered from an "excess of democracy," these reformers—often the same men who reacted also against labor militancy and the "unscientific" distribution of public and private charity—pushed for changes in the way elections were held, and, above all, for a tightening of voter eligibility. Their critique resonated with concerns about the disreputability that many upper- and middle-class Americans found at the heart of the rude republic, and their arguments found considerable support among respectable people in the cities and countryside of every region. From the 1870s through the early decades of the twentieth century nearly every state participated in what Frances Fox Piven and Richard Cloward have called "the reconstruction of the legal and procedural underpinnings" of voter participation.[11] State legislatures and constitutional conventions moved to restrict the

franchise by tightening procedures for voter registration, by regulating the voting of recently naturalized citizens, and by instituting poll taxes and voter
literacy tests. In the process, according to Piven and Cloward, they changed
the United States from one of the easiest nations in which to vote, into one of
the most difficult.

The use of poll taxes and literacy tests by southern states to disfranchise
black citizens is legendary.[12] Also well known to historians are efforts made by
states outside the South to reduce the numbers of troublesome voters, sometimes by means of poll taxes, and sometimes by instituting and controlling
voter registration. Between 1876 and 1912 about half the states in the North
and West amended their constitutions to authorize the registration of voters,
and in a number of instances the new clauses and laws clearly reflect what
we have called the urbanization of political consciousness—the increasingly
widespread association in people's minds of political manipulation and corruption within the immigrant and other poor neighborhoods of cities. New Jersey,
for example, required personal voter registration in the seven cities in the state
with populations exceeding twenty thousand. In New York, despite the claim
of one delegate that "the lowest slums of the meanest cities produce no public
enemies more malign than those fly-gobbling clodhoppers of the crossroads,"
the constitutional convention of 1894 required only those who lived in cities
of five thousand or more to register in person. (Southern states, too, could
demonstrate the same concern: in 1891, Texas adopted a law requiring voter
registration in cities larger than ten thousand.)[13] Some new laws focused on
the immigrants themselves; or, more accurately, the parties' manipulation of
newcomers. In 1874 Pennsylvania barred from the polls any man who had
been naturalized less than thirty days before an election. Twenty years later,
New York's constitutional convention upped the ante to ninety days. Learning
that more than seven out of every nine persons who were naturalized became
citizens in the month of October, convention delegates tried to take the process
"out of the hands of campaign committees," and to shift the initiative away
from "persons who are desirous merely of making voters, and not of making
citizens."[14] The convention's majority clearly felt that democracy would not
suffer from the absence of those voters the parties did not rush to naturalize
in the last days of the campaign.

Except in the South, where the dominant Democrats were delighted to im-
plement laws they had passed for the removal of African-American Republicans
from voter lists, the new regulations apparently had little immediate impact
on vote totals. Registration laws and poll taxes did not in themselves wrest
control of elections from party professionals and their workers (this would
occur more gradually, with the introduction of state-printed ballots, voting
booths and machines, and rules regulating political activity at polling places),
and in many places "weak and ineffectual" laws, as historian Peter Argersinger
has called them, were circumvented or ignored with relative ease.[15] It is im-

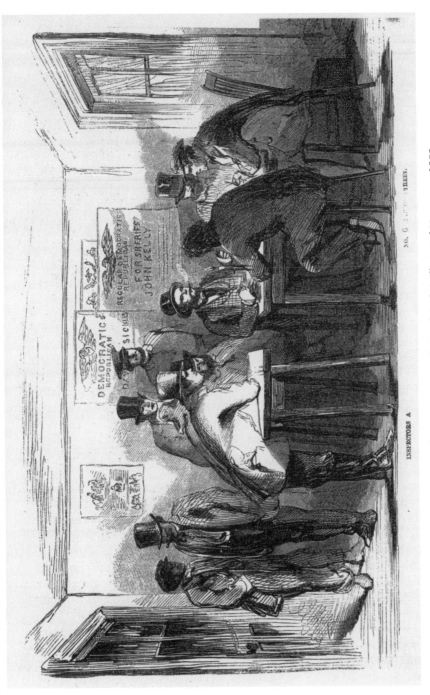

8.2. Election clerks and inspectors at work. *Frank Leslie's Illustrated Newspaper*, 1858.

portant to understand that the new procedures and regulations were imple-
mented and enforced by the very ward and precinct party men they were
designed to control (an explanation, perhaps, of why the party politicians sit-
ting in state legislatures and constitutional conventions voted for these laws in
the first place). Registration clerkships and local magistracies were, in most
places, patronage appointments, and election inspectors continued to be
named directly by the political parties themselves—a policy, one might say, of
appointing rival foxes to guard the chicken house. "The man who has the
inspectors on his side," wrote Thomas Kinsella in the Brooklyn Eagle in 1880,
"is in no danger of finding the people recorded against him."[16] The culture and
practice of killing chickens ran deeply among political foxes, who found ways
around the law and each other, and of colluding in the kill when necessary. In
Pennsylvania, for example, unregistered voters could be taken to a friendly
magistrate on election day to swear to their qualifications and procure certifi-
cates. In Deerfield Township and in the fourth ward of Scranton, according to
the testimony of election judges, about 10 percent of the voters had become
eligible in this way in elections held in 1871 and 1872. "Get a handkerchief
washed there," advised William Davis to his friend George Smith when the
latter wanted to establish residency and register in Forest County a week before
the election of 1876.[17] Loopholes of this sort discouraged election officials from
challenging voters, and there could be unhappy consequences of attempting
to play by the new rather than the old rules of the game. An election judge in
Scranton's ninth ward described with some consternation what happened
when a zealous Democratic election inspector demanded to see the naturalization papers of one voter he expected to vote Republican. The Republican inspector immediately began to challenge every voter he believed to be a Democrat, requiring the Democrat to challenge all the Republicans in turn. "The
result was, they had to go home and get their papers—some of them a mile."[18]
Neither party profited from this unnecessary alienation of voters, and one can
be sure that there were few such challenges in Scranton's ninth ward the next
time around.

And yet the new laws did make election-day mobilization more difficult and
more costly for the parties, and in the long run these laws would contribute
to declining vote totals. Registration laws, and regulations concerning the timing of naturalization, added to the tasks of party workers, who could not always
count on their opponents to allow votes unsupported by the proper documents. Poll taxes created similar tasks, and a not inconsiderable new expense.
Testimony from a disputed election in the third state senatorial district in Philadelphia provides a close view of how one state's new poll tax could add to the
parties' burden, and complicate their relations with voters. In Pennsylvania,
an adult male citizen became eligible to vote upon payment of any state or
county tax within two years of an election. Those men left out by this provision
could qualify by paying a fifty-cent poll tax and by bringing the receipt to the

polls on election day. To minimize fraud, the poll tax had to be paid no earlier than two months, and no later than one month, prior to the election. The tax could be paid at the office of the local receiver of taxes, or in any of several temporary offices set up in the neighborhoods of large cities. Young men of twenty-one or twenty-two were exempt from the poll tax, even if they paid no other taxes.

Testimony following the disputed 1888 senatorial election between Francis Osbourn, the Republican, and Charles Devlin, the Democrat, reveals the extra burden of effort and money the poll tax placed on the political parties. Before the tax was enacted it had sufficed to list party voters and make sure they reached the polls with a properly prepared ballot. Now it was necessary to see that taxes were paid and duly certified, which required earlier ward and precinct organization and additional visits to individual voters. Many citizens, to be sure, paid the tax without any prodding or assistance from their party. Thomas Holloway, for example, was a committed voter who waited so long at the office of the receiver of taxes that he missed chapel services at the University of Pennsylvania, where he was a student. Others, however, including some who objected on principle, did not pay the tax. "Hold on a minute!" James Sheridan exclaimed. "I want all hands to pay attention to what I am going to say. I put in three years in the United States service." Less principled, but certainly more numerous, were those simply unwilling to take the time or pay the money that would entitle them to vote. The task, and often the expense, then fell to the parties.[19]

Party officials began by collecting money to defray the tax from the men who attended the meetings of campaign clubs, and in poll-tax states this was no doubt one of the reasons clubs continued to be organized in the face of a declining campaign spectacle. At a Democratic gathering at Steuben Hall at Fifth and Thompson streets, Frank Weibel was asked to contribute fifty cents: "I did not ask what it was for." John Irvin paid his poll tax at the Garfield Club, where the tax receiver actually set up shop for a time. But most voters could not be reached in this way: of the thousands of voters who were interviewed in this case, no more than a dozen claimed that they had paid their tax at a political club. Precinct politicians, therefore, had to find the vast majority of delinquents in the streets or at home. The experience of Wilson Allen was probably typical. He was sought out by politically active firemen to make sure his tax was paid. "I have been living around here for several years," Allen testified, "and of course I know a good many friends there, and they always make mention to me before the election have I got a tax receipt, and if I have not got one they send me one."[20]

As Allen's testimony suggests, many voters expected their party to pay the poll tax for them, and as long as a voter's allegiance was known, precinct politicians were willing to do so. Michael Dougherty was told to pay "what I felt like paying," and the Democratic Party would pay the rest: "that is the custom." F. J. Heppe was prepared to pay his half dollar at the Republican club until a friend told him "he could get it for nothing." It did not take long for the naive to learn that the party would pick up the tab. "Everybody knows that the tax is paid by the [party] committee," Frank Wild told investigators. How many men regularly availed themselves of the party's treasury in this way is impossible to specify, but we do have a reliable accounting of the magnitude of one party's involvement in the securing of poll-tax receipts for its voters during one election year. J. Dallas Hall, chief clerk to the receiver of taxes in Philadelphia, testified in the *Osbourn vs. Devlin* case that the Philadelphia Democratic Committee paid twenty-two thousand dollars in poll-tax assessments in 1888, enough to qualify 44,000 voters, or nearly half of the 92,786 Philadelphians who cast Democratic ballots that year. As many of these actual voters had qualified by paying other levies (and as some were young men not liable under the poll-tax law), we must conclude that the committee collected and paid—or simply paid—for the vast majority of those Democrats who were subject to the poll tax.[21] Republicans almost certainly had comparable arrangements for collecting funds, paying taxes, and distributing receipts.

Despite strenuous efforts and significant expense, the parties did not reach everyone, and this compelled party workers to encourage voting by those they knew had not paid the tax (implicating themselves, we might add, in an illegal activity that deepened the perception of parties as corrupt). Several voters testified that precinct politicians invited them to vote even after having been told that they had paid no tax. H. B. Somers swore that he had "not intended voting. I was called for at my home two or three times, and I voted." James Morrow voted for Osbourn even though he, like Somers, had not paid the poll tax. "The reason of that," he testified, "is that I have to work until half-past seven o'clock, and I did not intend to vote, and they would have me vote, and of course I told them I had no tax receipt, and I had not time to look up one, and they said it will be all right. I said well, I will take your word for it. So I went on with it."[22] Morrow's ballot was not challenged, and neither were those of several others who voted in this way, but it is evident that the parties preferred earlier and better organization, and even the expense of paying poll taxes, to such blatant challenges to the new system. Also clear is their understanding that too many men would neither pay the tax nor vote if left on their own. "I have never bothered with politics," James Morrow explained at the conclusion of his testimony. "[M]y work takes up all my time." Thomas Kean had not paid the poll tax, and was not asked for his receipt when he voted. "If there had been any difficulty about it," he insisted, "I should not have voted, for I was not much interested in voting." Kean voted Republican, but "didn't examine the whole of the ticket." "I never bothered myself about a tax receipt," claimed John Ward, "and sometimes did not vote for anybody." Pressed by a party activist, he did vote in 1888, but told the committee "I never looked at the ticket or whom I voted for."[23]

Comments of this sort, many of which were incidental to the main line of questioning by investigative committees, give us a good sense, if not an accurate measure, of the apathy (and sometimes the skepticism and hostility) that underlay the disengagement of some citizens from political affairs—disengagement that in turn underlay the voter-mobilization practices that parties found so necessary and reformers so odious. They recur throughout the testimony of ordinary men before these committees, whether it related to poll taxes, registration, or voting. "I think as much as I have taken part in politics is to go to the polls and vote," stated bank teller Francis Maher, who also informed a New York committee that he would not even have done that much if he had encountered any difficulty or delay at the polls. Many others besides Maher told the committees, gently or otherwise, that they had other things to do, and little time or energy left over for politics. Thomas Francis, a railroad worker, "couldn't tell" anything about a state senatorial election, and learned the name of his party's candidate "on the way up to vote." "I go to my work at seven in the morning and go back at seven at night," he explained. Michael Davenport, a laborer, was a little more blunt: "It is my business that troubles me always, and not them things." David Leehardt bristled when questioned about what he did after he had deposited his vote: "I am not a politician," he declared (to questioners who obviously were); "I am a working man; I was working the whole day in the shop, and then I got out at twelve o'clock for my dinner; I cannot spare much time to vote, I must work, I have got a big family." George Knapp spent "less than a minute, not more than three minutes" at the polls; Richard Libby took "no more [time] than I could help" to vote his Republican ticket.[24]

Even party workers, who did have to give more than a few minutes to politics, could express a lack of interest in political affairs. In California, Edward Attridge responded negatively when asked if he was interested in the tariff. Was he in politics, then, for "whatever you can get out of it? A. I don't know what a man is in politics for. . . . I went over [to the Republicans] for good friends and to benefit myself" with a job on the police force. Attridge seems to have been a rather disreputable fellow, but candidate W. O. Banks thought him valuable enough to take him to see Governor Waterman to get assurances about patronage for him and his father. Neither the tariff nor any other issue interested James Lynch, who pocketed his salary and the money given him to peddle tickets: "I generally pick up all the loose change that is running around." E. P. Buckley, a real estate and insurance agent who had supported the Republicans for thirty-five years, told the committee that he had electioneered not out of any interest in Benjamin Harrison or the party platform, but because he had made a twenty-dollar bet on the state senate race. Louis Pistolisi explained that he accepted six dollars to work for Banks because he had nothing better to do. "My work is finished," Pistolisi explained to a Democratic Party worker (Pistolisi, recall, worked for the Republican candidate) who found him in a saloon "playing euchre with the boys" on the night before the election. "Well, come on boys, let's go up and have a drink on Sullivan," the Democrat responded. Neither man, we suppose, lost much sleep over the outcome of the election.[25]

Many voters testified to committees that they had voted only because they had been brought to the polls, or induced to go, by other people.[26] We have seen enough to know that these other people were often party workers, but they could also be family members, friends, or employers who were among the more committed party adherents or citizens. Many of the latter would have received party tickets in advance of the election, a practice (reflective of the old landscape of mobilization) that stimulated and enhanced their efforts to reach the less committed. Edward Adriance, a New York City dry-goods clerk, voted in response to a very personal and forceful influence. When the Republicans sent ballots to the house he shared with his father, Adriance "did not pay any attention to them at all." But when Mr. Adriance handed his son an envelope and said, "Ed, vote those tickets!" Adriance complied, even though he had no interest "in politics whatever." Nicholas Rossiter's son John was eligible to vote for the first time in the fall of 1888. Nicholas was certain John voted "because I took him up there by the coat collar and bid him cast it." Employers and supervisors could exercise a similar paternalism. James Seligman, a banker, selected tickets for his coachman, and went with him to the polls "so that he did not get cheated." When David Hayes told the boss spinner in his mill that he did not think he would vote because "I didn't like to climb the hill," Dennis Murray replied, "you had better go up and vote. . . ."[27] Friends were generally not so forceful, but a number of indifferent citizens testified that they voted only to accommodate a friend, or to go along with street-corner companions. Dwight Ruggles did so even though he was "indifferent about the election," and "cared nothing about voting any way." Ambrose Spencer "would not go across the street to vote for anyone," but did vote at the behest of a neighbor, as did Francis Seib, who "would not have voted at all, but a few neighbors come and invited me." As Charles Baxter stood on the corner with four or five friends, one declared he was going to vote for Clauson for assembly. Baxter "thought I might as well too." Patrick Kearney would not have voted in that same election in Manhattan in 1867, "only that Mr. Bryan McCahill and others were standing on the corner of Third Avenue and 49th Street" and McCahill stated that it would be as good to vote for Clauson "as some of those other loafers." "If he is such a man I will vote for him," Kearney announced, and he did.[28]

Political parties concerned themselves with this kind of nonchalance, but reformers worried more about ignorance, which they ascribed not only to those who were indifferent toward politics, but also to venal and easily manipulated partisans. Ignorance about candidates (especially those listed below the top line of electoral tickets) and an unthinking compliance with the pressures and favors of party workers are ubiquitous themes of the postelection testimony.

When asked by investigating committees whether they had read their ballots, significant numbers of voters stated that they had not, or were uncertain if they had, and a smaller but still significant number could not say that they knew who they had voted for. To be more precise, in the aftermath of four state legislative elections held in New York between 1868 and 1888, in districts ranging from Manhattan to the almost entirely rural east-central region of the state, 23 percent of the 766 men asked if they had read their ballots answered negatively, and another 8 percent were uncertain. Of 1,110 respondents to the question "Do you know who you voted for?" 11 percent admitted they did not, and 7 percent were uncertain. Interestingly, the highest proportions of negative and uncertain answers were among rural voters (52 percent of the east-central voters had not read or could not recall reading their ballots, while 28 percent of these voters could not say they knew who they had voted for), rather than those in the big city.[29] But they are at least fairly high everywhere, and they undoubtedly understate the actual amount of ignorance about candidates among voters. Many respondents were reluctant to admit to what was, in the context of a legislative committee hearing, an embarrassing truth. Some men surely learned the names of the contesting candidates on the way to the committee room; indeed, what may be most remarkable is that so many did not trouble themselves with gaining the information for sustaining so simple a bluff. The committees ordinarily did not attempt to break down affirmative answers with further probing, although we might also note that in a few cases they did so with little difficulty. Hugh Campbell, for example, told the committee that he had voted for Halpin for assembly in 1868, adding, "well, I can read." Counsel surprised him: "Just read there." Campbell tried bravado: "I won't read to please you." It didn't work: "Q. Can you read? A. No, I can't read. . . . That's where I am played out; a man gave me the tickets."[30] Moreover, a large number of affirmative respondents revealed that they had read only the top of the ticket, and that they had no interest in or knowledge of candidates below the top line. Robert Sandy, for example, knew that he had voted for Cleveland in 1888, but added "I cannot tell you anything more than that." James Beechey was "so entirely taken up with the [Harrison] part that I hardly noticed whom else was on the ticket." Asked who he voted for as state senator, F. G. Maurer, a painter, replied, "I voted for our President."[31]

As we have seen in earlier chapters, voter inattention to party tickets was frequently exploited by polling-place workers. Parties posted their complete tickets at the polls, often on prominent billboards, but it is clear that many voters did not take the time to verify that their ballots were "straight." There is considerable evidence in the testimony on disputed elections that ticket distributors who smuggled one or more of the wrong names onto a party ticket could count on fooling a fairly large number of voters. Sometimes a precinct worker would ask a voter to scratch a name and to substitute another, especially when the latter was that of a candidate from the neighborhood. More often he would simply alter the ticket himself, knowing that many voters would not notice the change. In the 1869 assembly race in Kings County, New York, for example, G. W. Reid gave out fifteen ballots with William C. Jones, the Democrat, pasted over William W. Goodrich, the Republican. "Of course," he disingenuously told the committee, "I thought they would look at the tickets and see who they were voting for; but it seems they did not." James Pauley claimed that a majority of the thirty Democrats to whom he gave tickets and accompanied "to the window" in 1873 knew that Joseph Ash was the Republican candidate for assembly: "Of course I didn't want to deceive them," he added. The committee, however, swore in several voters who had obtained their tickets from Pauley, and who claimed they had voted for John Faunce, the Democrat.[32] In some of the disputed elections the number of split tickets was very high, and there were few voters who testified that they had made the changes themselves, or even that they knew and approved of changes made by someone else. In the twentieth district of the ninth ward of Manhattan in 1870, the election inspector reported "over a hundred odd split tickets" out of 311 cast. Of 719 votes in the second election district of Middletown, Richmond County, New York, in 1868, the inspector counted 150 scratches and 40 pasted names. James Dunn, the deputy sheriff of San Francisco, may have exaggerated when he testified that there were "more scratched than there are straight tickets" in the 1888 election, but his comment reflects the concern of party professionals about the potential for bogus ballots to find their way into the box.[33] Party newspapers, as we have seen, invariably warned their readers of this possibility in the last issues before the election. We may assume that many of those who neglected to read their ballots were similarly inattentive to the party press.

The testimony of James Dunn and others suggests that ticket "scratching," and consequent split-ticket voting, may have been more widespread than has generally been recognized. This is significant, as historians have often pointed to straight-ticket voting (as evidenced by each party's nearly consistent vote totals for the various races in a given election) as evidence of a widespread and strong partisan commitment. However, vote totals alone do not tell us how much ticket splitting there was in an election. The minor variations we see in each party's vote tell us only of the net effect of what might have been a large number of nearly offsetting alterations in each direction. Were there, then, many such hidden scratched ballots in a typical nineteenth-century election? We must be careful about generalizing from disputed elections such as those we just observed in Manhattan, San Francisco, and New York's Richmond County—to the extent that the dispute revolved around the number of altered ballots, these elections were atypical with reference to this issue. But even these atypical elections suggest the likelihood of widespread split-ticket voting and, more importantly, tell us that ticket scratching was probably more frequently the deceptive act of poll workers than the deliberate act of individual voters. Perhaps, too, they suggest that straight-ticket voting was in some cases no more deliberate, but reflected the same willing acceptance of ballots from party workers, who in most elections offered their own party's unaltered ticket. Such a conclusion corresponds to the more extensive testimony of men who voted reluctantly or with nonchalance, who paid little attention to their ballots, and who could not even say whether or not they had voted a straight party ticket. It is this inattentiveness that seems to us most important of all. Among other things, it prevents us from assuming that an altered ballot was an act of political independence, or that a straight ticket invariably signified deep partisan commitment.

The "best men" who wished to restrict the franchise made much of the careless citizenship testified to so frequently in the legislative committee hearings, especially when it was exercised by "easily manipulated" recent immigrants. They could identify much evidence of that manipulation in the postelection testimony. The coachman Francis Zimmerman, for example, did not know whether he had voted for the Democrats or the Republicans. He had obtained his tickets from Cohen the harness maker, but understood nothing about them. Voting in an unfamiliar land was "too much" for him. "I am," he confessed, "too much of a stranger for this." Godfritz Lipkins, who had been in the country for eight years, could tell the committee very little about his vote in 1874. A man had handed him a paper, he remembered, but at the polls someone else "came and knocked me on the shoulder and said, 'Here, Dutchman, come and get something to drink.'" Lipkins told the committee he did not know what a Republican or a Democrat was, or how men gained office in America. "I like General Grant," he concluded. "I like him to be president." Fourteen years later John Steiger, who was interviewed in German, voted a ticket he could not read but thought was Republican. "Did you vote for Osbourn?" he was asked. "I know I voted for President Taylor," Steiger replied.[34] "Don't vote for General Taylor, for he is dead," a facetious editor might have advised.

The ignorance of American institutions on the part of recent immigrants was a significant problem to political reformers, but of equal or even greater importance to them was the ignorance of issues and candidates born of the unreflective, even hidebound partisanship of many voters, native and immigrant alike. What politicians and other activists considered a laudable commitment, reformers saw as the inability or unwillingness to engage in a thoughtful, independent citizenship, and a number of reform proposals were intended to weaken the hold of the parties over voters' minds and motivation. Civil-service reform, the Australian ballot, and the institution of citizen initiative, referendum, and recall were the most obvious of these, but others were no less relevant. The movement for civics instruction in American schools, for example, was predicated on the need to equip future voters with the knowledge that would allow them to make judgments about issues and candidates. More importantly, civics classes (which were introduced into many American high schools in the latter years of the century) would imbue young citizens with the value of political independence, beginning their political socialization with a value diametrically opposed to the central tenet of the political parties.[35] Having removed from the electorate some of those who they believed were the least equipped to vote, reformers tried to improve the performance of those who remained. Unthinking partisan loyalty was a principle target of both of these assaults on the practice of American politics.

Some witnesses in the disputed-election hearings did join their admissions of ignorance about candidates to firm statements of partisan allegiance. Bernard Maybeck, a wood carver, could not name a candidate he had voted for ("I am not a politician. . . . I went there from my business and back to my business"), but asserted instead that "when the time come, I vote with the party I know come up to my idea." Did Albert Weber vote for Halpin or Herrick for assemblyman? "I voted the Democratic ticket, that is all I know. . . . I didn't know there were two such men living as that." Did Cornelius Driscoll support Marsh or Decker? "I intended to vote the [Democratic] ticket Donovan gave me." "Here are two candidates," the committee's counsel asked saw mill worker Rufus Watson, "can you tell me which you voted for?" "I could," Watson replied, "if I knew their politics."[36] Reformers would have seized on statements such as these, and might quite reasonably have used them to claim that partisan loyalists, no less than others too marginal to express even a party preference, were inattentive to the ballots they cast. We must be more circumspect, however, in claiming that the partisan commitment of these men, and others like them, was itself slavish or thoughtless. Bernard Maybeck, though "not a politician" (he was one of many witnesses who went out of their way to say this), had an "idea" that his party had "come up to," and we cannot tell whether the committee would have gotten an earful or an empty stare if it had asked him to explain what that idea was. Rufus Watson's "if I knew their politics" might have referred to more than a party name. Maybeck's and Watson's knowledge of the names of party candidates—politicians chosen by other politicians at a party convention—might have been less important to them than the party principles and policies they could claim these candidates were obligated to protect and pursue. Principled partisanship, particularly on the part of a wood carver and a sawmill worker, was not something the "best men" were quick to recognize, but there is nothing that these partisan witnesses told the committees that precludes such an interpretation of their failure to know the names of candidates.

Political scientists have used the term "rational ignorance" to describe situations in which voters understand that adding to a limited knowledge about candidates is not worth the time and effort of doing so.[37] Perhaps some of the Gilded Age men who could not name the candidates they had voted for or against in state legislative races—the Bernard Maybecks and the Rufus Watsons—were being rational in this sense. Perhaps they did have a good "idea" of politics, and cast their votes accordingly. "Rational ignorance," however, could apply to parties as well as candidates, and by extension to the entire political system. If the political ideas of men such as Bernard Maybeck were informed and well considered, how often would either party come up to them? How often would these men, along with others who simply did not know or care, find themselves ignoring not merely candidates but politics in general? During the late nineteenth century as high a proportion of the electorate as in former times remained within the voting population, but the testimony of thousands of ordinary voters reveals, perhaps more clearly than any other surviving source, how qualified, how hesitant, and how casual the act of voting could be. Some men, as in the age of Tippecanoe, were careful, informed, and even determined in the act of voting, but others purchased the partisan "package" at a relatively low price of thought or effort. Still others were merely borne along by the tide—brought to the polls by a friend; dragged there by a party worker; bribed, duped, or intimidated into a particular vote once on the ground. Eventually, the reformers' assault on parties, voters, and the form and style of American elections would, in combination with other forces, reduce the proportion of voters back to Jacksonian levels and even lower, draining the political system of those least committed to it. The heirs of the disaffected and uncaring voters of the nineteenth century, no longer subject to the same degree and forms of pre-election and election-day pressure from the parties—and harder to find and to pester in the densely packed neighborhoods and sprawling suburbs of great cities—would more often express their political "idea" (or the absence of any) by staying home.

CONCLUSION: DEMOCRACY AND DISENGAGEMENT

When the parties controlled the polling place, voter turnout was very high. And when they lost that control, turnout declined. Does this suggest a falling off of participatory democracy, a "decline of popular politics" from the nineteenth century to the twentieth? We have been arguing, in effect, that the persisting decline in the percentage of voting Americans has been overburdened by historians who rely on the readily available, reassuringly quantifiable evidence of engagement that vote columns seem to provide, and who accept a straightforward association of voting with political engagement. Votes can be tabulated, and tabulations of votes can be compared, but how shall we tabulate and compare the different meanings—the different types and degrees of political attitude and feeling—that voters brought to the polls? How shall we add to this already problematic tabulation the other political activities and expressions of citizens who lived not merely on election day, and not only during the political season, but all the year round? As Sidney Verba and his colleagues have recently pointed out, the act of voting, which is a quantitatively fixed phenomenon within a given span of time, understates in highly varying degrees the political activity of citizens who attend meetings, write letters to legislators and editors, send contributions to parties, candidates, and pressure groups, or in other ways expand the political process beyond election day.[38] Can it not also be made to *overstate* the political engagement of those who, in varying degrees, decline or even actively resist knowledge of and involvement in political activities that are urged upon them by parties and by more committed citizens? Political historians of the nineteenth century have augmented their tabulations of voter turnout with other evidence of popular political participation, especially in the party-directed campaigns that preceded presidential elections. What they have been less attentive to is the evidence of qualified participation and of outright rejection. They have, for the most part, heard the cheers but not the sneers, and have taken very little note of silence.

America's democratic politics took shape in an age when small central and state governments contributed to (or intruded into) most people's lives in relatively remote, indirect, and minimal ways. The political parties developed modes of mobilizing large numbers of voters who did not have to care much about the outcome of elections, and the success of the parties' efforts relied on many things—from heroic candidates to election-day drinks—that had little to do with public policy. Some, of course, did care, and found in their party's package of ideas, symbols, and candidates an important representation of their own values. But for many Americans the political party was not a "natural lens through which to view the world." Large numbers, we believe, embraced the institutions and rituals of self-rule hesitantly, limiting their political engagement to brief periods, distancing themselves from the wire-pullers and office seekers who ran the parties to their own advantage, and resisting the intrusion of politics into the more sacred precincts of family, church, and community. Nearly everyone affirmed democracy itself, and most Americans accepted voting as a civic responsibility, but a much smaller number of citizens found in the party and its politicians an entirely satisfactory embodiment of democratic ideals; indeed, the party's reputation appears to have worsened as it extended its reach over the political process, absorbing preexisting personal networks of influence, introducing partisan considerations into local elections, and contributing to the decline and eventual abandonment of the "meeting-place democracy" that had functioned occasionally or regularly in many cities and towns, accomplishing various types of public business through nonpartisan assemblies of local citizens. Political engagement—increasingly, partisan engagement—was for some a serious business, for others an amusement or temporary diversion, and for still others an intrusion.

By the early 1850s, as Michael Holt has shown, alienation from the political parties deepened with the growing perception that little of importance separated them as organizers of policy or doctrine.[39] This would change, however, as the "peculiar issue" of slavery intruded itself into the political system with increasing force, eventuating in the still more peculiar issues of secession and war. The Civil War in particular energized the political feelings and commitment of many Americans who had never before been deeply engaged in public affairs, and it is interesting to note that it is in the context of the more intense politics of the great civil crisis that Abraham Lincoln, concluding his brief remarks at the new military cemetery on what had been the Gettysburg battlefield, articulated the most eloquent possible definition of participatory democracy. It is seldom if ever noticed that Lincoln's famous last sentence was in an important sense contestable. The war was being fought to save the Union, not democracy, and white Southerners would no doubt claim that their Confederacy, no less than the Yankee Union, functioned (or would function in peacetime) as a "government of the people, by the people, and for the people." But Lincoln found an excellent moment for identifying the Unionist cause and the American political nation with a democracy that was engaging more citizens in public affairs than it had ever before succeeded in doing. It was a masterful perception.

The Civil War changed many things in American life, but it did not entirely transform patterns of political activity and commitment, and it did not seem to bring the nation significantly closer to Lincoln's ideal. Even before the war had ended, but especially after, long-settled attitudes reasserted themselves, and the more active and relevant central government that grew out of the war reinforced many of the perceptions that discouraged political engagement, even while it stimulated some people to take a greater interest in what the government was doing. The well-publicized peculations of the Gilded Age alienated many, but so in a different way did government expansion itself. "The more complex and extravagant government becomes," argued Henry George in 1879, "the more it gets to be a power distinct from and independent of the people, and the more difficult does it become to bring questions of real public policy to a popular decision." The problem, under these conditions, lay with the "average American voter," who "has prejudices, party feelings, general notions of a certain kind, but [who] gives to the fundamental questions of government not much more thought than a street-car horse does to the profits of the line."[40] George was pleading a case, but it was by no means peculiar that his solution to the fundamental problems of an industrializing, urbanizing, and increasingly unequal society was a simple one that skirted and even undermined existing political institutions, including the parties that he, like so many others, derided as remote and corrupt.[41] This was, as we have seen, a great age for dramatically simple proposals that bypassed parties and most or all other aspects of the existing political process.

We have encountered citizens of Henry George's era who were as thoughtless as a streetcar horse, and we have met others whose serious grappling with public issues generated by the more active government of the Gilded Age complicated their relations to their party and to the political system. The Civil War veteran Washington Marsh became interested in national politics when his pension became an important part of his livelihood. But his awakened interest remained focused on this one issue, which he discussed in his diary in personal, not public terms, and in a way that suggests further alienation from his political party and from politics in general. William B. Pratt's political interests were wider, less self-centered, and of much longer standing, but even this most avid of citizens experienced difficulties with the way political men were conducting the new government. Pratt's diary, and the shift of his public writing from political to agricultural newspapers and subjects, reveal a greater attachment to extrapolitical organizations than to his political party, and an increasing skepticism toward politics in general. Marsh and Pratt were but two men of millions in Gilded Age America, and their diaries only begin to suggest the variant responses of attentive men and women to evolving public issues. However, read in conjunction with other diaries, and other types of sources, they do allow us reasonably to conclude that this was not an era of increasing political engagement.

We have argued in many different ways that the massive turnouts in nineteenth-century elections mask the highly variable relations of Americans to their politics—relations that included detachment as well as commitment, skepticism as well as belief, disgust as well as enthusiasm—and the relatively clear divide between the majority of franchised citizens who turned only episodically and often in qualified ways to political matters, and the minority who made politics their trade, their passion, or their refuge. The rules, processes, and landscapes of electoral politics in the nineteenth century may have made political parties effective engines of voter mobilization, but the parties in turn did not necessarily engender effective, satisfied, or deeply engaged voters. Were there, then, too many votes in the nineteenth century? We would not join the political reformers in blaming the voting masses for a politics too often characterized by ignorance, cynical manipulation, and the insiders' game of service and reward, but would identify instead a different kind of failure, not too much voting (indeed, considering those still outside the electorate, there was surely too little), but an insufficient result for the attention and the efforts of those who went to the polls, and a corresponding reduction or qualification of popular political commitment. To critical European observers of America, writes Robert Wiebe, "politics not government was the purpose of politics. . . . [I]t had no logic to it other than its own perpetuation."[42] This may have been too harsh a judgment, but it calls upon us to recognize significant gaps in the relation between politics and public policy that Americans of the nineteenth century themselves perceived and reacted to with varying degrees of disapproval. At its best, writes Arthur Schlesinger, Jr., democratic politics is about "the search for remedy," a characterization that in fact suits too few of the political processes and players we have reviewed here.[43] In this important sense, there was a dearth, not an excess, of democracy in the rude republic of the nineteenth century.

This is, we realize, an unusually critical, even unsettling, view of the first generations of democratic self-rule in America. On the other hand, moderating our view of political engagement in the age of spectacular campaigns and high voter turnout allows us to challenge the still more troubling trajectory of democratic declension. If we can agree that there was no golden age to envy, perhaps we can refrain from using the nineteenth century as a club with which to beat subsequent generations of declining voter turnout. Voting is a different phenomenon from what it was in the nineteenth century, and so, too, are the electorate, the modes of campaigning, the institutions (including parties, lobbies, and pressure groups of all sorts) that surround and support the electoral process, and, not least, government itself. Are we interested citizens? To this simple question there can only be a complex answer, just as there is only a complex answer—one we have tried to provide here—to the same question applied to the nineteenth century. Just as surely, there is no simply understood trajectory in the longer history of American participatory democracy.

Notes

Introduction
The View from Clifford's Window

1. Nathaniel Hawthorne, *The House of the Seven Gables* (1851; Columbus, Ohio, 1965), pp. 199–200.

2. Jean H. Baker, *Affairs of Party: The Political Culture of Northern Democrats in the Mid-Nineteenth Century* (Ithaca, N.Y., 1983), pp. 23, 269, 271.

3. William E. Gienapp, " 'Politics Seem to Enter into Everything': Political Culture in the North, 1840–1860," in Stephen E. Maizlish and John J. Kushma, eds., *Essays on American Antebellum Politics, 1840–1860* (College Station, Tex., 1982), p. 66; Michael E. McGerr, *The Decline of Popular Politics: The American North, 1865–1928* (New York, 1986), p. 13.

4. Robert H. Wiebe, *Self-Rule: A Cultural History of American Democracy* (Chicago, 1995), pp. 74, 81.

5. McGerr, *Decline of Popular Politics*, p. 17.

6. Wiebe, *Self-Rule*, p. 74; Joel H. Silbey, *The American Political Nation, 1838–1893* (Stanford, Calif., 1991), p. 48.

7. By Lex Renda, for example, in *Running on the Record: Civil-War Era Politics in New Hampshire* (Charlottesville, Va., 1997): "The nineteenth century often seems a golden age of politics when elections were exciting, voters participated in droves, . . . there was little breathing space between political events [and] parties sought to keep voters' attention fixed on politics" (p. 7). The antebellum era, in particular (unsullied by the more famous political scandals of the post–Civil War era, and the period in which mass-based parties and campaigns first took shape), seems to earn this designation. William Gienapp observes that many post–Civil War Americans looked back on the antebellum decades as a "golden age." Gienapp, " 'Politics Seem to Enter into Everything,' " p. 65.

8. Influential works that discuss these qualifications within the traditional framework of extensive popular political engagement include Richard P. McCormick, *The Second Party System: Party Formation in the Jacksonian Era* (Chapel Hill, N.C., 1966); William E. Gienapp, *The Origins of the Republican Party, 1852–1856* (New York, 1987); Paul Kleppner, *Who Voted?: The Dynamics of Electoral Turnout, 1870–1890* (New York, 1982); Peter H. Argersinger, *Structure, Process, and Party: Essays in American Political History* (Armonk, N.Y., 1982); Silbey, *American Political Nation*. More challenging to this framework are Ronald P. Formisano, *The Transformation of Political Culture: Massachusetts Parties, 1790s–1840s* (New York, 1983; Formisano, "Deferential-Participant Politics: The Early Republic's Political Culture, 1789–1840," *American Political Science Review* 68 (1974): 473–87; Edward Pessen, *Jacksonian America: Society, Personality, and Politics* (Homewood, Ill., 1969); Paul Bourke and Donald DeBats, *Washington County: Politics and Community in Antebellum America* (Baltimore, 1995); Kenneth J. Winkle, *The Politics of Community: Migration and Politics in Antebellum Ohio* (Cambridge, England, 1988).

9. The most important exception, in our view, is Formisano's discussion of geopolitical cores and peripheries in *The Transformation of Political Culture*. Based on a reading of correspondence, Lewis O. Saum finds a "comparative indifference" toward politics on the part of ordinary antebellum Americans; Lewis O. Saum, *The Popular Mood of Pre–Civil War America* (Westport, Conn., 1980), pp. 143–74. Political scientists have on occasion probed variations in political engagement among contemporary electorates. Lester Milbrath, for example, divides the electorate into "spectators," "transitional activists," and "gladiatorial activists." See Milbrath, *Political Participation* (Chicago, 1965).

10. Mary P. Ryan, *Civic Wars: Democracy and Public Life in the American City during the Nineteenth Century* (Berkeley, Calif., 1997).

11. Jean H. Baker, "Politics, Paradigms, and Public Culture," *Journal of American History* 84, no. 3 (December 1997): 898–99.

12. Sidney Verba, Kay Lehman Schlozman, and Henry E. Brady, in *Voice and Equality: Civic Voluntarism in American Politics* (Cambridge, Mass., 1995), define political participation as "activity that has the intent or effect of influencing government action—either directly by affecting the making or implementation of public policy or indirectly by influencing the selection of people who make those policies" (p. 38). This is, as will soon be evident, an even more narrow definition than we intend, but we share the focus on government, and especially that part of it directly responsive to public elections.

13. Richard Carwardine, *Evangelicals and Politics in Antebellum America* (New Haven, Conn. 1993), esp. chap. 7. An even stronger connection is made by Nathan O. Hatch, in *The Democratization of Christianity* (New Haven, Conn., 1989).

14. Mark Y. Hanley, *Beyond a Christian Commonwealth: The Protestant Quarrel with the American Republic, 1830–1860* (Chapel Hill, N.C., 1994), p. 45.

15. Wiebe, *Self-Rule*, p. 61.

16. Gienapp, " 'Politics Seem to Enter into Everything,' " p. 43. Gienapp observes that complaints such as these "should not be taken at face value" (p. 44), and in other instances, too, introduces but then dismisses evidence of skepticism or disengagement that we believe should be taken more seriously.

17. On the oratorical dimensions of this crisis, see Kenneth Cmiel, *Democratic Eloquence: The Fight over Popular Speech in Nineteenth-Century America* (Berkeley, Calif., 1990). Cmiel argues persuasively that traditional conceptions of refinement of language were linked to an aristocratic notion of the holistic self, which in turn was an important foundation for elitist political authority. Hence, aristocratic attacks on oratorical vulgarity expressed a fundamental discomfort with democracy as a system in which respectable people could continue to exercise authority.

18. These new environments and experiences are described at greater length in Stuart M. Blumin, *The Emergence of the Middle Class: Social Experience in the American City, 1760–1900* (Cambridge, England, 1989).

19. Richard L. Bushman, *The Refinement of America: Persons, Houses, Cities* (New York,

1992). Bushman's text should be compared to Richard B. Stott's illuminating discussion of decidedly ungenteel "jolly fellows," in both rural and urban America, in his introduction to William Otter, *History of My Own Times*, ed. Richard B. Stott (Ithaca, N.Y., 1995).

20. Ibid., p. 208.

21. Joyce Oldham Appleby, *Liberalism and Republicanism in the Historical Imagination* (Cambridge, Mass., 1992); Louis Hartz, *The Liberal Tradition in America: An Interpretation of American Political Thought Since the Revolution* (New York, 1955); Oscar Handlin and Lilian Handlin, *Liberty in America, 1600 to the Present* (New York, 1986); Lawrence Frederick Kohl, *The Politics of Individualism: Parties and the American Character in the Jacksonian Era* (New York, 1989).

22. This is another historian's word: Sam Bass Warner, Jr., *The Private City: Philadelphia in Three Periods of its Growth* (Philadelphia, 1968).

23. James C. Davies provides this nicely phrased perspective: "People generally do not turn to politics to satisfy hunger and to gain love, self-esteem and self-actualization; they go to the food market, pursue members of the opposite sex, show friends what they have done and lose themselves in handicrafts, fishing or contemplation—with rarely a thought about politics. If achievement of these goals is threatened by other individuals or groups too powerful to be dealt with privately, people then turn to politics to secure these ends." Davies, *Human Nature in Politics: The Dynamics of Political Behavior* (New York, 1963), p. 10.

24. Richard Hofstadter, *The Idea of a Party System: The Rise of a Legitimate Opposition in the United States, 1780–1840* (Berkeley, Calif., 1969).

25. William Burlie Brown, *The People's Choice: The Presidential Image in the Campaign Biography* (Baton Rouge, La., 1960), p. 110.

26. Baker, *Affairs of Party*, p. 71.

27. Ibid., p. 107.

28. Kohl, *The Politics of Individualism*, p. 14. Kohl's study of party rhetoric and doctrine continues a long tradition that includes influential studies such as Marvin Meyers, *The Jacksonian Persuasion: Politics and Belief* (Stanford, Calif., 1957); Eric Foner, *Free Soil, Free Labor, Free Men: The Ideology of the Republican Party before*

the Civil War (New York, 1970); Major L. Wilson, *Space, Time, and Freedom: The Quest for Nationality and the Irrepressible Conflict, 1815–1861* (Westport, Conn., 1974); and Daniel Walker Howe, *The Political Culture of the American Whigs* (Chicago, 1979).

29. Our approach to partisan newspapers differs significantly from that of many political historians. Lex Renda recently explicated what appears to be a common assumption about the political content of these papers. "Party spokesmen," he argues, "would not have printed extended discussions of legislative debates in newspapers, given speeches on the partisan dimensions of public policy developments, or rehashed evidence about candidates and party records on issues unless they thought such approaches would influence voters." Renda, *Running on the Record*, p. 4. This is a characterization we will question at some length below.

30. Ezra Cornell to Mary Ann Cornell and their children, July 28, 1844, Ezra Cornell Papers, Rare and Manuscript Collections, Carl A. Kroch Library, Cornell University.

Chapter 1
Political Innovation and Popular Response in Jack Downing's America

1. Willi Paul Adams, *The First American Constitutions: Republican Ideology and the Making of the State Constitutions in the Revolutionary Era*, trans. Rita Kimber and Robert Kimber (Chapel Hill, N.C., 1980); Marc W. Kruman, *Between Authority and Liberty: State Constitution Making in Revolutionary America* (Chapel Hill, N.C., 1997); Jackson Turner Main, *The Sovereign States, 1775–1783* (New York, 1973); Forrest McDonald, *E Pluribus Unum: The Formation of the American Republic, 1776–1790* (Boston, 1965).

2. Gordon S. Wood, *The Radicalism of the American Revolution* (New York, 1992).

3. Ronald P. Formisano, *The Transformation of Political Culture: Massachusetts Parties, 1790s–1840s* (New York, 1983), p. 17.

4. Walter Dean Burnham, "Elections as Democratic Institutions," in Kay Lehman Schlozman, ed., *Elections in America* (Boston, 1987), pp. 34–35. Burnham's tabulations for

congressional and gubernatorial elections apply only to presidential election years, and represent national averages. Voter turnout in individual districts and states, in these and other years, was occasionally significantly higher.

5. Formisano, *The Transformation of Political Culture*, esp. pp. 128–35; and Formisano, "Deferential-Participant Politics: The Early Republic's Political Culture, 1789–1840," *American Political Science Review* 68 (1974): 473–87.

6. Edmund S. Morgan, *Inventing the People: The Rise of Popular Sovereignty in England and America* (New York, 1988), p. 306.

7. Ibid.

8. Alexis de Tocqueville, *Democracy in America* (London, 1835), vol. 2, pp. 135–38.

9. These notes are cited in George Wilson Pierson, *Tocqueville in America* (New York, 1938; Baltimore, 1996), p. 653. Pierson's book, a classic in its own right, is a brilliant analysis of Tocqueville's strengths and weaknesses as a social and political observer. Pierson points frequently to the power of Tocqueville's French experience and point of view in shaping his reaction to conditions in America, and to a propensity for generalization that too often overrode the necessity of close and accurate observation. Tocqueville, in other words, was often wrong, and the emblematic statement we have quoted in the previous paragraph is a good example of how both of his major biases could lead to a serious, if compelling, exaggeration. More recently, Michael Schudson has observed that most of Tocqueville's statements about the "feverish" engagement of Americans in politics are to be found in the first volume of *Democracy in America*; in the second volume we find Americans who are selfishly removed from public affairs. "Would the real American please stand up!" Schudson asks. "Which of the Tocquevilles are we to credit?" See Schudson, *The Good Citizen: A History of American Civic Life* (New York, 1998), pp. 134–35.

10. Pierson, *Tocqueville in America*, p. 370.

11. Richard T. McCormick, *The Second American Party System: Party Formation in the Jacksonian Era* (Chapel Hill, N.C., 1966), p. 343. The standard study of suffrage expansion is Chilton Williamson, *American Suffrage: From Property to Democracy, 1760–1860* (Princeton, N.J., 1960).

12. On the emergence of the presidential nominating convention see James S. Chase, *The Emergence of the Presidential Nominating Convention, 1789–1832* (Urbana, Ill., 1973).

13. McCormick, *Second American Party System*, pp. 347–49. See also Chase, *The Emergence of the Presidential Nominating Convention*, p. 291.

14. Williamson, *American Suffrage*, p. 205.

15. McCormick, *Second American Party System*, p. 344.

16. *Sixth Census; or, Enumeration of the Inhabitants of the United States . . . in 1840* (Washington, 1841), pp. 40–41, 338–39, 114–15, 235–36. The absence of townships in Georgia and other southern states made the county the basic unit of local political organization; hence, our noting Richmond County's population here.

17. Kingston's Democratic paper was the *Ulster Republican*. See the issues of March 18, March 25, May 27, August 19, August 26, September 23, 1840; September 29 and October 6, 1841; and March 23, August 24, August 31, September 21, October 5, October 12, 1842. For Whig activities see the (Kingston) *Political Reformer*, March 25, June 24, July 8, July 29, August 26, September 23, 1840; and the *Kingston Democratic Journal*, March 24, September 29, October 6, 1841; and March 23, August 24, August 31, September 14, September 21, September 28, October 12, 1842.

18. *Greenfield Gazette and Mercury* (the Whig paper, renamed *Greenfield Gazette and Courier* at the end of 1841), June 9, September 1, September 22, October 13, 1840; May 4, September 28, November 2, 1841; and September 6, September 27, October 18, 1842; *Franklin Democrat*, August 11, September 29, October 6, October 20, 1840; February 16, August 10, August 17, September 21, October 26, November 2, 1841; and March 1, August 23, 1842.

19. *Marietta Intelligencer*, January 30, March 5, May 28, June 18, July 23, July 30, August 13, 1840; and April 8, April 29, May 27, June 24, 1841.

20. On elitism in Georgia politics, see Donald A. DeBats, "Elites and Masses: Political Structure and Behavior in Ante-Bellum Georgia," (Ph.D. diss., University of Wisconsin, 1973). DeBats writes, for example, that political leaders in Georgia assumed a "trusteeship" over their constituents that denied the right of constituent instruction to elected officials. "Indeed, at times Georgia's political leaders expressed considerable disdain for their constituents' opinions" (p. 225).

21. *Augusta Daily Chronicle and Sentinel* (the State Rights, or Whig paper), April 22, April 24, May 27, August 28, December 1, 1840; August 14, August 24, October 8, October 9, October 11, 1841; and May 5, May 12, May 16, June 16, July 16, August 1, October 5, 1852; *Augusta Daily Constitutionalist* (the Democratic paper), February 11, May 2, May 5, May 26, June 16, June 20, July 11, August 13, September 15, September 19, 1840; and August 25, 1842.

22. *Augusta Daily Chronicle and Sentinel*, April 24, May 18, May 20, May 23, May 27, June 6, June 9, June 13, July 16, August 24, September 10, September 21, September 23, October 28, 1840; (Kingston) *Political Reformer*, April 1, April 15, May 20, May 27, June 10, July 1, July 8, July 15, August 12, 1840; *Ulster Republican*, June 17, August 26, September 9, 1840; see also, *Marietta Intelligencer*, March 5, March 12, 1840.

23. *Franklin Democrat*, May 12, 1840; *Marietta Intelligencer*, April 16, May 28, June 4, November 15, 1840; (Kingston) *Political Reformer*, November 4, 1840; *Greenfield Gazette and Courier*, November 10, 1840.

24. *Ulster Republican*, November 18, 1840.

25. *Kingston Democratic Journal*, March 24, 1841.

26. *Franklin Democrat*, May 12, July 7, 1840.

27. *Marietta Intelligencer*, January 30, 1840; (Kingston) *Political Reformer*, June 24, August 12, 1840; *Augusta Daily Constitutionalist*, May 24, 1840.

28. *Augusta Daily Chronicle and Sentinel*, January 5, 1841; *Marietta Intelligencer*, October 21, 1841.

29. *Augusta Daily Chronicle and Sentinel*, August 24, August 30, 1841.

30. *Kingston Democratic Journal*, October 13, 1841; *Ulster Republican*, October 13, October 6, 1841, and September 14, September 21, 1842.

31. *Ulster Republican*, January 6, 1841.

32. *Marietta Intelligencer*, March 5, December 10, 1840; (Kingston) *Political Reformer*, May 27, September 30, 1840; *Augusta Daily Chronicle and Sentinel*, May 20, May 21, May 23, June 9, June 13, August 24, September 10, September 23, 1840.

33. A contemporary study finds that people "sign petitions mostly out of simple courtesy, and the key to understanding who signs petitions is to identify who is most likely to encounter the people who circulate them." Steven J. Rosenstone and John Mark Hansen, *Mobilization, Participation, and Democracy in America* (New York, 1993), p. 82.

34. Stuart M. Blumin, *The Urban Threshold: Growth and Change in a Nineteenth-Century American Community* (Chicago, 1976), pp. 141–43.

35. *The Augusta Directory and City Advertiser for 1841* (Augusta, Ga., 1841). One obvious use of the city directory would be to create an occupational profile of political leaders and activists. We were able to find 375 of those Augustans who appeared in the newspapers in a political context. Of these, 10 percent were professionals (a small majority were lawyers, but there were a large number of physicians as well), 57 percent were businessmen, 20 percent were clerical workers, and 13 percent were artisans. There are two significant difficulties with these tabulations, however. One is that the directory excludes "planters" and other farmers, who, as we will see later, constituted an important element of Richmond County's political community. The other is that the directory provides no means of separating out from the artisanal group those whose operations were large enough to place them within the community of nonmanual businessmen. The second of these problems disappears when we consider the occupations of the smaller group of political leaders. Of the thirty-three whose occupations we located in the directory, twelve were professionals (eight lawyers and four doctors), twenty were businessmen, and one was a clerk. Nevertheless, we will not attempt to probe the relations between socioeconomic and political hierarchies here, but will take this subject up later, with respect to the politics of the 1850s.

36. We use the date 1840 here because the residential and occupational data for the 1841

directory were almost certainly collected in 1840. City directories were usually published very early in the year of their imprint, or even in the previous year. It is possible that this 1841 directory actually appeared in 1840.

37. *Greenfield Gazette and Mercury*, November 10, 1840.

38. *Augusta Daily Constitutionalist*, October 23, 1841.

39. The quotation is from a letter from Samuel Medary of Ohio to Martin Van Buren. See Robert Gunderson, *The Log Cabin Campaign* (Lexington, Ky., 1957), 122.

40. Quoted in *Marietta Intelligencer*, June 11, 1840.

41. *Augusta Daily Chronicle and Sentinel*, November 29, 1841.

42. Ibid., November 10, 1840.

43. Curtis Porter to William C. Bouck, November 20, 1840, William C. Bouck Papers, Rare and Manuscript Collections, Carl A. Kroch Library, Cornell University. Unless otherwise stated, all unpublished letters and diaries cited in this chapter are drawn from this depository.

44. Gunderson, *Log Cabin Campaign*, 109.

45. William Nisbet Chambers, "The Election of 1840," in *The History of American Presidential Elections, 1789–1968*, ed. Arthur M. Schlesinger, Jr. (New York, 1985), vol. 2, p. 645.

46. Michael F. Holt, "The Election of 1840, Voter Mobilization, and the Emergence of the Second American Party System," in *A Master's Due: Essays in Honor of David Herbert Donald*, ed. William J. Cooper et al. (Baton Rouge, La., 1985), pp. 16–58. But see Ronald P. Formisano's response to this essay, "The New Political History and the Election of 1840," *Journal of Interdisciplinary History* 23, no. 4 (Spring 1993): 661–82.

47. Richard L. McCormick, *The Party Period and Public Policy: American Politics from the Age of Jackson to the Progressive Era* (New York, 1986), p. 204.

48. William J. Novak has recently argued (primarily from court cases) that American government in this era continued traditional practices of intervening actively in the marketplace and in public morals. Nearly all the practices he cites, however, were those at the local level of governance; few, if any, involved pol-

icy-making or administration on the Federal or state levels. See Novak, *The People's Welfare: Law and Regulation in Nineteenth-Century America* (Chapel Hill, N.C., 1996).

49. Both the humbugging and the turning away are themes of a letter written four years later by one politically active Whig to another. The people, wrote J. J. Speed, "love to be humbuged and cheated and chose to elect James K Polk . . . . I suppose you felt as I did, grieved and disappointed but it is useless to mourn on what cannot be avoided and I should now like to hear that you are doing a successful business and likely to be in a situation to set Polk times at defiance." J. J. Speed to Ezra Cornell, December 1, 1844, Ezra Cornell Papers.

50. Formisano, *The Transformation of Political Culture*, 362–63; Silbey, *American Political Nation, 1838–1893* (Stanford, Calif., 1991), p. 53. The Illinois instructions, printed in Silbey, were drafted by Abraham Lincoln.

51. *Franklin Democrat*, August 25, 1840.

52. We calculated these figures from the data in Svend Petersen, *A Statistical History of the American Presidential Elections* (New York, 1963), pp. 21–22, 25. The comparison is based on fourteen of the fifteen states in which Harrison electors ran in 1836. The fifteenth, Michigan, had not yet achieved statehood in 1832.

53. Our source for Jack Downing is *The Select Letters of Major Jack Downing, of the Downingville Militia, Away Down East, in the State of Maine. Written by Himself* (Philadelphia, 1834). Like many of the Jack Downing compilations, this one includes a number of Smith's original "letters" alongside others written by imitators, of whom there were many. The best known of these imitators was the Whig editor of the *New York Daily Advertiser*, Charles Augustus Davis, and since a number of the letters in our volume are taken from the *Advertiser* it is likely that Davis, not Smith, was the book's compiler. It little matters. Jack Downing quickly became a folk figure identifiable with a narrow and consistent set of motifs. Davis's Jack, though more explicitly anti-Jackson, is essentially the same as Smith's. The quotation is from page 3.

54. Ibid., p. 4.

55. Ibid., p. 30.

56. Ibid., p. 34.

57. Ibid., p. 44.

58. Ibid., p. 57.

59. Richard Henry Dana, *Two Years before the Mast* (Boston, 1869), p. 413.

60. *The Statistical History of the United States: From Colonial Times to the Present* (Stamford, Conn., 1965), p. 710.

61. Ibid., pp. 10, 710.

62. Patronage as a political motivation suffuses the public and private writings of antebellum Americans, but it has a much smaller place in historical accounts of the era. It might be noted, for example, that the term "patronage" does not appear in the index of the books by Jean Baker, Robert Wiebe, and Joel Silbey we have cited above. A recent and notable exception is Michael F. Holt, *The Rise and Fall of the American Whig Party: Jacksonian Politics and the Onset of the Civil War* (New York, 1999), especially chapter 13, "Patronage Is a Dangerous Element of Power." Holt argues that government jobs were attractive at a time when laborers made a dollar a day when they could find work, and when most skilled artisans earned less than six hundred dollars a year. Therefore, patronage gave politicians an edge over intraparty rivals in the struggle for control over the party's organizational apparatus.

63. DeAlva Stanwood Alexander, *A Political History of the State of New York*, vol. 2, *1833–1861* (New York, 1906), pp. 54–57.

64. William H. Brown to William C Bouck, October 12, 1843; L. H. Nicolls to Bouck, November 26, 1842; William Colman to Bouck, November 19, 1841; William R. Anderson to Bouck, January 29, 1844; C. W. Bouck to Bouck, January 12, 1842; S. L. Holmes to Bouck, June 14, 1845; John D. Lawyer to Bouck, November 26, 1842; William Deitz to Bouck, December 5, 1842; Bouck Papers.

65. John W. Edmonds to Bouck, August 16, 1844; George Carlyle to Bouck, February 23, 1843; E. D. Essnor to Bouck, February 26, 1844; Bouck Papers.

66. P. J. House to Bouck, August 5, 1842; Samuel Beardsley to Bouck, July 23, 1842; Beardsley to Bouck, August 2, 1842; Demosthenes Lawyer to Bouck, April 14, 1846; Bouck Papers.

67. A. Keyser to Bouck, May 22, 1843; P. Granden to Bouck, October 31, 1842; S. L. Holmes to Bouck, June 14, 1845; A. B. Hamilton to Bouck, November 27, 1843; Bouck Papers.

68. John Staats to Bouck, August 21, 1844, Bouck Papers.

69. Staats to Bouck, June 8, 1847; Staats to Bouck, September 15, 1847; Staats to Bouck, October 18, 1847; Bouck Papers.

70. Staats to Bouck, December 29, 1847; Staats to Bouck, January 11, 1851; Staats to Bouck, February 2, 1853; Staats to Bouck, August 1,1857; Bouck Papers.

71. Staats to Bouck, March 9, 1858, Bouck Papers.

72. Staats to Bouck, February 2, 1854, Bouck Papers.

73. John W. Edmunds conveyed to Bouck both the effects of the current hard times, and the ongoing presence even in good times of office-seekers motivated by economic misfortune: "The truth is that in this city the disasters of the last few years have thrown a vast number of people out of employment & they are seeking for office as a means of keeping body & soul together. . . . This class always numerous enough to produce a good deal of effect, is now numerous beyond all former precedent. . . ." John W. Edmunds to Bouck, September 15, 1842, Bouck Papers.

74. Staats to Bouck, December 29, 1847; Staats to Bouck, January 11, 1851; Bouck Papers.

75. Formisano, *The Transformation of Political Culture*, p. 266.

76. Ibid., p. 267.

Chapter 2
The Maturing Party System

1. Joel H. Silbey, *The American Political Nation, 1838–1893* (Stanford, Calif., 1991), pp. 8–9.

2. *Kingston Democratic Journal*, May 5, 1852, August 10, 1859; *Marion Buckeye Eagle*, August 2, 1850; *Weekly Dubuque Tribune*, April 30, 1851, May 8, 1850; *Greenfield Gazette and Courier*, October 19, 1841.

3. *Franklin Democrat*, June 1 and 8, 1860.

4. Ibid., October 14, 1850; *Greenfield Gazette and Courier*, October 12, 1858; *Kingston Democratic Journal*, September 7, 1859.

5. *Franklin Democrat*, August 10, 1860.

6. Ibid., August 9, 1858; *Kingston Democratic Journal*, September 7, 1859; July 25, 1860; *Ulster Republican*, December 31, 1851.

7. *Marietta Intelligencer*, May 27, 1841.

8. *Marion Democratic Mirror*, September 3, 1852, and September 29, 1859; *Marion Republican*, March 1, 1860. For Republican claims of full township representation at county conventions, see September 30, 1858 (where the convention is described as "one of the fullest we have had for years"), September 29, 1859, and September 13, 1860.

9. *Dubuque Daily Times*, June 5, 1858; *Dubuque Herald*, May 12, 1860; *Dubuque Miners' Express*, March 20, 1850.

10. *Dubuque Daily Times*, March 21, 1859.

11. *Augusta Daily Constitutionalist*, June 5, 18, 22, and 24, July 16, 1859; *Clarksville Jeffersonian*, January 11 and July 18, 1860.

12. *Opelousas Courier*, May 19, 1860.

13. *Dubuque Daily Times*, August 25, 1859.

14. *Franklin Democrat*, July 18, 1859.

15. *Clarksville Chronicle*, October 1, 1858.

16. *Ulster Republican*, December 31, 1851.

17. *Augusta Daily Constitutionalist*, March 1, 1860.

18. *Opelousas Courier*, October 2, 1858.

19. Although most historians pay little attention to the character of nominating caucuses and conventions, some see a give and take between the people and the professionals as the distinguishing characteristic of the nomination system. See, for example, Silbey, *American Political Nation*, pp. 60, 121, 221; and Silbey, *The Partisan Imperative: The Dynamics of American Politics before the Civil War* (New York, 1985), p. 65.

20. A good example of this may be found in the *Augusta Daily Chronicle and Sentinel*, April 29, 1860, which describes a Constitutional Union county convention for selecting delegates to a state convention. The delegate committee retired "for a few moments," and then offered a list of no fewer than twenty delegates, all of whom were approved.

21. *Franklin Democrat*, October 18, 1858.

22. Hugh White to Will White, October 25, 1859, Hugh White Papers, Rare and Manuscript Collections, Carl A. Kroch Library, Cornell University. Unless otherwise stated, all unpublished letters and diaries cited in this chapter are drawn from this depository.

23. S. J. Hathaway, Jr., to S. J. Hathaway, September 21, 1840; Samuel Hathaway to Cal-

vin Hathaway, December 19, 1851; Hathaway Papers.

24. Thomas Jeffrey, *State Parties and National Politics: North Carolina, 1815–1861* (Athens, Ga., 1989), pp. 100–101.

25. Ebenezer Lafayette Dohoney, *An Average American* (Paris, Texas, 1907), pp. 56–57.

26. Samuel Love to Ezra Cornell, October 31, 1859, Ezra Cornell Papers.

27. *Rondout Courier*, October 31, 1851.

28. *Augusta Daily Chronicle and Sentinel*, January 5, 1850.

29. *Augusta Daily Constitutionalist*, April 3, 1858.

30. *Augusta Daily Chronicle and Sentinel*, April 7, 1860.

31. Ibid., April 11, 1860.

32. *Marion Republican*, May 24, May 31, June 30, September 20, October 18, November 15, 1860; *Marion Democratic Mirror*, November 1, 1860.

33. *Greenfield Gazette and Courier*, June 28, August 2, September 6, 1852.

34. *Franklin Democrat*, October 18, 1852.

35. *Greenfield Gazette and Courier*, September 15, September 22, October 13, October 27, November 3, 1851.

36. *Rondout Courier*, June 27 and September 12, 1851.

37. *Augusta Daily Constitutionalist*, September 21, 1859.

38. The best of the recent descriptions of antebellum campaign spectacles, McGerr, *Decline of Popular Politics*, pp. 22–99, incorporates only presidential campaigns.

39. *Marion Democratic Mirror*, August 16, 1860.

40. *Dubuque Herald*, October 9, 1860.

41. Gustave Koerner, *Memoirs* (Cedar Rapids, Iowa, 1909), vol. 2, pp. 434–35. This incident underscores the argument of Michael Schudson that the partisan campaign spectacle of this era failed to develop an adequate sphere for serious public discourse. Referring to an incident that has been mythologized in ways suggestive of a "golden age" of discourse as well as of popular engagement, he writes that to "infer nineteenth-century politics from the Lincoln-Douglas debates would be something like characterizing American politics in the 1970s by the fact that the impeachment debates in the House Judiciary Committee were broadcast live on television and discussed widely and fervently among people of all walks of life. All these events were extraordinary; none of them represents the normal political discourse of its era." Michael Schudson, "Was There Ever a Public Sphere? If So, When?: Reflections on the American Case," in Craig Calhoun, ed., *Habermas and the Public Sphere* (Cambridge, Mass., 1992), p. 160.

42. *Marion Republican*, August 23 and June 30, 1860.

43. *Dubuque Herald*, September 15, 1860.

44. *Marion Democratic Mirror*, August 16, 1860.

45. *Marion Republican*, September 20, 1860.

46. *Marion Democratic Mirror*, May 24, 1860.

47. *Marion Republican*, July 12, 1860.

48. *Marion Democratic Mirror*, July 19, 1860.

49. *Greenfield Gazette and Courier*, June 25, 1860.

50. *Ulster Republican*, January 26, 1859.

51. *Kingston Democratic Journal*, August 25, 1858.

52. See, for example, *Greenfield Gazette and Courier*, September 30, 1850; October 20, 1851; October 4, 1852; October 11, 1858; and October 3, 1859; *Franklin Democrat*, September 21, 1860.

53. *Franklin Democrat*, May 4, 1860. This event provides a perspective from which to assess Andrew W. Robertson's observation, in *The Language of Democracy: Political Rhetoric in the United States and Britain, 1790–1900* (Ithaca, N.Y., 1995), p. 15, that in the nineteenth century an "attentive national audience" followed congressional debate "the way succeeding generations follow sports playoffs."

54. R. H. Duell to E. B. Morgan, October 28, 1850; William Beach to Morgan, October 26, 1850; James Lash to Morgan, November 2, 1850; J. C. Lawyer to Morgan, November 1, 1850; R. H. Duell to Morgan, November 9, 1850; George Cook to Morgan, November 7, 1850; E. B. Morgan Papers.

55. U. B. Judd to Morgan, October 22, 1850; E. B. Cobb to Morgan, n.d.; Calvin B. Morgan to Morgan. U.S. Bureau of the Census, seventh census, manuscript population schedules, Cayuga County, New York, National Archives microfilm.

56. Jacob Schoonmaker to Morgan, October 25, 1850; U. B. Judd to Morgan, November 28, 1850.

57. Silbey, *American Political Nation*, p. 145; *Marion Democratic Mirror*, April 22, 1852, and December 3, 1852; *Marion Buckeye Eagle*, April 10, 1851, and October 18, 1850.

58. One interesting issue we will not examine here is the motivation and the character of political engagement on the part of excluded groups seeking inclusion in the electorate. Judith N. Shklar has argued that these groups tended to pursue inclusion as an end in itself; more specifically, as "an effort to break down excluding barriers to recognition, rather than an aspiration to civic participation as a deeply involving activity." Judith N. Shklar, *American Citizenship: The Quest for Inclusion* (Cambridge, Mass., 1991), p. 3.

59. *Augusta Daily Chronicle and Sentinel*, October 30 and November 4, 1860; *Clarksville Chronicle*, November 2, 1860; *Kingston Democratic Journal*, October 27, 1858.

60. After their defeat in 1840, Democrats quickly copied the Whigs in issuing precise instructions to local parties. See, for example, the instructions issued in October of 1842 by the New York State Democratic Central Committee, in the Hathaway Papers, cited above.

61. N. Bailey to Morgan, November 1, 1850, Morgan Papers.

62. Walter Dean Burnham, in "The Changing Shape of the American Political Universe," *American Political Science Review* 59 (1965), observes that "turnout was consistently higher and much less subject to variation in rural counties . . . than in either industrial, mining or metropolitan counties" at least until the 1930s (p. 15). Turnout was by then declining in all areas, of course, but it remained highest in rural counties.

63. Henry S. Randall to Calvin Hathaway, October, 1846, Hathaway Papers.

64. *Marion Republican*, October 13, 1859.

65. *Dubuque Daily Times*, August 19, 1859.

66. Benjamin Ketcham to William C. Bouck, February 7, 1844, William C. Bouck Papers. Bouck's own local election-day expense record in 1846 included the cost of dinners for four men and the price of two pounds of candy. Expenses, William. C. Bouck, April 28, 1846.

67. There are numerous discussions of " 'lection day" and its enemies. See, for example, the brief but good description of this phenomenon in one New England town in Paul G. Faler, *Mechanics and Manufacturers in the Early Industrial Revolution: Lynn, Massachusetts, 1780–1860* (Albany, 1981), pp. 126–30.

68. Marcus Mills ("Brick") Pomeroy, *Journey of Life* (New York, 1890), p. 141.

69. Dohoney, *An Average American*, p. 58. Transactions of this sort did not always work out. When Fletcher was given the shoes, he voted the Democratic ticket. Seeing this, "the unreasonable Whig knocked him down and took the shoes off of him." Ibid.

70. Ibid., p. 59.

71. N. Bailey to E. B. Morgan, November 4, 1850, Morgan Papers.

72. R. H. Duell to Morgan, November 9, 1850.

73. Mary N. Bartlett to Henry Wright, November 16, 1844, H. and D. Metzger Family Papers.

74. Reprinted in the *Franklin Democrat*, November 23, 1860. William Gienapp notes that "betting on elections was common," and that "large sums of money changed hands." See William E. Gienapp, " 'Politics Seem to Enter into Everything': Political Culture in the North, 1840–1860," in *Essays on American Antebellum Politics, 1840–1860*, ed. Stephen E. Maizlish and John J. Kushma (College Station, Tex., 1982), p. 32.

75. *New York State Assembly Documents: 1840*, vol. 7, no. 291, pp. 23–69.

76. *Greenfield Gazette and Courier*, November 1, 1858.

77. F. G. Day to E. B. Morgan, November 4, 1850; D. F. Randolph to Morgan, November 8, 1850; R. H. Duell to Morgan; Morgan Papers.

78. *Augusta Daily Constitutionalist*, November 6, 1852. We cannot determine the numbers of voters who split their tickets through ignorance or indifference, or even deliberately. Ticket splitting operated in both directions; hence, its full dimensions are not revealed in aggregate voting. Several election inspectors testified about split tickets before a committee of the New York State Assembly. One Yates County inspector found 60 split tickets out of 357 total votes in his election district in 1851. *New York State Assembly Documents, 1851*, vol.

3, no. 55 (Albany, 1851), p. 28. See our further discussion of this issue in chapter 8, below.

79. *Clarksville Jeffersonian*, November 10, 1858.

80. *New York State Assembly Documents, 1840* (Albany, 1840), pp. 23–69.

81. *New York State Assembly Documents, 1850*, vol. 4, no. 67 (Albany, 1850), p. 50.

82. *New York State Assembly Documents, 1840*, pp. 23–69.

83. *New York State Assembly Documents, 1846*, vol. 2, no. 45 (Albany, 1846), pp. 38–39.

84. *New York State Assembly Documents, 1848*, vol. 5, no. 147 (Albany, 1848), pp. 32.

85. *New York State Assembly Documents, 1840*, pp. 23–69.

86. Maurice Duverger long ago made this distinction between the party and other organizations in *Political Parties: Their Organization and Activity in the Modern State* (New York, 1954). Philip J. Ethington has more recently pointed to the distinction between ordinary party "members" and the activist core, as well as to the "hibernation" of the party between campaigns. Philip J. Ethington, *The Public City: The Political Construction of Urban Life in San Francisco, 1850–1900* (Cambridge, England, 1994), pp. 70–71.

87. On this fundamental alteration, see Jon C. Teaford, *The Municipal Revolution in America: Origins of Modern Urban Government, 1650–1825* (Chicago, 1975).

88. *Clarksville Chronicle*, August 12, 1859.

89. For a similar perspective on the effects of party development in England, see James Vernon, *Politics and the People: A Study in English Political Culture, c. 1815–1867* (Cambridge, England, 1993).

90. *Clarksville Jeffersonian*, November 11, 1860.

91. Joshua Gamson, *Claims to Fame: Celebrity in Contemporary America* (Berkeley, Calif., 1994).

92. T. J. Jackson Lears, in *Fables of Abundance: A Cultural History of Advertising in America* (New York, 1994), discusses a pervasive "problem of influence" in nineteenth-century America, and notes increasingly shrill warnings against duplicity in major American magazines during the 1840s and 1850s.

93. Neil Harris, *Humbug: The Art of P. T. Barnum* (Boston, 1973), pp. 61–62. Our discussion of Barnum and the meaning of political "humbug" should be compared to Ronald P. Formisano, *The Transformation of Political Culture: Massachusetts Parties, 1790s–1840s* (New York, 1983), p. 326.

94. *Ulster Republican*, December 4, 1850.

95. *Franklin Democrat*, September 21, 1860.

96. *Frank Leslie's Illustrated Newspaper*, vol. 6, no. 2, November 13, 1858.

97. Michael E. McGerr, *The Decline of Popular Politics: The American North, 1865–1928* (New York, 1986), p. 13.

Chapter 3
Political Men

1. Kenneth J. Winkle, *The Politics of Community: Migration and Politics in Antebellum Ohio* (Cambridge, England, 1988).

2. Paul Bourke and Donald DeBats, *Washington County: Politics and Community in Antebellum America* (Baltimore, 1995), p. 149.

3. The exclusion from most newspaper listings of campaign club members who were not officers is not as serious an omission as it might at first seem. Even more than in most other antebellum organizations, the ratio of officers to total members in these clubs was very high, and in some of them new officers were elected (and reported to the party paper) every month during the campaign. It appears to have been a deliberate strategy to elect as many members as possible to some official post, in order to bind the membership more closely to the club, the party, and the campaign, and to increase the chances that the club itself would remain active until the election was over.

4. Three men in the group of 110 were listed in the census with artisanal occupational titles, but their reported wealth strongly suggests that these men were, in reality, manufacturers, retailers, or nonmanual businessmen of some sort. They are: a "carriage maker" whose property placed him in the upper 5 percent in the distribution of wealth among adult white males; a "butcher" who placed in the upper decile; and a "gunsmith" in the upper quintile. For a discussion of manufacturing and retailing "artisans" and the sometimes misleading nature of artisanal labels in historical sources, see Stu-

art M. Blumin, *The Emergence of the Middle Class: Social Experience in the American City, 1760–1900* (Cambridge, England, 1989), pp. 68–73.

5. Julian Cumming, a thirty-year-old lawyer, reported no property to the census marshal, but his father Henry reported $140,000. W. P. Crawford, a propertyless twenty-nine-year-old planter, was the son of George W. Crawford, whose fortune reached $225,000. The Cummings and the Crawfords had long been among Augusta's most influential political families. John Phinizy, Jr., was a propertyless lawyer of thirty-nine, but John Phinizy, Sr., reported $140,000. Both were leaders of the local Democratic Party.

6. Kenneth J. Winkle, "The Voters of Lincoln's Springfield: Migration and Political Participation in an Antebellum City," *Journal of Social History* 25, no. 3 (Spring 1992): 596, 604. See also Winkle, *The Politics of Community*, p. 96.

7. As we saw in chapter 1, Augusta was divided into wards, and the Whigs did form ward-based campaign clubs during the 1840 campaign. Both parties would develop ward-based nomination systems for city elections in the years that followed. But for other elections, and despite occasional efforts to create a more localized party infrastructure, the county remained the basic level of political organization in Augusta.

8. Dubuque, in this way, resembled larger cities with ward-based political organizations. Using a method similar to our own, Anthony Gronowicz has recently counted 2,391 active Democrats in New York City (perhaps 2 or 3 percent of the adult male population) in the presidential election year of 1844. As many as 40 percent of these active party men, according to Gronowicz, were skilled and unskilled workers who entered the party through ward organizations. New York City's Democratic party was perhaps the most elaborately organized local political organization in the nation. See Gronowicz, *Race and Class Politics in New York City Before the Civil War* (Boston, 1998), p. 115.

9. We would add, too, that in each of our eastern towns there were identifiable families of partisan activists—Cumming, Crawford, Phinizy, in Augusta; Grennell, Griswold, Nims, in Greenfield; Hasbrouck, Hardenberg, Suydam, in Kingston; to cite several examples—in which leadership passed frequently from father to son. None of these transitions occurred during the 1850s, however, so there is no need to adjust the leadership turnover we have observed to account for transitions within powerful families.

10. Ansel J. McCall to James F. Chamberlain, November 20, 1842, McCall Family Papers, Rare and Manuscript Collections, Carl A. Kroch Library, Cornell University. Unless otherwise stated, all unpublished letters and diaries cited in this chapter are drawn from this depository.

11. McCall to Chamberlain, September 15, 1840.

12. Gerard Gawalt observes that there were sixteen lawyers among the eighteen congressmen from Massachusetts in 1839, and estimates that at least half of the lawyers in Massachusetts during the era had sought elective office at some point in their careers. See Gerard W. Gawalt, *The Promise of Power: The Emergence of the Legal Profession in Massachusetts, 1760–1840* (Westport, Conn., 1979), pp. 85, 68.

13. James M. Bouck to William C. Bouck, January 1834, William C. Bouck Papers.

14. Ibid.

15. Timothy R. Mahoney has recently traced midwestern lawyers across extensive judicial circuits, tabulating their miles of travel and months spent away from home, and exploring the cosmopolitan professional (and political) communities they created amongst themselves. Lawyers did less of this in more settled regions, but were everywhere more likely than most of their neighbors to form extralocal associations. See Mahoney, *Provincial Lives: Middle-class Experience in the Antebellum Middle West* (New York, 1999), pp. 168–212.

16. These numbers permit a calculation different from but related to those that probe the social structure of political activism in the above text. The sixteen political leaders constituted 19 percent of those men in the highest decile of reported total wealth. This is a high proportion of the community's wealthy men, considering how small a group exercised political leadership. At the same time, 26 percent (twenty-two) of the men in the highest wealth

decile were not active at all in party politics, which means also that nearly three-quarters of the men in this upper decile were active in their party at some level.

17. For a slightly different analysis of Kingston's church leaders during the entire decade, see Stuart M. Blumin, "Church and Community: A Case-Study of Lay Leadership in Nineteenth-Century America," *New York History* 61 (1975): 393–408.

18. George E. Cole, *Early Oregon: 1850 to 1860* (n.p., 1905), pp. 67–68.

19. C. W. Hall, *Threescore Years and Ten* (Cincinnati, 1884), p. 41; Mifflin Wister Gibbs, *Shadow and Light* (Washington, 1902), p. 51; Marcus Mills ("Brick") Pomeroy, *Journey of Life* (New York, 1890), p. 157; Gustave Koerner, *Memoirs* (Cedar Rapids, Iowa, 1909), vol. 1, pp. 594–95, 597–98.

20. Levi Leighton, *Autobiography* (Portland, Maine, 1890), pp. 83–93; Mrs. Sarah Agnes Pryor, *My Day: Reminiscences of a Long Life* (New York, 1909), p. 316; Hall, *Threescore Years and Ten*, pp. 83, 93; Charles Reemelin, *Life of Charles Reemelin* (Cincinnati, 1892), p. 105.

21. *Davy Crockett's Own Story As Written by Himself* (New York, 1955), pp. 128, 261.

22. *Dubuque Miners' Express*, June 19, 1850; *Franklin Democrat*, August 12, 1859. Note how late in the year the latter warning was issued. The 1852 presidential campaign really did last "but a few months"—no more than three—in Greenfield. It was not significantly longer in other places.

23. *Marion Buckeye Eagle*, August 19, 1852. See also Kingston's *Rondout Courier*, October 19, 1860: "We offer no apology to our readers for filling so much of the second page of this paper, during the campaign, with political matter."

24. *Dubuque Weekly Times*, March 17, 1859.

25. *Dubuque Herald*, December 8, 1860.

26. *Augusta Daily Constitutionalist*, February 11, 1859; *Marion Democratic Mirror*, January 6, 1859.

27. *Marion Democratic Mirror*, August 2, 1860. See also February 9, 1860; April 5, 1860.

28. *Dubuque Daily Times*, July 19, 1859.

29. *Clarksville Jeffersonian*, May 5, 1852.

30. *Weekly Dubuque Tribune*, February 11, 1852.

31. Ibid., January 22, 1851.

32. *Dubuque Herald*, December 29, 1860.

33. *Franklin Democrat*, March 7, 1859; *Ulster Republican*, March 17, 1852.

34. Will Cross to Jesse Cross, March 19, 1856, Hugh White Papers.

35. This kind of political "flexibility" could be exercised by others who wrote for the partisan press. Ezra Cornell, for one, explained to his family (at the very height of the 1844 presidential campaign), how he set his strong Whig identity to one side when it came to writing newspaper "editorials" to promote his business: "When I write for the Atlas, Advertiser or Courier I give them a Whiggish hue, for the Post Mail etc I blacken them a little with Loco Focoism, not so much in either case to make them unpalatable for the fence men. So you see I am wielding a two-edged sword." Ezra Cornell to Mary Ann Cornell and their children, October 27, 1844, Ezra Cornell Papers.

36. Michael F. Holt, *The Political Crisis of the 1850s* (New York, 1978), esp. pp. 132–38, 163–66. The quoted phrases are from Tyler Anbinder, *Nativism and Slavery: The Northern Know-Nothings and the Politics of the 1850s* (New York, 1992), pp. 47–48.

37. For a recent discussion of such Young American extravagances, see Edward L. Widmer, *Young America: The Flowering of Democracy in New York City* (New York, 1999).

38. Ansel J. McCall to James S. McLaury, August 28, 1838, McCall Family Papers.

39. McLaury to McCall, April 19, 1839; October 22, 1840.

40. For example, McLaury to McCall, December 28, 1843; January 29, 1853.

41. McLaury to McCall, September 26, 1853.

42. James F. Chamberlain to McCall, May 27, 1838.

43. Chamberlain to McCall, February 18, 1846.

44. Chamberlain to McCall, November 15, 1848.

45. Chamberlain to McCall, September 20, 1851.

46. Chamberlain to McCall, September 14, 1854; September 27, 1854.

47. Chamberlain to McCall, October 14, 1851.

48. Chamberlain to McCall, November 5, 1859.

49. McCall to Chamberlain, September 1, 1853; October 23, 1853; November 5, 1853.

50. In 1885 McCall wrote, in reference to President Cleveland's threats to abandon the spoils system: "If a man wants friends he must stand by them. Without friends he can do nothing." McCall to C. A. Loomis, March 14, 1885. See also McCall's comments about Cleveland, civil service reform, and the consequences of the 1888 election, in McCall to Loomis, March 26, 1889.

51. McCall to Chamberlain, September 17, 1854.

52. McCall to Chamberlain, March 22, 1857.

53. McCall to Chamberlain, April 4, 1857.

54. McCall to Chamberlain, July 20, 1856.

55. McCall to Chamberlain, January 16, 1853; Chamberlain to McCall, February 16, 1853.

56. McCall to Chamberlain, November 14, 1852.

57. Chamberlain to McCall, December 15, 1859; April 27, 1860; May 24, 1860; McCall to Chamberlain, December 20, 1859; February 14, 1860.

58. Paula Baker, *The Moral Frameworks of Public Life: Gender, Politics, and the State in Rural New York, 1870–1930* (New York, 1991), p. 34.

59. Ibid., p. 31.

60. For a good discussion of the contrast between middle-class respectability and working-class honor that draws upon these elements of the working-class saloon, see Elliot J. Gorn, *The Manly Art: Bare-Knuckle Prize Fighting in America* (Ithaca, N.Y., 1986), pp. 129–47. Richard B. Stott extends the contrast in *Workers in the Metropolis: Class, Ethnicity, and Youth in Antebellum New York City* (Ithaca, 1990), pp. 247–76.

61. W. W. Clayton, *History of Steuben County, New York* . . . (Philadelphia, 1879), p. 74.

Chapter 4
A World beyond Politics

1. William H. Price, *Clement Falconer; or, The Memoirs of a Young Whig*, 2 vols. (Baltimore, 1838).

2. The microfilmed titles are listed in Lyle H. Wright, *American Fiction 1774–1850: A Contribution toward a Bibliography* (San Marino,

Calif., 1969); and in Wright, *American Fiction, 1851–1875* (San Marino, 1965). The "best-" and "better-" seller lists are in Frank Luther Mott, *Golden Multitudes: The Story of Best Sellers in the United States* (New York, 1947), pp. 306–308.

3. Laurence Neville, *Edith Allen; or, Sketches of Life in Virginia* (Richmond, Va., 1855), p. 129. It is sometimes argued that the domestic novels of this era were read almost exclusively by women, and, therefore, not by voting citizens. Ronald J. Zboray, in *A Fictive People: Antebellum Economic Development and the American Reading Public* (New York, 1993), has found, however, that men and women checked such novels out of the New York Society Library in very similar proportions to their overall reading during the 1840s and 1850s (see p. 164), and our own research in nineteenth-century diaries reveals numerous references by male diarists to domestic novels. Moreover, we find no significant differences in the treatment of politics between domestic novels and any other fictional genre.

4. T. S. Arthur, *Agnes; or, The Possessed. A Revelation of Mesmerism* (Philadelphia, 1848). See pp. 33, 68, 75. Several of our novels make this apolitical connection between liberty or freedom and religion. See, for example, J. P. Brace, *Tales of the Devils* (Hartford, 1846), p. 136: "Man is free, and prayer is the free man's defense against demons."

5. Mrs. Emma D. E. N. Southworth, *The Curse of Clifton: A Tale of Expiation and Redemption*, 2 vols. (Philadelphia, 1853). See vol. 1, p. 60, vol. 2, pp. 98–101.

6. Cornelius Mathews, *Chanticleer: A Thanksgiving Story of the Peabody Family* (Boston, 1850), p. 57.

7. Ibid., p. 98.

8. Ibid., p. 51.

9. E. C. Z. Judson, *English Tom: or, The Smuggler's Secret. A Tale of Ship and Shore* (New York, 1858), pp. 5–6.

10. George Payson, *Totemwell* (New York, 1854), pp. 127–28.

11. Sylvester Judd, *Richard Edney and the Governor's Family. A Rus-Urban Tale, Simple and Popular, Yet Cultured and Noble, of Morals, Sentiment, and Life, Practically Treated and Pleasantly Illustrated Containing, also, Hints on Being Good and Doing Good* (Boston, 1850), pp. 54–55.

12. Ibid., p. 78.

13. Ibid., pp. 146–47.

14. Ibid., pp. 149–50.

15. Ibid., p. 149.

16. Ibid., p. 153.

17. Timothy Shay Arthur, *Ten Nights in a Bar-Room, and What I Saw There* (Boston, 1854), p. 46.

18. George Lippard, *The Quaker City* (1845; Philadelphia, 1876), pp. 409, 139.

19. Ibid., p. 338.

20. Harriet Beecher Stowe, *Uncle Tom's Cabin* (1852; Boston, 1960), pp. 85–86.

21. E. D. E. N. Southworth, *The Hidden Hand; or, Capitola the Madcap* (1859; New Brunswick, N.J., 1988), p. 150.

22. E. D. E. N. Southworth, *The Fatal Marriage*, 2 vols. (Philadelphia,1863), vol. 2, p. 408.

23. Augusta Jane Evans, *Beulah*, ed. Elizabeth Fox-Genovese, (1859; Baton Rouge, 1992), pp. 117, 372.

24. Brace, *Tales of the Devils*, pp. 246–72. The quotations are on pp. 246, 271, 272.

25. Rhoda Elizabeth White, *Portraits of My Married Friends; or, A Peep into Hymen's Kingdom* (New York, 1858), pp. 50, 52 ff.

26. Sophia L. Little, *Thrice through the Furnace: A Tale of the Times of the Iron Hoof* (Pawtucket, R.I., 1852).

27. Ada M. Field, *Altha; or, Shells from the Strand* (Boston, 1856).

28. A. D. Milne, *Uncle Sam's Farm Fence* (New York, 1854), p. 245.

29. Elizabeth Johns, *American Genre Painting: The Politics of Everyday Life* (New Haven, Conn., 1991), pp. 7–12.

30. Ibid., p. 41.

31. Ibid., pp. 47–54.

32. Ibid., p. 59. Edward L. Widmer points out that Mount did return to politics for one more canvas, *The Herald in the Country*, also known as *The Politics of 1852, or Who Let Down the Bars*, painted in 1853. Widmer also argues that Mount was an ardent, lifelong Democrat. See Widmer, *Young America: The Flowering of Democracy in New York City* (New York, 1999), p. 132.

33. Nancy Rash, in *The Painting and Politics of George Caleb Bingham* (New Haven, Conn., 1991), observes that in *The County Election* "serious figures far outnumbered the louts." (p. 130) At the same time she acknowledges the various ways Bingham emphasizes the fallen-down drunk in *The Verdict of the People*, as well as other elements of all three paintings that complicate and darken his comprehensive representation of the political process. William H. Truettner, in *The West as America: Reinterpreting Images of the Frontier, 1820–1920* (Washington, 1991), similarly acknowledges, and then subordinates, Bingham's darker themes: "Bingham's pictures . . . introduce all the drawbacks of an 'open system'—the deals, profiteering, hustling, class influence, and disenfranchisement of minorities—but the artist ultimately channels the energy of the electorate into a pictorial design that resolves conflicting elements. His composition proclaims that the system works." (p. 32) Truettner compares Bingham's optimism with the more skeptical *Politics in an Oyster House* of Richard Caton Woodville (p. 33), who was one of a very few other painters of American political scenes. On Bingham's political paintings, see also: Barbara S. Groseclose, "Painting, Politics, and George Caleb Bingham," *American Art Journal* 10 (1978): 4–19; and Gail E. Husch, "George Caleb Bingham's *The County Election*: Whig Tribute to the Will of the People," *American Art Journal* 19 (1987): 4–22.

34. David M. Lubin's attempt to find political meaning (alongside manifold other meanings) in Bingham's *Daniel Boone Escorting Settlers through the Cumberland Gap* (1851–52) reminds us that paintings can be "political" even when explicitly political events are not represented, and even in the absence of detailed and easily decoded political allegory. Bingham's *Boone*, and his commercially more successful western river scenes as well, can be said to exemplify Bingham's Whig view of the proper course of national expansion. See Lubin, *Picturing a Nation: Art and Social Change in Nineteenth-Century America* (New Haven, Conn., 1994), pp. 55–105, and Rash, *Painting and Politics*, pp. 40–65. Our interest here, however, is in perceptions and representations of the political *process* as a set of practices and events, increasingly organized by political parties, in which Americans could choose to participate in various ways and degrees. Our focus, therefore, is on this more specific kind of representation—of partisan politics "at work" in campaigns and elections—rather than on un-

derlying ideologies, values, and power relations that can also be called political.

35. *Currier & Ives: A Catalogue Raisonné*, 2 vols. (Detroit, 1984). Of the 7,500 items in this catalog, approximately 3,500 are dated, and of these 1,167 are dated before 1861. If undated prints were produced in the same proportion to dated prints throughout the firm's history (it ceased publishing new prints in 1898), then the total antebellum output would have been approximately 2,500. We offer an upper estimate of 3,000 to reflect the possibility that the firm dated greater numbers of its lithographs as its production became more systematized after the Civil War.

36. Roy King and Burke Davis, *The World of Currier & Ives* (New York, 1968), p. 8.

37. Harry T. Peters, *Currier & Ives: Printmakers to the American People* (Garden City, N.Y., 1942), p. 34.

38. *Gleason's Pictorial Drawing Room Companion*, vol. 11, no. 5, October 11, 1856. *Gleason's* claimed a "gala" crowd of one hundred thousand for this event.

39. Ibid., vol. 3, no 17, October 23, 1852, p. 269.

40. Ibid., vol. 3, no. 23, December 4, 1852, p. 353.

41. Ibid., vol. 4, no. 14, April 2, 1853, p. 219.

42. Ibid., vol. 5, no. 23, December 3, 1853, pp. 374–75.

43. In its inaugural editorial, *Frank Leslie's* acknowledged *Gleason's* (now *Ballou's*) as the only successful pictorial weekly, but justified its own appearance in terms of the latter's technical inability to keep up with events: "It has not . . . the artistic facilities for seizing promptly and illustrating the passing events of the day." *Frank Leslie's Illustratred Newspaper*, vol. 1, no. 1, December 15, 1855.

44. Ibid., vol. 10, no. 255, October 13, 1860; *Harper's Weekly*, vol. 4, no. 198, October 13, 1860.

45. *Frank Leslie's*, vol. 2, no. 31, July 12, 1856.

46. Mary N. Bartlett to Henry Wright, November 16 and November 22, 1844, H. and D. Metzger Family Papers, Rare and Manuscript Collections, Carl A. Kroch Library, Cornell University. Unless otherwise stated, all unpublished letters and diaries cited in this chapter are drawn from this depository.

47. Ann McCall to Ansel J. McCall, November 12, 1834; July 15, 1835; McCall Family Papers.

48. Elizabeth Hathaway to Sarah Whiting, January 15, 1854; Vigne Hathaway to Elizabeth Hathaway, February 4, 1854; Elizabeth Hathaway to Sarah Whiting, May 28, 1852; Hathaway Family Papers. Many other letters written by and to Elizabeth Hathaway between 1848 and 1856 could be cited to demonstrate her political engagement.

49. "Sister Phebe" to Ezra Cornell, Thanksgiving 1846; Rebecca Chace to Ezra Cornell, September 21, 1856; Ezra Cornell Papers.

50. Annie Osborne to "My own dear Cousin," November 4, 1856, John and Jacob Camp Family Papers.

51. Julia Clapp to Miss Butler, May 15, 1842, Kernan Family Papers.

52. In an interesting recent essay, Elizabeth Varon observes that, from the Tippecanoe campaign onward, women were active in partisan politics, especially by attending rallies and presenting banners. Following the 1844 presidential election, Virginia Whig women established an association for commemorating Henry Clay's service to the country, and succeeded in enrolling 2,236 members from among the state's women. Elizabeth R. Varon, "Tippecanoe and the Ladies, Too: White Women and Party Politics in Antebellum Virginia," *Journal of American History* 82 (1995): 494–521. "Partisanship was indeed a consuming passion and pastime for antebellum Americans," concludes Varon, and "wives, mothers, daughters, and sisters . . . were an integral part of the new American political culture" (pp. 517–18). Women's political enthusiasm clearly does need more recognition, as do the various other political attitudes of both women and men. How, for example, shall we understand the political engagement of the scores of thousands of Virginia women who did *not* join the Clay Association?

53. We selected and read nearly fifty manuscript diaries, mostly from the excellent collection in the Rare and Manuscript Collections at Cornell, but including as well several from two of our representative towns, Augusta and Greenfield. Fourteen of these diaries were writ-

ten partly or entirely before the Civil War. We read as well several published diaries. Some of the diaries cover brief periods of only a year or two, but others record many years—up to a half-century—of their authors' lives.

54. John Bower diary, August 29, November 5, April 2, 1844, John Bower Papers.

55. Ibid., January 26 and 31, 1844.

56. Philo Munn diary, March 7, 1836, Philo Munn Papers, Historic Deerfield Library.

57. Ibid., October 10, October 21, November 16, 1834; November 5 and 12, 1848.

58. "A Diary of the Travels of William G. Randle, Daguerrotypist, of Henry County, Tennessee: 1852," *Tennessee Historical Magazine* 9 (1925): 195–208. Diaries published in scholarly journals are generally excerpted or abridged, which diminishes their usefulness to this type of analysis. Randle's diary is one of a very few that we found complete enough to use with confidence.

59. Julius C. Robbins diary, May 13, July 4, November 9, 1840, Julius C. Robbins Papers, Historic Deerfield Library.

60. Ibid., February 20, 23, and 24, April 13 and 24, May 5, June 17, 1842.

61. *Greenfield Gazette and Mercury*, November 10, 1840. See chapter 1.

62. Robbins diary, March 4, September 25, 1844; May 4, 1846; November 7, 1848; March 5, 1849; October 1, 1851; November 2, 1852; March 7, 1853; March 6, 1854; September 20, October 20, November 3 and 6, 1860.

63. Ibid., November 22, 1855.

64. Robert Brown Fiddis diary, October 23, 25, 29, November 5, 6, 8, 12, 1842, Robert Brown Fiddis Papers.

65. Edward Jenner Carpenter diary, August 8, September 25, October 10, November 4, 5, 8, 9, 11, 12, 13, 14, December 9, 1844; March 3 and 4, 1845; Edward Jenner Carpenter Papers, Historic Deerfield Library. A more extensive discussion of Carpenter is included in Richard D. Brown, *Knowledge Is Power: The Diffusion of Information in Early America, 1700–1865* (New York, 1989), pp. 230–35.

66. Samuel A. Mariner diary, November 6, 1855, Samuel A. Mariner Papers.

67. Two other young men's diaries reflect engagement in a presidential campaign, and in the case of one we can trace the cooling of political passion in the older man. W. W. Hayden

of Williamstown, Massachusetts, and William G. Markham, of Rush (near Rochester), New York, were both Wide-Awakes in 1860. Hayden's diary is brief (it resumes for a time during the Civil War), but Markham's extends for many years. Markham, who was a prosperous sheep farmer and businessman who became deeply involved after the war in state and national wool growers' associations, developed political connections in conjunction with his business affairs that alone precluded political disengagement. But, as we will see later when we discuss his diary and career in greater detail, this wealthy and sophisticated western New Yorker never repeated his experience as an active partisan in the last antebellum election. W. W. Hayden diary, April 6, May 17, 18, 21, 23, October 2, November 6, 7, 1860, Hayden Papers; William G. Markham diary, August 27, September 1, 13, 27, October 15, 18, November 1, 5, 6, 8, 1860, Markham Papers.

68. "The Memoirs of Dr. Samuel Beach Bradley," pp. 27, 21, 23, Samuel Beach Bradley Papers.

69. Samuel Beach Bradley diary, Bradley Papers.

70. William B. Pratt diary, November 8, 16, December 5, 1842; March 3, October 30, November 5, October 18, 1, 1844; Pratt Family Papers.

71. Ibid., April 8, September 8, October 1, 13, April 23, 1846.

72. Ibid., February 14, 1854.

73. Ibid., February 11, 1857.

74. This phase of Pratt's political life can be followed through his diary, and through newspaper clippings and obituaries in a bound volume in the Pratt family papers. One of the obituaries was authored by Pratt's fellow Steuben County Democrat, Ansel J. McCall.

75. Pratt Family Papers.

76. Pratt diary, September 6, 11, 1844; January 5, 1846.

77. Ibid., October 24, 1854.

Chapter 5
Civil Crisis and the Developing State

1. James F. Chamberlain to Ansel J. McCall, June 27, 1862; May 23, 1861; September 17, 1863; December 15, 1886; McCall to Chamberlain, July 21, 1861; June 6, 1865; McCall

Family Papers, Rare and Manuscript Collections, Carl A. Kroch Library, Cornell University. Unless otherwise stated, all unpublished letters and diaries cited in this chapter are drawn from this depository.

2. William B. Pratt diary, December 22, 1860, Pratt Family Papers.

3. Walt Whitman, *The Eighteenth Presidency!* ed. Edward F. Grier (Lawrence, Kans., 1956), pp. 19–20, 22, 28–29. Whitman's title refers to the eighteenth presidential term; that is, the one to be filled in the upcoming 1856 election. This tract appears not to have been published in Whitman's lifetime, although it did get as far as printer's proof, and several passages from it were incorporated into Whitman's other works (see the editor's introduction, p. 16). Our colleague Barry Maxwell brought this text to our attention. It may be useful here to observe Vivien Hart's distinction between political alienation, which often produces apathy toward the political system, and distrust, which can result in an active, vocal expression of the discrepancy between political practices and ideals. Vivien Hart, *Distrust and Democracy: Political Distrust in Britain and America* (Cambridge, England, 1978). Albert O. Hirshman makes a similar distinction between "exit" and "voice": dissatisfied "shoppers" (for commercial, political, or other organizational "products") who are inert or conscious mainly of price, merely accept the product or "exit"; those conscious mainly of quality exercise "voice" to express dissatisfaction. Albert O. Hirschman, *Exit, Voice, and Loyalty: Response to Decline in Firms, Organizations and States* (Cambridge, Mass., 1970). Whitman, we might say, was more distrustful than alienated, and certainly exercised "voice."

4. Chamberlain to McCall, March 25, 1861, McCall Family Papers.

5. Chamberlain, McCall, Pratt, and others we call upon in this chapter were all northerners, a regional bias that is justified, we believe, by the fact that these were the men (and women) who remained within the American political system, responding to the political process organized by the Republican and Democratic parties, throughout the sectional crisis. How different from their political feelings and responses were those of the southerners we exclude? The latter may have been especially suspicious of political parties and processes, as George C. Rable suggests, but if so this was a difference of degree, not of kind. We have been arguing throughout this book that skepticism and hostility directed toward political parties was a national phenomenon, not a sectional one, at least until the war began. If the war itself created sectional divergence, it was in part because the Confederacy, newly created and utterly consumed by the war effort, did not (or did not have time to) create a partisan system of the sort that all southern political leaders had experienced before secession. See George C. Rable, *The Confederate Republic: A Revolution against Politics* (Chapel Hill, N.C., 1994). See also Eric L. McKitrick, "Party Politics and the Union and Confederate War Efforts," in William Nisbet Chambers and Walter Dean Burnham, eds., *The American Party Systems: Stages of Political Development* (New York, 1967), pp. 117–51.

6. The analysis of the religious and other extrapolitical foundations of political abolitionism stretches from Gilbert Hobbes Barnes, *The Anti-Slavery Impulse, 1830–1844* (1933; New York, 1964), to Richard Carwardine, *Evangelicals and Politics in Antebellum America* (New Haven, Conn., 1993).

7. Michael F. Holt, *The Political Crisis of the 1850s* (New York, 1978).

8. Again, see ibid., and Tyler Anbinder, *Nativism and Slavery: The Northern Know Nothings and the Politics of the 1850s* (New York, 1992).

9. Hugh White to William White, April 25, 1861, Hugh White Papers.

10. Pratt diary, July 31, August 23 and 24, 1861.

11. Ibid., July 23, 1861; February 13, 1862. Several of the published obituaries included in the Pratt family papers comment on Pratt's wartime contributions as town supervisor.

12. Charles McCarthy to Andrew Wall, August 19, 1861, Wall Family Papers.

13. Henry D. Locke diary, June 13, July 13, 1863, H. Emmons Ogden Family Papers.

14. James McPherson, *What They Fought For, 1861–1865* (Baton Rouge, La., 1994), p. 46. McPherson points out that officers are overrepresented in his samples (constituting 47 percent of his Confederate sample, and 35 percent of his Union sample), as are slaveholders among the Confederates and professional and other white-collar men among the Yankees.

These were probably the men most likely to discuss ideological questions (40 percent of each sample did so), but might not have been so much more likely than other men to have expressed patriotic sentiments.

15. Julius Skelton to Hattie Skelton, September 20, 1861, Julius Skelton Papers.

16. George Collins to Kate Collins, November 16, October 21, 1863; George Collins to "My dear Mother," February 1, 1863; Collins Family Papers.

17. John T. Andrews to Homer Andrews, January 10, December 26, 1864, Andrews Family Papers.

18. Quoted in Mary Dearing, Veterans in Politics: The Story of the GAR (Baton Rouge, La., 1952), p. 48.

19. J. W. Fitzpatrick to John Kernan, July 1864, Francis Kernan Papers.

20. William G. Markham diary, September 2 and 3, 1861; July 14, August 5, 8, 10, 13, 1862; August 7, 9, 31, September 10, 12, 1863, Markham Papers.

21. W. W. Hayden diary, August 18 and 24, November 3, 1863, Hayden Papers.

22. Ibid., November 13, 1863.

23. George Thompson to Ansel J. McCall, October 31, 1865, McCall Family Papers.

24. James F. Chamberlain to McCall, April 11, 1862, McCall Family Papers.

25. Mary Ann Collins to George Collins, October 5, 9, 16, 26, 1862, Collins Family Papers. Collins's wife, Kate, also wrote to him about politics: Kate Collins to George Collins, July 14, 22, August 9, October 18, 1863.

26. Lizzie Camp to Jacob A. Camp, March 29, August 9, 1861; Emily B. Schuyler to Lizzie Camp, April 23, 1863 [1862?], and March 7, 1864; John and Jacob Camp Family Papers.

27. Em Andrews to John T. Andrews, October 16, 18, 20, 28, November 7, 15, 1864, John T. Andrews Papers.

28. Henry D. Locke diary, 1863.

29. Jacob A. Camp to Lizzie Camp, June 8, 1861, John and Jacob Camp Family Papers.

30. Dubuque Daily Times, May 21, 28, 1864.

31. Dubuque Herald, May 18, July 15, 1864.

32. Kingston Argus, November 23, 1864.

33. Dubuque Herald, August 30, March 16, 1864; Dubuque Daily Times, August 15, 1865.

34. Greenfield Gazette and Courier, August 28, 1865.

35. Ibid., January 30, March 20, August 14, 1865.

36. Ibid., December 12, 1864.

37. Ibid., November 6, 1865. For criticism of political preaching in the more Democratic Dubuque, see Dubuque Herald, October 8, December 20, 1864.

38. Joel H. Silbey, A Respectable Minority: The Democratic Party in the Civil War Era, 1860–1868 (New York, 1977).

39. Greenfield Gazette and Courier, February 6, 1865.

40. Dubuque Herald, June 16, 1865.

41. Ibid., March 12, 1864; Dubuque Daily Times, March 15, 1864; Dubuque Daily Times, March 4, 29, 1866. The Democrats wanted to be sure that the board would not establish a Negro school at public expense, an assurance the Republicans were evidently unwilling to give. The Democrats themselves divided on the issue. One Copperhead, the Herald reported, "says that if such schools are established 'niggers' will flock here in swarms to get 'larnin' and the gas will need to be kept lighted all day to find the way through town. A democrat is asked if he would not rather have them by themselves than mixed with whites, and on this appeal several have signed the petition. On the other hand, it is argued that there is no employment here for any more darkies, and no danger of their coming." Dubuque Herald, February 2, 1866. See also February 28, March 1, 3, 13, 1866. Eventually, as befits the disengagement that began with the end of the war, one ticket was agreed on.

42. Dubuque Daily Times, August 26, September 23, 1864.

43. Ibid., September 19, 1864.

44. Ibid., June 29, 1864; Dubuque Herald, April 26, July 4, July 6, 1865. Of course, when exslave H. H. Thomas lectured at Globe Hall (the first "gentleman of color" to do so) only "rampant republicans were present." And when blacks celebrated the anniversary of Emancipation Day in the West Indies with a picnic, "There was Clem and Sam, Dinah and Phillis—shades of all colors, from the light-haired brunette, to the coal black rose, dressed up in silks and white dresses and highly scented with Eau De Cologne." No Democrats, we are quite certain, attended. Ibid., June 17, August 2, 1865.

45. Kingston Argus, September 7, 1864.

46. Ibid., September 14, 1864.

47. Ibid., March 16, 1864.

48. Ibid., November 23, 30, 1864.

49. Ibid., December 21, 1864.

50. Ibid., February 1, 1865.

51. Ibid., March 1, 1865. For the editor's denial that the paper printed the wrong date for Curtis's lecture on purpose, see ibid., February 15, 1865.

52. In 1865 the celebration of the Fourth fizzled in Marion, apparently because Democrats chose not to participate. *Marion Independent*, July 6, 1865.

53. *Marion Democratic Mirror*, March 2, 1865.

54. Ibid., November 23, 1865.

55. *Dubuque Daily Times*, March 30, December 14, November 21, 1866; *Dubuque Herald*, December 3, 1865; *Greenfield Gazette and Courier*, March 5, 1866.

56. See, for example, *Marion Independent*, September 14, 1865; *Marion Democratic Mirror*, July 27, August 3, 1865.

57. *Greenfield Gazette and Courier*, October 23, 1865; October 31,1864.

58. *Marion Democratic Mirror*, August 15, 1865.

59. *Dubuque Herald*, August 30, 1864; August 16, September 20, October 1, 1865.

60. William B. Pratt diary, August 29, 1862; William G. Markham diary, April 23, October 7, 1861; September 6, October 25, 1862. Markham attended war meetings in two different villages (East Avon and Rush) near his family's farm.

61. *Greenfield Gazette and Courier*, July 18,1864.

62. *Kingston Argus*, June 14, 1865.

63. Ibid., September 14, 1864; *Dubuque Daily Times*, October 30, 1864.

64. Ernest Duvergier de Hauranne, *Huit mois en Amérique: Lettres et notes de voyages, 1864–1865*, ed. and trans. Ralph H. Bowen, as *A Frenchman in Lincoln's America*, 2 vols. (Chicago, 1974), vol. 1, pp. 346, 384–85. We would like to thank our friend and colleague Alain Seznec for bringing this text to our attention.

65. William B. Pratt diary, September 24, October 1, 29, 1864. For reports of campaign "fizzles," see *Dubuque Daily Times*, August 26, 1864; *Dubuque Herald*, October 12, 1864.

66. Duvergier de Hauranne, *Huit mois en Amérique*, vol. 1, p. 98.

67. Ibid. p. 282.

68. Ibid. pp. 283, 285.

69. Ibid. p. 391.

70. *Kentucky Documents, 1865* (Lexington, 1865), vol. 1, no. 10, pp. 8–9, 11, 18; vol. 1, no. 12, pp. 34–35, 50, 62. Soldiers could be intimidated, too, by their own officers. John Bailey, a thirty-two-year-old quartermaster sergeant in the Kentucky Cavalry, was told on election day that Colonel Johnson knew that of all the soldiers under his command only he and one other had not yet voted. Bailey, who was probably a Democrat, had decided not to vote, but changed his mind: "I knew that if I failed to vote and vote the way I did, I would incur the displeasure of all my officers." The image of Colonel Johnson as a kind of ward captain, keeping track of those who had voted, and sending emissaries to bring in those who had not, is a striking one. Ibid., vol. 1, no. 13, pp. 16–17.

71. *Appendix to the Journals of the Senate and Assembly of the State of California, 1863* (Sacramento, 1863), no. 18, pp. 5, 15, 19.

72. *Documents of the New York State Senate, 1864* (Albany, 1864) vol. 2, no. 14, pp. 22, 106, 197, 209, 211, 367, 530.

73. *Documents of the New York State Senate, 1865* (Albany, 1865), vol. 7, no. 132, pp. 48, 86–88, 229.

74. Ibid., pp. 234, 325–28.

75. Ibid., pp. 11, 26, 38, 40.

76. *Documents of the New York State Senate, 1865* , vol. 7, no. 132, pp. 107–109, 180, 198, 351, 386; *Documents of the New York State Senate, 1864*, vol. 2, no. 14, pp. 896–97.

77. See, for example, Morris Fiorina, *Retrospective Voting in American National Elections* (New Haven, Conn., 1981).

78. *Marion Independent*, September 14, 1865; *Dubuque Daily Times*, August 16, 1866. See also "The Democratic Party," in *Dubuque Daily Times*, June 9, 1866.

79. *Pennsylvania Legislative Documents, 1870* (Harrisburg, 1870), vol. 1, no. 28, pp. 1, 217.

80. *Finley vs. Nichols: Contested Election 1889* (Harrisburg, Pa., 1889), p. 655; *Proceedings in the Matter of the Contested Election of Osbourn vs. Devlin before the Committee on Elections of the*

Senate of Pennsylvania (Harrisburg, 1889), vol. 1, p. 2292.

81. *Dubuque Herald*, January 12, 19, 23, May 8, 1864; *Marion Independent*, March 16, 1865.

82. *Kingston Argus*, November 2, 1864; *Dubuque Herald*, June 29, 1864.

83. *Kingston Argus*, August 30, 1865.

84. *Dubuque Herald*, June 11, 1865.

85. *Marion Democratic Mirror*, May 10, 1866; *Kingston Argus*, August 29, 1866; *Dubuque Herald*, February 17, 1865; May 2, 1866.

86. *Greenfield Gazette and Courier*, March 21, October 10, 1864; *Kingston Democratic Journal*, July 12, November 29, 1865. The *Dubuque Daily Times* (July 12, 1864) even found a way to win sympathy for government bureaucrats through a strategy we would call "waving the bloody skirt": The three hundred ladies in the Treasury Department, the *Times* editor argued, were "mostly the wives and widows of our soldiers, dependent on their industry for support and on their fair fame for their social position." Copperhead charges that they had turned the department "into a seraglio, or into a den of bacchanalian orgies," were not only false and scandalous, but unpatriotic.

87. *Dubuque Daily Times*, July 11, 1864. On January 16, 1864, the *Times* reported that "a large delegation of the heaviest taxpayers" in Muscatine had asked the board of supervisors "to *increase* their taxes so that a larger amount might be spent on the suffering families of soldiers."

88. Heather Cox Richardson, *The Greatest Nation of the Earth: Republican Economic Policies during the Civil War* (Cambridge, Mass., 1997).

89. *Dubuque Daily Times*, July 23, 30, 1864; *Marion Independent*, May 25, 1865; *Kingston Democratic Journal*, February 8, 1865.

90. *Kingston Democratic Journal*, July 6, 1864.

91. Ibid., November 29, 1865.

92. Ibid., November 2, 1864; September 13, 1865; October 31, 1866. See also *Marion Independent*, March 29, 1866; *Dubuque Daily Times*, February 10, October 19, 1866.

93. Theda Skocpol *Protecting Soldiers and Mothers: The Political Origins of Social Policy in the United States* (Cambridge, Mass., 1992).

Chapter 6
People and Politics

1. Albion Tourgee, *A Fool's Errand* (1880; New York, 1966); George Koehler, *Nick Putzel; or, Arthur Gurney's Ruin* (Philadelphia, 1881); John Hay, *The Bread-Winners: A Social Study* (New York, 1884); Edward P. Roe, *An Original Belle* (New York, 1885); Thomas Norwood, *Plutocracy; or, American White Slavery* (New York, 1888); Edward Bellamy, *Looking Backward, 2000–1887* (1888; New York, 1960); Lewis H. Watson, *Not to the Swift: A Tale of Two Continents* (New York, 1891); David Ross Locke, *The Demagogue: A Political Novel* (Boston, 1891); Mark Twain and Charles Dudley Warner, *The Gilded Age: A Tale of Today* (Hartford, 1873). Approximately 120 of the 200 best-selling and randomly selected novels we read were published between 1861 and 1900. See chapter 4 for a discussion of our method for selecting these books.

2. Robert Lee Taylor, *A Yale Man: A Novel* (New York, 1896), p. 34.

3. Charles W. Jay, *My New Home in Northern Michigan, and Other Tales* (Trenton, N.J., 1874), p. 13.

4. Edward Everett Hale, *Mr. Tangier's Vacation* (Boston, 1888), pp. 42–43. The notion of General Logan's speaking to the whole county at a political caucus is a curious one, especially in New England, where caucuses were held only on the town level. Could Hale's inaccurate use of this term suggest an increase in the distance between the author (and possibly his readership) and the political process?

5. William Dean Howells, *The Rise of Silas Lapham* (1885; New York, 1963), pp. 187–88, 74.

6. Robert J. Burdette, *Chimes from a Jester's Bells* (Indianapolis and Kansas City, 1897), p. 191.

7. Stephen Crane, *The Red Badge of Courage* (1895; New York, 1976).

8. In his preface, Roe identifies "power," to be portrayed as the deliberate development of individuality on the part of a young woman, as the central idea of his novel. Here again (as in the way Timothy Shay Arthur and others earlier utilized "liberty") is an apolitical formulation of

a profoundly political concept. See Roe, *An Original Belle*, preface and p. 44.

9. Bellamy, *Looking Backward*, p. 89. There actually is a Congress in Bellamy's utopia, but it is nothing like the institution created by the U.S. Constitution.

10. Ibid., pp. 118, 120, 129. Retirees over the age of forty-five also vote in "exceedingly lively" elections of the generals of their guilds (p. 133). There is, however, no hint of a political party in this process.

11. Kenneth M. Roemer, in *The Obsolete Necessity: America in Utopian Writings, 1888–1900* (Kent, Ohio, 1976), documents the burst of Utopian writing in this period, and discusses the "Minerva-like stability" that Utopian authors offered without recourse to political solutions of fundamental problems.

12. The standard history of post–Civil War civil-service reform is Ari Hoogenboom, *Outlawing the Spoils: A History of the Civil Service Reform Movement, 1865–1883* (Urbana, Ill., 1968).

13. Benjamin Perley Poore, *The West Point Cadet; or, The Turns of Fortune's Wheel* (Boston, 1863).

14. Burdette, *Chimes from a Jester's Bells*, p. 172.

15. Thomas Hayden Hawkins, *Drifting* (Denver, 1892), p. 31.

16. Hale, *Mr. Tangier's Vacation*, p. 95.

17. Hay, *The Bread-Winners*, p. 246.

18. Horatio Alger, *Ragged Dick* (1868; New York, 1962), pp. 144, 123. Alger takes aim at congressmen, too, occasionally (see, for example, pp. 178–79), but it is the mayor and the city council that most frequently represent politics for the author and his hero.

19. Koehler, *Nick Putzel*, pp. 58, 63, 28, 86–87, 298–99.

20. Jon C. Teaford, *The Unheralded Triumph: City Government in America, 1870–1900* (Baltimore, 1984).

21. Paul Boyer, *Urban Masses and the Social Order in America, 1820–1920* (Cambridge, Mass., 1978; Robert Bremner, *From the Depths: The Discovery of Poverty in the United States* (New York, 1956).

22. Robert Henry Newell, *Orpheus Kerr Papers* (New York, 1870), vol. 2, p. 199.

23. Finley Peter Dunne, *Mr. Dooley in the Hearts of His Countrymen* (1899; New York, 1969), pp. 24–25.

24. Ibid., p. 111.

25. Finley Peter Dunne, *Mr. Dooley in Peace and War* (Boston 1899), pp. 112–13, 220–22.

26. Jay, *My New Home*.

27. Charles Farrar Browne, *The Complete Works of Artemus Ward* (New York, 1898), pp. 42, 148.

28. Newell, *Orpheus Kerr Papers*, vol. 1, pp. 164, 251.

29. Norwood, *Plutocracy*, p. 105.

30. Locke, *The Demagogue*, pp. 197–206.

31. John Carboy, *Kicked into Good Luck* (New York, 1872), pp. 26–28.

32. Ellis Horton, *The Hoosier Practitioner* (Indianapolis, 1888), pp. 121–22.

33. Ibid., p. 151.

34. Koehler, *Nick Putzel*, pp. 300–305.

35. Lewis H. Bond, *One Year in Briartown* (Cincinnati, 1879), pp. 199–206.

36. Finley Peter Dunne, *Mr. Dooley's Opinions* (New York, 1906), pp. 109–110. This sketch was obviously written six years before publication in this collection.

37. Of the 111 presidential portraits published during these thirty-eight years, 78 were representations of Lincoln or Grant. A slightly smaller number of presidential portraits (107) had been published during the twenty-six years preceding the war.

38. Dunne, *Mr. Dooley's Opinions*, p. 171.

39. We examined every illustration in *Harper's Weekly* during five three-year periods beginning toward the end of the war: 1864–66, 1872–74, 1880–82, 1888–90, and 1896–98. We also examined a shorter run of issues of the magazine's old competitor, *Frank Leslie's Illustrated*.

40. The widely publicized fact that Garfield's assassin, Charles Guiteau, was a disappointed office-seeker inspired *Harper's* and others to connect the assassination with the spoils system. See Hoogenboom, *Outlawing the Spoils*, p. 209.

41. Richard Ohmann, in *Selling Culture: Magazines, Markets, and Class at the Turn of the Century* (New York, 1996), argues, moreover, that other magazines not as reliant on caricatures and other illustrations tended to avoid

politics as a violation of the "class-coded decorum of a family magazine. . . . Party politics, in any case, was a mug's game." *McClure's*, for example, came no closer to politics during the 1896 campaign than the printing of articles on Lincoln, Grant, and Gladstone (see pp. 254–55). Ohmann's study should remind us that there were many magazines published throughout the nineteenth century that avoided politics in this way.

42. *Harper's Weekly*, September 21, November 9, 1872.

43. *Frank Leslie's Illustrated Newspaper*, May 18, 1872.

44. *Harper's Weekly*, October 24, 1874.

45. Ibid., April 23, 1881.

46. Ibid., May 21, 1881.

47. Ibid., November 11, 1882.

48. Ibid., May 2, 1874.

49. Ibid., August 11, 1865.

50. Samuel Beach Bradley Papers, Rare and Manuscript Collections, Carl A. Kroch Library, Cornell University (unless otherwise stated, all unpublished letters and diaries cited in this chapter are drawn from this depository). See Bradley's diary, November 6, 1872; and November 7, 1876; and Bradley to William Bradley, May 31, September 20, November 12, December 2, 1872.

51. William B. Pratt diary, February 8, 1871; January 2,1872; October 9, November 4, 1873; February 7, 1874, Pratt Family Papers. See also, *Prattsburgh News*, October 23, 30, 1873; February 5, 1874.

52. Pratt diary, November 2, 1884. Eleven straight losers is a remarkable record. Pratt, recall, was a Whig and a Republican before becoming a Democrat just in time for that party's six consecutive losses in presidential elections. The only time Pratt's party's candidate won was in 1848. There happens to be no diary for that year, but what Pratt is telling us thirty-six years later is that he had bolted the party in 1848, presumably to vote for the Free Soil candidate, Martin Van Buren. This may have been part, perhaps even a big part, of the reason why his rise within the Steuben County Whig party was cut short.

53. Ibid., September 16, 1877.

54. *Prattsburgh News*, October 30, 1873.

55. William G. Markham diary, February 28, March 3, 1874, Markham Papers.

56. Ibid., January 31, February 11, 1874; January 7, 13, February 17, 1875; January 5, 12, 19, March 8,1876; February 13, 1877.

57. Ibid., August 1, 4, September 1, 1879.

58. See, for example, ibid., October 27, 1880.

59. J. W. Hobbs diary, George W. Hobbs diary, Hobbs Family Papers.

60. Edwin D. Lyons diary, Lyons Papers.

61. Isaac Purdy diary, Purdy Papers.

62. Washington Marsh diary, November 7, 1865, Marsh Papers.

63. Ibid., August 28, October 31, 1867, February 11, 1873.

64. Ibid., November 4, 1879.

65. Ibid., February 10, 1883.

66. Ibid., February 12, 1884.

67. Ibid., August 28, November 6, 14, 1888; February 11, 1889; January 27, 1890.

68. Ibid., November 8, 1888.

69. Ibid., November 8, 1893; November 8, 1894; October 22, 25, 1896.

70. Ibid., March 20, 1897.

71. William Seward Brooks diary, March 14, 1876, Brooks Papers; John C. Berry diary, November 5, 1889, Berry Papers; C. A. Cullings diary, November 8, 1892, Cullings Papers.

72. We were able to mitigate somewhat this inevitable bias by conducting our diary research primarily within the superb collection at Cornell, which includes many diaries written by ordinary people. Most of these people were upstate New York farmers and villagers, and if our concentration in the Cornell collection introduces a regional bias (we would prefer to think of it as a regional case study), it is well worth the mitigation of the class bias that limits most historical diary samples.

Chapter 7
Leviathan

1. Voting for third parties did not exceed 3.5 percent in post–Civil War presidential elections until 1892, when the People's Party polled 10.9 percent. See Joel H. Silbey, *The American Political Nation, 1838–1893* (Stanford, Calif., 1991), p. 210. By referring in our chapter title to the political party as "Leviathan," we mean to refer also, if indirectly, to Richard Bensel's application of Hobbes's famous metaphor to post–Civil War national government. See

Richard Bensel, *Yankee Leviathan: The Origins of Central State Authority in America, 1859–1877* (New York, 1991).

2. The only significant departure from this norm was in the Grant-Greeley contest of 1872, when 72 percent of the electorate voted. Turnout would begin its long-term decline after 1888, but in 1892 it was still a quite respectable 76 percent. Ibid., p. 145.

3. Michael E. McGerr, *The Decline of Popular Politics: The American North, 1865–1928* (New York, 1986).

4. *Augusta Daily Chronicle and Constitutionalist*, June 2, 1880. That party newspapers did continue to exaggerate the appeal of this and other aspects of the political campaign is nicely captured in a letter written by Ulysses S. Grant from Galena, Illinois, in 1868: "A person would not know there was a stirring canvas going on if it were not for the accounts we read in the papers." Quoted in Robert Dallek, *Hail to the Chief: The Making and Unmaking of American Presidents* (New York, 1996), p. 151.

5. *Greenfield Gazette and Courier*, September 19, October 24, 1881; September 25, October 23, 1882. It should be recalled that nominations were generally made quite late in Franklin County.

6. *Syracuse Morning Standard*, March 4, 1881; *Dubuque Herald*, June 14, 23, 1881; October 13, 1880. The Republican county convention in Dubuque in August of 1880 should have had 111 delegates, but only 50 votes were cast. See *Dubuque Daily Times*, August 14, 1880.

7. *Graham Leader*, June 1, 1882.

8. *Marion Democratic Mirror*, June 30, 1881. This convention also resolved that all the Democratic members of the county bar, along with four county officers, would constitute the delegation to the upcoming judicial convention.

9. *Greenfield Gazette and Courier*, April 5, 1880.

10. *Augusta Daily Chronicle and Constitutionalist*, August 11, 1882.

11. *Graham Leader*, July 2, August 13, 1880.

12. *Placer Weekly Argus*, March 27, 1880; *Placer Herald*, May 8, 1880.

13. *Marion Democratic Mirror*, July 18, 1880.

14. This characterization of Georgia (and by implication the rest of the former Confederacy) as "one-party" is somewhat premature, in the sense that widespread disenfranchisement of African-American voters had not yet occurred. In Augusta the latter were able to accumulate fairly respectable vote totals for the Republican Party in 1880. But the Republicans in the post-Reconstruction era were never in a position to win in Augusta; indeed, we can measure their hopelessness by the very fact that the Democratic paper regularly reported the details of Republican conventions and other meetings, usually without bothering to attack or ridicule the Republicans as though they were a credible threat. As nearly all white men in Augusta (and elsewhere in the South) voted Democratic, and nearly all black men voted Republican, it may be best to characterize the South as having a pair of racially segregated one-party systems, one in control of all elections, the other in the role of providing a vehicle for political expression and activism on the part of an essentially powerless African-American community. Populism, as C. Vann Woodward claimed long ago, may briefly have threatened this imbalance, but the South soon thereafter sank into a very long period of truly one-party (and one-race) rule. Our use of "one-party" in this early period is justified, we believe, by the fact that Republicans were no more able to win an election in Georgia in 1880 than they were in 1900 or 1950.

15. *Augusta Daily Chronicle and Constitutionalist*, March 26, July 2, July 7, August 25, 1880.

16. Ibid., July 20–23, August 25, 29, 1880; September 3, December 3, 1882.

17. *Syracuse Morning Standard*, February 8, 1881, February 13, 18, August 22, 1882.

18. *Placer Weekly Argus*, April 17, 1880.

19. *Greenfield Gazette and Courier*, November 18, 1881.

20. *Syracuse Morning Standard*, April 13, 1880; *Syracuse Courier*, May 16, 1881; *Dubuque Daily Times*, August 13, 1882.

21. *Greenfield Gazette and Courier*, September 18, 1882; *Graham Leader*, May 7, 28, 1880.

22. *Dubuque Herald*, April 25, 1880; *Placer Weekly Argus*, May 15, 1880.

23. *Marion Independent*, March 22, April 7, 1881.

24. *Greenfield Gazette and Courier*, March 22, 1880.

25. *Dubuque Daily Times*, October 13, 1880.

26. *Augusta Daily Chronicle and Constitutionalist*, May 30, June 7, 1882.

27. *Greenfield Gazette and Courier*, August 30, 1880.

28. *Dubuque Daily Times*, October 5, 1882.

29. *Augusta Daily Chronicle and Constitutionalist*, September 28, 1882.

30. Ibid, November 2, 1882.

31. *Syracuse Morning Standard*, March 10, 1880.

32. *Marion Democratic Mirror*, October 7, 1880; August 18, 1881.

33. *Syracuse Morning Standard*, June 6, 1882.

34. Ibid, June 30, 1882.

35. *Graham Leader*, July 27, 1882.

36. *Placer Herald*, October 4, 1882.

37. *Syracuse Morning Standard*, November 28, 1881.

38. *Graham Leader*, October 19, 1882.

39. *Dubuque Daily Times*, December 7, 1880. Nearly every man you meet, opined the *Augusta Daily Chronicle and Constitutionalist* on December 8, 1881, has not read the President's Message "but is going to! Tomorrow never comes."

40. *Syracuse Courier*, October 29, 1880.

41. *Greenfield Gazette and Courier*, November 8, 1880. The *Gazette and Courier*, on July 5, 1880, had appealed to civic boosterism, not partisanship or principle, as a spur to citizens to organize a ratification rally for Garfield, noting that the absence of one is "a very enterprising state of things for a county seat with a growing and grasping neighbor over the river."

42. Ibid, October 30, November 6, 13, 1882. In 1881 the *Gazette and Courier* disagreed with the argument that annual elections helped keep the masses enlightened. "Who, we would ask, is better off, and who has been instructed by this year's campaign?" November 7, 1881.

43. *Augusta Daily Chronicle and Constitutionalist*, September 27, 1882. In Augusta in 1880 24 whites and 1,438 blacks voted for Garfield, 32 blacks and 2,170 whites for Hancock.

44. Ibid, September 2, 9, 1882.

45. Ibid, September 10, 19, October 5, 1882.

46. *Marion Democratic Mirror*, July 1, August 26, September 9, 16, 30, 1880; October 14, 1881.

47. *Marion Independent*, July 29, September 9, 30, October 28, 1880.

48. *Graham Leader*, July 8, 1881; *Placer Weekly Argus*, July 3, 1882.

49. *Graham Leader*, May 21, 28, September 24, October 29, November 12, 1880.

50. *Placer Herald*, June 26, July 24, September 18, October 2, 1880.

51. *Placer Weekly Argus*, June 19, September 11, 25, October 16, 23, 1880; November 11, 1882.

52. *Dubuque Herald*, August 8, September 23, October 7, 1880. There is some evidence that a club was established in the third ward.

53. Compare ibid., September 19, October 21, 1880, with *Dubuque Daily Times*, September 19, October 21, 1880. For attractions see *Dubuque Herald*, October 2, 28, 1880.

54. *Dubuque Herald*, December 29, 1880.

55. *Dubuque Daily Times*, August 10, September 19, October 17, 20, November 3, 1880.

56. Ibid., November 5, 1882. The Republicans also welcomed the ladies into campaigns. In 1882, to the dismay of Democrats, women entered with a vengeance in an election on the prohibition of alcohol. "In several localities," the *Herald* reported, "the polls were so surrounded by women, ministers, and partisans generally that many were deterred from voting. "There was never an election so surrounded by such terrorism" (July 6, 1882).

57. *Syracuse Daily Courier*, August 16, October 4, 13, 1880.

58. *Syracuse Morning Standard*, January 22, 24, March 18, June 16, 25, 29, July 13, 14, August 10, 1880.

59. Ethnic and other such clubs manifest the continuing erosion in the cities of what Mary Ryan has called, perhaps with some exaggeration, the "integrative sociability" of urban public life before the reshaping of politics by the second party system. See Ryan, *Civic Wars: Democracy and Public Life in the American City during the Nineteenth Century* (Berkeley, Calif., 1997), p. 309. "There are five Americans, two Germans and four Irishmen on the Democratic ticket, and all good capable men, and don't you forget it," the *Dubuque Herald* asserted on September 22, 1881. The next day the *Herald*, not-

ing that at the recent county convention there were fifty-two Germans, fifty-six Irishmen, and seven Americans, declared that "all nationalities should be recognized in the distribution of local offices." Ethnic clubs did not, however, always signal a party's openness to minority groups. During the 1890s in Brooklyn, according to Henry Claflin Wells, immigrants "were not welcomed into the ward associations, but were instead herded into satellite, ethnically specific organizations and affiliates whose principal function was issuing endorsements of party tickets." Henry Claflin Wells, *Urban Political Development and the Power of Local Groups: A Case Study of Politics in South Brooklyn, 1865–1935* (Ann Arbor, Mich., 1988), p. 145.

60. McGerr, *The Decline of Popular Politics*, pp. 107–137. McGerr implies that "the sense that elections held a special place in public life ebbed away" because sensational and independent newspapers replaced partisan publications (p. 126).

61. Quoted in Mark Summers, *The Press Gang: Newspapers and Politics, 1865–1878* (Chapel Hill, N.C., 1994), p. 61.

62. *Syracuse Morning Standard*, July 8, 1881, April 1, 1882; September 9, 1881. The rival *Courier* opined that "nothing but an earthquake or a revolution could arouse the people from the apathy that has settled down on them" (November 8, 1881).

63. *Dubuque Herald*, March 24, 1880; October 1, 1882.

64. *Dubuque Daily Times*, February 26, 1882.

65. *Syracuse Morning Standard*, November 8, 1882.

66. *Dubuque Herald*, November 7, 1880; *Syracuse Morning Standard*, November 4, 1880; *Syracuse Courier*, July 11, 1880.

67. *Placer Weekly Argus*, July 22, October 14, 1882.

68. *Graham Leader*, June 4, August 20, September 10, 1880; August 5, 1881; May 5, 1882.

69. This latter phenomenon is particularly well defined in Burton J. Bledstein, *The Culture of Professionalism: The Middle Class and the Development of Higher Education in America* (New York, 1976).

70. As in the earlier periods, reportage of formal party roles was very nearly complete.

Attendees at local caucuses and ordinary members of campaign clubs were still not reported, but the newspapers also suggest that neither form of partisan gathering was well attended by those who were not pulling wires. Our files for the analysis of the 1880–82 election cycle range in size from 142 (of whom 62 were politically active) in Auburn, to 3,182 (of whom 1,757 were politically active) in Syracuse. Together, the files describe the political and other local institutional activity of 8,854 men, of whom 4,894 are identifiable in some way with political activity. Again we should emphasize that comparisons of our file to the local population reported on the proximate Federal census (1880) overstate the proportions of activists to the whole (and unknowable) number of men who resided in the community during some portion of the three-year election cycle.

71. There are actually twenty-eight Democratic Party leaders in our file, but one is not listed in the Augusta city directory, which is our source of occupational information for political and communal activists in Augusta and in our other larger towns. In the absence of a census index, it proved unfeasible to link these large files to the hundreds of pages of the manuscript population schedules for Augusta, Dubuque, and Syracuse, and in any case the census of 1880 is a less rich source of relevant information than is the census of 1860. The city directories of the three cities proved to be quite inclusive, and the proportions of our files we were able to link with them compare favorably with equivalent census link proportions in our smaller towns, and in previous election cycles.

72. The Republicans' conventions and other meetings, and the names of their officers, delegates, and nominees for office, were regularly reported in the Democratic paper, often without editorial comment, occasionally accompanied by a brief note to the effect that the true home of Augusta's black men was in the Democratic party.

73. There were also five Republican leaders who could not be found in the city directory.

74. Amy Bridges, *A City in the Republic: Antebellum New York and the Origins of Machine Politics* (New York, 1984); Jon C. Teaford, *The Unheralded Triumph: City Government in America, 1870–1900* (Baltimore, 1984).

75. Theodore Roosevelt, *An Autobiography* (New York, 1919), p. 63.

76. Lamont later joined the staff of Governor Grover Cleveland, became Cleveland's private secretary during the latter's first term as President, and, during Cleveland's second term, was appointed Secretary of War.

77. Diedrich Willers, Jr., to Daniel S. Lamont, March 28, 1876; William W. Gordon to E. K. Apgar, March 28, 1876; Daniel S. Lamont Papers, Rare and Manuscript Collections, Carl A. Kroch Library, Cornell University. Unless otherwise stated, all unpublished letters and diaries cited in this chapter are drawn from this depository.

78. A. T. Ney to Lamont, October 22, 1876; John Rankine to Lamont, November 13, 1876; D. Magone to Lamont, May 25, 1877. Before he moved to Albany Lamont was himself a local party organizer, responsible to state Democratic leaders. In 1869, Samuel J. Tilden instructed him to supply the names and addresses "of at least *ten* earnest and active democrats in *each election district* of your town. The selection should be made of those . . . who are willing to undertake the labor necessary to organize our party and bring out the vote at the coming election." S. J. Tilden to My Dear Sir [Daniel Lamont], September 25, 1869.

79. B. B. Jones to Lamont, December 27, 1875; John Courtney, Jr., to Lamont, August 24, September 13, 1883. Not all of the appeals for patronage in this era were written by men, even when men were the intended beneficiaries. In 1872, for example, Anna Lowe wrote her congressman to ask for help in influencing the state governor to appoint her father, who was "worn down physically by the uncertainty of a NY lawyer's life," to a city judgeship in Brooklyn. Ten years later, Mrs. J. H. Mattimore wrote for an appointment for her husband. "I have a large family to see to," she explained, "& we need his assistance." Women who wrote letters of this sort frequently apologized for mixing in politics, and, like many men, framed their appeals in terms of the well-being of their families. Anna Lowe to F. Kernan, April 7, 1872; Mrs. J. H. Mattimore to Kernan, Francis Kernan Papers.

80. *Pennsylvania Legislative Documents, 1873*, vol. 1, no. 8 (Harrisburg, 1873), p. 811;

Documents of the New York State Assembly, 1867, vol. 4, no. 65 (Albany, 1867), p. 240.

81. *Documents of the New York State Assembly, 1890*, vol. 12, no. 83 (Albany, 1890), p. 794; *Appendix to the Journals of the Assembly and Senate of California, 1889*, vol. 7, no. 4 (Sacramento, 1889), p. 338.

82. *Documents of the New York State Assembly, 1869*, vol. 9, no. 139 (Albany, 1869), p. 90; *Documents of the New York State Assembly, 1890*, vol. 12, no. 83, p. 438; *Pennsylvania Legislative Documents: 1870*, no. 28 (Harrisburg, 1870), pp. 1227–33.

83. Madison Contested Election, 1868, General Assembly Papers of Connecticut, Connecticut State Library, pp. 412, 414, 432–40, 712.

84. *Proceedings in the Matter of the Contested Election of Osbourn vs Devlin before the Committee on Elections of the Senate of Pennsylvania*, vol. 2 (Harrisburg, 1889), pp. 1930–31; *Documents of the New York State Assembly, 1873*, vol. 4, no. 51 (Albany, 1873), p. 26. That the pressure on voters by party operatives was deeply embedded in the popular consciousness is evident in the commentary in several Dubuque newspapers about "elections" at churches and fairs. The editor of the *Dubuque Herald*, for example, warned in 1880 that the contest for most popular teamster or wood dealer was becoming lively because "it is understood that certain parties are working outside." A year later the *Daily Times* noted that during the vote for the most popular young lady at the St. Patrick's Fair, "the different friends of the three contestants occupied prominent positions near the judges' stand, and pushed in the bills at a lively rate." Americans, it seems, could not visualize elections without the presence and influence of partisan workers. *Dubuque Herald*, December 17, 1880; *Dubuque Daily Times*, January 7, 1882.

85. *Documents of the New York State Assembly, 1869*, vol. 9, no. 139, pp. 31, 117.

86. *Appendix to the Journals of the Senate and Assembly of California, 1889*, vol. 7, no. 4, pp. 31, 219, 243–50. For the North End Social Club, an Irish organization of thirty men, Banks was asked at Lilkendy's saloon to put twenty dollars over the bar and to pay another ten for a group photograph. His advisers told

him not to waste his money on men certain to vote for his Democratic opponent. Ibid., p. 50.

87. We derive the phrase "ritual partisan loyalty" from Leon Fink, *Progressive Intellectuals and the Dilemma of Democratic Commitment* (Cambridge, Mass., 1997), p. 27.

Chapter 8
An Excess and a Dearth of Democracy

1. *Report of the Proceedings in the Case of the United States vs. Charles J. Guiteau* (Washington, 1882), vol. 1, p. 896.

2. Ibid., pp. 124–26.

3. Insanity was the essential defense, insisted upon by Guiteau's lawyer (who was also his brother-in-law), but resisted by Guiteau himself. The best discussion of the medical aspects of the trial is Charles E. Rosenberg, *The Trial of the Assassin Guiteau: Psychiatry and Law in the Gilded Age* (Chicago, 1968).

4. *United States vs. Guiteau*, vol. 1, p. 131.

5. Ibid., p. 589.

6. Ibid., pp. 602, 645–50, 946. Guiteau himself claimed that several important politicians gave him their support, but none testified at the trial that he had done so. Such support would have been unlikely, but so too would any admission of it at an assassin's trial.

7. Ibid., p. 648.

8. Ibid., pp. 122, 131.

9. Michael Schudson, *The Good Citizen: A History of American Civic Life* (New York, 1998), pp. 154–55. The classic portrayal of a turn-of-the-century politician's breezy (but we believe rather nervous and edgy) dismissal of civil-service reform is William L. Riordon, *Plunkitt of Tammany Hall: A Serious of Very Plain Talks on Very Practical Politics* . . . (1905; New York, 1963).

10. When "specific or divisible incentives" are available, James Q. Wilson argues, "a measure of control attaches to their use, such that individual performance can be rewarded or punished regardless of what others may do. A general or durable incentive . . . may depend on the efforts of many. . . . Everyone gets it or none. Therefore no person has any compelling reason to work hard for it. If he knows his candidate may win or lose regardless of what he does, he need not work at all." James Q. Wil-

son, *The Amateur Democrat: Club Politics in Three Cities* (Chicago, 1962), p. 170.

11. Frances Fox Piven and Richard Cloward, *Why Americans Don't Vote* (New York, 1988), p. 65.

12. The most detailed account of this process is J. Morgan Kousser, *The Shaping of Southern Politics: Suffrage Restriction and the Establishment of the One-Party South, 1880–1910* (New Haven, Conn., 1974). While the focus of Kousser's and others' analyses is properly on black disfranchisement, W. E. B. Du Bois, writing shortly after the turn of the century, makes the unusual additional observation that many of "the better class of Negroes" in the North were removing themselves from an increasingly disreputable political system, "leaving the careless and venal of their race to exercise their rights as voters." See W. E. Burghhardt Du Bois, *The Souls of Black Folk: Essays and Sketches* (Chicago, 1903), p. 174. Du Bois detested black disfranchisement, and disapproved of African Americans of the North who squandered the franchise. His remarks, though, remind us that political engagement varied among African Americans just as it did among European Americans, and that it responded in similar ways to political practices and events.

13. Piven and Cloward, *Why Americans Don't Vote*, p. 91; *Revised Record of the Constitutional Convention of the State of New York, May 8, 1894–September 29, 1894*, vol. 4 (Albany, 1900), p. 103; *Constitution of the State of New York—Annotated* (Albany, 1899), p. 150; *Vernon's Annotated Texas Statutes* (Kansas City, 1927), pp. 455–56.

14. *Purdon's Pennsylvania Statutes Annotated* (Philadelphia, 1961), p. 93; *Revised Record* . . . *New York*, vol. 3, pp. 935–36, vol. 4, pp. 462, 467.

15. Peter H. Argersinger, *Structure, Process, and Party: Essays in American Political History* (Armonk, N.Y., 1982), p. 47.

16. Quoted in Harold Syrett, *The City of Brooklyn, 1865–1898: A Political History* (New York, 1944), p. 97.

17. *Pennsylvania Legislative Documents, 1872*, vol. 2, no. 10 (Harrisburg, 1872), p. 1314; *Pennsylvania Legislative Documents, 1873*, vol. 2, no. 13 (Harrisburg, 1873), pp. 332–33,

345; *Pennsylvania Legislative Documents, 1877,* vol. 3, no. 16 (Harrisburg, 1877), p. 1217.

18. *Pennsylvania Legislative Documents, 1873,* vol. 3, no. 16, p. 344.

19. *Proceedings in the Matter of the Contested Election of Osbourn vs. Devlin before the Committee on Elections of the Senate of Pennsylvania* (Harrisburg, 1889), vol. 1, pp. 744–45, 1035.

20. Ibid., pp. 523, 1920, 3248, 3256.

21. Ibid., pp. 1727–30.

22. Ibid., pp. 1534, 2048, 2580.

23. Ibid., pp. 3437–38, 3618.

24. *Documents of the New York State Senate, 1875,* vol. 3, no. 47 (Albany, 1875), pp. 70, 96, 266; *Documents of the New York State Assembly, 1868,* vol. 10, no. 128 (Albany, 1868), p. 67; *Documents of the New York State Assembly, 1867,* vol. 4, no. 65 (Albany, 1867), pp. 183, 198.

25. *Appendix to the Journals of the Senate and Assembly of California, 1889,* vol. 7, no. 4 (Sacramento, 1889), pp. 159–60, 175, 183, 214, 243–50.

26. Indications of this are available, of course, in other sources as well. In New Jersey, for example, political boss Frank Hague estimated that a "full fifty percent of the voters have got to be coaxed or dragged to the polls." Quoted in John F. Reynolds, *Testing Democracy: Electoral Behavior and Progressive Reform in New Jersey, 1880–1920* (Chapel Hill, N.C., 1988), p. 124. Reynolds himself estimates that from one-fifth to one-third of the electorate in the 1880s expected to be paid one to three dollars for turning out at the polls (p. 54).

27. *Documents of the New York State Assembly, 1867,* vol. 4, no. 65, pp. 13, 35–36; *Proceedings in the Matter of the Contested Election of Osbourn vs. Devlin,* vol. 1, p. 1507; *Documents of the New York State Assembly, 1872,* vol. 3, no. 50 (Albany, 1872), p. 220; *Documents of the New York State Assembly, 1890,* vol. 12, no. 83 (Albany, 1890), p. 1115.

28. *Documents of the New York State Assembly, 1867,* vol. 4, no. 65, p. 155; *Documents of the New York State Assembly, 1868,* vol. 10, no. 128, p. 111; *Documents of the New York State Assembly, 1873,* vol. 4, no. 51 (Albany, 1873), p. 23; *Documents of the New York State Assembly, 1868,* vol. 10, no. 128, pp. 149, 158; *Proceedings in the Matter of the Contested Election of Osbourn vs. Devlin,* vol. 1, p. 1005.

29. *Documents of the New York State Assembly, 1870,* vol. 11, no. 209 (Albany, 1870); *Documents of the New York State Senate, 1875,* vol. 5, no. 69; *Documents of the New York State Assembly, 1890,* vol. 12, no. 83.

30. *Documents of the New York State Assembly, 1869,* vol. 9, no. 139 (Albany, 1869), p. 226.

31. *Pennsylvania Legislative Documents, 1873,* vol. 2, no. 13, p. 507; *Proceedings in the Matter of the Contested Election of Osbourn vs. Devlin,* vol. 1, p. 1115; *Documents of the New York State Senate, 1875,* vol. 5, no. 69, p. 164.

32. *Documents of the New York State Assembly, 1870,* vol. 11, no. 209, p. 19; *Pennsylvania Legislative Documents, 1873,* vol. 1, no. 8, pp. 811–12.

33. *Documents of the New York State Assembly, 1871,* vol. 3, no. 27 (Albany, 1871), p. 32; *Documents of the New York State Assembly, 1869,* vol. 7, no. 103, p. 15; *Appendix to the Journals of the Senate and Assembly of California, 1889,* vol. 7, no. 4, pp. 71–72.

34. *Documents of the New York State Assembly, 1872,* vol. 3, no. 50, p. 143; *Documents of the New York State Senate, 1875,* vol. 5, no. 69, pp. 79–82; *Proceedings in the Matter of the Contested Election of Osbourn vs. Devlin,* vol. 1, p. 3424.

35. For a relatively recent discussion of these ideas and motives, see Robert B. Westbrook, *John Dewey and American Democracy* (Ithaca, N.Y., 1991).

36. *Documents of the New York State Assembly, 1867,* vol. 4, no. 65, pp. 68–69; *Documents of the New York State Assembly, 1869,* vol. 9, no. 139, p. 232; ibid., vol. 7, no. 103, p. 108; *Documents of the New York State Senate, 1875,* vol. 5, no. 69, p. 164.

37. See Robert E. Goodwin, *Manipulatory Politics* (New Haven, Conn., 1980). Samuel L. Popkin has written in similar terms of "low information rationality." See Popkin, *The Reasoning Voter: Communication and Persuasion in Presidential Campaigning* (Chicago, 1991).

38. Sidney Verba, Kay Lehman Schlozman, and Henry E. Brady, *Voice and Equality: Civic Voluntarism in American Politics* (Cambridge, Mass., 1995), pp. 181–82.

39. Michael F. Holt, *The Political Crisis of the 1850s* (New York, 1978).

40. Henry George, *Progress and Poverty* (New York, 1879), p. 303.

41. Ibid., pp. 533–34. As in an earlier era, some Americans sought the solution in third parties that were at once part of and external to a political system they found unresponsive or hostile to their needs. Vivien Hart is but one historian who has described the Populists in these terms: "In America, the Populists showed how profoundly loyal citizenship could generate both a biting criticism of the political system and a logical programme of reform, and they seemed but an exaggerated example of an endemic American trait of disaffection with politics." Vivien Hart, *Distrust and Democracy: Political Distrust in Britain and America* (New York, 1978), pp. 129–30.

42. Robert H. Wiebe, *Self-Rule: A Cultural History of American Democracry* (Chicago, 1995), p. 64.

43. Quoted in E. J. Dionne, Jr., *Why Americans Hate Politics* (New York, 1991), p. 10.

Index

Page numbers in boldface type refer to illustrations.